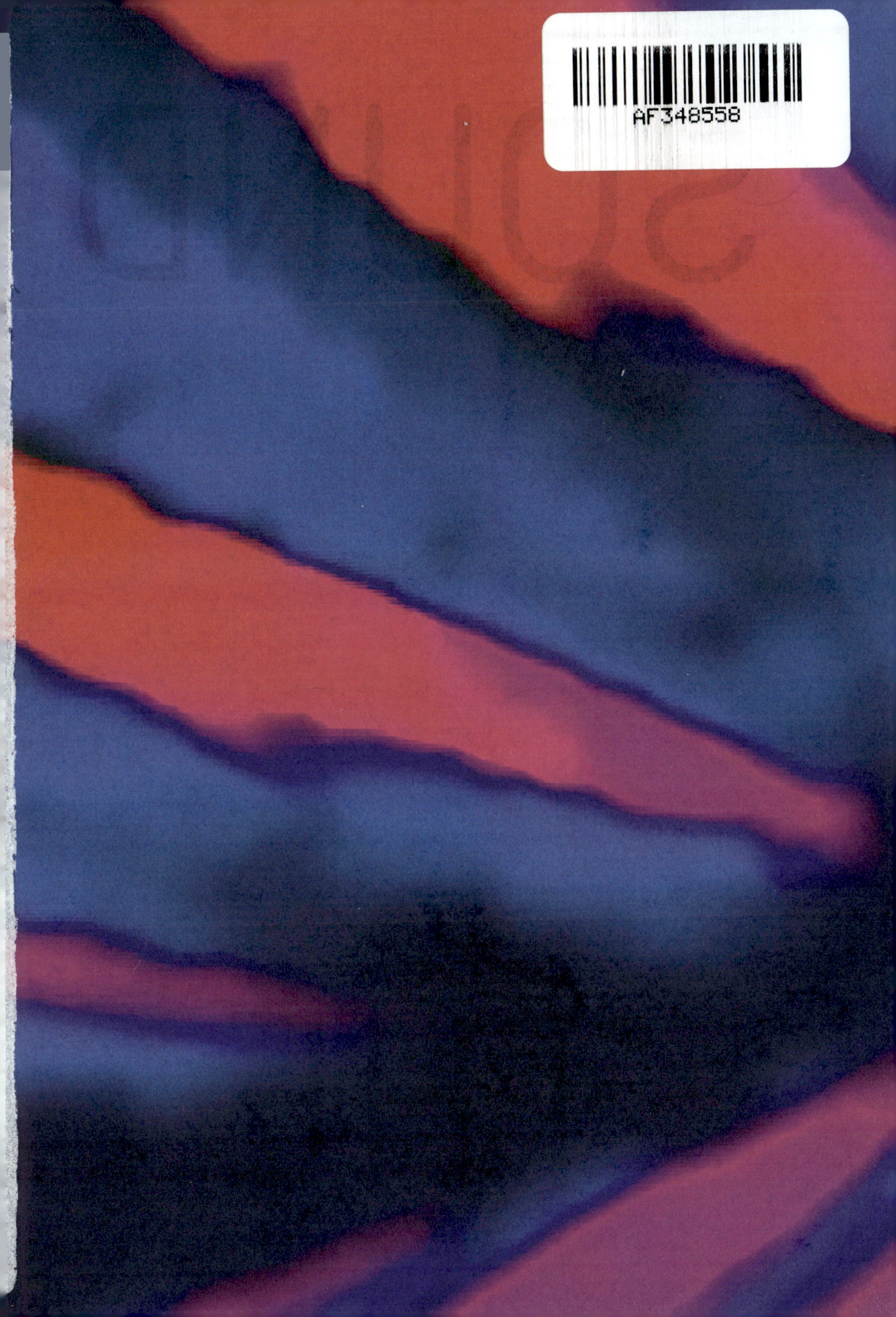

AF348558

SOUND

THE

OF

BREAK

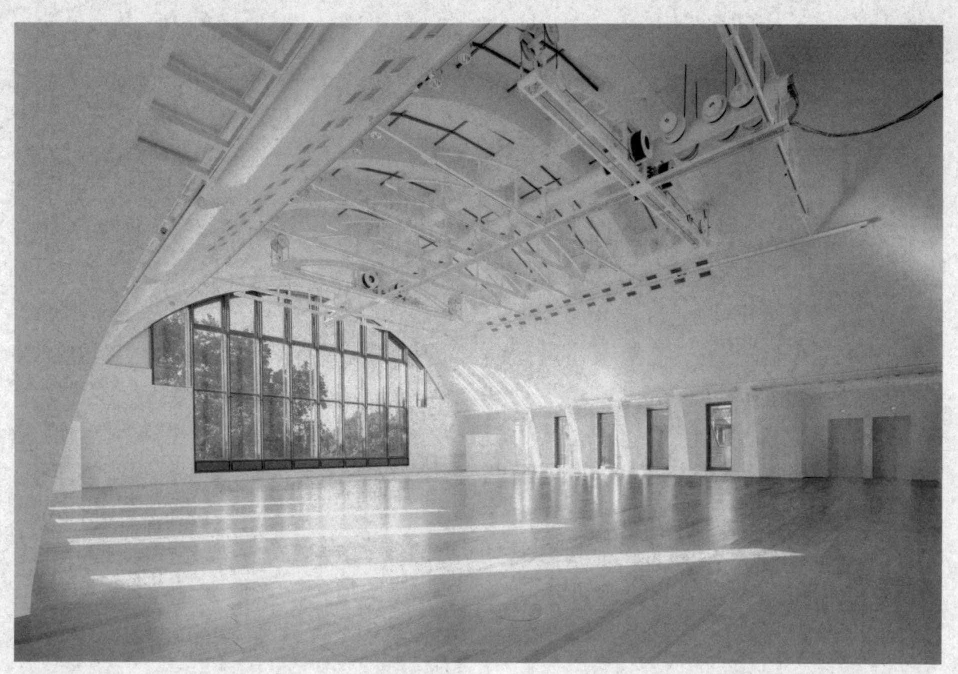

Schirn Kunsthalle Frankfurt

Friends of the Schirn Kunsthalle Frankfurt e.V.

The SCHIRN FRIENDS are delighted to be able to support the Schirn Kunsthalle Frankfurt in the realization of the solo exhibition *Elizabeth Price SOUND OF THE BREAK*. Elizabeth Price's video works present a captivating interplay of image, text, and music. With a keen sense for the particularities and nuances of technological innovation and vernacular speech, and a discerning eye for cultural and historical contexts, Price uncovers highly original, often idiosyncratic narratives. She offers surprising perspectives to develop incisive analyses of gender and power relations out of mundane details.

It is a great pleasure to welcome the Turner Prize winner to the Schirn. With this project, the Schirn Kunsthalle Frankfurt once again lives up to its aspiration of enabling audiences both in Frankfurt and internationally to directly engage with important international contemporary positions. As the SCHIRN FRIENDS, we are happy to support the team in this endeavor.

Antje Conzelmann
Chairwoman, Friends of the Schirn Kunsthalle
Frankfurt e.V.

Die Ausstellung wird gefördert durch / The exhibition is supported by

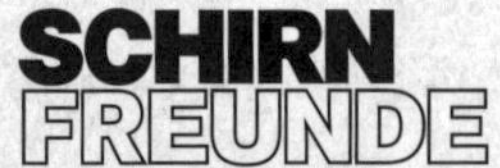

GRUSSWORT

Verein der Freunde der Schirn Kunsthalle
Frankfurt e.V.

Die SCHIRN FREUNDE sind hocherfreut, die Schirn
Kunsthalle Frankfurt bei der Realisierung der Einzel-
ausstellung *Elizabeth Price SOUND OF THE BREAK*
unterstützen zu können. Elizabeth Prices Videoarbeiten
zeigen ein fesselndes Zusammenspiel von Bild, Text und
Musik. Mit feinem Gespür für die Besonderheiten und
Nuancen der technologischen Innovation und der Umgangs-
sprache sowie einem scharfen Blick für den kulturellen
und historischen Kontext spürt Price höchst origi-
nelle, oft eigenwillige Erzählungen auf. Sie eröffnet
überraschende Perspektiven, um aus unbedeutenden
Details pointierte Studien über Geschlechter- und
Machtverhältnisse zu entwickeln.

Es ist uns eine große Freude, die Turner-Prize-
Gewinnerin in der Schirn willkommen zu heißen. Mit diesem Projekt wird die Schirn Kunsthalle Frankfurt erneut
ihrem Anspruch gerecht, dem Frankfurter sowie dem
internationalen Publikum die direkte Auseinandersetzung
mit wichtigen internationalen zeitgenössischen Positionen zu ermöglichen. Bei diesem Anliegen stehen wir
als Verein der SCHIRN FREUNDE dem Team gerne zur Seite.

Antje Conzelmann
Vorstandsvorsitzende des Vereins der Freunde der
Schirn Kunsthalle Frankfurt e.V.

Elizabeth Price's video works are densely layered:
they open up narratives, single out objects as well
as stories, and get to the bottom of the relationships
between them. Price combines photographs, archival
materials, documents, text, graphics, animation,
and sound in her works. She personally describes her
works as hybrid forms that exist between PowerPoint
presentations, video animations, and commercials;
they might also be melodramas like those seen at the
cinema. The different elements are brought together
according to an overarching order determined by
the artist. New contexts emerge through the visible
and audible narrative of the videos. Music and
voice impart a distinctive rhythm to the digital
collages. In addition to all this, there is the
audio atmosphere of a technological-synthetic voice-
over, which evokes computer-generated tutorials.

Die Videoarbeiten von Elizabeth Price sind dicht und
vielschichtig, sie eröffnen Erzählungen, heben Dinge
und Geschichten hervor und gehen den Beziehungen
zwischen ihnen auf den Grund. Price verbindet in ihren
Arbeiten Fotografien, Archivmaterialien, Dokumente,
Text, Grafik, Animation und Sound. Sie selbst charak-
terisiert ihre Werke als Mischformate zwischen Power-
Point-Präsentation, Videoanimation und Werbefilm,
es könnten auch Melodramen wie im Kino sein. Anhand
einer übergreifenden, von der Künstlerin arrangierten
Ordnung werden die unterschiedlichen Elemente zusammen-
geführt. Über die sichtbare und hörbare Erzählung der
Videos ergeben sich neue Zusammenhänge. Den digitalen
Collagen wird mit Musik und Stimme ein spezieller
Rhythmus verliehen. Dazu kommt die Klangatmosphäre
eines technisch-synthetischen Voice-overs, das stark
an computergenerierte Tutorials erinnert.

Price creates moving text and image montages, split screens, and textual superimpositions. The artist takes a critical view of linear narrative logic and makes this visible by presenting synchronous narrative threads that run through real and fictional places, allowing for many things to happen simultaneously and on different levels of a single moment. This demands great attention, while also promising a wealth of insights. Indeed, her approach to digital deconstruction corresponds to a revolutionary resistance: it is not unambiguous symbols, the propaganda of the obvious, that are of interest to the artist, but rather the rereading of data, the observation of marginal notes and secondary information. To be precise, Price examines the fine print of the information age, its data packets and their encoding, and then explains the correlations she has discovered. In other words, information is a string of signs that must be brought into meaningful contexts – because they would otherwise simply stand in space as empty signifiers. In her work, Price focuses on seemingly insignificant objects, unheard voices, and blind spots in our perception. Through her selection and digital processing of the material, Price also addresses issues relating to power and gender relations, raising questions about social representation: her artistic organization of things functions as a visualized poststructuralism, which here, as art, becomes a master class in signs and signifiers.

Price reviews our traditional systems of order with regard to work, gender, power, and social visibility. Her themes range from the patterns on neckties to the myths surrounding automobiles and dancing stiletto heels.

    Es entstehen bewegte Text- und Bildmontagen, Split-
screens und Überschreibungen. Die Künstlerin kritisiert
die Logik der linearen Erzählung und macht dies anhand
synchron verlaufender Erzählstränge durch reale und
fiktionale Orte sichtbar, das heißt, vieles passiert
gleichzeitig und auf verschiedenen Ebenen des einen
Augenblicks. Das verlangt viel Aufmerksamkeit und ver-
spricht viel Erkenntnisgewinn. Denn dieses Verfahren
einer digitalen Dekonstruktion entspricht einem revolu-
tionären Widerstand: Nicht die eindeutigen Zeichen,
die Propaganda des Offensichtlichen sind für die Künstlerin von Interesse, sondern die Relektüre von Daten,
die Beobachtung von Randnotizen und Sekundärinformation.
Genau genommen schaut Price nach dem Kleingedruckten
des Informationszeitalters, nach den Datenpaketen und
deren Codierung und erklärt von ihr entdeckte Zusammenhänge. Informationen sind also Zeichenketten, die in
sinnstiftende Kontexte gebracht werden müssen – weil
sie sonst als leere Signifikanten einfach im Raum
stehen. Price richtet in ihren Arbeiten den Fokus auf
scheinbar unbedeutende Objekte, ungehörte Stimmen und
blinde Flecken unserer Wahrnehmung. Durch ihre Auswahl
und die digitale Bearbeitung des Materials führt sie
auch Fragen nach Macht- und Geschlechterverhältnissen
vor Augen, fragt nach sozialer Repräsentation: Ihre
künstlerische Ordnung der Dinge wirkt wie ein bildge-
wordener Poststrukturalismus, der hier als Kunst zum
Lehrstück über Zeichen und Bezeichnendes wird.
    Price kritisiert unsere tradierten Ordnungssysteme
in Hinblick auf Arbeit, Geschlecht, Macht und gesell-
schaftliche Sichtbarkeit. Thematisch spannt sie dabei
den Bogen von Mustern auf Krawatten bis zum Mythos
des Automobils und tanzenden Stöckelschuhen.

Price's works are neither documentary nor conventionally narrative video art. They are based on a conceptual way of working that focuses on the connection between text and image. Artistic practices such as those of Barbara Kruger and Jenny Holzer have used typography to alter the perception of letters as carriers of meaning. The history of graphic art, such as its usage of collage and photomontage, are also relevant to Price's works. Likewise, the cartoon montages of Pop Art and works of Institutional Critique are important references. Beyond art history and its forms, Price's work is guided by questions about society that are informed by cultural studies. In her works, she brings together technology and nature, the digital and the analog, truth and fiction. The artist invites her audience to observe the simultaneity of the nonsimultaneous, leading us to startling pictorial collisions.

I am very grateful, first and foremost, to Elizabeth Price for her trust and willingness to develop the exhibition and the accompanying catalog together with us, and to very specifically conceive them both for our spaces. We are particularly pleased to be able to show here in Frankfurt her new work *UNDERFOOT*, created in 2022. I would like to thank Dominic Paterson, curator at The Hunterian, and The Hunterian for the loan of *UNDERFOOT*, as well the work's co-commissioner, Panel. The Schirn is also presenting, for the first time ever, four of Price's video lectures, made during the Covid lockdowns. In these lectures, Elizabeth Price explains her artistic practice and methodology, and clearly presents the various layers of her complex compositions.

Ihre Arbeiten sind keine dokumentarische oder
konventionell erzählende Videokunst. Ihnen liegt eine
konzeptuelle Arbeitsweise zugrunde, die die Verbindung von Text und Bild ins Zentrum rückt. Künstlerische
Positionen wie Barbara Kruger oder Jenny Holzer haben
mit Schriftbildern die Wahrnehmung von Buchstaben
als Bedeutungsträger verändert. Auch die Geschichte
der grafischen Kunst, wie Collage- und Fotomontage-
techniken, spielt für Prices Arbeiten eine wichtige
Rolle. Ebenso sind Cartoon-Montagen der Pop-Art oder die
institutionskritische Konzeptkunst wichtige Referenzen.
Jenseits der Kunstgeschichte und deren Formen sind
kulturwissenschaftliche Fragen an die Gesellschaft für
Price wegleitend.

Die Künstlerin führt in ihren Arbeiten Technik und
Natur, das Digitale und das Analoge, Wahrheit und
Fiktion zusammen. Sie lädt ihr Publikum zur Beobachtung der Gleichzeitigkeit des Ungleichzeitigen ein
und führt uns zu überraschenden Bildkollisionen.

Mein großer Dank geht zuallererst an Elizabeth Price
für ihr Vertrauen und die Bereitschaft, die Ausstellung und den begleitenden Katalog mit uns gemeinsam
zu entwickeln und ganz gezielt für unsere Räume zu
erdenken. Besonders freut es uns, dass wir ihre neue,
im Jahr 2022 entstandene Arbeit *UNDERFOOT* zeigen können.
Ganz besonderen Dank möchte ich The Hunterian und Panel
für die Leihgabe von *UNDERFOOT* aussprechen, in deren
Auftrag die Arbeit entstanden ist. Maßgeblich beteiligt
daran war Dominic Paterson, Kurator der Hunterian
Art Gallery. Erstmals überhaupt präsentiert werden in
der Schirn vier von Prices Videovorträgen, die während der Corona-Lockdowns entstanden sind. In diesen
Vorträgen erläutert die Künstlerin ihre Arbeitsweise

The ongoing support of our sponsors and partners is essential for the realization of our extensive projects. We are particularly grateful to the Verein der Freunde der Schirn Kunsthalle e.V. (SCHIRN FRIENDS) and its more than two thousand members. As a major pillar of support, it consistently facilitates the presentations of important contemporary positions, which are typical of the museum's program. The SCHIRN FRIENDS and its board of directors have not only supported the exhibition financially, but have also taken a great interest in the development of the project. I would like to thank Antje Conzelmann, the chairwoman of the association, as well as the entire board and the managing team, Tamara von Clary and Alexandra Enzensberger. I would also like to thank Samsung Electronics, our technology partner for this exhibition, for their generous support. Furthermore, I thank the City of Frankfurt for its ongoing support of our work at the Schirn, and, as representative of all the decision makers, the head of the Department of Culture, Ina Hartwig.

I am particularly grateful to the curator of the exhibition, Matthias Ulrich, who conceived the exhibition for the Schirn and realized it in the most compelling way. He was assisted with tremendous dedication by Marie Oucherif in her role as curatorial assistant. I would also like to sincerely thank her for her immense support in the preparation and implementation of the exhibition.

I thank Blake Williams for his enriching text contribution to the catalog. For the outstanding design of this catalog, I would like to thank Eva Kellenberger and Sebastian White of Kellenberger–White, London. I thank Michael Ammann and Susie Hondl for the translations

und Methodik und fächert die unterschiedlichsten Ebenen ihrer komplexen Kompositionen weiter auf.

Bedeutend für die Realisierung unserer umfangreichen Projekte ist die fortwährende Unterstützung durch unsere Förder:innen und Partner:innen. Besonderer Dank gebührt dem Verein der Freunde der Schirn Kunsthalle e.V. mit seinen über 2.000 Mitgliedern, der als große Säule der Unterstützung immer wieder auch die für die Programmatik des Hauses typischen Präsentationen wichtiger zeitgenössischer Positionen ermöglicht. So haben der Verein und sein Vorstand die Ausstellung nicht nur finanziell unterstützt, sondern mit großem Interesse den Werdegang des Projekts begleitet. Stellvertretend gilt mein großer Dank Antje Conzelmann als Vorstandsvorsitzender des Vereins sowie dem gesamten Vorstand und der Geschäftsführung mit Tamara von Clary und Alexandra Enzensberger. Samsung Electronics, unserem Technikpartner für diese Ausstellung, gebührt ebenfalls mein Dank für die großzügige Unterstützung. Ich danke außerdem der Stadt Frankfurt für ihre kontinuierliche Unterstützung unserer Arbeit in der Schirn, stellvertretend für alle Entscheidungsträger der Kulturdezernentin Ina Hartwig.

Mein besonderer Dank geht an den Kurator der Ausstellung, Matthias Ulrich, der diese für die Schirn erdacht und auf höchst überzeugende Weise umgesetzt hat. Mit größtem Engagement stand ihm als kuratorische Assistentin Marie Oucherif zur Seite. Auch ihr möchte ich für die großartige Unterstützung bei der Ausstellungsvorbereitung und -umsetzung herzlich danken.

Blake Williams danke ich für seinen bereichernden Textbeitrag zum Katalog. Für die herausragende Gestaltung dieses Katalogs gilt mein Dank Eva Kellenberger

of the texts. I am grateful to Annette Siegel and
Andrew Wagner for their attentive editing. I am
furthermore especially grateful to Mousse Publishing,
in particular Ilaria Bombelli, for their excellent
cooperation. I would like to thank Sam Kim for the suc-
cessful exhibition graphics, as well as Stephen Holmes,
and Markus Berger, Satis n Fy, for their technological
conception and general support.

Without the dedicated team at the Schirn, this
impressive exhibition and the accompanying publication
would not have been possible. For this, I would like to
express my tremendous gratitude to the entire staff,
especially to the deputy director and head of exhibitions, Esther Schlicht. I would like to thank Christian
Teltz and Oliver Taschke for the complex technical
coordination; Elke Walter, Karin Grüning, and Fanny
Bengsch for overseeing the exhibition's organization;
and Luise Leyer for her work as assistant to the
deputy director. Luise Bachmann, Heike Stumpf, and
Angelika Schäfer have been responsible for the marketing and design of the campaign, for which I thank them.
I also wish to thank Johanna Pulz, Julia Bastian,
Maya Röttger, and Thea Stroh for their coordination
of the exhibition's public relations. I further thank
Natalie Storelli for coordinating and supervising the
publication and Julia Schaake for editing the *SCHIRN
MAG*. For the accompanying mediation program, I am
most grateful to Laura Heeg with Simone Boscheinen,
Olga Schätz, Anna Haag, and Sarah Schweizer. The development and implementation of the exhibition's events
is owed to Ute Seiffert and Vivien Shahzad. I would
like to thank Miriam Werner and Corinna Fröhling for
their coordination of the support of the partners

und Sebastian White von Kellenberger-White, London.
Die Übersetzungen der Texte sind Michael Ammann
und Susie Hondl zu verdanken. Annette Siegel und
Andrew Wagner danke ich für das aufmerksame Lektorat.
Mein besonderer Dank gilt außerdem Mousse Publishing,
insbesondere Ilaria Bombelli, für die gute Zusammenarbeit. Ich danke für die gelungene Ausstellungsgrafik Sam Kim, sowie Stephen Holmes und Markus Berger,
Satis n Fy, für die Konzipierung und Unterstützung
in allen technischen Belangen.

Ohne das engagierte Team der Schirn wäre auch diese
eindrucksvolle Ausstellung nicht zustande gekommen.
Dafür möchte ich allen Mitarbeiter:innen meinen großen
Dank aussprechen, besonders der stellvertretenden
Direktorin und Ausstellungsleiterin Esther Schlicht.
Christian Teltz und Oliver Taschke danke ich für die
komplexe technische Koordination, Elke Walter, Karin
Grüning und Fanny Bengsch in der Organisation sowie
Luise Leyer als Assistentin der Ausstellungsleitung.
Luise Bachmann, Heike Stumpf und Angelika Schäfer
möchte ich für das Marketing und die Gestaltung der Kam-
pagne danken, Johanna Pulz, Julia Bastian, Maya Röttger
und Thea Stroh für die Pressearbeit. Darüber hinaus
danke ich Natalie Storelli für die Koordination der
Publikation sowie Julia Schaake für die Redaktion des
SCHIRN MAG. Mein Dank gilt außerdem Laura Heeg mit
Simone Boscheinen, Olga Schätz, Anna Haag und Sarah
Schweizer für das begleitende Vermittlungsprogramm sowie
Ute Seiffert und Vivien Shahzad für die Entwicklung
und Umsetzung der Veranstaltungen. Miriam Werner und
Corinna Fröhling danke ich für die Koordination sowie
die Betreuung der Partner:innen und Förder:innen.
Ebenso gilt mein Dank Heike Berndt, Boris Deckelmann und

and sponsors. Likewise, I would like to thank Heike
Berndt, Boris Deckelmann, and Tanja Mayer in the
Schirn's administration, as well as Kerstin Lehmann
for her assistance in a large variety of matters.
Finally, I would like to thank Andreas Gundermann,
Stefan Schell, Rosaria La Tona and the facility
services team, and Bettina Beyermann and Vanessa
Bernhardt at the reception desk, as well as all the
other Schirn staff members who were involved in
the realization of this extensive project.

Sebastian Baden
Director
Schirn Kunsthalle Frankfurt

Tanja Mayer in der Verwaltung der Schirn sowie Kerstin
Lehmann für die Assistenz in zahlreichen Belangen.
Abschließend möchte ich Andreas Gundermann, Stefan
Schell, Rosaria La Tona und dem Team der Gebäude-
reinigung, Bettina Beyermann und Vanessa Bernhardt am
Empfang sowie allen weiteren Mitarbeiter:innen der
Schirn danken, die an der Realisierung dieses Projekts
beteiligt waren.

Sebastian Baden
Direktor
Schirn Kunsthalle Frankfurt

FOLLOW YOU

The interlinking of data, of words into a sentence,
of images into a movie, of threads into a rug, is at
its heart an everyday practice, which relies on rules
to create orders: scientific, linguistic, cinemato-
graphic, and so on. Digital technology enables a
liberation from these constraints, allowing everything
to be interconnected to everything else.

Elizabeth Price's video works, or rather moving-image
works, navigate the dynamic contexts of technology,
labor, gender, and politics. They form a flexible
architecture of images to create a linguistic narrative
that sits like a floor in a multistory building. On
other levels there are collections of various things,
such as objects and artifacts, photographs and videos,
and music samples. As if free-floating, these levels
are interwoven on the computer with the help of a video-
editing program; like individual pieces of furniture,

FOLLOW YOU

Das Verknüpfen von Daten miteinander, von Wörtern zu
einem Satz, von Bildern zu einem Film, von Fäden
zu einem Teppich, ist im Grunde eine alltägliche Praxis
und wird durch Regeln in Ordnungen überführt: wissen-
schaftliche, bürokratische, kinematografische usw.
Mittels digitaler Technologie findet eine Befreiung
aus solchen Zwängen statt, und alles kann mit allem
verbunden werden.
   Die Video- oder besser gesagt Bewegtbild-Arbeiten
von Elizabeth Price bewegen sich in einem Spannungsfeld
aus Technologie, Arbeit, Geschlecht und Politik. Sie
bilden eine flexible, aus Bildern bestehende Architektur für die sprachliche Erzählung, die wie eine Etage
in einem mehrstöckigen Haus angesiedelt ist. In weiteren Stockwerken befinden sich Sammlungen unterschiedlicher Dinge, etwa von Gegenständen und Artefakten,
von Fotografien und von Videos oder von Musiksamples.

each element is placed in a room. The completed house
eventually appears as a temporal structure that
only ever makes visible the active pieces of furniture
on each level, while the inactive ones are waiting
to be used or only exist to complete the house. As
I write this, I am reminded of Georges Perec's *Life:
A User's Manual*, which portrays a large apartment building through the sometimes microscopic observations
of objects and people residing within it. Chapter by
chapter, the author reconstructs the individual stories
of the house's inhabitants, occasionally getting lost
in detail, sometimes establishing connections between residents, and sometimes drifting away to other
times and places – all while avoiding any form of
hierarchy or linear narrative structure.

In Elizabeth Price's multilayered building, each
story is a collage composed of many individual
parts – both acoustic and visual – that are positioned,
as it were, side by side and one above the other,
merging into one voice only to drift apart again the
next moment. The rhythmic movement of the various individual voices lends Price's building a distinctive
sound and a musically shaped identity. The entirety of
the material Price uses to make a video is stored
on her computer, sometimes arriving there through the
process of digitization, which is a prominent subject
in her work. As parameters of the digital, recording and
arranging or assembling are equally relevant to forms
of writing as well as filmmaking. Price places impor-
tance on rendering visible the transformations of the
digital; in the simplest version of this, a PC sleeping
in the darkness of her studio might come to life,
its booting-up sound transformed into a speaking voice.

Wie freischwebende Ebenen werden sie am Computer mithilfe eines Videobearbeitungsprogramms miteinander
verwoben und jedes Element wie einzelne Möbelstücke
in einem Raum abgestellt. Das fertiggestellte Haus
erscheint schließlich als ein zeitliches Gebilde,
das immer nur die aktiven Möbelstücke der jeweiligen
Ebenen sichtbar macht, während die inaktiven auf ihren
Einsatz warten oder nur zur Vervollständigung des Hauses
da sind. Jetzt, wo ich das schreibe, erinnert mich
das an Georges Perecs *Das Leben. Gebrauchsanweisung*
(orig.: *La vie mode d'emploi*), in dem ein großes
Mehrfamilienhaus anhand der teilweise mikrosko-
pischen Beobachtungen von Dingen und Menschen in den
einzelnen Wohnungen dargestellt wird. Kapitel für
Kapitel rekonstruiert der Autor darin die individu-
ellen Geschichten der Hausbewohner:innen, verliert
sich manchmal in Details, stellt manchmal Verbindungen
zwischen Bewohner:innen her, treibt manchmal weg in
andere Zeiten und an andere Orte und unterbindet jede
Form von Hierarchie und linearer Erzählform.

In dem vielschichtigen Gebäude von Elizabeth Price
ist jede Geschichte eine Collage aus vielen – akustischen wie visuellen – Einzelstimmen, die gewisser-
maßen neben- und übereinander angesiedelt sind, sich
zu einer Stimme vermischen und im nächsten Moment
wieder auseinanderdriften. Die rhythmisierte Bewegung
der verschiedenen Einzelstimmen verleiht dem
Price'schen Gebäude einen spezifischen Sound und eine
musikalisch geformte Identität. Das gesamte Material,
mit dem Price ein Video macht, befindet sich in ihrem
Computer, gelangt mitunter dorthin über den Prozess
der Digitalisierung, der ein wesentliches Kennzei-
chen ihrer Arbeit ist. Aufnehmen und Arrangieren bzw.

Technology and the manifestations made through it are thus cast in a contingent and interdependent form that is never brought to a conclusion.

Each of Elizabeth Price's works is based on extensive research, which finds her sifting through archives and collections of materials. This specific approach lends each work a distinct identity, its content related to the historically documented events that the artifacts bear witness to. In *NIGHT OF THE WORLD* (2023), for instance, her point of departure is the accidental sinking of a cargo ship carrying luxury cars in the English Channel in 2002. *A RESTORATION* (2016) finds its basis in the collection of Sir Arthur Evans, the archaeologist who is considered to have discovered the ancient Greek city of Knossos. The artist's personal collection of neckties from the 1970s and 1980s and a used edition of German sexologist Reimut Reiche's *Sexuality and Class Struggle* are, in turn, the objects of investigation in *FELT TIP* (2018). In each of these cases, what is most significant for Price is the marginal, minoritarian position of these elements within official historiographies, or rather the gradual invisibility of the voices narrating the events. Price reawakens the past, however, not just as a historian interested in incidental events, but in order to expose traces in each history that have been shaped by apparatuses of power and persist well into our present day. The ecstatically orchestrated mixture of text, sound, and image muddies the past beyond recognition and infects it with a new energy that is at once sad, seductive, and anarchistic.

In her videos, which deconstruct and phantasmagorically reconstruct existing narratives, Elizabeth Price

Zusammenstellen sind, als Parameter des Digitalen,
für Formen des Schreibens und des Filmemachens gleicher-
maßen relevant. Für Price ist es wichtig, die Trans-
formationen des Digitalen sichtbar zu machen, wofür im
einfachsten Fall auch schon mal ein im Dunkeln ihres
Studios schlafender PC zum Leben erwacht und sein
hochfahrender Ton sich in eine sprechende Stimme
verwandelt. Auf diese Weise werden Technologie und die
durch sie vorgenommenen Manifestationen in eine
kontingente und interdependente Form gegossen, ohne
diese abzuschließen.

Jede einzelne Arbeit von Elizabeth Price basiert
auf einer umfassenden Recherche, Sichtung von Archiven
und Materialsammlungen. Diese spezifische Herangehens-
weise verleiht den Arbeiten eine je distinkte Identität,
sie adressiert ihren Inhalt an die historisch belegten
Ereignisse, von denen die Artefakte Zeugnis ablegen.
In *NIGHT OF THE WORLD* (2023) beispielsweise nimmt sie
den Unfall eines Frachtschiffes im Ärmelkanal, welches
im Jahr 2002 mit einer großen Menge von Luxusautos an
Bord untergegangen ist, zum Ausgangspunkt. Die Sammlung des Archäologen Sir Arthur Evans, der als Entdecker
der griechischen Stadt Knossos gilt, ist die Grundlage
für die Arbeit *A RESTORATION* (2016). Die persönliche
Sammlung der Künstlerin von Krawatten aus den 1970er-
und 1980er- Jahren sowie eine gebrauchte Ausgabe
von *Sexualität und Klassenkampf* des deutschen Sexual-
forschers Reimut Reiche sind wiederum die Untersuchung-
sgegenstände in der Arbeit *FELT TIP* (2018). Bedeutsam
für Elizabeth Price sind in allen Fällen die nebensäch-
liche, minoritäre Stellung dieser Elemente innerhalb
der offiziellen Geschichtsschreibung sowie die graduelle
Unsichtbarkeit der die Ereignisse erzählenden Stimmen.

uses technology both as her artistic medium and as
a structuring device in work processes, as well as a
language-generating tool in the events she examines.
Technology, or rather the technological developments of
the twentieth and twenty-first centuries, becomes
a theme for the artist both in terms of the medium she
uses and in terms of societal transformations, particularly changes in human labor. Initially, Price began her
artistic-editorial project with PowerPoint, a program
widely used by companies for presentations; she now
works with a video-editing program that allows her
to retain PowerPoint's aesthetics. Like PowerPoint,
she can design one page after the other, but she can
now make each page many times more complex, individually
editing each of the contained elements – music, voice,
text, and both still and moving image. One recurring
motif is the way the world of work has changed as
a result of digitization, the migration of manual labor
to developing countries with low wages (as in the
textile and iron industries), and the growth of information work, office work, and administration. Evoking
the former industrial society, Price depicts information
society as follows: at the bottom is the (data) repository, above is the administration, and at the top
is the management or executive department. Elizabeth
Price tends to focus on the administration, in part
because it is predominantly female and carries with it
the long memory of gender inequality. The administration
is given assignments that require it to delve into the
existing data repository, where it extracts and collates
the appropriate data. Other assignments run in the
opposite direction, with new data being brought to the
right place in the data storage. This is how data

Price erweckt die Vergangenheit jedoch nicht nur als
an nebensächlichen Ereignissen interessierte Histori-
kerin, sondern um in jeder von ihnen Spuren sichtbar
zu machen, die bis in unsere Tage fortwirken und von
Machtapparaten geprägt sind. Das ekstatisch inszenierte
Gemisch aus Text, Sound und Bild trübt die Vergangenheit bis zur Unkenntlichkeit und infiziert sie mit
neuer Energie, die zugleich traurig, verführerisch und
anarchistisch ist.

Elizabeth Price benutzt für ihre Erzählungen, die
die vorhandenen Erzählungen dekonstruieren und phantas-
magorisch wiederaufbauen, Technologie sowohl als ihr
künstlerisches Arbeitsmittel als auch als strukturie-
rendes Verfahren in Arbeitsabläufen oder als Sprache
generierendes Werkzeug in den von ihr untersuchten
Ereignissen. Technologie, oder besser gesagt die technologischen Entwicklungen des 20. und 21. Jahrhunderts,
thematisiert die Künstlerin sowohl in Bezug auf das
von ihr verwendete Medium als auch auf gesellschaftliche Veränderungen, insbesondere Veränderungen
der menschlichen Arbeit. Ausgehend von einem in Unternehmen für Präsentationen verbreiteten Programm
namens Power Point, mit dem Price ihr künstlerisch-
editorisches Projekt begann, arbeitet sie heute mit
einem Videobearbeitungsprogramm, mit dem sie die
Ästhetik von Power Point beibehalten, also Seite für
Seite nacheinander gestalten, jedoch jede Seite um
ein Vielfaches komplexer ausstatten und alle zum Einsatz
kommenden Elemente – Musik, Stimme, Text, stilles
Bild und bewegtes Bild – einzeln bearbeiten kann. Ein
wiederkehrendes Motiv ist die durch die Digitalisierung veränderte Arbeitswelt, das Abwandern der manuellen
Arbeit in Schwellenländer mit geringen Löhnen, in der

is digitized, as with the artifacts from around 1900
that were discovered during excavations in Crete,
and which can now be viewed on the websites of the
Ashmolean and Pitt Rivers museums in Oxford. In
A RESTORATION, Price uses the digitized artifacts and
drawings of the reconstructed architecture of Knossos
to tell the story from the point of view of the administrators, themselves digital workers who, in order
to escape the monotony of work, surreptitiously move
some of the data aside in order to "[cultivate]
a garden, in a remote corner of the server." It is
as if one were witnessing a revolt 2.0 in the making,
exactly following the path of the reconstructed
history of the creation of Knossos – only from a
different perspective.

The choir, which functions as a kind of signature
in Elizabeth Price's works, and has played a recurring role since at least 2011, serves to create a
polyphonic authorship, a kind of "Us" that becomes the
subject of her videos' narratives and cannot be assigned
unambiguously to a single source. Such an Us permits
a collage of different voices, including that of the
artist, turning multiple perspectives into the organ
of a group. Price introduced the choir in detail in the
three-part work *THE WOOLWORTHS CHOIR OF 1979* (2012),
which begins with a stylistic description of the Gothic
choir, continues with concert recordings of the
American girl group the Shangri-Las, and culminates
in the 1979 fire at the Woolworths department store
in Manchester, where firefighters, store employees,
and others of those present during the incident each
have their say. The merging of many voices into
a unified voice, which Price chooses to be spoken by

Textilindustrie etwa oder der Eisenindustrie, und
die Zunahme der Informationsarbeit, Büroarbeit
und Verwaltung. Analog zur ehemaligen Industriegesell-
schaft skizziert Price die Informationsgesellschaft
wie folgt: Unten befindet sich der (Daten-)Speicher,
darüber die Administration und oben das Management oder
die Exekutive. Elizabeth Price widmet sich in der
Regel der Administration, auch deswegen, weil sie über-
wiegend weiblich besetzt ist und *das lange Gedächtnis*
der Ungleichheit der Geschlechter mit sich herumträgt.
Der Administration werden Aufträge erteilt, die sie
in den vorhandenen Datenspeicher führen, wo sie
die passenden Daten entnimmt und zusammenführt.
Andere Aufträge verlaufen umgekehrt, neue Daten werden
an die richtige Stelle im Datenspeicher gebracht.
Auf diese Weise geschieht die Digitalisierung von Daten,
etwa von Artefakten aus den Jahren um 1900, die bei
Ausgrabungen auf Kreta entdeckt wurden und heute auf
der Website des Ashmolean und des Pitt Rivers Museum
in Oxford anzuschauen sind. In *A RESTORATION* erzählt
Price anhand der digitalisierten Artefakte und Zeichnungen der rekonstruierten Architektur von Knossos
die Geschichte aus Sicht der Administration, ihrerseits
digitale Arbeiterinnen, die, um der Arbeitsmonotonie
zu entfliehen, einige der Daten unbeobachtet zur
Seite schaffen, um damit »in einer abgelegenen Ecke
des Servers einen Garten zu kultivieren« (orig.: »We are
cultivating a garden, in a remote corner of the server«). Es ist, als würde man einer sich gerade formie-
renden 2.0-Revolte beiwohnen, die exakt das befolgt,
was die rekonstruierte Entstehungsgeschichte von
Knossos aufgeschrieben hat – nur aus einer anderen
Perspektive.

a digital voice, subverts hierarchy and replaces it
with an alternative narrative. The choir motif can also
be applied to the work's visual dimension, where its
heterogeneous collection is unified through digital
animation, suspending both temporal and spatial dis-
tinctions. Wherever the images might come from, and
whatever date they bear, the only thing that matters
to Elizabeth Price is the transformation of the present
and its problematic interplay of technology and culture.
The best manifestation of a currently widespread
debate about the state of the human in the context of
the post-human is found in *NIGHT OF THE WORLD*, which
Price made using only a few elements. The focus here
is on the car as a mass product and status symbol,
nowadays ambivalently caught between economy and
ecology. Initially only hinted at through the cockpit's
high-tech blue-and-red displays, BMW sports cars
and limousines float gracefully and effortlessly across
the otherwise empty black space in the video's second
part. The cars are the talking Us, lecturing with
"realistic sound" about their "athletic" and "energetic"
bodies, "attractive" forms, "intuitive operation,"
"exquisite interface" and "super-controlled glide."
These objects, spruced up as if for presentation and
alluringly revolving with welcoming open doors,
are transformed in the artist's hands into active
subjects who, equipped with advertising copy, perform
an increasingly euphoric dance to Genesis's "Follow You
Follow Me." The cars experience their vivification
at the moment of their demise, and one can almost hear
the car asking us: Will you follow me?

Matthias Ulrich

Der Chor, der in der Arbeit von Elizabeth Price eine Art von Signatur darstellt und spätestens seit 2011 eine wiederkehrende Rolle spielt, dient der Kreation einer vielstimmigen Autor:innenschaft, eines Wir, das das Subjekt der Erzählungen in ihren Videoarbeiten ist und sich nicht eindeutig und einer einzigen Quelle zuordnen lässt. Ein solches Wir ermöglicht die Collage unterschiedlicher Stimmen, die der Künstlerin mit eingeschlossen, um mehrere Perspektiven zum Organ einer Gruppe zu machen. Ausführlich eingeführt hat Price den Chor in der dreiteiligen Arbeit *THE WOOLWORTHS CHOIR OF 1979* (2012), die mit einer stilgeschichtlichen Beschreibung des gotischen Chors anfängt, sich mit Konzertaufnahmen der US-amerikanischen Girlgroup The Shangri-Las fortsetzt und schließlich beim Brand des Woolworth-Kaufhauses in Manchester 1979 mündet, wo direkt betroffene Feuerwehrleute, Kaufhaus-Mitarbeiter:innen und beim Unglück Anwesende zu Wort kommen. Die Auflösung vieler Stimmen in einer unisono vorgetragenen Stimme, die Price in ihren Arbeiten durch eine digitale Stimme sprechen lässt, unterwandert die Hierarchie und stellt an ihrer statt eine alternative Erzählung vor. Das Chormotiv lässt sich auch auf den Bildbereich übertragen, dessen heterogene Sammlung durch die digitale Animation vereinheitlicht wird, mit der zeitliche wie auch räumliche Unterschiede außer Kraft gesetzt werden. Wo auch immer die Bilder herkommen und welches Datum sie auch tragen, für Elizabeth Price zählt alleine die Transformation der Gegenwart und deren zu problematisierendes Zusammenspiel von Technologie und Kultur. Bestes Beispiel einer aktuell breit geführten Debatte über den Zustand des Humanen im Feld des

Post-Humanen bietet *NIGHT OF THE WORLD*, das Price mit
nur wenigen zum Einsatz kommenden Elementen hergestellt hat. Das ambivalent zwischen Ökonomie und Ökolo-
gie im Heute angekommene Massen- und Statusprodukt
Auto steht hier im Mittelpunkt. Anfangs nur angedeutet
durch die im Cockpit verbauten, blau und rot leuchtenden High-Tech-Displays, navigieren im zweiten Teil
BMW-Sportwagen und -Limousinen anmutig und schwerelos
über den ansonsten leeren schwarzen Projektionsraum.
Die Autos sind das sprechende Wir, das mit realisti-
schem Klang über seinen sportlichen und energetischen
Körper, attraktive Formen, intuitive Bedienung, perfekte
Schnittstellen und superkontrollierten Gleitdrang
doziert. Die wie auf Präsentationsshows herausgeputzt
und mit einladend offenen Türen begehrlich sich drehenden Objekte werden in den Händen der Künstlerin
zu den aktiven, mit Werbetext-Terminologie ausgestat-
teten Subjekten eines zunehmend euphorischer und zu
Follow You Follow Me von Genesis tanzenden Balletts.
Ihre Verlebendigung erfahren die Autos im Moment ihres
Untergangs, und fast hört man das Auto uns fragen:
Will you follow me?

Matthias Ulrich

Elizabeth Price has said that she decides when a
piece is finished "when I feel, in some way, that the
density of all [my] material is expressed through
the narrative."[1] This matter-of-fact, perfectly pragma-
tic insight about conclusions is worth opening with
for at least two reasons: First, it alludes to the
anxiety of writing about her practice at all, to the
problem of trying to contain the ever-refracting angles
found in each of her videos, from which one could
approach, contextualize, and articulate a body of work
that is itself a model of lucid complexity. Articul-
ation, indeed, is one of her primary concerns, which
is embodied by body-less choruses of loquacious narrators who can't stop (re-)directing the viewer toward
the ever-broadening contexts for each piece's subject.
These works are also distinguished by their subversive appropriation of corporate slideshow aesthetics

EIN LANGES GEDÄCHTNIS

Elizabeth Price hat einmal gesagt, sie entscheide, wann ein Werk fertig sei, »wenn ich irgendwie spüre, dass die Dichte [meines] gesamten Materials auf narrativer Ebene zum Ausdruck kommt«.[1] Es lohnt sich aus mindestens zwei Gründen, mit dieser nüchternen und vollkommen pragmatischen Erkenntnis über das Fertigwerden zu beginnen: Erstens spielt sie auf die Angst davor an, überhaupt über ihr Schaffen zu schreiben, auf das Problem, die sich immer wieder brechenden Blickwinkel erfassen zu wollen, die sich in jedem ihrer Videos finden und von denen aus man sich einem Œuvre, das selbst ein Modell klarer Komplexität ist, nähern, es kontextualisieren und artikulieren könnte. Artikulation ist eigentlich eines ihrer Hauptanliegen. Es wird von körperlosen Chören redseliger Erzähler:innen verkörpert, die die Betrachtenden unablässig auf die sich permanent erweiternden Kontexte

– declarative texts that appear in boxes floating atop
a parade of archival images, CGI diagrams, and both
found and original video footage. Price deploys these
aesthetics to mount a unique mode of Institutional
Critique that addresses her concerns with social hierarchies, gender, language, technology, and memory.
Testifying to the sheer depth of her work, this exhibition also presents several video lectures that Price
produced during the pandemic. Closer to traditional
artist statements and exegeses, these presentations
unpack the thought processes and production workflows
that she navigated while developing her projects'
wells of objects, data, and overlapping narratives
– without mitigating the respective works' delicate
constructions and essential mysteries.

The second reason to begin with a point about end-
ings is that doing so perhaps invokes one of the
paradoxical qualities encompassed in all of Price's
work, which I think distinguishes it from that of
her peers and forebears. Specifically, she constructs
her videos' arguments in a simultaneously rational
and irrational register that allows them to resist
closure, despite their linear form; they begin, they
end, and still they continue. These works challenge our
impulse to seek the origin of things (of objects,
ideas, and words), because an origin (like an ending)
is where alternatives and future suppositions are
eliminated, the point from which everything springs
forth or into which it collapses. A Deleuzian touch
runs through her practice, rooted in its singular
address to the viewer that is at once dogmatic and ped-
agogic, a packaging and an unfolding that achieves
what the philosopher described in his conception of

des Themas der jeweiligen Arbeit verweisen. Die Werke kennzeichnet auch eine subversive Aneignung der Ästhetik von Bildschirmpräsentationen in Unternehmen – mit erklärenden, in Kästen erscheinenden Texten, die über einer Abfolge von Archivbildern, computer-animierten Grafiken und gefundenen oder eigenen Videosequenzen erscheinen. Price setzt diese Ästhetik ein, um eine einzigartige Form von Institutionskritik zu entwickeln, die ihre Anliegen in Bezug auf gesell-schaftliche Hierarchien, Gender, Sprache, Technik und Erinnerung thematisiert. Um die beeindruckende Tiefe ihres Schaffens zu verdeutlichen, präsentiert die Ausstellung auch einige Videovorträge, die Price während der Pandemie produziert hat. Die Präsenta-tionen ähneln gängigen Statements und Werkinter-pretationen von Kunstschaffenden und bieten Einblicke in die Denkprozesse und Produktionsabläufe bei der Entwicklung der ihren Projekten zugrunde liegenden Objekte, Daten und sich überkreuzenden Erzählungen – ohne dabei die empfindlichen Konstruktionen und zen-tralen Rätsel der Werke zu beschädigen.

Der zweite Grund für die Entscheidung, mit einem Satz über das Fertigwerden zu beginnen, hängt damit zusammen, dass damit vielleicht eine der paradoxen Qualitäten angesprochen wird, die Prices gesamtes Werk durchziehen und durch die es sich meiner Ansicht nach von dem ihrer Zeitgenoss:innen und Vorläufer:innen abhebt. Konkreter gesagt verorten sich die Thesen in ihren Videos in einem zugleich rationalen und irratio-nalen Register, was es ihnen trotz ihrer linearen Form ermöglicht, unabgeschlossen zu bleiben. Sie haben einen Anfang und ein Ende, und doch bestehen sie weiter. Die Arbeiten stellen unseren Drang infrage, den Ursprung von

the "image of thought." An image of thought – that is,
the desire or trigger that prompts a cognitive
journey, wherever it may lead – precedes thinking and
is therefore theoretical. But, as a concept, it has
so much in common with the experience of Price's
art that I'm tempted to say, in the distinctive vernacular of her narrators: Yes, here it is, in material
form: philosophical commencement and recommencement;
a field of difference and repetition, generatively
opening up avenues for new narratives, new structures,
new systems that directly oppose the social and
economic realities that make the history of knowledge
feel fixed, finite, and dead.

Which begs the question: How? Let's start with the
earliest work in the exhibition, *NIGHT OF THE WORLD*,
the original iteration of which was produced in 2012,
the same year that Price won the Turner Prize for her
ecstatic video *THE WOOLWORTHS CHOIR OF 1979*. Like
that piece, *NIGHT OF THE WORLD* (2023) is a single-
channel projection that tells a history of an actual
event – in this case, the sinking of a cargo ship
laden with new luxury vehicles off the British Isles
in 2002 – taking fanciful digressions to include
potentially real and certainly imagined episodes in its
narrative. A hallmark of Price's style is the use of
animated onscreen text that appropriates advertising
lingo – a trait that immediately links her with a
previous generation of text-based conceptual artists
like Barbara Kruger and Jenny Holzer. In firm and
affirmation-heavy intonations, red text emerges line
by line on a black screen to ominously declare,
"You don't have to see something to know it is there."
Subsequent lines encourage viewers to "Relax into an

Dingen (von Objekten, Ideen oder Wörtern) zu suchen,
denn an einem Ursprung (wie an einem Endpunkt)
sind jegliche Alternativen oder Annahmen über die
Zukunft aufgehoben; es ist jener Punkt, an dem alles
seinen Anfang nimmt oder in den alles hineinstürzt.
Ein Deleuze'sches Moment durchzieht ihr Schaffen.
Es beruht auf der einzigartigen Weise, das Publikum
anzusprechen, zugleich dogmatisch und pädagogisch,
sich verschließend und sich entfaltend. Sie schafft
das, was der Philosoph mit seinem Begriff vom »Bild des
Denkens« beschrieben hat. Ein Bild des Denkens – das
heißt der Wunsch oder Auslöser, der eine geistige
Reise anregt, wo auch immer sie hinführen mag – geht
dem Denken voraus und ist daher etwas Theoretisches.
Aber als Konzept hat es so viel mit der Erfahrung von
Prices Kunst gemein, dass ich versucht bin, im unver-
kennbaren Jargon ihrer Erzählstimmen zu sagen: Ja,
hier ist er, in seiner materiellen Gestalt: der philo-
sophische Beginn und Neubeginn; ein Feld der Differenz
und Wiederholung, das generativ neue Erzählungen,
neue Strukturen, neue Systeme ermöglicht. Diese
widersetzen sich unmittelbar den gesellschaftlichen
und ökonomischen Realitäten, welche die Wissensge-
schichte festgefahren, begrenzt und tot wirken lassen.
   Was die Frage nach dem Wie aufwirft. Beginnen
wir mit dem frühesten Werk in der Ausstellung, *NIGHT
OF THE WORLD*, dessen ursprüngliche Fassung 2012
entstand, dem Jahr, in dem Price für ihr ekstatisches
Video *THE WOOLWORTHS CHOIR OF 1979* mit dem Turner
Prize ausgezeichnet wurde. Wie diese Arbeit ist auch
NIGHT OF THE WORLD (2023) eine 1-Kanal-Videoprojektion,
die die Geschichte einer tatsächlichen Begebenheit erzählt – nämlich den Untergang eines mit Luxusfahrzeugen

advanced spatial concept," followed by what reads like
quotations culled from a contemporary car commercial
and visual graphics of a vehicle dashboard. "There are
different rules here," we're told, and indeed, viewers
will find themselves positioned as consumers, well
beneath the consumer-learner position we typically
adopt whenever we enter a gallery or museum space.
From the jump, the disembodied "voice" of NIGHT OF THE
WORLD postures beyond and above us, surrounds us,
to authoritatively sync itself to both our sensory and
cognitive functions. It thinks for and before us,
prefacing numerous statements with "Yes," as if to
demonstrate that the narrator (and by extension
the artwork itself) not only agrees with our thoughts,
but has already anticipated them.

Once the narrator becomes audible – with its
announcement that the vehicle is equipped with freely
programmable and intelligent memory keys that are
able to combine voice and visual display – Price takes
NIGHT OF THE WORLD into more expressive territory.
An inoffensive alt-rock instrumental track kicks in,
and the montage accelerates through a cluster of
vibrantly saturated, unfocused shots of the entertainment panel and the dash's speedometer, its dial
spinning and glowing to sell us that bustling after-
hours social life so desired by the overworked
working class. Though decked out to dazzle users with
"the shimmering effect of cool high-tech," the
vehicles ultimately meet a different fate. They drift
to the bottom of the Atlantic – a narrative development introduced by pixelated images of the sunken cars
that looks like a cross between snuff films and the
deep sea drone footage that comprises James Cameron's

beladenen Frachtschiffs vor den Britischen Inseln im Jahr 2002. Sie schweift dabei in fantasievolle Exkurse ab und verwebt in der Geschichte potenziell wahre mit offenkundig erfundenen Anekdoten. Ein Markenzeichen von Prices Stil ist die Verwendung von animiertem, Werbejargon aufgreifendem Text im Bild – ein Merkmal, das eine unmittelbare Verbindung zu einer früheren Generation textbasierter Konzeptkünstlerinnen wie Barbara Kruger oder Jenny Holzer herstellt. In festem und stark bekräftigendem Tonfall erscheint auf einem schwarzen Bildschirm Zeile für Zeile roter Text, der auf unheilvolle Weise verkündet: »Man muss eine Sache nicht sehen, um zu wissen, dass sie da ist.« Die folgenden Zeilen ermutigen dazu, sich »in ein fortschrittliches Raumkonzept« hinein zu entspannen, gefolgt von Textzeilen, die wie Zitate aus einer aktuellen Autowerbung oder vom Display am Armaturenbrett eines Fahrzeugs wirken. »Hier gelten andere Regeln«, wird uns gesagt, und tatsächlich finden sich die Betrachter:innen in der Position von Konsument:innen wieder, deutlich unterhalb der Position als Konsument:innen und Lernende, die wir gewöhnlich beim Betreten eines Ausstellungs- oder Museumsraums einnehmen. Von Anfang an ist die körperlose »Stimme« von *NIGHT OF THE WORLD* um uns und über uns, umgibt uns, um sich schließlich gebieterisch mit unseren sensorischen und kognitiven Funktionen zu synchronisieren. Sie denkt für und vor uns, wobei sie zahlreichen Erklärungen zunächst ein »Ja,« voranstellt, als wolle sie demonstrieren, dass die Erzählinstanz (und im weiteren Sinne das Kunstwerk selbst) unseren Gedanken nicht nur zustimmt, sondern sie bereits vorausgesehen hat.

Ghosts of the Abyss (2003). Detached from fulfilling their intended use, the vehicles instead reconstitute themselves as an underwater balletic dance troupe. In its liberation of its subjects from the prepenned histories their designers programmed for them, *NIGHT OF THE WORLD* stops just short of launching into a full-on disquisition on object-oriented ontology. The vehicles' AI learns and adapts to their new context, remapping their narrative outside of the rote system that says everything will live out its life in the same way. It is telling and in no way incidental that this freedom manifests itself in Price's piece only when the object becomes removed from its societal context, outside of time and space at the bottom of the ocean floor.

Spatial metaphors, in fact, play a major role in every piece in this exhibition. The triumphant dual-projection work *A RESTORATION* (2016) – its two channels combining to form an enveloping, superwide frame – concerns the drawings, photographs, and other visual representations that Sir Arthur Evans made of his excavation of the ancient city of Knossos. The archive at the Ashmolean Museum, which is one of the oldest museums in the world, doubly functions as a historical narrative of representational media, with its materials including near every archival standard across its centuries of existence – from drawings to etchings to photographs, from daguerreotypes to megapixels. Keen to the fact that earlier documentary technologies (namely, drawings) were especially susceptible to human intervention, Price noticed that Evans's understanding of Knossos and their civilization was informed by his own interventions in the archive: the lines he

    Sobald die Erzählstimme zu hören ist – mit ihrem
Hinweis, dass das Fahrzeug mit frei programmier-
baren und intelligenten Datenspeichern ausgestattet
ist, mit denen sich Stimme und visuelle Darstellung kombinieren lassen – überführt Price *NIGHT OF
THE WORLD* in einen expressiveren Bereich. Unaufdring-
liche, instrumentale Alternative-Rock-Musik setzt
ein, und die Montage beschleunigt sich in mehreren
farbstark gesättigten, unscharfen Aufnahmen des
Bedienungsfelds für das Entertainment-System und des
Tachometers im Armaturenbrett. Das Ziffernblatt wirbelt
herum und leuchtet, um uns jenes pulsierende feier-
abendliche Sozialleben vorzugaukeln, nach dem sich
die überarbeitete Arbeiterklasse so sehr sehnt.
Wenngleich die Fahrzeuge herausgeputzt sind, um ihre
Nutzer:innen mit dem »schimmernden Effekt coolen
Hightechs« zu blenden, wird ihnen ein anderes Schicksal
zuteil. Sie sinken auf den Grund des Atlantiks
– eine narrative Entwicklung, die durch verpixelte
Bilder der gesunkenen Autos angekündigt wird, die wie
eine Kreuzung von Snuff-Filmen mit den Tiefseedrohnen-
Aufnahmen aus James Camerons *Ghost of the Abyss* (2003)
wirken. Befreit von der Erfüllung ihres eigent-
lichen Zwecks, formieren sich die Fahrzeuge statt-
dessen neu zu einer Unterwasserballett-Tanztruppe.
Durch die Befreiung der Subjekte in *NIGHT OF THE WORLD*
von den vorgezeichneten Geschichten, die ihre
Designer für sie programmiert hatten, wird die Arbeit
fast zu einer vollständigen Abhandlung über objekt-
orientierte Ontologie. Die KI der Fahrzeuge lernt und
passt sich ihrer neuen Umgebung an; sie fasst
dazu ihre Geschichte neu, außerhalb des routinemäßigen
Verfahrens, dem zufolge alles auf die gleiche Weise

extended, the gaps he filled, and the language he used.
Rather than mount an exposition of Evans's violence
to history, Price critiques it from a parallel point.
As in *NIGHT OF THE WORLD*, the piece is narrated by
a chorus of sentient AI – in this case, a group of
administrators overseeing the Ashmolean's digital
database – and once again they run away with (and from)
their programmed assignment. Their telling of Knossos
begins by outlining a gathering they are organizing
in the present, before transforming into a thesis on
the structural fractures observed on certain drinking
vessels. The conclusion upon which they arrive – that
the breaks were made for their sound, announcing
a change in the law (of the world) – is a compelling
interpretation, though it is unmistakably fiction.
Price hasn't cleaned up Evans's mess so much as added
to the noise. The narrator's authority, backed by
that of the institution, is perhaps too powerful to
overthrow; it will suffice, then, to cast it further
into doubt.

    FELT TIP (2018) may initially seem more modest
than *A RESTORATION*. It runs half the duration, and its
subject (an isolated history of men's neckties) is,
relative to the preservation of an ancient civilization, comparatively narrow – and quite literally so.
Price cheekily mimics the necktie's dimensions in the
work's form; here, she once again employs dual projection, now with both projectors oriented vertically
to compose an almost comically slender frame. "When
dealing with the managerial class," declares Price's
administrator-narrators, "there is nothing quite as
sharp as a very stupid joke." Indeed, *FELT TIP* is one
of Price's funniest and most overtly political works.

ablaufen soll. Es ist bezeichnend und keineswegs ein
Zufall, dass sich diese Freiheit in Prices Arbeit
nur dann manifestiert, wenn das Objekt – nun außerhalb
von Zeit und Raum und am Meeresgrund – seinem gesellschaftlichen Kontext enthoben ist.

Im Grunde genommen spielen Raummetaphern in jeder
Arbeit der Ausstellung eine zentrale Rolle. Die tri-
umphale Doppelprojektions-Arbeit *A RESTORATION* (2016)
– deren zwei Kanäle so kombiniert sind, dass sie
einen umfassenden superbreiten Rahmen bilden – befasst
sich mit den Zeichnungen, Fotografien und anderen
visuellen Darstellungen, die Sir Arthur Evans von seiner Ausgrabung der antiken Stadt Knossos angefertigt
hat. Das Archiv des Ashmolean Museum, eines der ältes-
ten Museen der Welt, fungiert in doppelter Hinsicht
als historische Erzählung von Darstellungsmedien,
da die im Verlauf seiner jahrhundertelangen Existenz
angesammelten Materialien fast jeden archivarischen
Standard vertreten – von Zeichnungen zu Radierungen und
Fotografien, von Daguerreotypien bis hin zu Megapixeln.
Price ist sich der Tatsache bewusst, dass frühere
Dokumentationstechniken (insbesondere Zeichnungen)
besonders anfällig für menschliche Eingriffe waren,
und stellte fest, dass Evans' Verständnis von Knossos
und der dortigen Zivilisation von seinen eigenen
Eingriffen ins Archiv beeinflusst war: von den Linien,
die er verlängerte, den Lücken, die er füllte,
und der Sprache, die er benutzte. Anstatt die Gewalt
herauszustellen, die Evans der Geschichte antut, kritisiert Price diese von einem parallelen Standpunkt aus.
Wie in *NIGHT OF THE WORLD* ist auch die Erzählinstanz
dieser Arbeit eine vielstimmige, empfindungsfähige KI
– in diesem Fall eine Gruppe von Administrator:innen,

The necktie has long gestured toward on-going lega-
cies of social and class imbalances – an insignia that
implicitly conveys membership within an elite social
club, evoking both racial (white) and gendered (male)
privilege. But when the managerial class's demographics
broadened in the 1970s and 1980s, the garment's func-
tion as a status symbol was thrown into crisis. Price's
database-dwelling narrators see the humor in power
upended (not to mention the spectacle of the necktie's
resemblance to a giant phallus), and conjure their own
theory of its new agenda.

The history the narrators tell is hyperbolic and
conjectural as ever, situated both in that which
they lack (touch) and in their trade (memory). Puns
and language games dominate their pronouncements
since, yes, they're funny, but also because etymology
is just as integral as any history within Price's
archaeological system. If we are to get to the bottom
of what happened, or how we got here, or what else
could have been, we can only do so by tracing and
retracing the complex nature of the past's present
conditions. In this spirit, *FELT TIP*'s narrators
– who may well be speaking to us from after the Sing-
ularity – describe for us a resemblance they've found
between the geometric designs on the era's neckties
and computer memory chips (one imagines, their ances-
tors). Their "short history" becomes a long (...long
...) memory, which reminds them of the *longue durée*
– the French Annales school's macroscopic brand of
historiography that considers broader trends and social
structures alongside any particular biography or event
in their accounts of the past. The narrators adopt
a similar preference for patterns and repetitions,

die die digitale Datenbank des Ashmolean Museum
pflegen. Erneut laufen diese mit (und von) ihrer pro-
grammierten Aufgabe davon. Ihre Erzählung von Knossos
beginnt mit der Beschreibung einer Versammlung, die
sie in der Gegenwart organisieren, und verwandelt sich
schließlich in eine Abhandlung über die an bestimm-
ten Trinkgefäßen beobachteten strukturellen Brüche.
Das Fazit, zu dem sie kommen – dass die Gefäße zerbrochen wurden wegen des dabei entstehenden Klangs, der
einen Wandel im Gesetz (der Welt) ankündigt –, ist eine
überzeugende Interpretation, aber dennoch eindeutig
eine Fiktion. Statt Evans' Durcheinander zu bereinigen,
hat Price es vielmehr noch verschlimmert. Die Auto-
rität der Erzählinstanz, ihrerseits von derjenigen
der Institution gestützt, ist vielleicht zu machtvoll,
um überwunden zu werden; es sollte also genügen,
sie weiter in Zweifel zu ziehen.
  FELT TIP (2018) mag auf den ersten Blick schlichter
wirken als *A RESTORATION*. Die Laufzeit der Arbeit
ist nur halb so lang, und ihr Thema (eine isolierte
Geschichte der Krawatte) ist im Vergleich zur Frage
der Erhaltung einer antiken Zivilisation relativ schmal
– und zwar im wahrsten Sinne des Wortes. Mit der
Gestalt des Werks greift Price augenzwinkernd die Kra-
wattenform auf; sie verwendet auch hier wieder eine
Doppelprojektion, richtet nun allerdings beide
Projektoren vertikal aus, wodurch eine derart schmale
Projektionsfläche entsteht, dass es fast komisch wirkt.
»Im Umgang mit der Managerebene«, erklärt Prices
Erzählstimme der Administrator:innen, gibt es »nichts
Schärferes als sehr schlechte Witze«. Und in der Tat
gehört *FELT TIP* nicht nur zu Prices humorvollsten
Arbeiten, sondern auch zu jenen, die am unverhohlensten

directing us toward unfrequented routes through the necktie's history so they can reclaim it as an empower- ing (rather than merely classist) form of attire. The past, looped and entangled around itself in this telling, is made once again present – that is, *felt* – by its very reorganization.

Context, which is arguably the primary subject of Price's work, is always (re-)constructed in the present tense, and her latest piece, *UNDERFOOT* (2022), is possibly her purest expression of this sentiment yet. Here, Price fixates on the floors of Glasgow's landmark Mitchell Library, a palace of self-directed learning and inquiry. Much like the piece itself, the space is sound sensitive, structurally vertical, and a container of intersecting thoughts, agendas, and routes through an essentially infinite supply of information. Libraries need silence, and Price here fully mutes her narrators' voices for the first time since her light-sensitive dual-projection video *SUNLIGHT* (2013). We read their rhythmically delivered texts onscreen and hear only their fingers clicking their keyboards – yet another instance of Price emphasizing the digital (i.e. pha- langes) as ballast for the removal of the corpus. There is a body *somewhere*, but we only sense its traces. Fitting, then, that *UNDERFOOT* would circuitously land its attention on the building's various styles of carpeting, which absorbs and tempers stray sounds, bears visitors' physical presence (their footprints), and is itself the fruit of machines operated by so many invisible designers, creators, and workers. Trefoils, quatrefoils, and trellises abound, as do wreaths, pinecones, and peonies. Echoing the administrator's opening gambit in *A RESTORATION*, the carpet designs

politisch sind. Die Krawatte ist seit Langem schon
ein Symbol anhaltender sozialer und klassenbedingter
Ungleichheit – ein Abzeichen, das implizit die Mit-
gliedschaft in einem elitären Gesellschaftsklub
kommuniziert und dabei auf ein auf Herkunft (weiß) und
Geschlecht (männlich) beruhendes Privileg verweist.
Aber als die Zusammensetzung der Managerebene in den
1970er- und 1980er-Jahren vielfältiger wurde, geriet
das Kleidungsstück in seiner Funktion als Statussymbol
in eine Krise. Prices die Datenbank bewohnende Erzäh-
ler:innen erkennen den Witz in der umgestürzten Macht
(ganz zu schweigen von der spektakulären Ähnlichkeit der Krawatte mit einem riesigen Phallus) und
zaubern ihre ganz eigene Theorie über deren neue Agenda
aus dem Hut.

Die von den Erzähler:innen vorgetragene Geschichte
ist wie immer übertrieben und spekulativ und situ-
iert sich zugleich in dem, was ihnen fehlt (Kontakt),
und in ihrem Handwerk (Erinnerung). Wortwitze und
Sprachspiele herrschen in ihren Äußerungen vor, denn
ja, sie sind lustig, aber auch deswegen, weil in
Prices archäologischem System die Etymologie genauso
grundlegend ist wie jegliche Art von Geschichte.
Wenn wir herausfinden sollen, was geschehen ist oder
wie wir hierhergekommen sind oder was sonst noch
hätte passieren können, kann das nur gelingen, wenn
wir das komplexe Wesen der in der Vergangenheit gegen-
wärtigen Bedingungen nachzeichnen und nachvollziehen.
In diesem Sinne beschreiben uns die Erzähler:innen
von *FELT TIP* – die möglicherweise aus einer Zeit nach
der Singularität zu uns sprechen – eine von ihnen
festgestellte Ähnlichkeit zwischen den geometrischen
Mustern auf den Krawatten jener Epoche und Speicherchips

cultivate a garden, not for their ornament, but because
they are soft and therefore quiet. As it was with the
necktie designs in *FELT TIP*, images are never simply
aesthetically arbitrary, but exist to cue other sensual
responses in the beholder, including their intuition.

Indeed, Price understands that an image is never
simply an image, and so she again takes us deeper.
Plunging down, through radiant digital (i.e. computer-
generated) renderings of the ostensibly flat textile
designs – "through the flora and foliage, the petals
and the leaves ... the rhizomes, and rhizoids, and
rhizines" – we hone in on the next dynamic layer
of *UNDERFOOT*'s complex: the loom, its multi-color scan
lines, and, crucially, the workers (almost always
women) who operate it. And it's here that the video
cartwheels and ends, in a charged, poetic gesture that
tilts our gaze up toward the looping chain of spools
passing above the worker, forming a new "abundant and
empty" garden in the ceiling – the implications of
which are left in ominous suspension. In Price's work,
a history is never elaborate enough to escape the social
mechanisms at the base of its roots. Were it content to
merely vigorously untangle these networks for viewers,
her videos would be noble and essential enough. But it's
Price's refusal to let history stay linear, to become
closed within a stable, resolved argument, that allows
her investigations to induce a state of cognitive
euphoria. Through provoking the viewers to always con-
struct, deconstruct, and reconstruct our understandings
of the present, Price's videos encourage us to see
what other highs we might unearth.

Blake Williams

von Computern (die ihre Vorfahren sein könnten). Ihre
»kurze Geschichte« wird zu einem langen (...langen...)
Gedächtnis, das sie an die Longue durée erinnert
– jene makroskopische Art der Geschichtsschreibung
der französischen Annales-Schule, die in ihren Darstellungen der Vergangenheit neben einzelnen Biografien
oder Ereignissen auch allgemeinere Tendenzen und
gesellschaftliche Strukturen berücksichtigt. Die
Erzähler:innen folgen einer ähnlichen Vorliebe für
Muster und Wiederholungen und führen uns auf ungewöhn-
lichen Wegen durch die Geschichte der Krawatte, um sie
sich als ermächtigendes (statt nur Klassenunterschiede
markierendes) Kleidungsstück wieder anzueignen. Die
Vergangenheit, in dieser Erzählung ineinander gewunden
und verwickelt, wird gerade durch ihre Neuausrichtung
erneut präsent gemacht – das heißt, gefühlt.

   Kontext ist wohl das zentrale Thema von Prices
Arbeiten, und er wird immer im Präsens (neu) geschaffen; in ihrer jüngsten Arbeit, *UNDERFOOT* (2022),
kommt diese Idee vielleicht auf bisher deutlichste
Weise zum Ausdruck. Hier fokussiert Price auf die
einzelnen Ebenen der Mitchell Library, eines Glasgower
Wahrzeichens, das ein Palast selbstständigen Lernens
und Forschens ist. Ähnlich wie die Arbeit selbst ist
der Raum geräuschempfindlich, vertikal strukturiert
und ein Behältnis für sich kreuzende Gedanken, Agenden
und Wege durch einen letztlich unendlichen Vorrat
an Informationen. Bibliotheken sind auf Stille ange-
wiesen, und so lässt Price hier erstmals seit ihrer
lichtempfindlichen Video-Doppelprojektion *SUNLIGHT*
(2013) die Stimmen ihrer Erzählinstanzen verstummen.
Wir lesen ihre rhythmisch vorgebrachten Texte auf
dem Bildschirm und hören nur das Klicken ihrer Finger

1 "FVU FRAMES: Elizabeth Price, 'Felt Tip', 2018,"
   interview, Film and Video Umbrella, December 5,
   2018, video, 7:19, https://youtu.be/do-2st7-rWU.

Blake Williams is an artist, filmmaker, and writer based in Toronto, Canada, where he cofounded the production company BlueMagenta Films. He also regularly contributed to *Cinema Scope* and *Filmmaker* magazines, and has recently worked as an assistant programmer for MDFF Selects and Big Ears Festival. His shorts, features, and video installations have been screened and exhibited at the Toronto International Film Festival, Berlinale, New York Film Festival, Locarno Festival, Jeonju International Film Festival, Internationale Kurzfilmtage Oberhausen, FIDMarseille, Cinéma du Réel, and the Museum of Modern Art in New York.

auf der Tastatur – ein weiteres Beispiel dafür,
wie Price das Digitale dem abwesenden Körper gegen-
überstellt – in diesem Fall die körperlosen, digitalen
Texte dem Geräusch der tippenden Fingerspitzen.
Irgendwo ist ein Körper vorhanden, aber wir bemerken
nur seine Spuren. So ist es nur angemessen, dass
UNDERFOOT die Aufmerksamkeit umständlich auf die ver-
schiedenen Teppichböden im Gebäude lenkt, welche
Störgeräusche absorbieren und dämpfen, die physische
Präsenz des Publikums (er-)tragen und selbst das
Produkt von Maschinen sind, die von einer großen
Anzahl unsichtbarer Designer:innen, Gestalter:innen
und Arbeiter:innen bedient werden. Dreipass-, Vierpass-
und Flechtwerk-Ornamente gibt es in Hülle und Fülle,
ebenso wie Kränze, Tannenzapfen und Pfingstrosen.
Den eröffnenden Schachzug der Administrator:innen aus
A RESTORATION aufgreifend, bilden die Teppich-Designs
einen Garten, nicht der Ornamente wegen, sondern
weil sie weich sind und daher auch still. Wie bei den
Krawatten-Designs von *FELT TIP* unterliegen die
Bilder nie einfach bloß einer ästhetischen Willkür,
sondern sind deshalb vorhanden, um in den Betrachtenden andere sinnliche Reaktionen auszulösen, inklusive
ihrer Intuition.

Tatsächlich versteht Price, dass ein Bild nie einfach ein Bild ist, und so nimmt sie uns auch hier mit
auf eine tiefere Ebene. Indem wir hinabtauchen, durch
die strahlenden digitalen (also computergenerierten)
Bilder der vermeintlich flachen Textildesigns – »durch
die Pflanzen und das Blattwerk, die Blütenblätter und
das Laub [...] die Rhizome und Rhizoide und Rhizine« –,
nehmen wir die nächste dynamische Ebene des Komplexes
von *UNDERFOOT* in den Blick: den Webstuhl mit seinen

Blake Williams ist Künstler, Filmemacher und Autor
und lebt in Toronto, Kanada, wo er die Produktionsfirma
BlueMagenta Films mitgegründet hat. Er schreibt regel-
mäßig Beiträge für die Zeitschriften *Cinema Scope*
und *Filmmaker*. Zuletzt hat er als Programmassistent für
MDFF Selects und das Big Ears Festival gearbeitet.
Seine Kurzfilme, Spielfilme und Videoinstallationen
wurden auf dem Toronto International Film Festival,
der Berlinale, dem New York Film Festival, dem Locarno
Festival, dem Jeonju International Film Festival,
den Internationalen Kurzfilmtagen Oberhausen, dem
FIDMarseille, dem Filmfestival Cinéma du Réel sowie im
Museum of Modern Art in New York gezeigt und ausgestellt.

vielfarbigen Linien und vor allem die Arbeiter:innen
(fast immer Frauen), die ihn bedienen. Und an dieser
Stelle schlägt das Video ein Rad und endet schließlich
in einer aufgeladenen, poetischen Geste, die unseren
Blick nach oben lenkt, in Richtung der schleifen-
förmigen Kette von Spulen. Diese zieht über dem/der
Arbeiter:in vorbei und bildet an der Decke einen neuen,
»üppigen und leeren« Garten – dessen Implikationen
in einer unheilvollen Schwebe gehalten werden. Die
Geschichten in Prices Arbeiten sind nie ausgefeilt
genug, um den gesellschaftlichen Mechanismen zu ent-
kommen, in denen sie wurzeln. Würde sie sich lediglich
damit begnügen, diese Netzwerke für die Betrachtenden
entschlossen zu entwirren, wären ihre Videos auch
dann schon aller Ehren wert und von Bedeutung. Aber
erst dadurch, dass Price der Geschichte ihre Lineari-
tät abspricht und verhindert, dass diese zu einer
unabänderlichen, geklärten These gerinnt, können ihre
Recherchen einen Zustand kognitiver Euphorie auslösen.
Prices Videos regen uns immer wieder dazu an, unsere
Vorstellung von der Gegenwart zu konstruieren, dekonstruieren und rekonstruieren, und ermutigen uns
so dazu, zu erkennen, welch andere Höhepunkte wir
entdecken könnten.

Blake Williams

1   »FVU FRAMES: Elizabeth Price, ›Felt Tip‹, 2018«,
    Interview, Film and Video Umbrella, 5.12.2018,
    Video, 7:19, https://youtu.be/do-2st7-rWU.

SOUND OF THE BREAK

The title of this show refers to the shattering of a
glass goblet that occurs in the final moments of
A RESTORATION (2016).

That goblet is a digital object based on a real
artefact dating from 1750, which is still intact
and on display in the Ashmolean Museum in Oxford.
The slightly shocking idea of ruining this antique was
prompted by another group of artefacts in the same
collection. These are unfired clay figurines dating
from 3000 BC, which were created in order to be
destroyed. Or, at least, this is one theory about their
purpose: they were ritually broken to mark a contract.

Who knows whether this is true. But it's an idea
that flies, is it not? We humans do break things to
announce a new state of affairs: a bottle on the side
of a new boat, a glass under a shoe at a wedding.
And the literal damage – of the bottle or the glass

DER KLANG DES ZERBRECHENS

Der Titel dieser Ausstellung nimmt Bezug auf das Zerbrechen eines Glaskelchs, das sich in den letzten Augenblicken von *A RESTORATION* (2016) ereignet.

Dieser Kelch ist ein digitales Objekt und beruht auf einem echten Artefakt aus dem Jahr 1750, das nach wie vor intakt ist und im Ashmolean Museum in Oxford ausgestellt wird. Die ein wenig schockierende Vorstellung, diese Antiquität zu zerstören, wurde durch eine andere Gruppe von Objekten aus derselben Sammlung inspiriert. Es handelt sich dabei um Figuren aus ungebranntem Ton aus der Zeit um 3000 v. Chr., die hergestellt wurden, um zerstört zu werden. Zumindest ist das eine Theorie über ihren möglichen Zweck: Sie wurden rituell zerbrochen, um einen Vertrag zu besiegeln.

Wer weiß, ob das stimmt? Aber es ist doch eine Idee, die verfängt, oder nicht? Wir Menschen pflegen ja durchaus Sachen zu zerbrechen, um einen neuen Stand der

- is only part of the point, the rest being the abrupt
percussive sound created. This marks the exact point
in time of the change, the moment after which there is
no going back.

Abrupt sound is also used without breakage to mark
profound, irreversible changes in both secular and
religious ceremonials. Examples that come to my
mind include the sharp strike of the Judge's gavel to
announce a judgement, or the high-pitched chime of
a handbell to mark the transubstantiation of the
host in a Catholic mass.

I use sound in my art to mark change, choice,
consequence in formal as well as political terms.
I will use a finger snap to denote an edit, a hand-
clap to announce the departure of an image from
the screen. I will use a melodic progression or crescendo to mark a shift from one body of material
to another, from an analysis to a lament. I accompany
elevated museum artefacts with camp electronic tunes
- in blunt and deliberate riposte to a hierarchy of
form. Sometimes I play a sound so loud in the gallery
that you can feel it. It is tangible. It is here
and now.

I often record the sounds made by the subjects of
my videos: the noise of a book creaking open, snap-
ping closed, landing with a flap and a slap on a desk;
the shuffle of photographs, the scratch of a pen,
the squeak of a sewing needle, the scrape of a phono-
graphic stylus. I often use the sound of things
working - computer hard drives starting up, cars
switching on - and the pressing into action of other
similarly complex mechanical, electronic, digital
things. These are frequently activated with the mere

Dinge zu verkünden: eine Flasche am Rumpf eines Schiffs,
um es zu taufen, ein Glas unter dem Schuh, wenn geheira-
tet wird. Und die eigentliche Beschädigung – der Flasche
oder des Glases – ist nur ein Teil der Pointe, der
Rest ist das plötzlich einsetzende perkussive Geräusch,
das dabei entsteht. Dieses markiert den exakten Zeit-
punkt des Übergangs, jenen Moment, nach dem es kein
Zurück mehr gibt.

Unvermittelt auftretende Klänge werden auch in
säkularen und religiösen Zeremonien eingesetzt, um von
tiefgreifenden, irreversiblen Wendungen zu künden
– allerdings ohne dass dabei etwas zerbrochen wird.
Ich denke dabei zum Beispiel an den scharfen Hammer-
schlag des Richters bei einer Urteilsverkündung
oder den hellen Klang der Handglocke bei der Wandlung
im katholischen Gottesdienst.

In meiner Kunst verwende ich Klang, um Veränderungen,
Entscheidungen und Konsequenzen sowohl in formaler
als auch politischer Hinsicht zu betonen. Ich nutze
etwa ein Fingerschnippen, um einen Schnitt hervor-
zuheben, oder ein Händeklatschen, um anzukündigen, dass
ein Bild gleich vom Bildschirm verschwindet. Ich setze
eine melodische Progression oder ein Crescendo ein,
um den Übergang von einem Themenkomplex zum anderen,
von einer Analyse zu einem Lamento kenntlich zu machen.
Ich unterlege erhabene Museumsartefakte mit theatrali-
scher elektronischer Musik – als unverblümte und bewusst
gewählte Retourkutsche auf die Hierarchie der Formen.
Manchmal lasse ich ein Geräusch so laut in der Galerie
erklingen, dass man es förmlich fühlen kann. Es ist
zu spüren. Es ist hier und jetzt.

Ich nehme oft die Geräusche der Gegenstände auf,
die in meinen Videos vorkommen: den Klang eines Buches,

touch of your index finger, a command often answered
by an ingratiating audio effect - PING! - as well
as the hum, hiss, and whirr of awakening machines.
I often use the sounds of me working, too: the click
of the return key to apply an effect, the clack of
the space bar rolling the video, the clatter that
accompanies the characters as text is typed on
the screen.

Yes, the idea of work itself is something I convey
through sound. The sound of labour, of production,
of executive command. But I also use sound to convey
something of the politics of social relations in
labour. I am very interested in this. Although there
aren't many humans in my videos, there is always
a group of narrators, and they are usually at work.
They are variously administrators, teachers, the
workforce of a museum, the committee of a library,
the guardians of a building. Sometimes they seem like
estate agents or salespeople. We never see them,
and sometimes they don't even speak, communicating
only through text, but they do have an expressive
range that exceeds writing. Their attitude, temper,
and mood is usually elaborated through sound.

I am interested in the work of making art. I believe
that the narrators of my videos are too, though they
might not name it as such. In each instance they defy
the limitations of their job descriptions. This is
not expressed in withdrawal. No, they do not refuse
to work. They do other work, their own work. They
produce a kind of supplement. More, not less. Oh yes!
Even when they are cars, they start to do something
else, something more ... something like mourning, something like protest, something like art.

wenn es knarrend aufgeklappt oder krachend zuge-
schlagen wird oder wenn es mit einem Knall auf dem
Schreibtisch landet; das Geräusch, wenn man Fotos
durchsieht, das Kratzen eines Stiftes, das leise
Quietschen einer Nähnadel, das Kratzen der Abtastnadel
eines Plattenspielers. Häufig verwende ich Geräusche
von Dingen, die gerade in Betrieb sind – hochfahrende
Computerfestplatten, anspringende Autos und andere,
ähnlich komplexe mechanische, elektronische, digitale
Geräte, die per Knopfdruck gestartet werden. Sie lassen
sich oft durch bloße Berührung mit dem Zeigefinger
in Gang setzen, einen Befehl, auf den häufig ein wohl-
wollend klingender Audioeffekt – PING! – folgt,
neben dem Brummen, Zischen oder Surren einer Maschine,
die zum Leben erwacht. Gerne nutze ich auch die
Geräusche, die bei meiner eigenen Arbeit entstehen:
das Klicken der Return-Taste, wenn ich einen Effekt
einbauen will, das Klacken der Leertaste, wenn ich ein
Video starte, das Klappern, das die einzelnen Buchstaben
begleitet, wenn ich etwas am Bildschirm schreibe.
    Ja, es ist die Idee des Arbeitens selbst, die ich
durch Klang vermittle. Durch den Klang einer Tätigkeit,
einer produktiven Handlung, einer Anordnung. Aber
ich verwende Klang auch, um etwas über die politischen
Dimensionen der sozialen Beziehungen in der Arbeitswelt zu vermitteln. Das interessiert mich sehr. Obwohl
nicht viele Menschen in meinen Videos vorkommen, gibt
es immer eine Gruppe von Erzähler:innen, und diese
arbeiten normalerweise. Sie kommen aus unterschiedlichen
Bereichen, sind Verwaltungsangestellte, Lehrer:innen,
die Belegschaft eines Museums, sind im Vorstand einer
Bibliothek oder Teil des Wachdienstes eines Gebäudes.
Manchmal wirken sie wie Immobilienmakler:innen oder

    Like most artists, I also do other work than art.
I have worked as an underground book-fetcher in
a University Library, as the administrator of a local
museum, as a teacher at school, college, and
University. I spent a year working in a peanut factory.
If this CV sounds a little like that of the narrators I create, I will admit it. But I would claim
this is not autobiographical as such. These are just
the worlds of work I have most closely observed.
    If sound can alert us to the existence of work,
this is in service of a wider, philosophical point:
sound accompanies matter. Things make sound. And the
sounds that things make in my videos are never
a backdrop, nor an ambient primer for human action.
The sounds that things make announce agency, both
theirs and ours. They mark the contract struck between
meaning and matter in the making of art or any
other kind of invention, which leaves neither material nor ideation intact. And they are one of the ways
that I declare to the viewer that video is not
an immaterial art.
    Digital video-editing interfaces often use the
language and iconography of physical making – cutting,
blending, rendering – in which we can see the bones
of old technologies. Perhaps they can also remind us
that the digital only ever exists through material
dependencies. I may use digital processes of composition, but this expresses a fascination with the grain
of physical things. Indeed, I mainly use projectors
and amplifiers to magnify: making small things large,
bringing them close. And whilst much of my time is
spent editing, I don't regard the digital files that
I export from those softwares as my art. It is only

Verkäufer:innen. Wir bekommen sie nie zu sehen, und
manchmal sprechen sie nicht einmal, sondern kommuni-
zieren nur durch die auf dem Bildschirm erscheinenden
Texte, aber sie verfügen über ein Spektrum an Aus-
drucksmöglichkeiten, das über die Ebene der Schrift-
lichkeit hinausgeht. Ihre innere Einstellung,
ihr Charakter und ihre Laune kommen normalerweise
klanglich zum Ausdruck.

Ich interessiere mich für die Arbeit, die darin
besteht, Kunst herzustellen. Ich glaube, das trifft
auch auf die Erzählinstanzen in meinen Videos zu, auch
wenn sie selbst es nicht so bezeichnen würden. Sie
setzen sich alle über die Grenzen ihres jeweiligen
Aufgabengebietes hinweg. Das kommt nicht etwa dadurch
zum Ausdruck, dass sie sich zurückziehen würden.
Nein, sie verweigern nicht ihre Arbeit. Sie leisten
andere Arbeit, ihre eigene Arbeit. Sie produzieren eine
Art Ergänzung. Mehr, nicht weniger. Oh ja! Selbst wenn
sie Autos sind, beginnen sie plötzlich damit, etwas
anderes zu machen, was eher ... was einer Art Trauer,
einer Art Protest, einer Art Kunst gleicht.

Wie die meisten Kunstschaffenden übe ich neben
der Kunst noch andere Tätigkeiten aus. Ich habe an
einer Universitätsbibliothek Bücher aus dem Depot im
Kellergeschoss geholt und war als Verwaltungsangestellte eines örtlichen Museums sowie als Lehrerin und
Hochschuldozentin tätig. Und einmal habe ich ein Jahr
lang in einer Erdnussfabrik gearbeitet. Wenn dieser
Lebenslauf ein bisschen nach denen meiner Erzähler:in-
nen klingt, dann muss ich das zugeben. Aber ich würde
behaupten, dass es nicht eigentlich autobiografisch
ist. Es sind einfach die Arbeitswelten, die ich aus
nächster Nähe erlebt habe.

when the sound strikes the walls of a room and the hot,
humming projectors illuminate the space, the seating,
the audience itself, that the work fully exists.

Perhaps this is why I do not think the experience of
video projection is easily captured in printed matter.
A full-bleed, double-page spread on glossy paper cannot
convey the sensual intensity of that luminous image.
So this book takes a different approach. It presents
the elements from which the exhibited videos are
composed – photographs, animation frames, source materials – while also disclosing aspects of the working
process. As you flip through this book, you move
through bodies of material in ways analogous to the
videos' timelines, attended with different but related
phenomena. The paper stock of this book, for example,
was selected primarily for its sound. It provides
an unusually loud, sibilant accompaniment to the turn
of each page.

Elizabeth Price

Wenn uns Klang auf die Existenz von Arbeit aufmerk-
sam machen kann, dient er auch einer umfassenderen
philosophischen Erkenntnis: Materie wird von Klang
begleitet. Dinge lassen Geräusche entstehen. Und die
Geräusche, die die Dinge in meinen Videos machen,
bilden nie bloß eine Kulisse oder einen Hintergrund für
menschliche Handlungen. Die Geräusche, die die Dinge
machen, künden von Handlungsfähigkeit, ihrer und
unserer. Sie stehen für den beim Kunstmachen oder jeder
anderen schöpferischen Tätigkeit zwischen Bedeutung
und Materie geschlossenen Vertrag, der weder Material
noch Ideenfindung unberührt lässt. Und sie sind eines
der Mittel, mit denen ich den Betrachtenden erkläre,
dass Video keine immaterielle Kunst ist.

Digitale Videobearbeitungs-Schnittstellen greifen
oft auf die Sprache und Ikonografie materieller
Arbeitsabläufe – wie »Schneiden«, »Mischen« oder
»Verputzen« (engl. *to render*) – zurück, in denen
die Überreste alter Techniken durchscheinen. Vielleicht können sie uns auch daran erinnern, dass das
Digitale immer nur in materiellen Bezügen existiert.
Mag sein, dass ich digitale Kompositionsverfahren
benutze, aber darin kommt letztlich meine Faszination
für die Elemente zum Ausdruck, aus denen die materi-
elle Welt zusammengesetzt ist. Tatsächlich benutze
ich Projektoren und Verstärker hauptsächlich zur
Vergrößerung: um kleine Dinge größer darzustellen,
sie heranzuholen. Und obwohl ich einen großen Teil
meiner Zeit mit digitaler Bearbeitung verbringe,
betrachte ich die Dateien, die ich aus den Programmen
exportiere, nicht als meine Kunst. Erst wenn der Klang
auf die Wände eines Raumes trifft, wenn die heißen,
brummenden Projektoren den Raum, die Sitzgelegenheiten

und das Publikum selbst in Licht tauchen, ist das Werk
vollumfänglich vorhanden.

Vielleicht aus diesem Grund bin ich der Ansicht,
dass die Erfahrung einer Videoprojektion sich nicht
leicht in gedruckter Form wiedergeben lässt. Selbst
eine Abbildung, die den ganzen Raum einer Hochglanz-
Doppelseite einnimmt, kann nicht die sinnliche
Intensität dieses leuchtenden Bildes vermitteln.
Die vorliegende Publikation folgt daher einem anderen
Ansatz. Sie präsentiert die Elemente, aus denen die
ausgestellten Videos bestehen – Fotoaufnahmen, Stand-
bilder aus Animationen, Ausgangsmaterialien –,
und legt gleichzeitig Aspekte des Arbeitsprozesses
offen. Als würde man der Timeline in einem der Videos
folgen, bewegt man sich beim Blättern durch das Buch
durch verschiedene Inhalte, die sich mit unterschiedlichen, aber verwandten Phänomenen befassen. Und so
wurde beispielsweise auch das Papier für dieses
Buch in erster Linie aufgrund seines Klangs ausge-
wählt: Blättert man eine Seite um, begleitet es
diesen Vorgang jeweils mit einem ungewöhnlich lauten,
zischenden Geräusch.

Elizabeth Price

A

RESTO

A

RATION

<u>A RESTORATION (2016)</u>

This video provides a hectic, hallucinatory survey
of the vast image archives of the Ashmolean Museum and
Pitt Rivers Museum in Oxford. It is narrated by
a chorus of self-proclaimed "museum administrators"
and features every type of visual document created
by the two museums in their long history of excavating
and collecting artifacts.

   Although the documents were originated in varied
media, they all appear here as digital artifacts.
And we encounter them only within the administrators'
computer file system, starting with thousands of
images created by Sir Arthur Evans, archaeologist and
first director of the Ashmolean (in its modern form).
The administrators show us photographs, drawings,
and paintings he created and commissioned during his
reckless restoration of Knossos, the Bronze Age city
on the island of Crete. They flip through these
images impatiently, using the twin projection screens
like the pages of a photo album. At other times,
the pictures stack up swiftly, like windows opening
on the desktop of a computer.

   Speaking as a combined synthetic voice, the administrators narrate the documents. They lead us through
Evans's project, satirically reconstructing his
destructive restoration of the ancient city. Then,
having rebuilt that ruin in their digital realm,
they adopt its mazy structure as an alternative repository for the museums' collections. This absurd
notion leads to a series of eccentric categorizations
and fantastical interpretative leaps.

Dieses Video bietet einen hektischen, halluzina-
torischen Überblick über die riesigen Bildarchive
des Ashmolean und des Pitt Rivers Museum in Oxford.
Es wird von einem Chor selbsternannter »Museums-
administrator:innen« als Erzählstimme begleitet und
zeigt alle Arten von Bilddokumenten, die von den
beiden Museen in ihrer langen Geschichte der Ausgrabung und Sammlung von Artefakten geschaffen wurden.

   Obwohl die Dokumente verschiedenste Medien umfassen,
erscheinen sie hier alle als digitale Artefakte. Und
wir begegnen ihnen nur innerhalb des Systems von
Computerdateien der Administrator:innen. Den Anfang
machen Tausende von Bildern, die Sir Arthur Evans,
Archäologe und erster Direktor des Ashmolean Museum
(in seiner heutigen Form), erstellt hat. Die Admi-
nistrator:innen zeigen uns Fotos, Zeichnungen und
Gemälde, die Evans während seiner rücksichtslosen
Restaurierung von Knossos, der bronzezeitlichen Stadt
auf der Insel Kreta, anfertigte oder in Auftrag gab.
Sie blättern ungeduldig durch diese Bilder und nutzen
die beiden Projektionsflächen wie die Seiten eines
Fotoalbums. In anderen Momenten stapeln sich die Bilder
in Windeseile, wie Fenster, die sich auf dem Desktop
eines Computers öffnen.

   Die Administrator:innen sprechen mit einer einzigen kombinierten synthetischen Stimme und berichten
über die Dokumente. Sie führen uns durch Evans' Projekt
und rekonstruieren auf satirische Weise seine zerstö-
rerische Restaurierung der antiken Stadt. Nachdem sie
die Ruine in ihrer digitalen Welt wiederaufgebaut

At one stage, they take us through each of the
museums' departments in sixty seconds by filtering one
of the few types of object common to all: the drinking vessel. This intoxicated dash starts with a
Minoan cup and concludes with a Jacobean wine glass
(which later gets noisily smashed). Later, they
imagine the mythic maze of Knossos as a giant cochlea
– the spiral chamber of the inner ear – and harvest
all of the sounds the thousands of museum objects
could possibly make. They orchestrate this cacophony
to restage the fall of both the ancient city and
Evans's project of restoration.

Folgende Seiten / Following pages:
Auswahl an Einzelbildern einer computergenerierten
Animation, die ein Faksimile eines jakobinischen
Weinglases aus der Zeit um 1750 zeigt. Medienbestand
von *A RESTORATION*. / Selection of frames from a
computer-generated animation featuring a facsimile of
a Jacobean wine glass, ca. 1750. Media asset of
A RESTORATION.

haben, übernehmen sie ihre verworrene Struktur als alternativen Aufbewahrungsort für die Sammlungen des Museums. Dieser absurde Gedanke führt zu einer Reihe von exzentrischen Kategorisierungen und fantastischen Interpretationssprüngen.

Einmal führen sie uns in 60 Sekunden durch alle Abteilungen des Museums, indem sie eine der wenigen Arten von Objekten herausfiltern, die in allen Sammlungen des Museums vertreten sind: das Trinkgefäß. Der Rausch beginnt mit einem minoischen Becher und endet mit einem jakobinischen Weinglas (das später geräuschvoll zerschlagen wird). Später stellen sie sich das mythische Labyrinth von Knossos als eine riesige Cochlea vor – die spiralförmige Kammer des Innenohrs – und sammeln alle Geräusche ein, die die Tausenden von Museumsobjekten erzeugen könnten. Sie inszenieren diese Kakophonie, um sowohl den Untergang der antiken Stadt als auch Evans' Restaurierungsprojekt neu zu inszenieren.

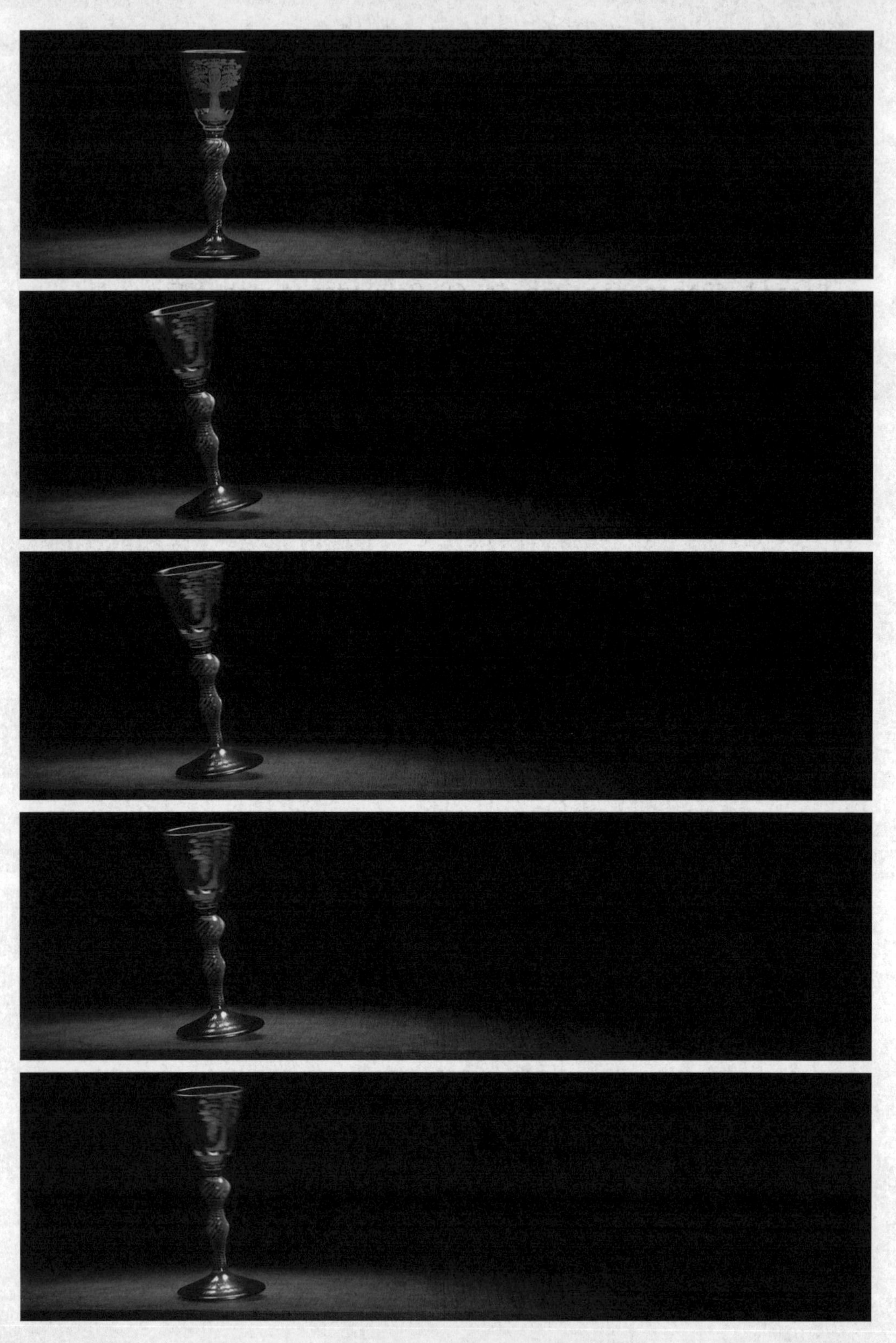

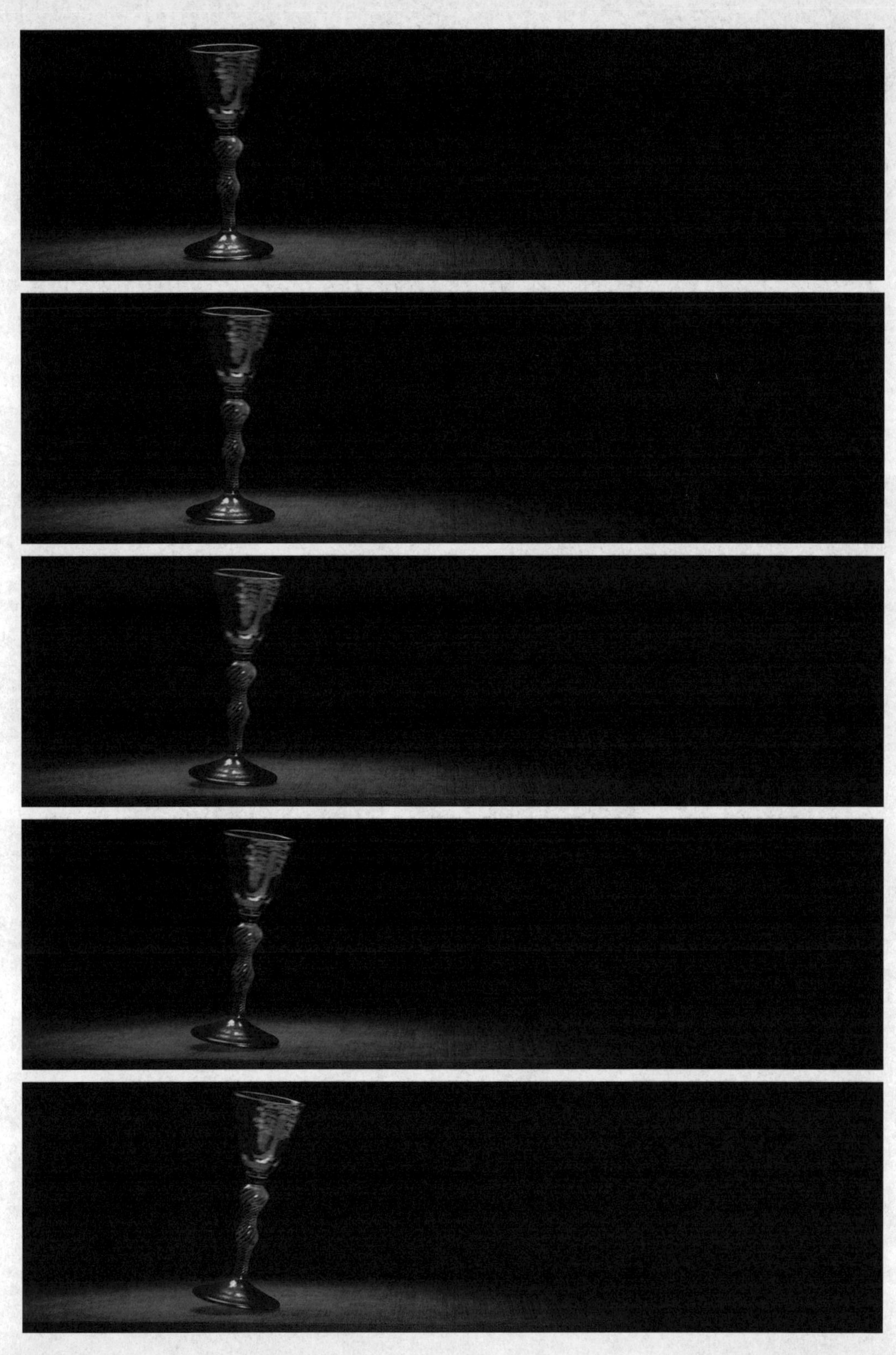

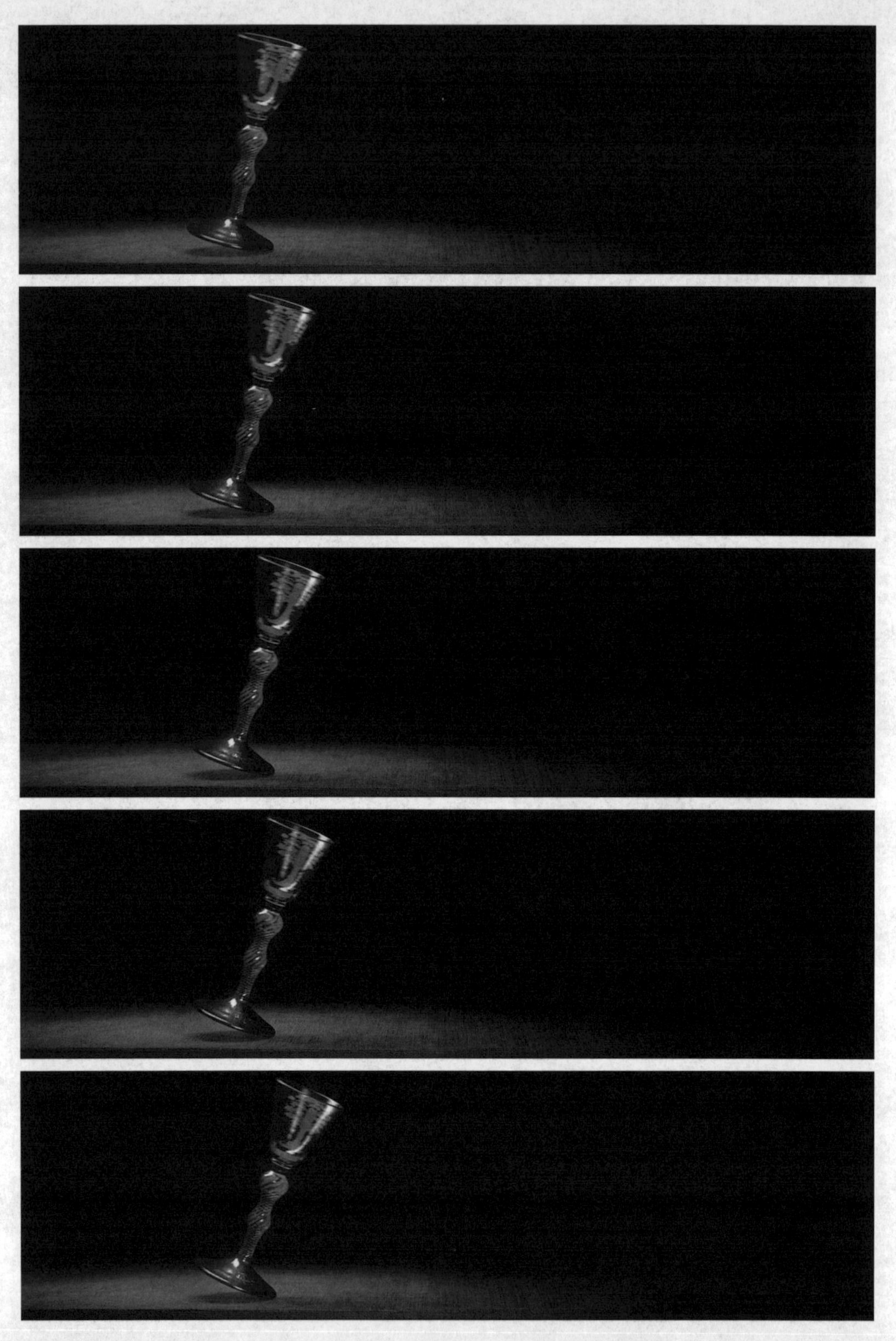

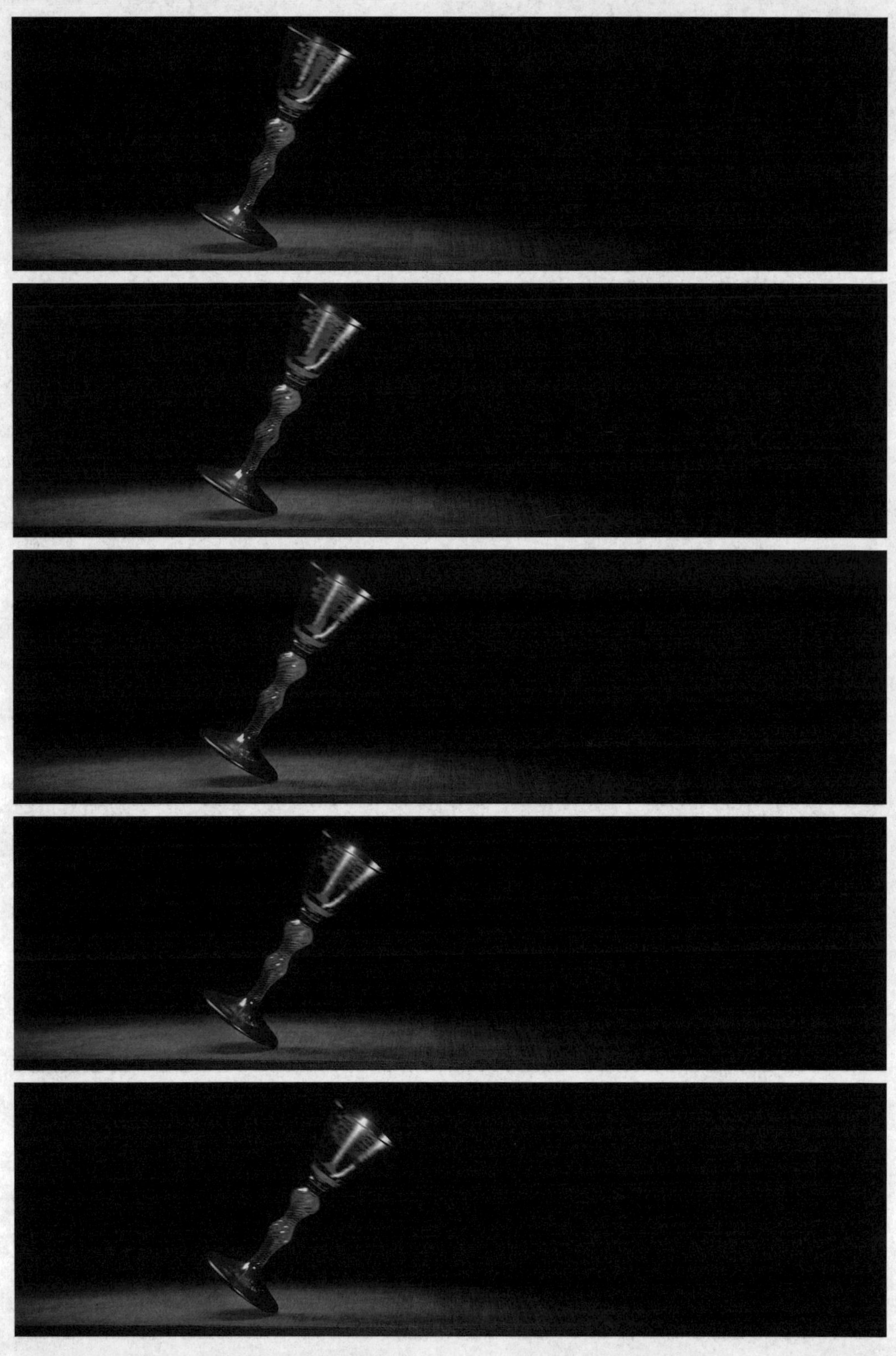

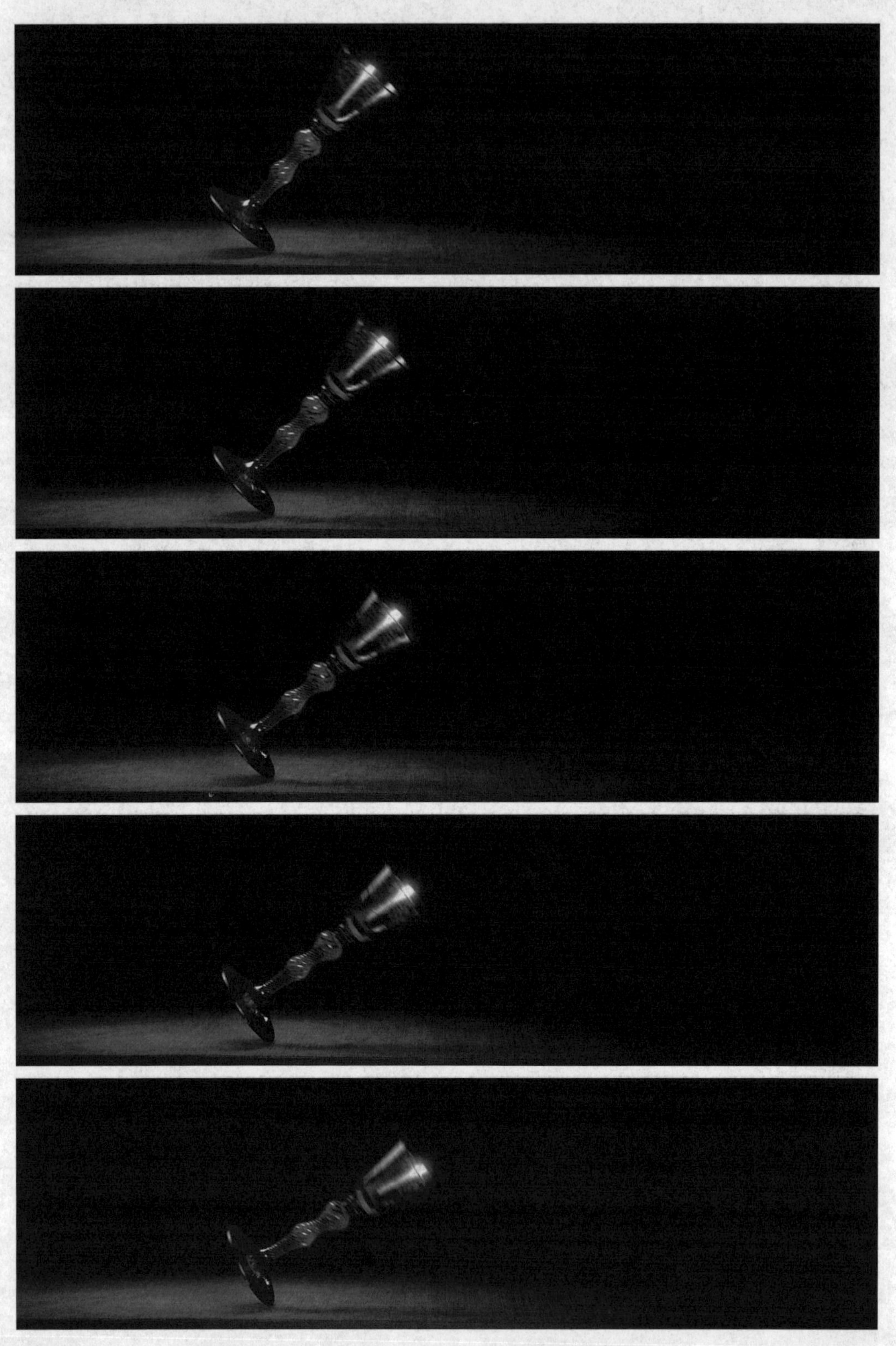

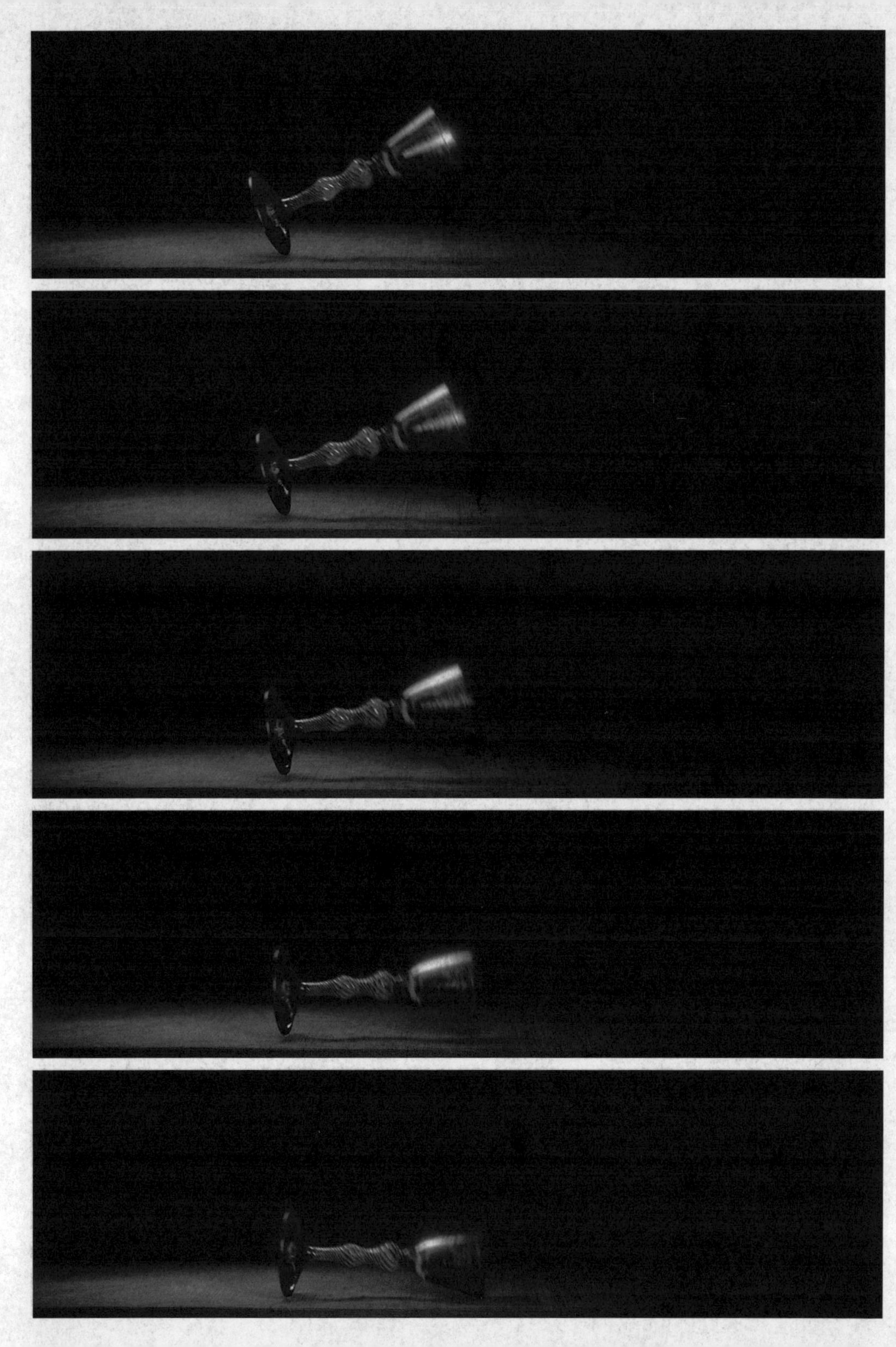

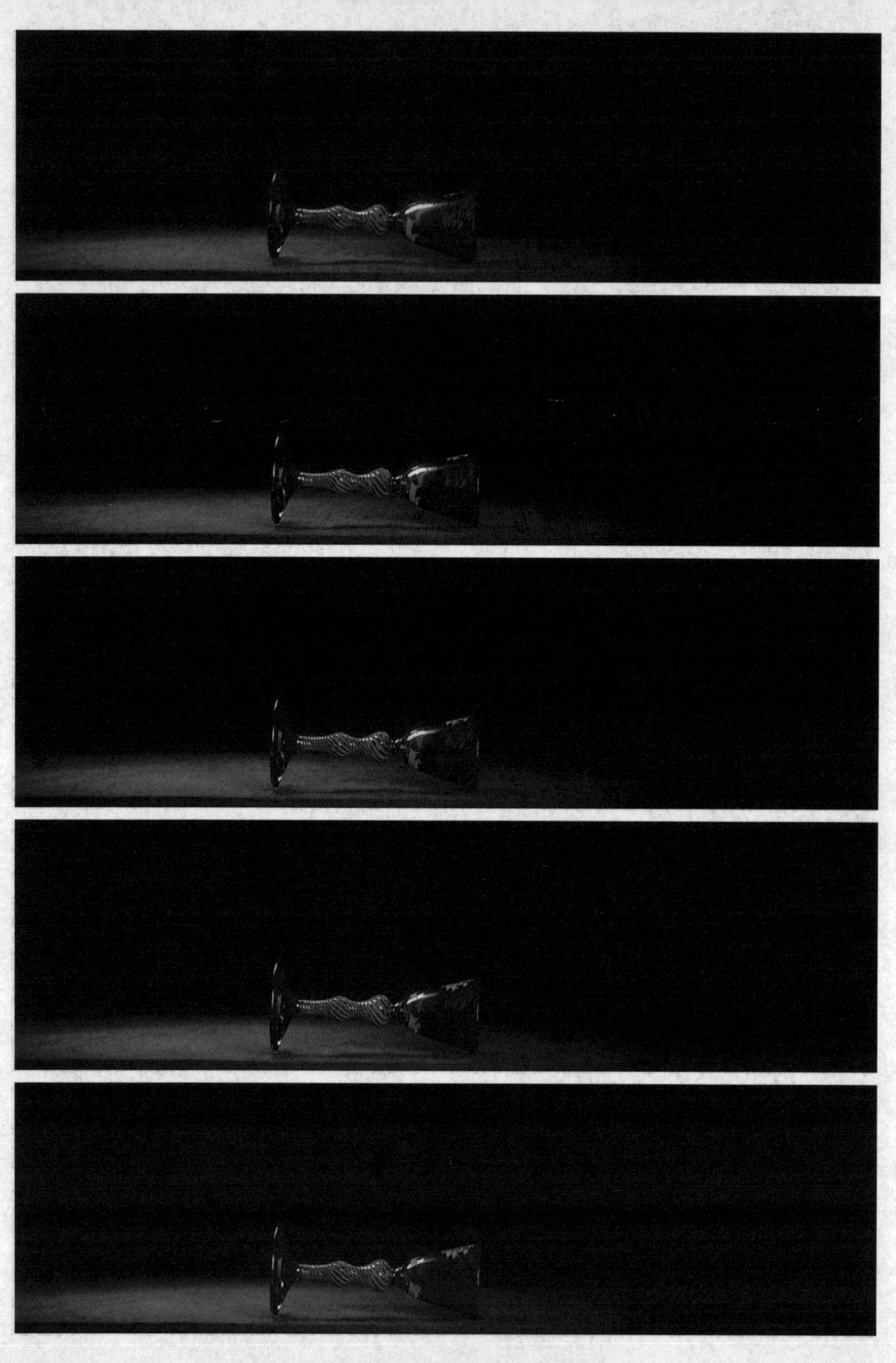

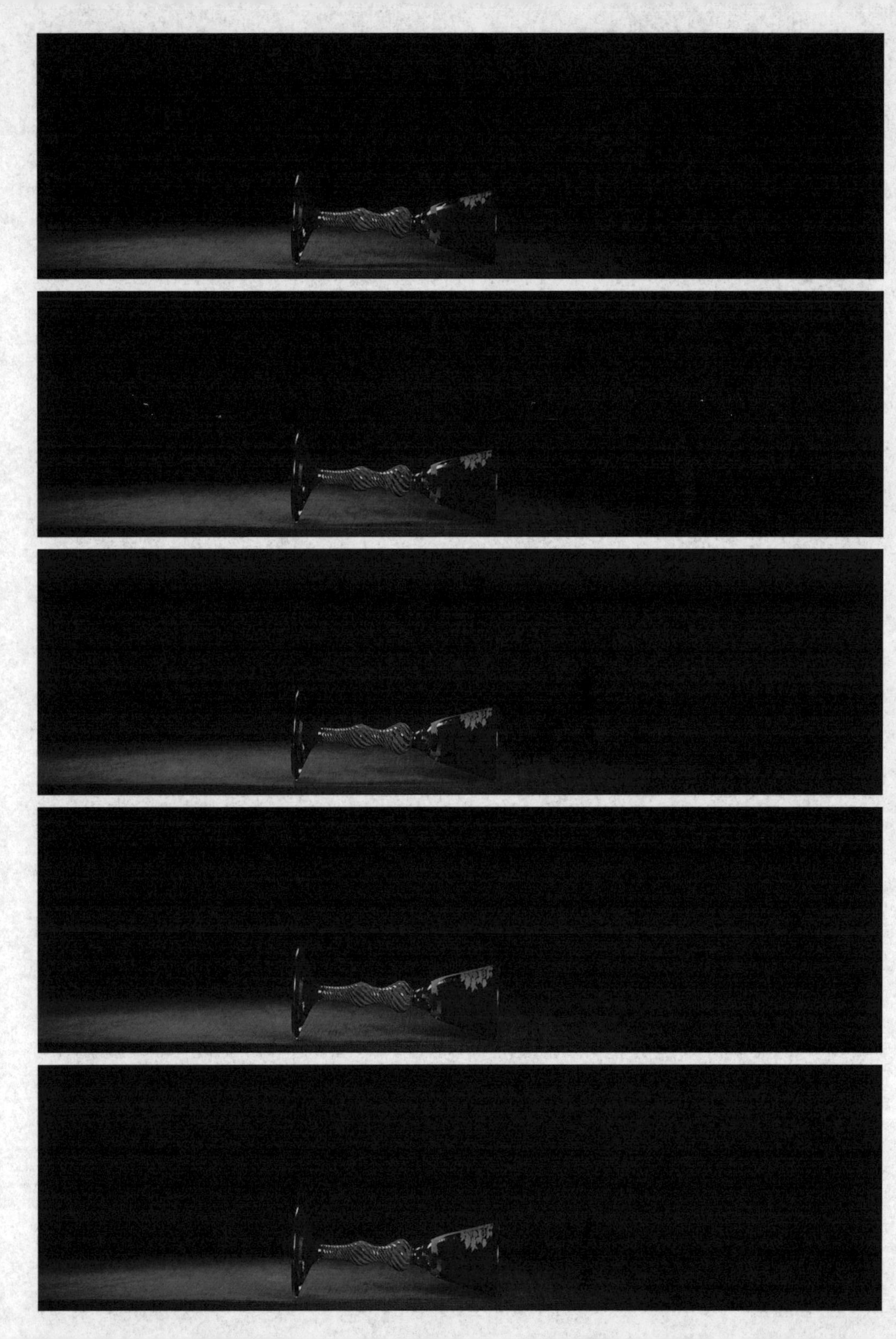

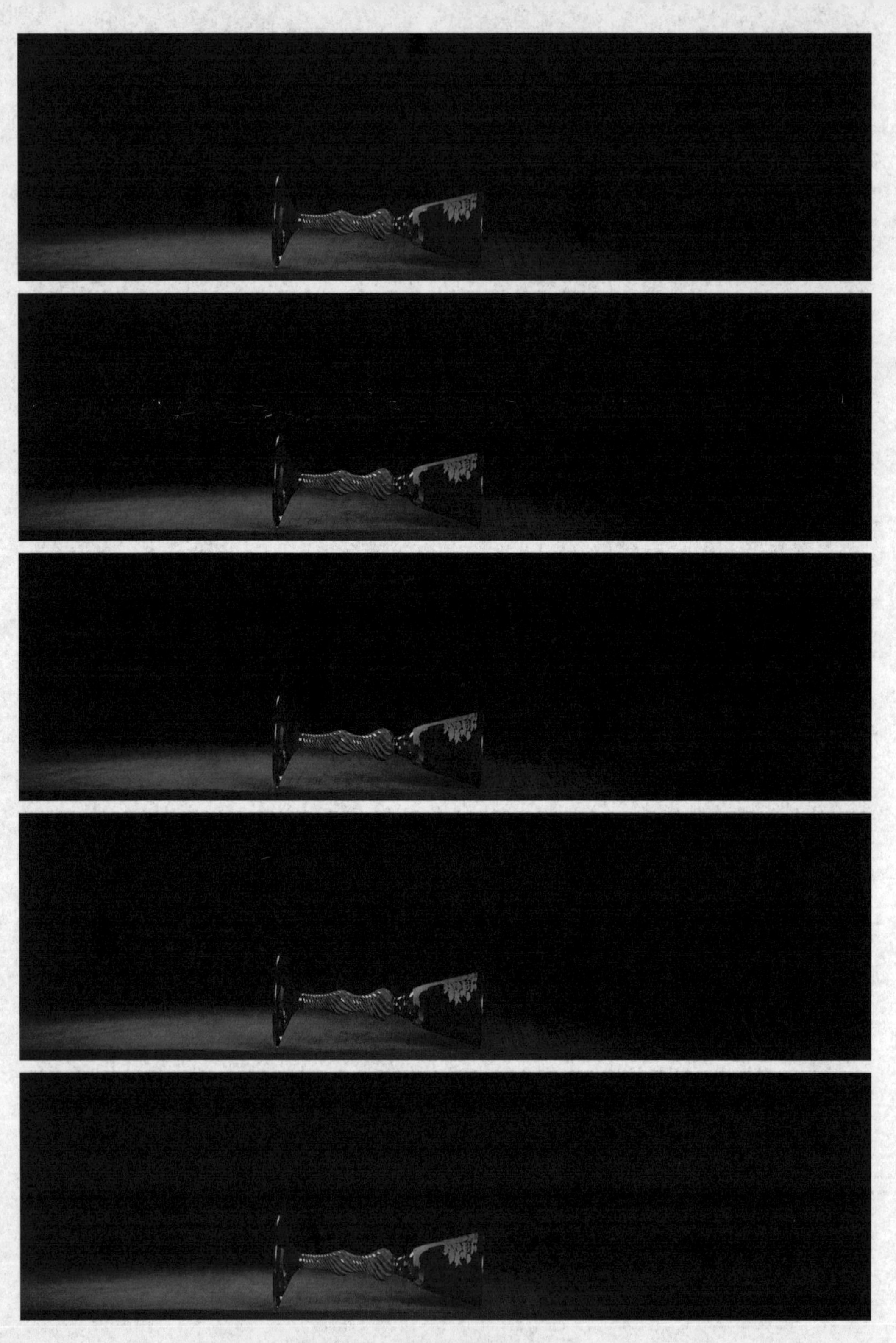

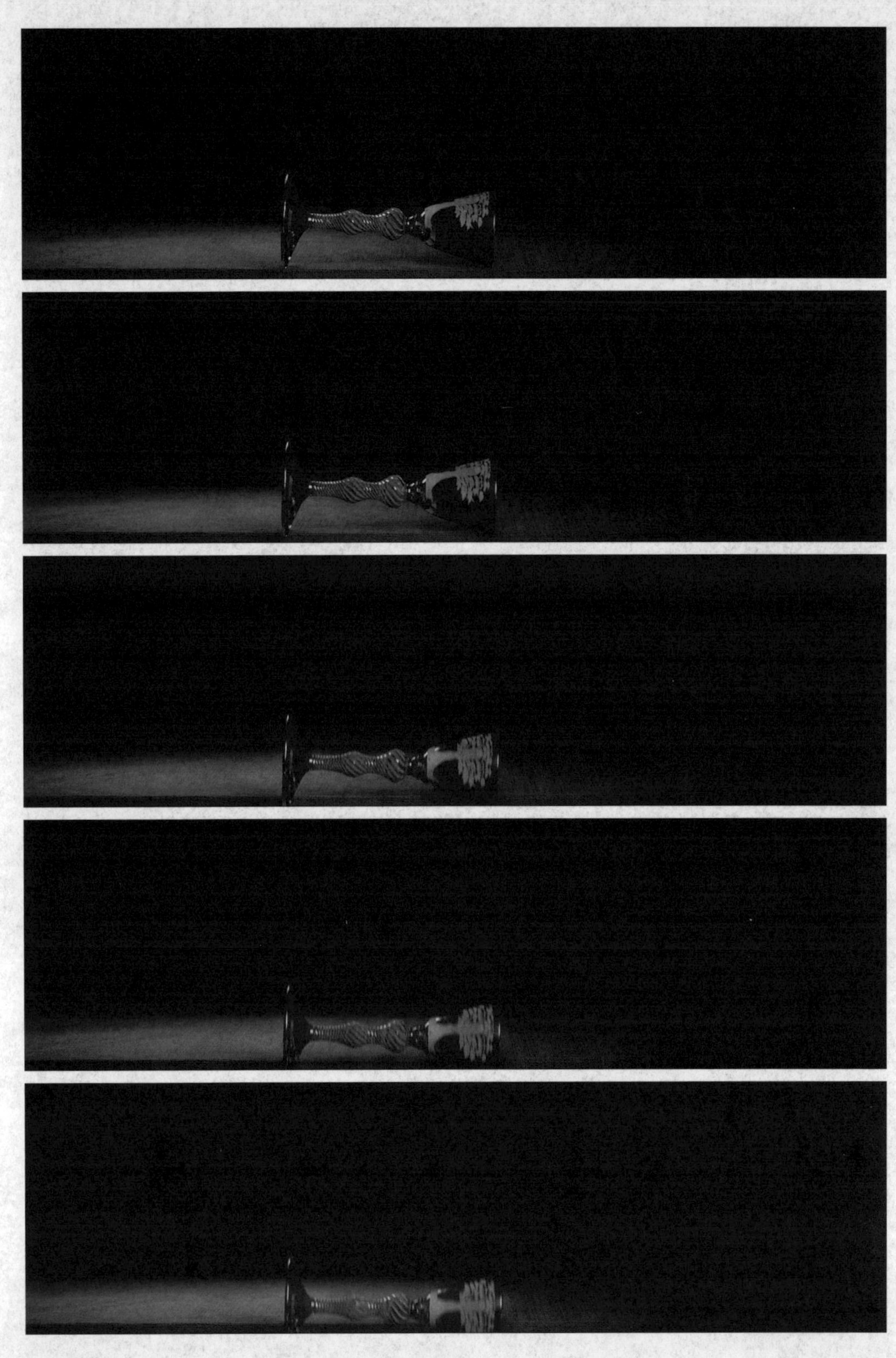

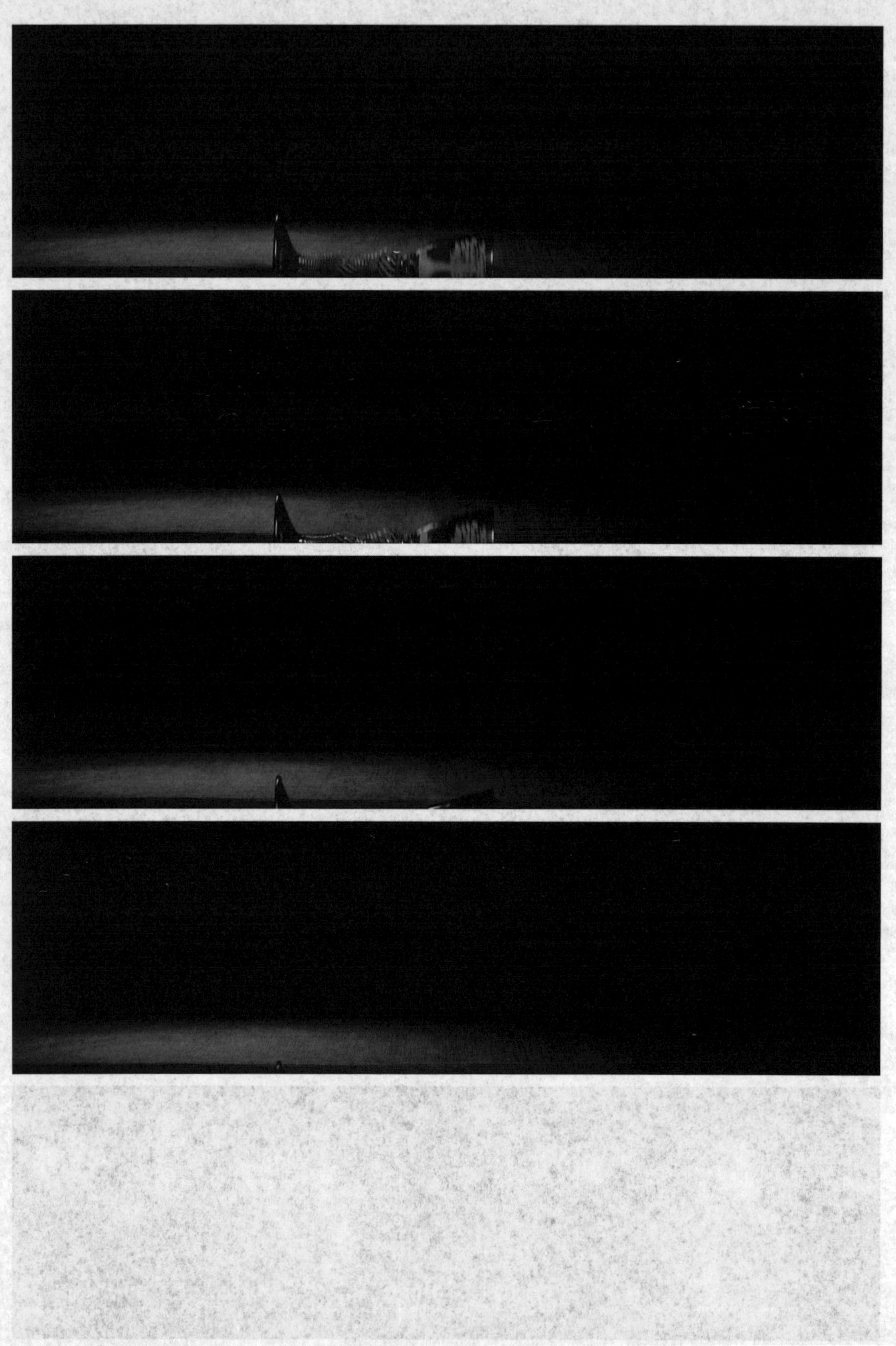

Timeline für die Bearbeitung, *A RESTORATION*
Bildschirm 1 und Audiomaster /
Editing Timeline, *A RESTORATION*
Screen one and audio master

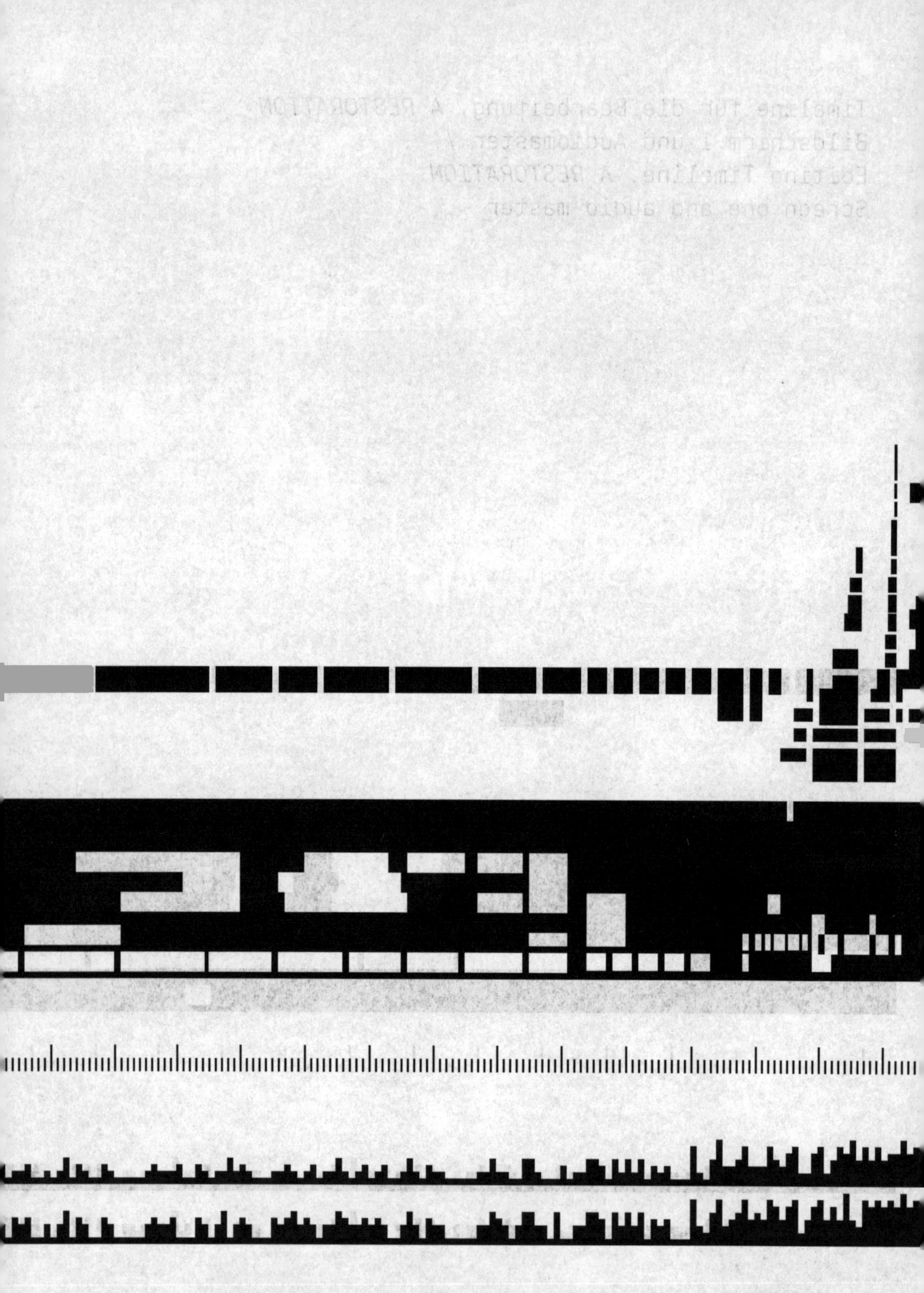

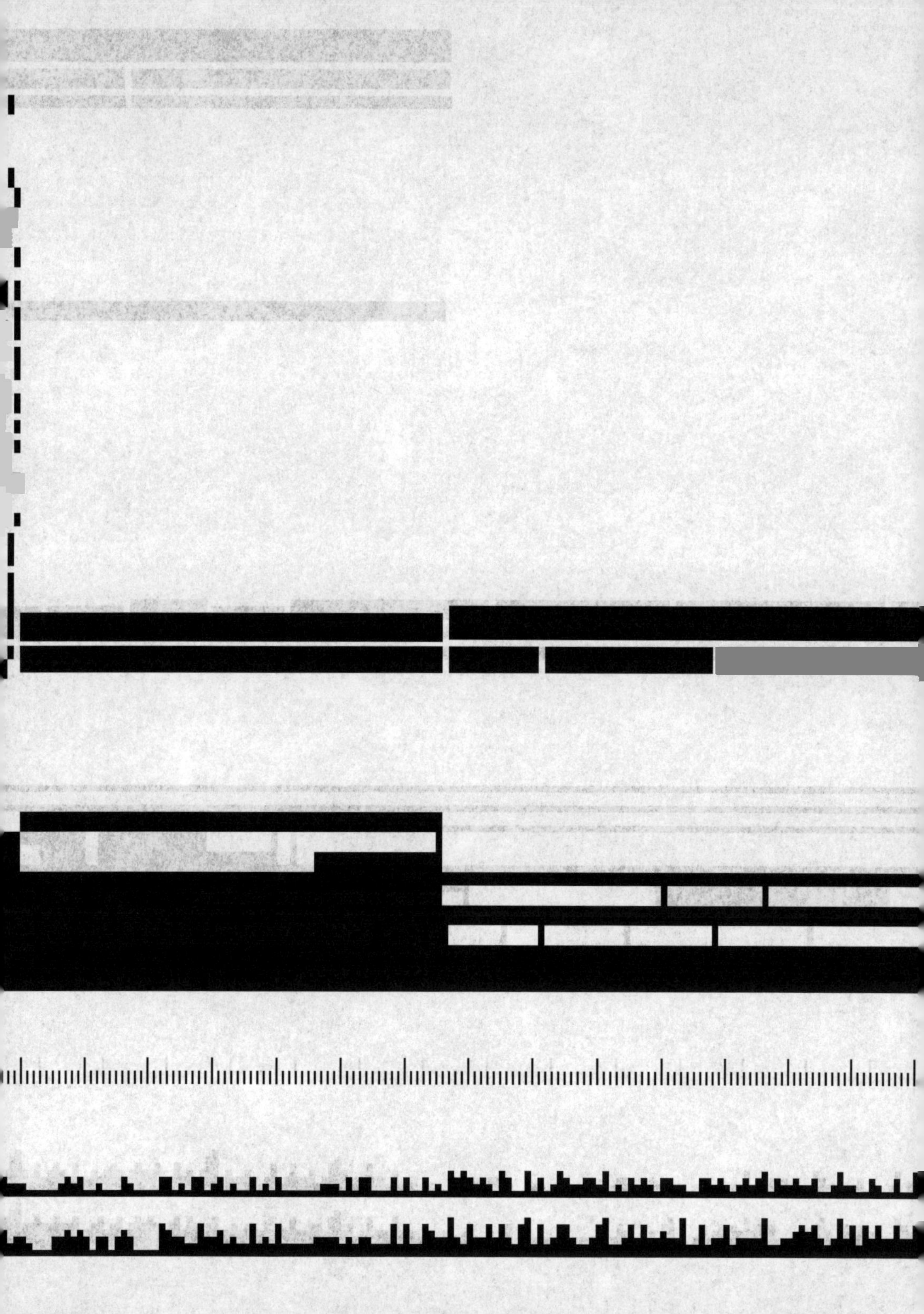

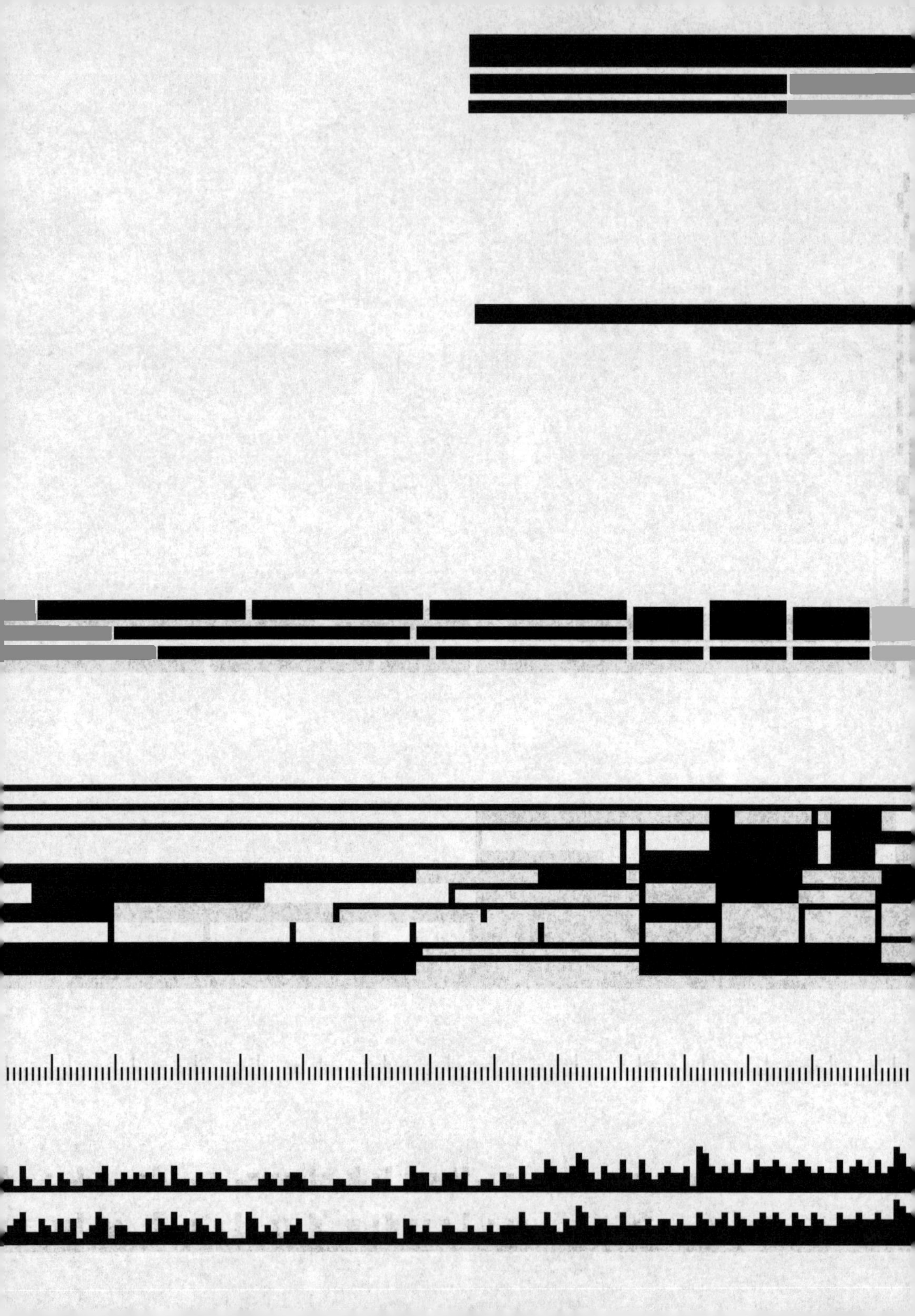

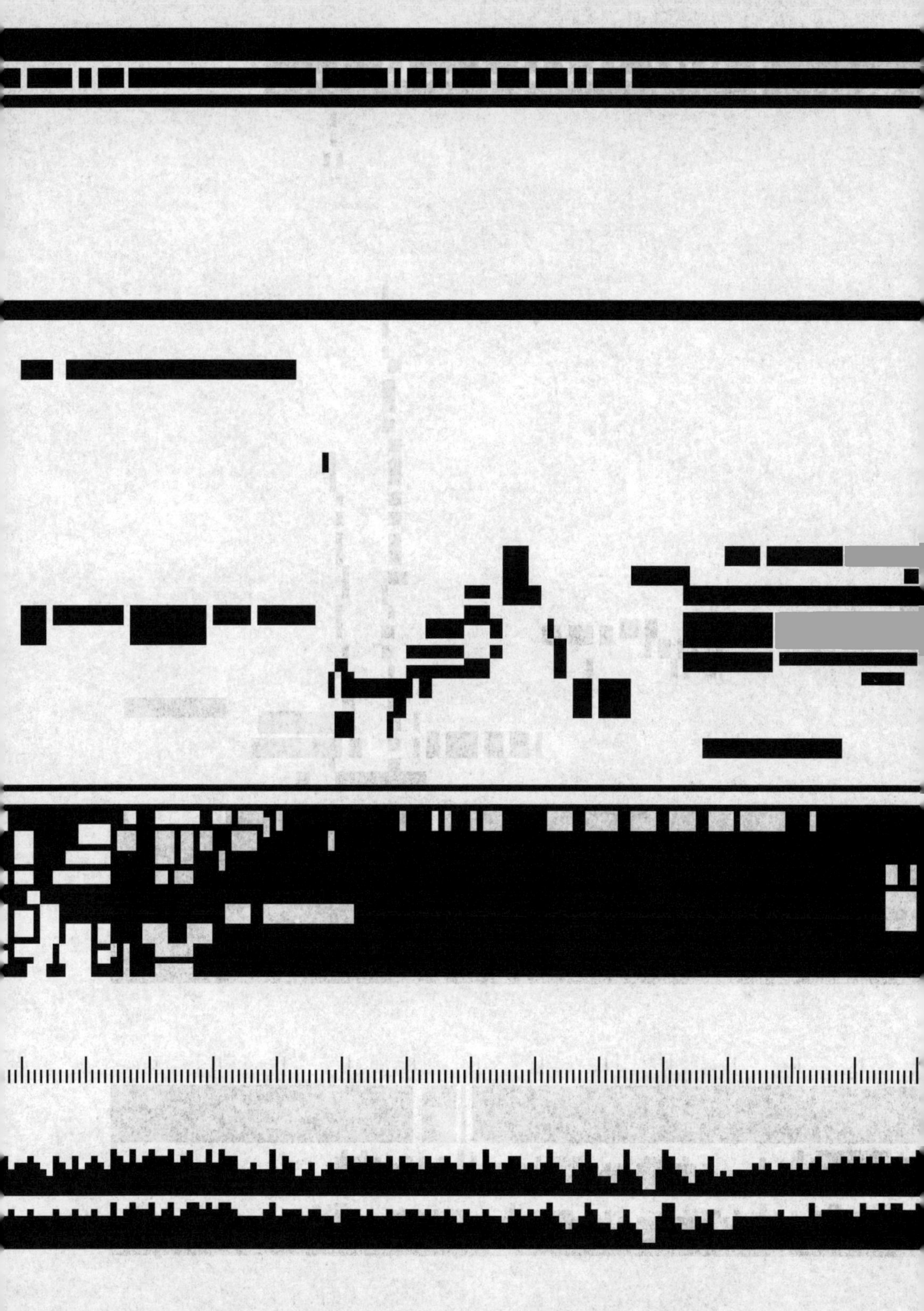

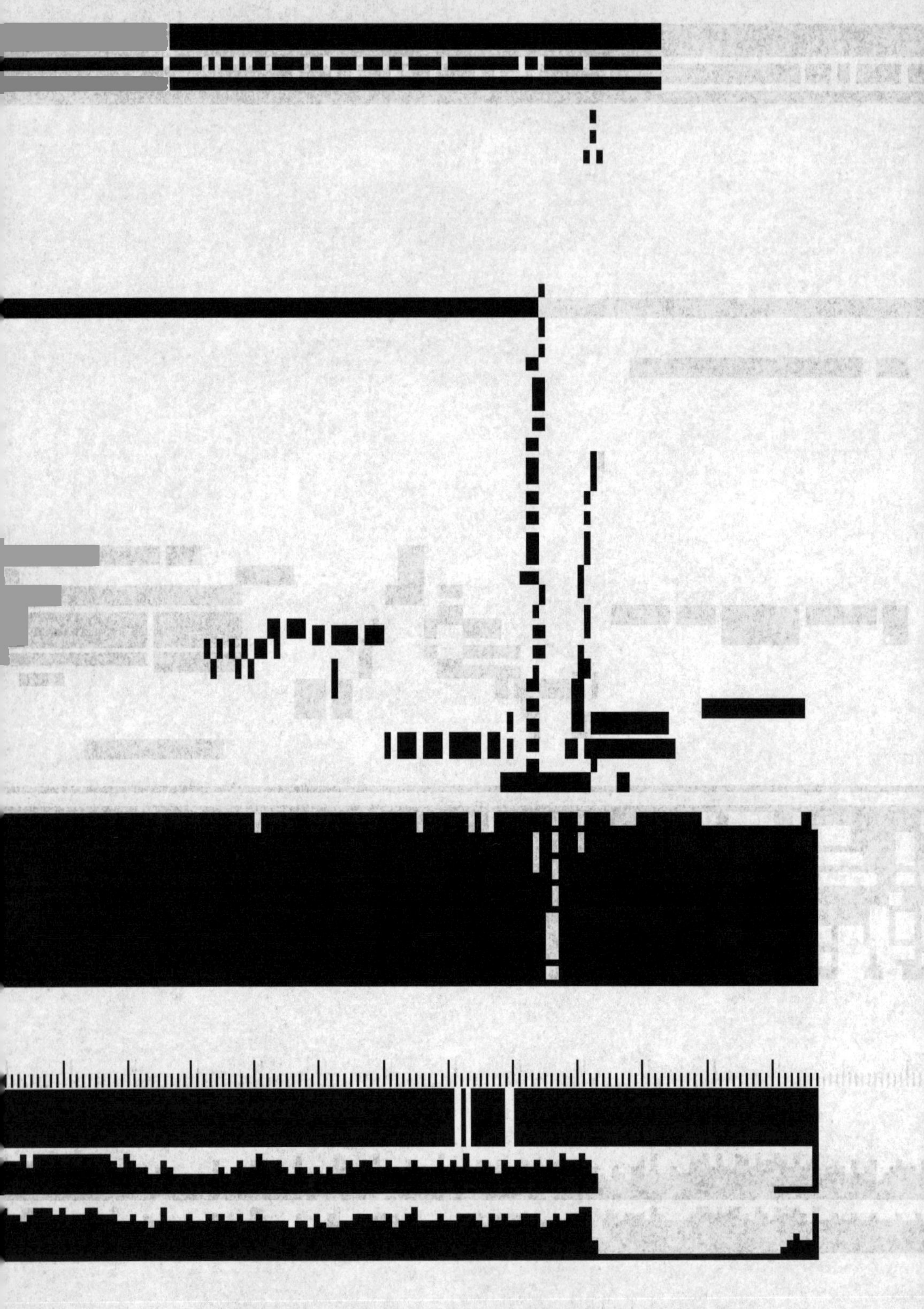

Timeline für die Bearbeitung,
A RESTORATION Bildschirm 2 /
Editing Timeline, *A RESTORATION*
Screen two

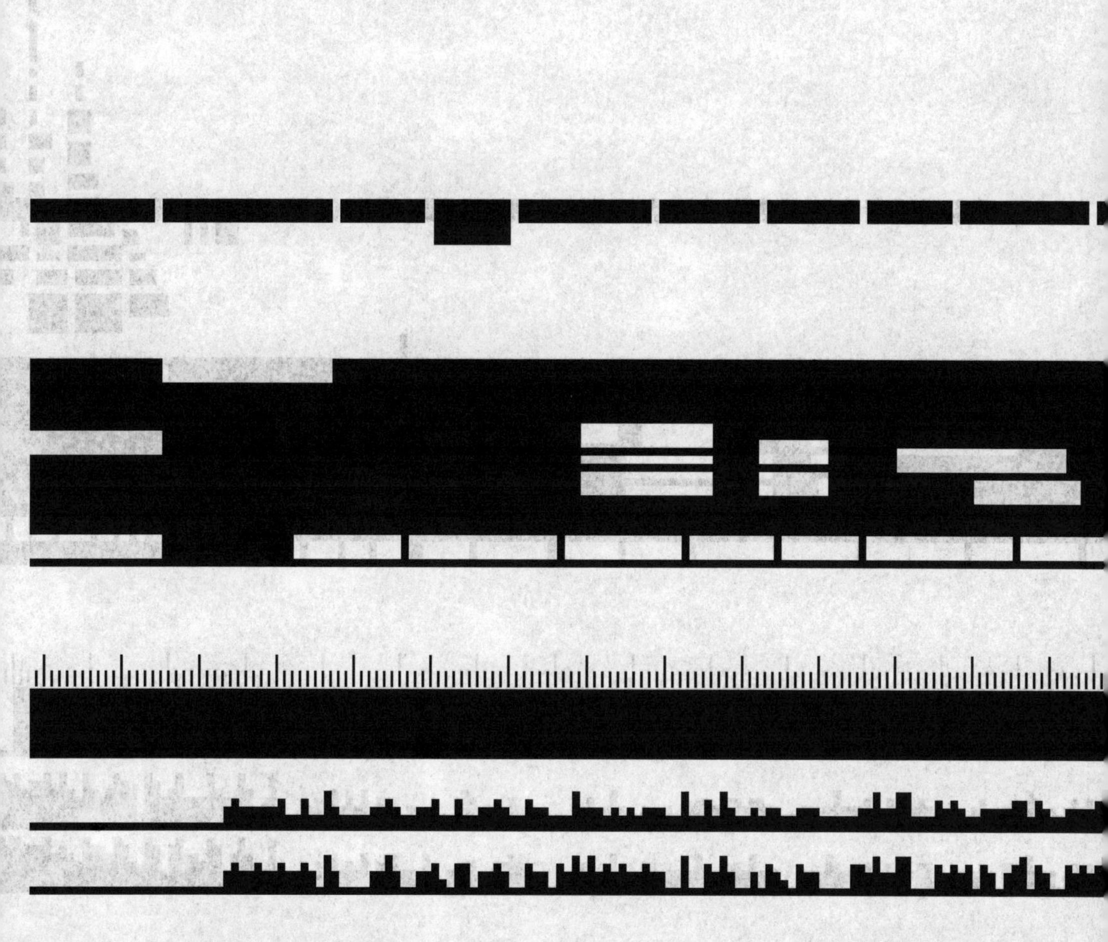

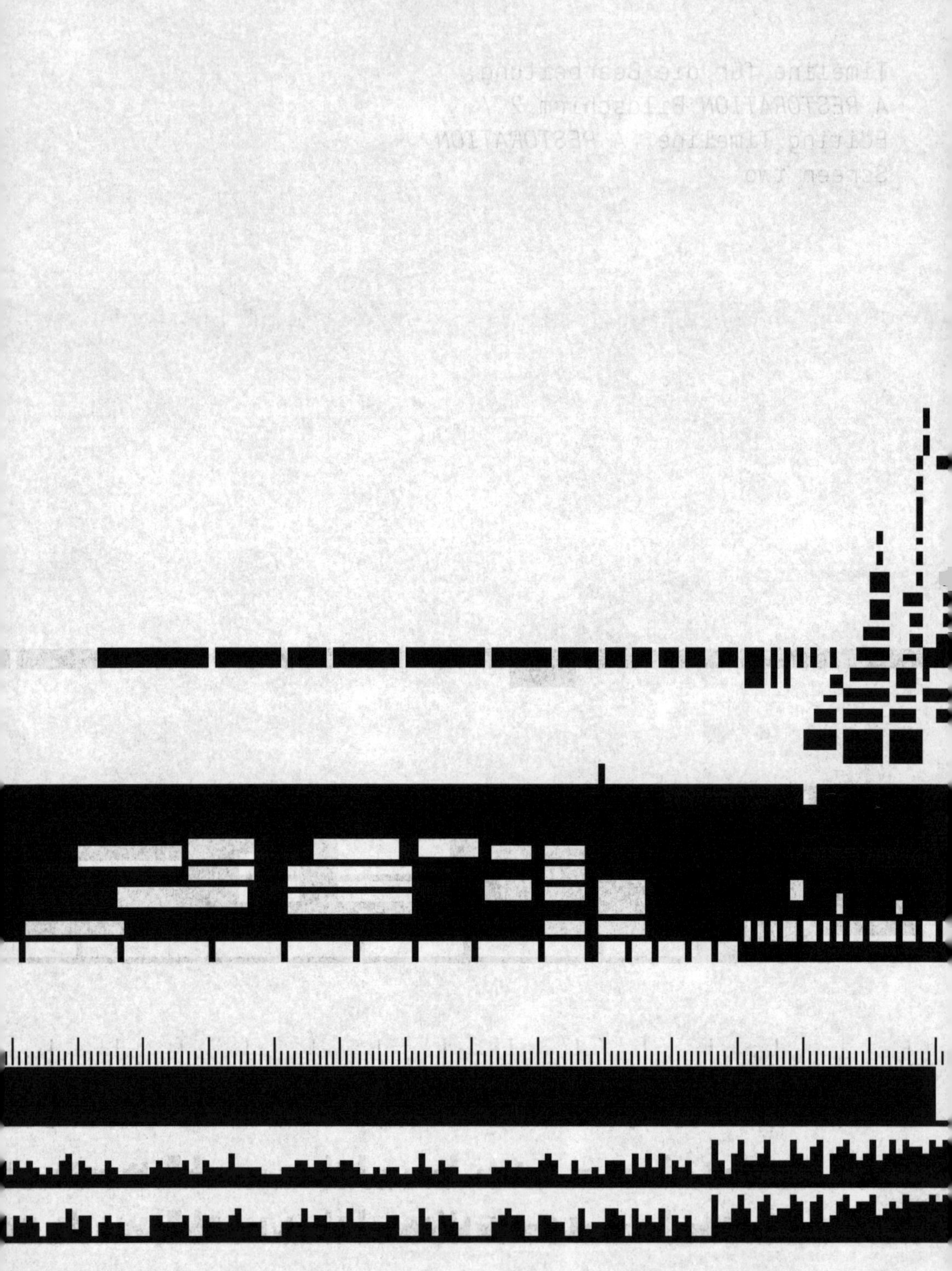

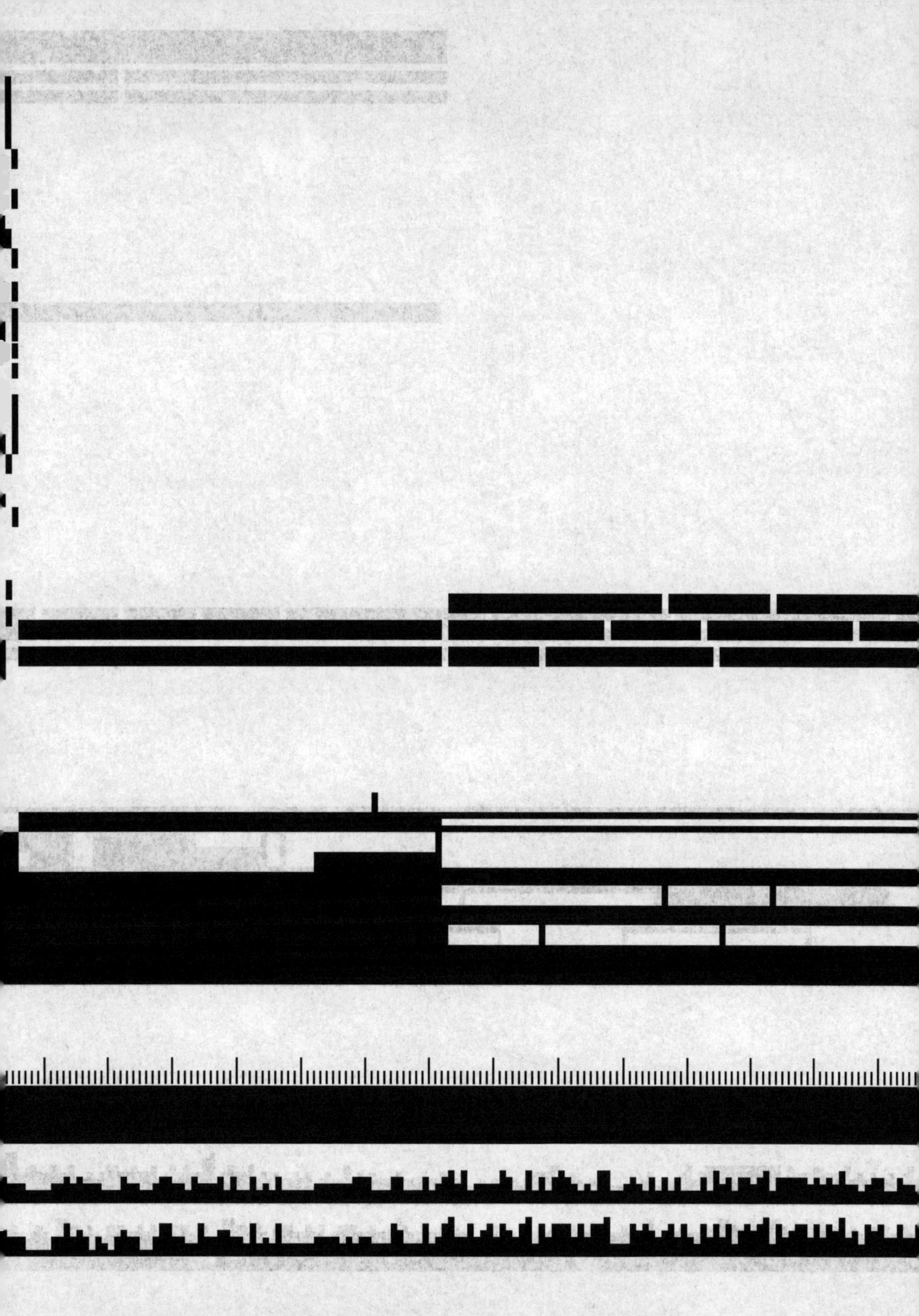

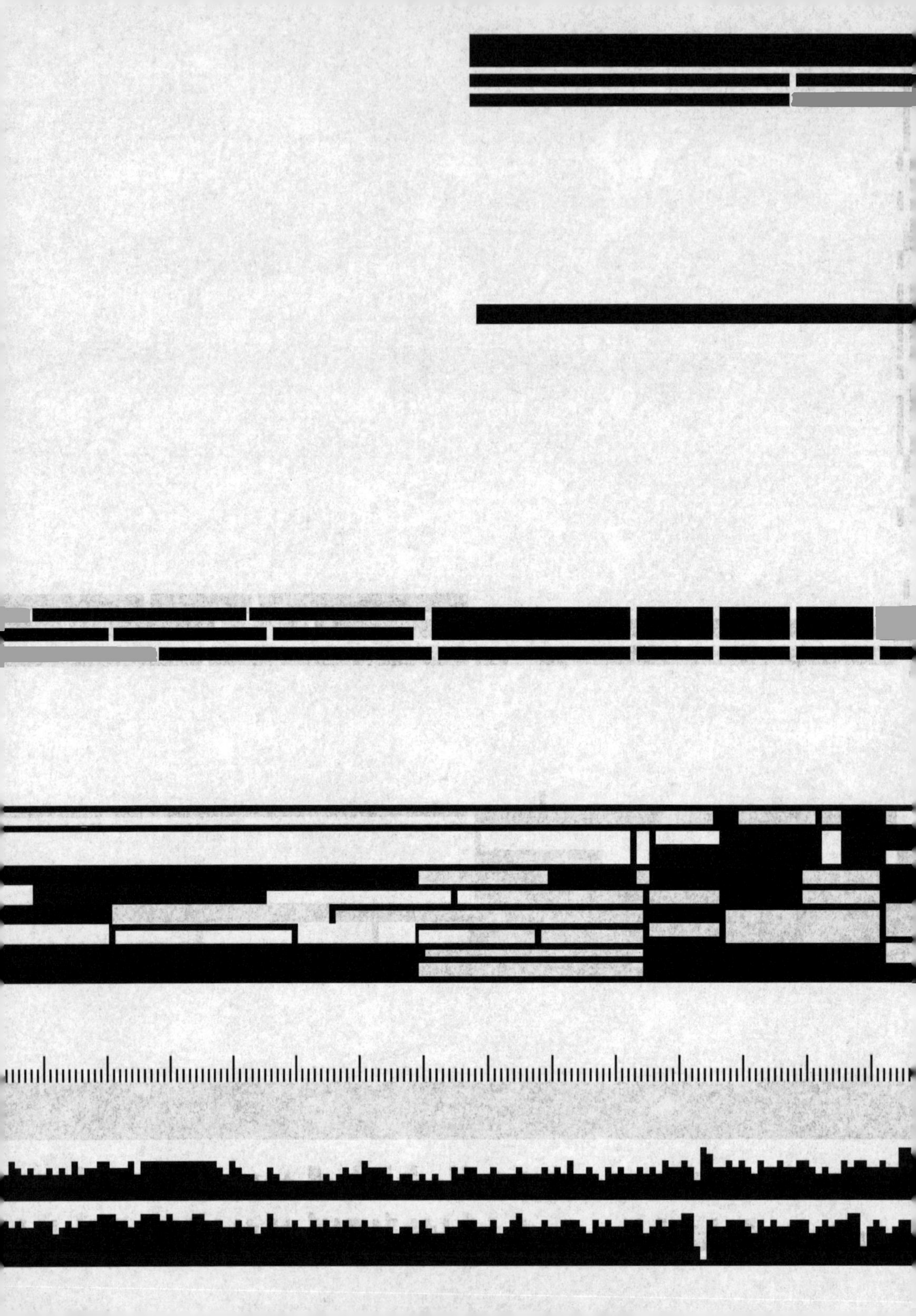

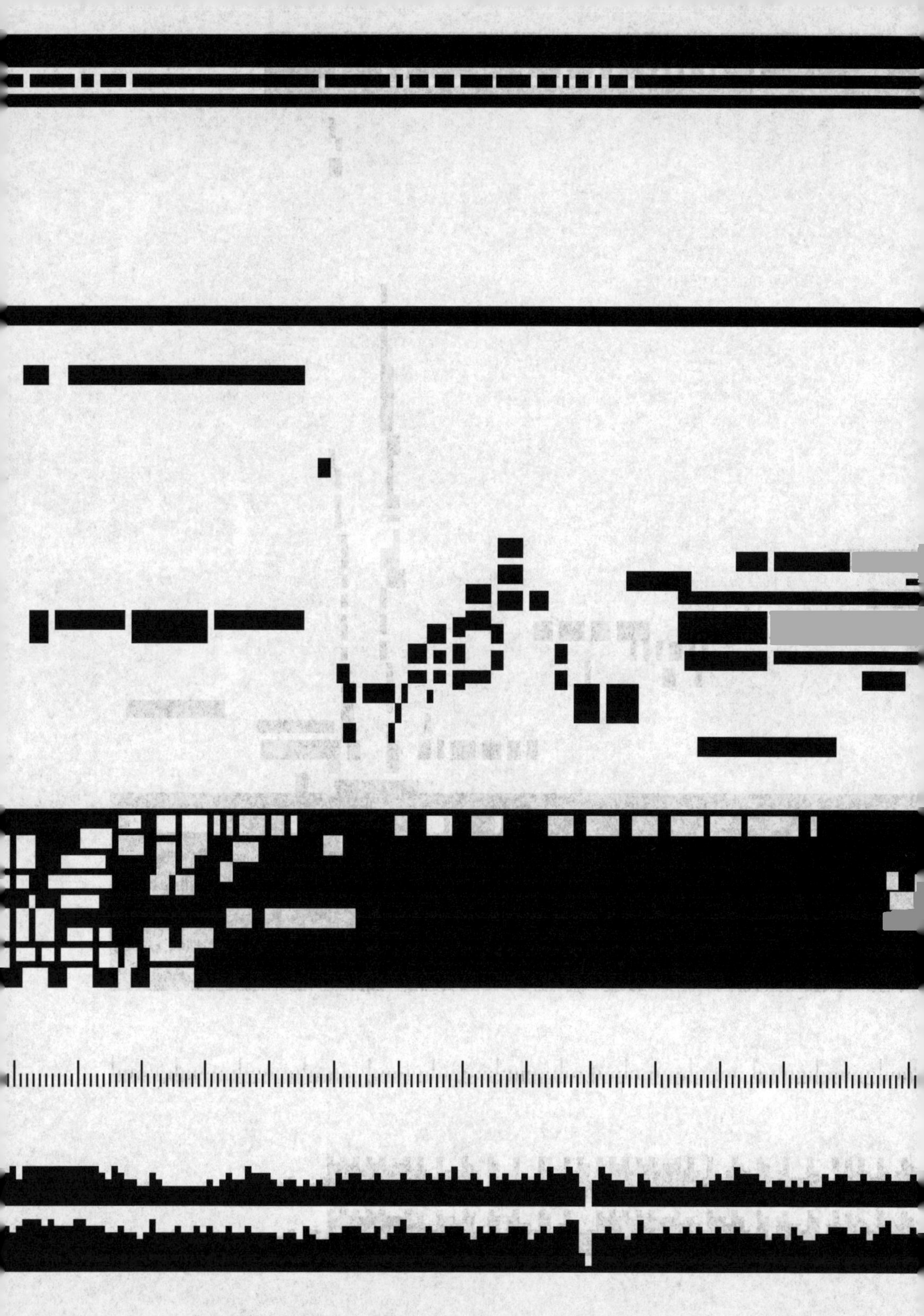

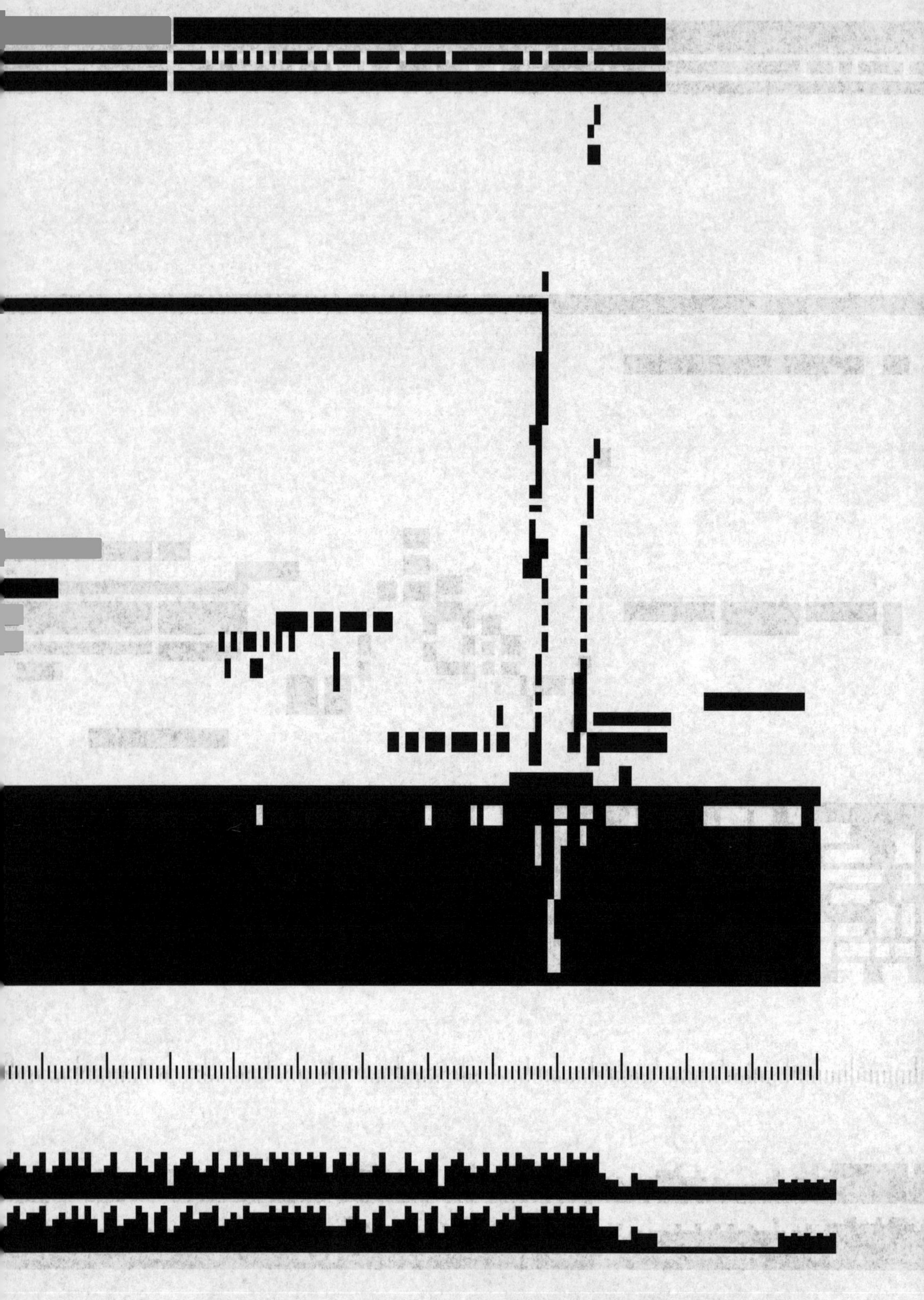

FELT

TIP

<u>FELT TIP (2018)</u>

This video features a collection of men's neckties
made between 1970 and 1990. Many of their designs
appear to incorporate imagery of computer networks,
interfaces, and memory chips. At the time, information
technology was revolutionizing the office workplace,
which perhaps explains this. But there are other connections: woven textiles and computing share a long
technical history. Indeed, the computer's ability to
"remember" is derived from the jacquard loom.
    FELT TIP draws on this history of data storage,
but also extends it into an imagined future: a corporate realm in which administrators are employed to
store documents in their own DNA. These administrators
– who are the narrators of the work – describe how
billions of bytes of data are written into the cells
of their fingertips.
    As a kind of therapy and a form of protest, the
administrators begin to collect images of men's neckties, which they regard as significant artifacts in
the history of hegemonic memory. They furtively annex
part of their fingertip data-stores for this purpose,
and use these images to elaborate on the enduring
class and gender hierarchies of office life.
    Their stories turn on a series of visual echoes
and substitutions. The weary phallic symbolism of
the tie is ignored in favor of its similarities to
the ink-pen nib, fingertip, stiletto, and tongue.
As they flip through these images, the administrators
swiftly segue from considering executive authority to
related matters of authorship, digital inscription,
and oral history.

<u>FELT TIP (2018)</u>

In diesem Video geht es um eine Sammlung von Herren-
krawatten, die zwischen 1970 und 1990 entstanden
sind. Viele ihrer Designs nehmen die Bildlichkeit
von Computernetzwerken, Schnittstellen und Speicherchips auf. Zur gleichen Zeit revolutionierte die
Informationstechnologie den Büroarbeitsplatz, was die
Motivik der Krawatten vielleicht erklärt. Aber es
gibt noch weitere Verbindungen: Gewebte Textilien und
Computertechnik haben eine lange gemeinsame technische Geschichte. In der Tat geht die Fähigkeit des
Computers, sich zu »erinnern«, auf den Jacquard-
Webstuhl zurück.

   FELT TIP greift auf die Geschichte der Daten-
speicherung zurück, weitet sie aber auch auf eine ima-
ginäre Zukunft aus: eine Unternehmenswelt, in der
Administrator:innen damit beschäftigt sind, Dokumente
in ihrer eigenen DNA zu speichern. Diese Adminis-
trator:innen – die die Erzähler:innen des Werks sind
– beschreiben, wie Milliarden von Bytes an Daten in
die Zellen ihrer Fingerspitzen eingeschrieben werden.

   Als eine Art Therapie und eine Form des Protests
beginnen die Administrator:innen, Bilder von Herren-
krawatten zu sammeln, die sie als bedeutende Artefakte
aus der Geschichte hegemonialer Erinnerung betrach-
ten. Zu diesem Zweck eignen sie sich heimlich einen
Teil ihrer Fingerspitzendatenspeicher an und ver-
wenden die Bilder, um die anhaltenden Klassen- und
Geschlechterhierarchien des Büroalltags zu erörtern.

   Ihre Geschichten drehen sich um eine Reihe von
visuellen Anklängen und Substitutionen. Die abgenutzte
phallische Symbolik der Krawatte wird zugunsten von

Word games are also used, ranging from bawdy jokes
to etymological references. Indeed, the administrators express themselves in a combination of slang,
innuendo, synonym, and rhyme. They draw upon the
roots of words – the digital (finger) in the digital
and the secret of the secretary – to propose a writing of fluid, heterogeneous meaning. Everything gets
mixed up, including languages themselves – English
with French, philosophy with pop – in the telling of
the tale.

Folgende Seiten / Following pages:
58 der 153 Fotografien, die Teil von *FELT TIP* sind. /
Fifty-eight of the 153 photographic images that are
media assets for *FELT TIP*.

Ähnlichkeiten mit der Füllfederspitze, der Finger-
spitze, dem Stilettoabsatz und der Zunge ausgeblendet.
Während sie die Bilder durchblättern, gehen die
Administrator:innen schnell von der Betrachtung der
Exekutive zu verwandten Fragen von Autorenschaft,
digitaler Einschreibung und mündlich überlieferter
Geschichte über.

Auch Wortspiele kommen vor: von derben Witzen
bis hin zu etymologischen Verweisen. In der Tat
drücken sich die Administrator:innen in einer
Kombination aus Slang, Anspielung, Synonym und Reim
aus. Sie greifen auf Wortwurzeln zurück – der Bezug
zum Finger (engl. *digit*) im Digitalen und das
Geheimnis (engl. *secret*) der Sekretärin – und bieten
damit ein Schreiben mit fließenden, heterogenen
Bedeutungen. Beim Erzählen der Geschichte gerät alles
durcheinander, auch die Sprachen selbst: Englisch
vermischt sich mit Französisch, Philosophie mit Pop.

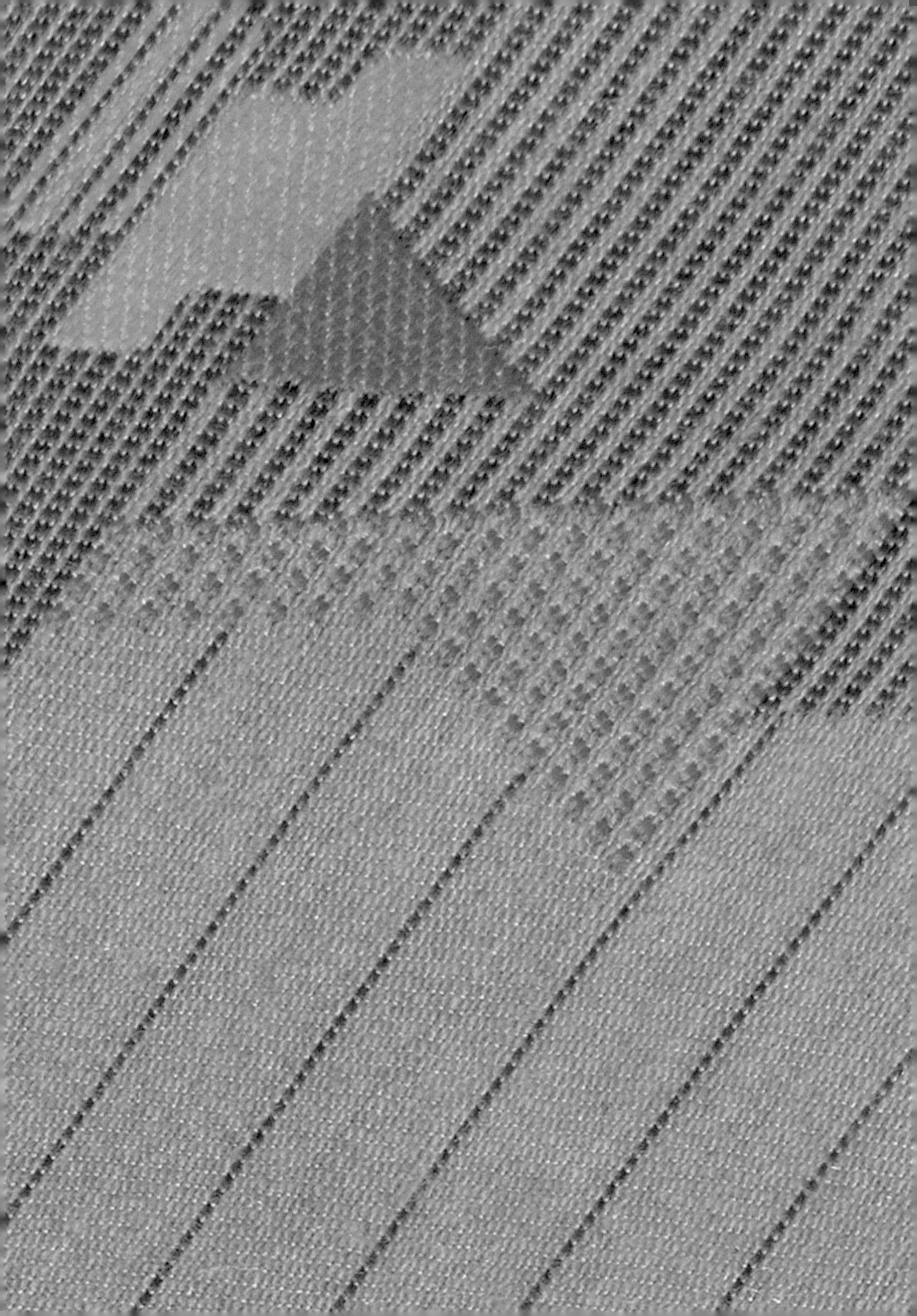

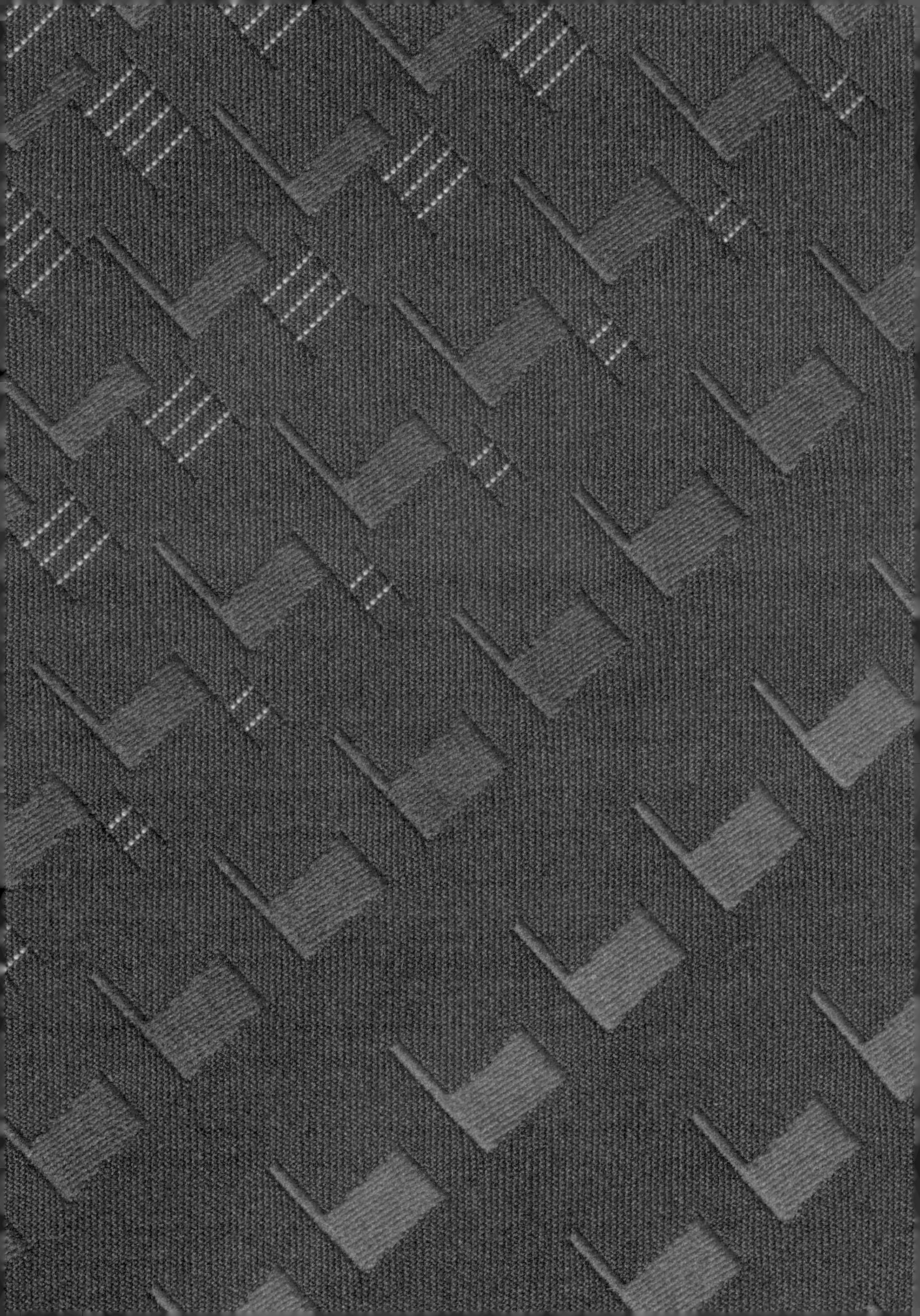

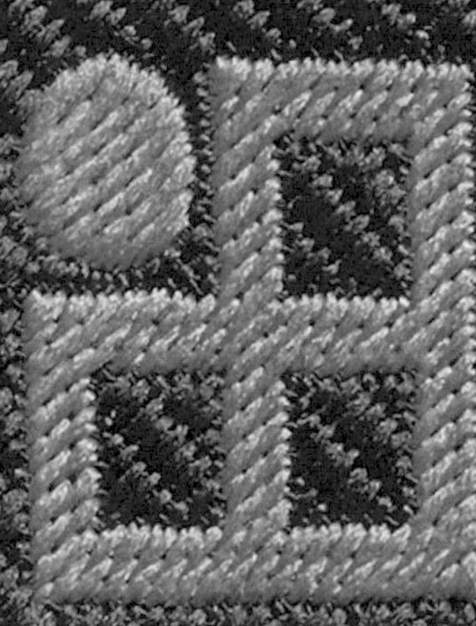

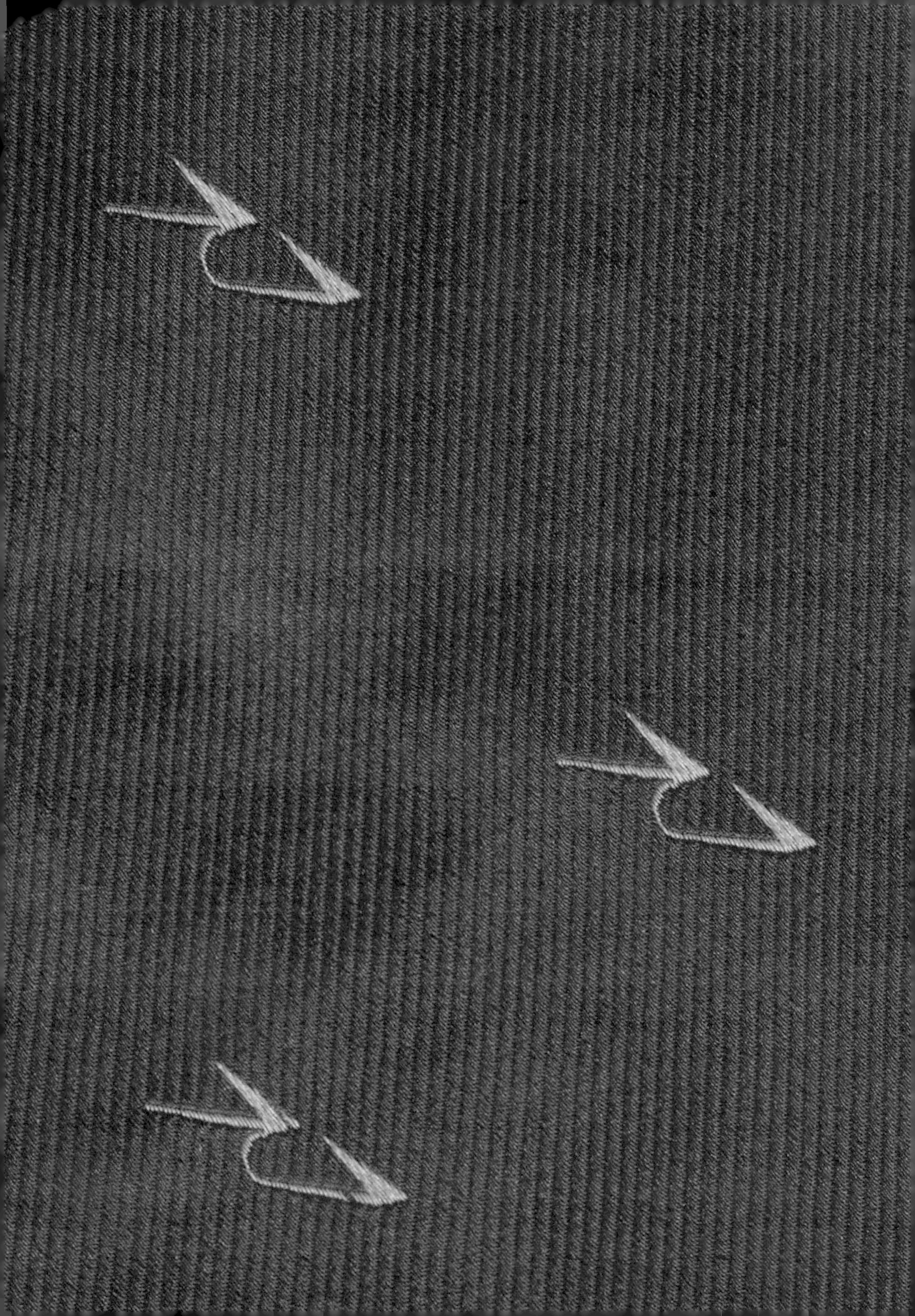

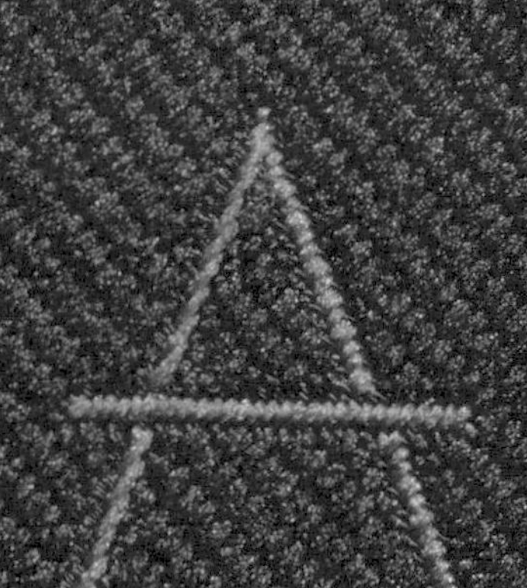

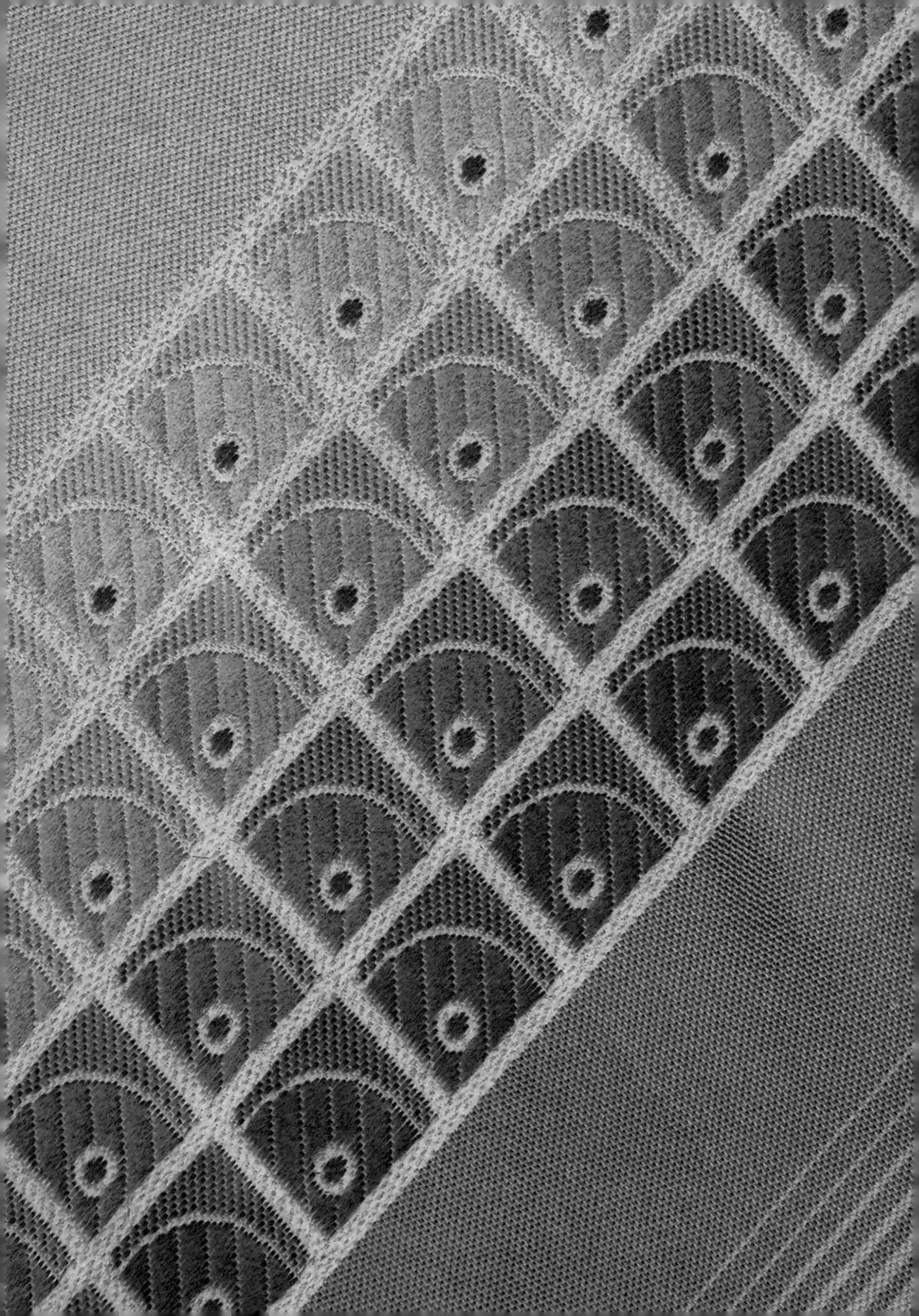

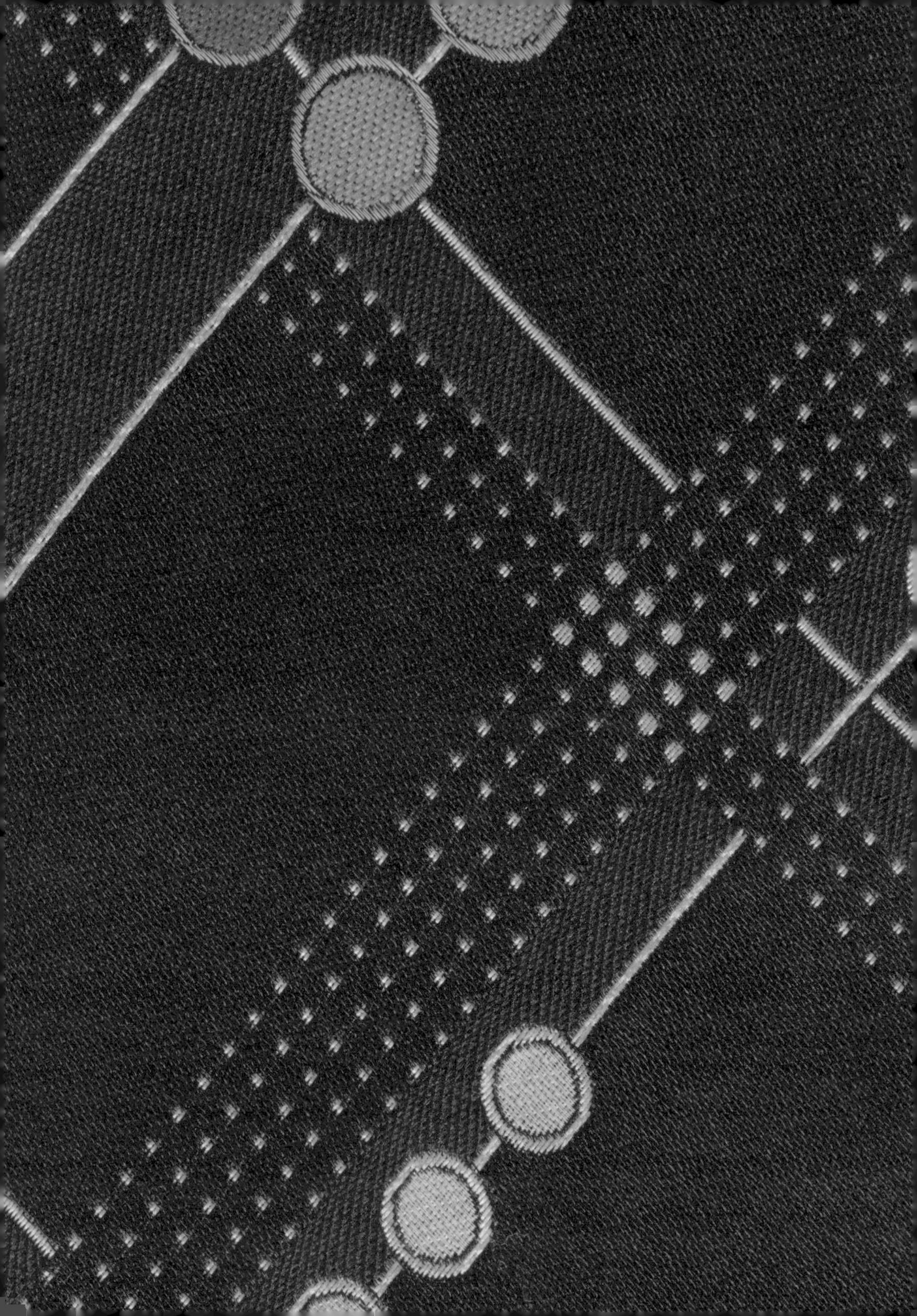

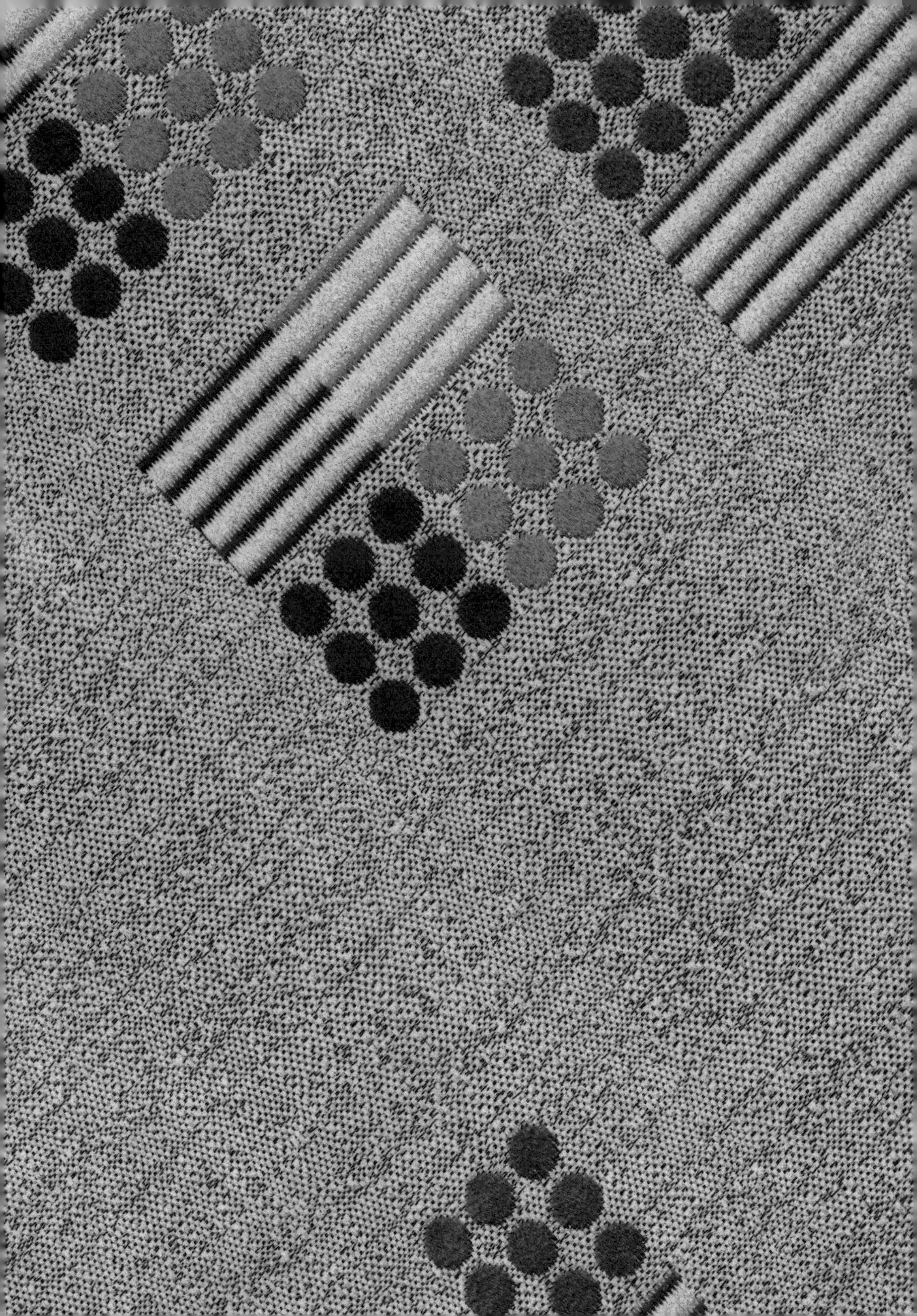

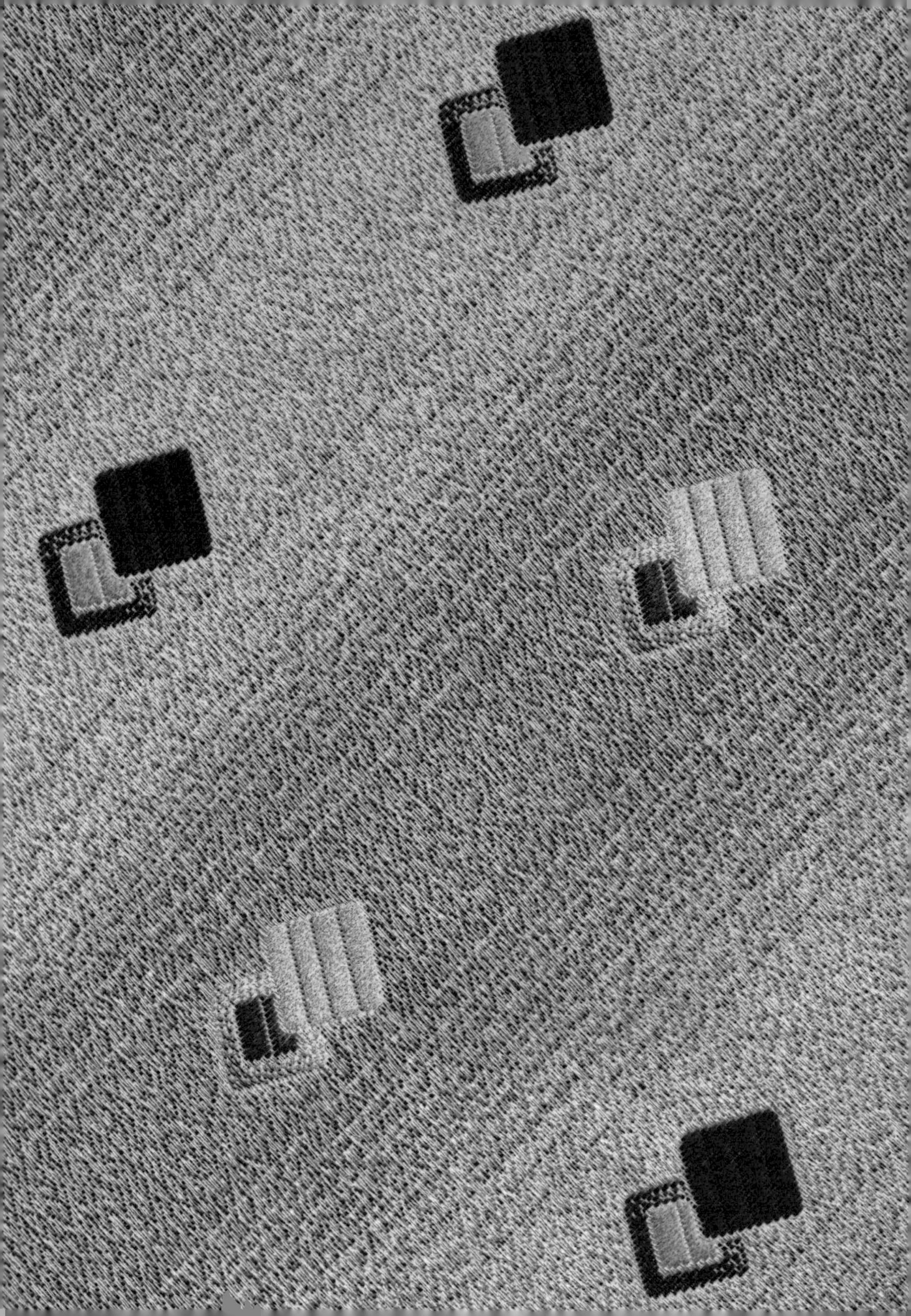

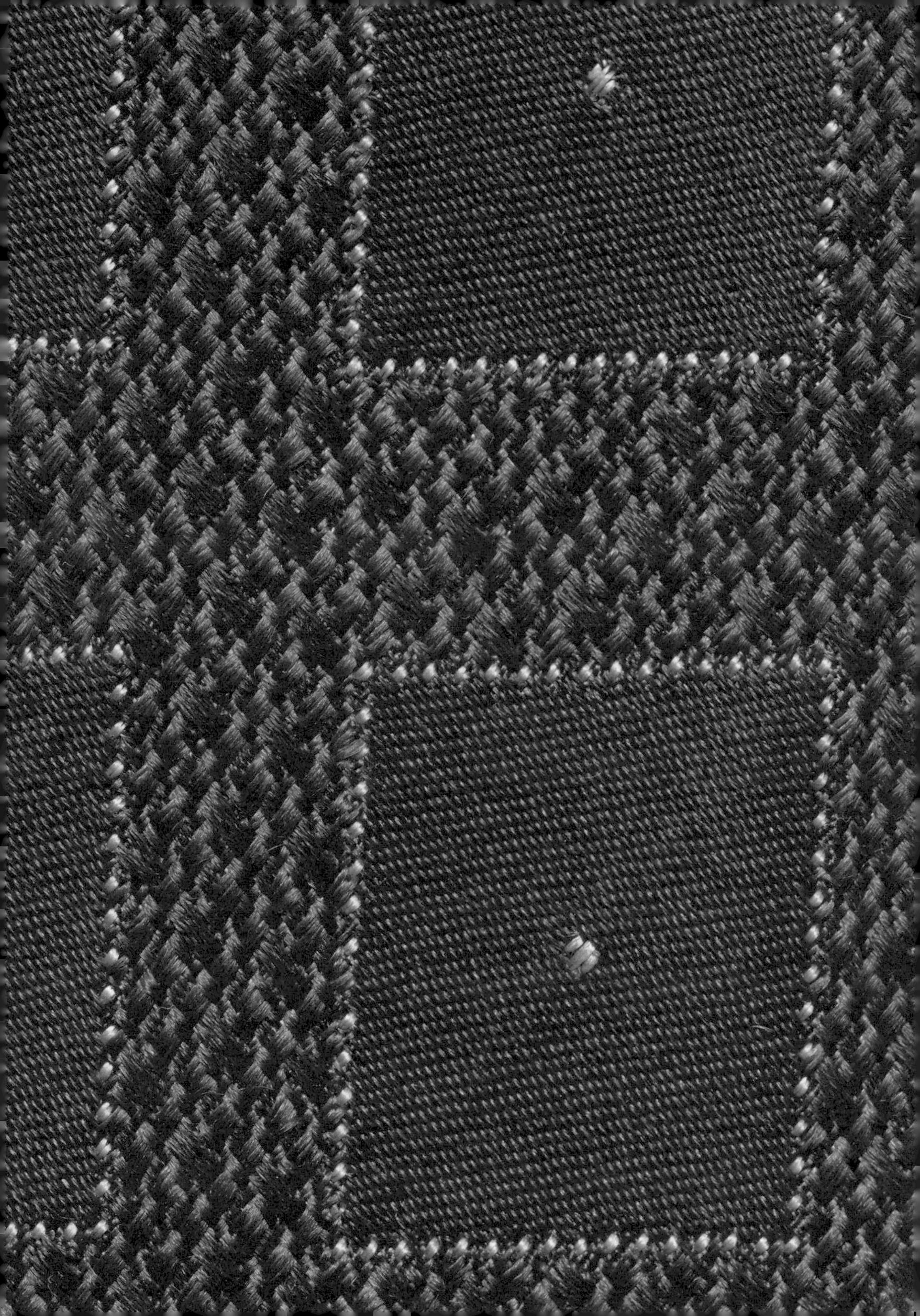

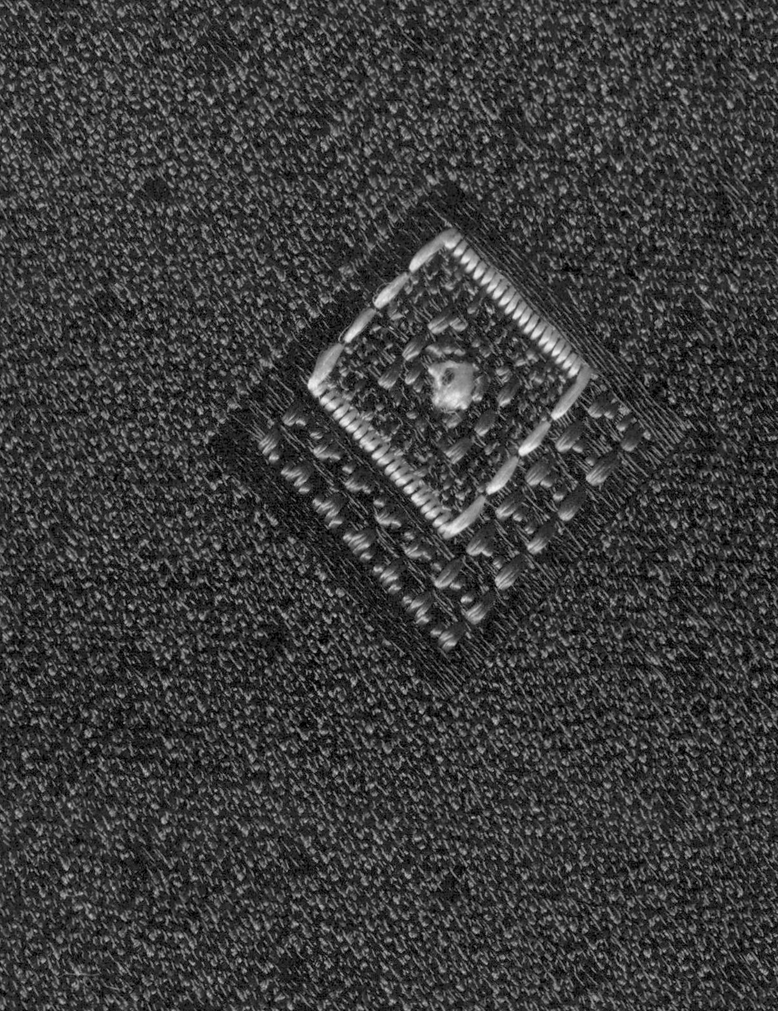

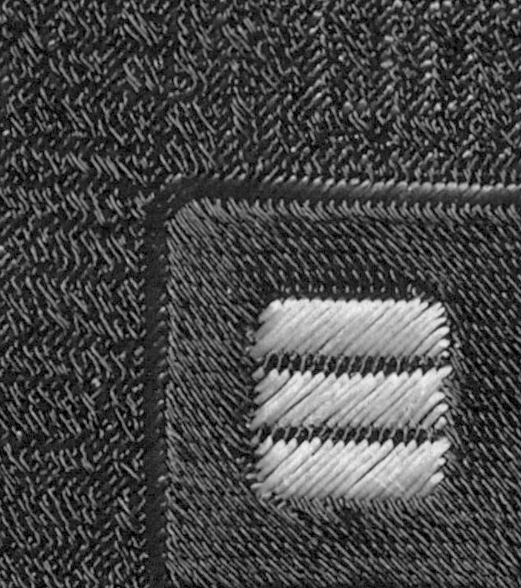

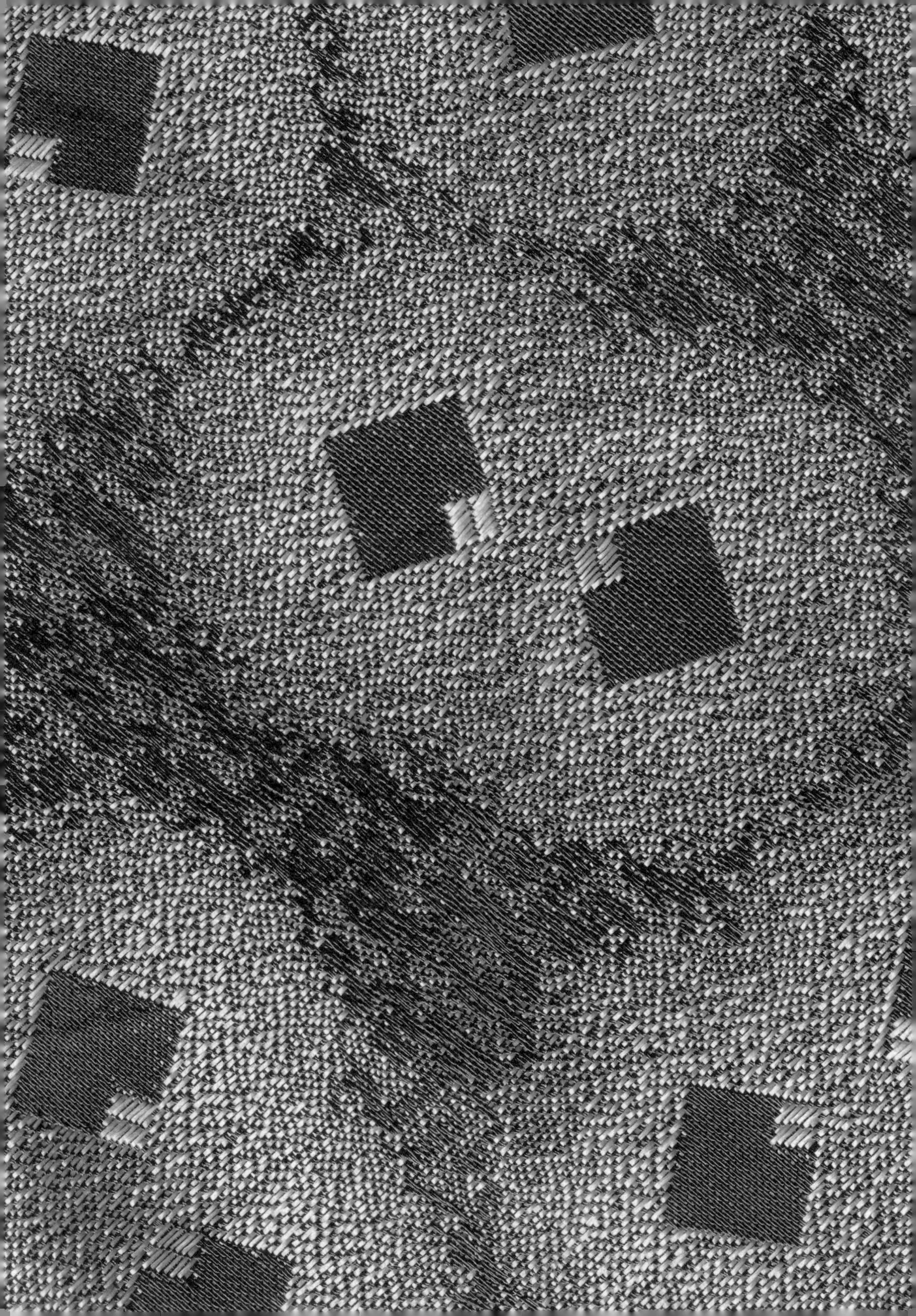

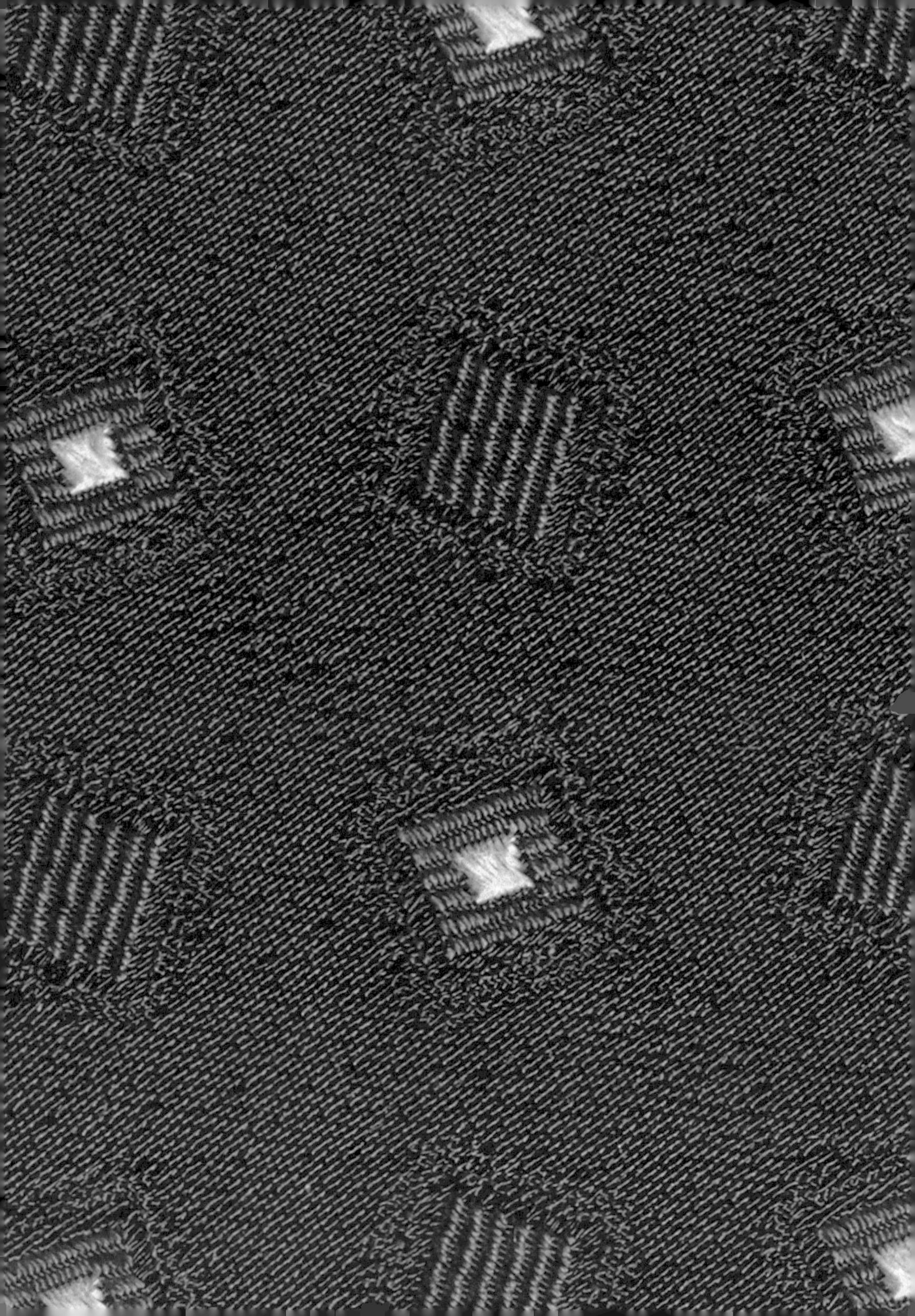

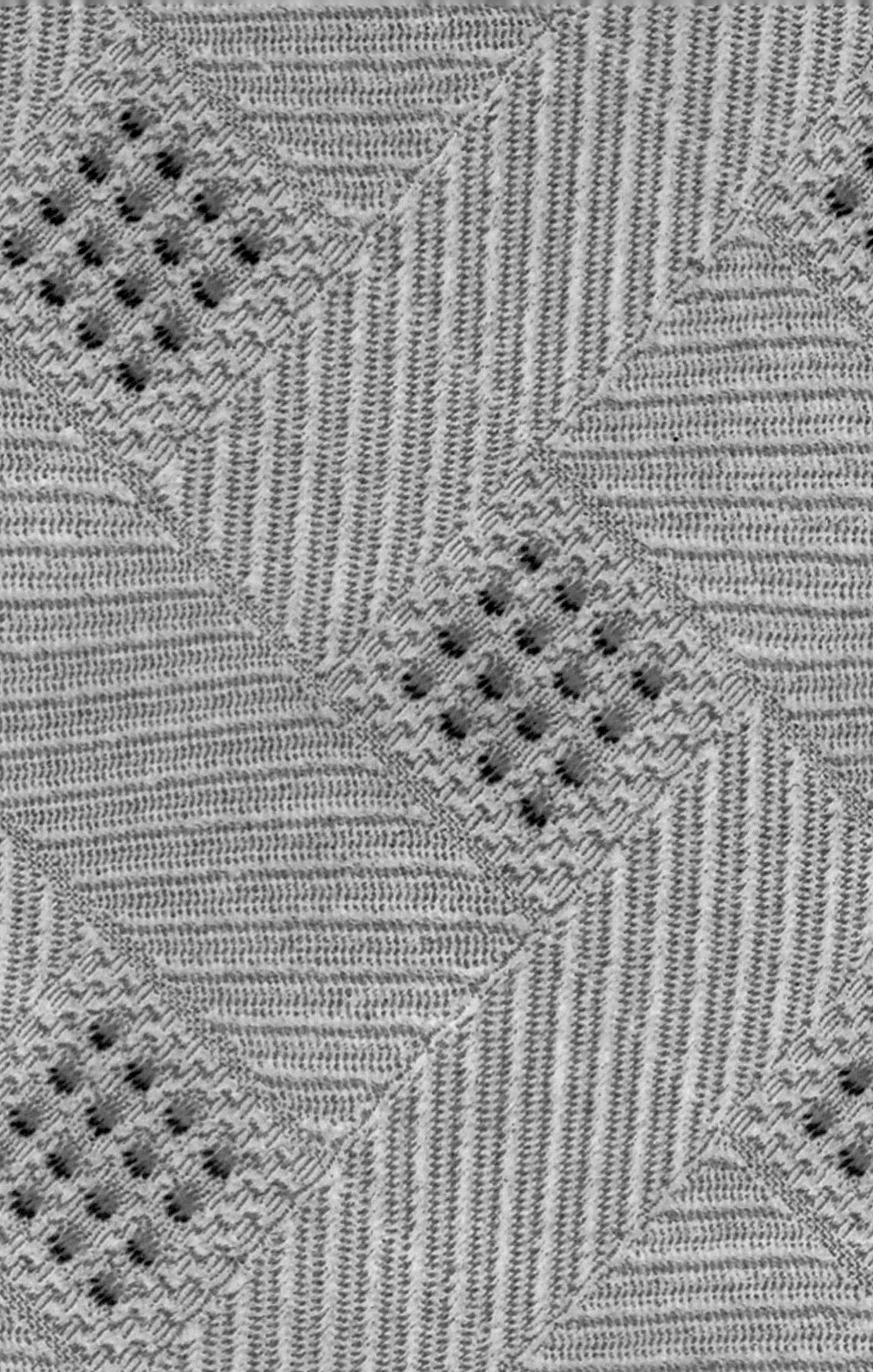

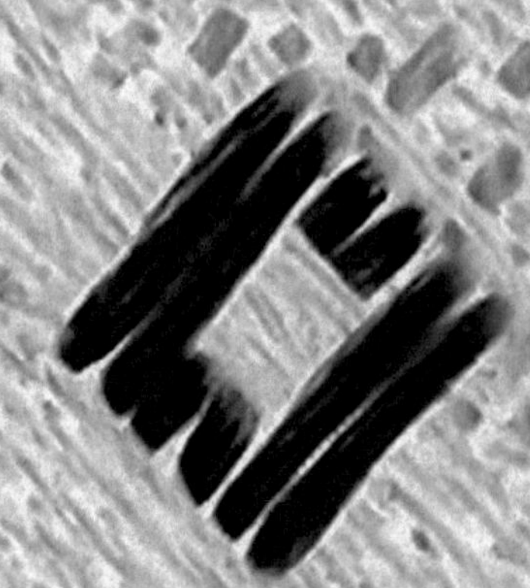

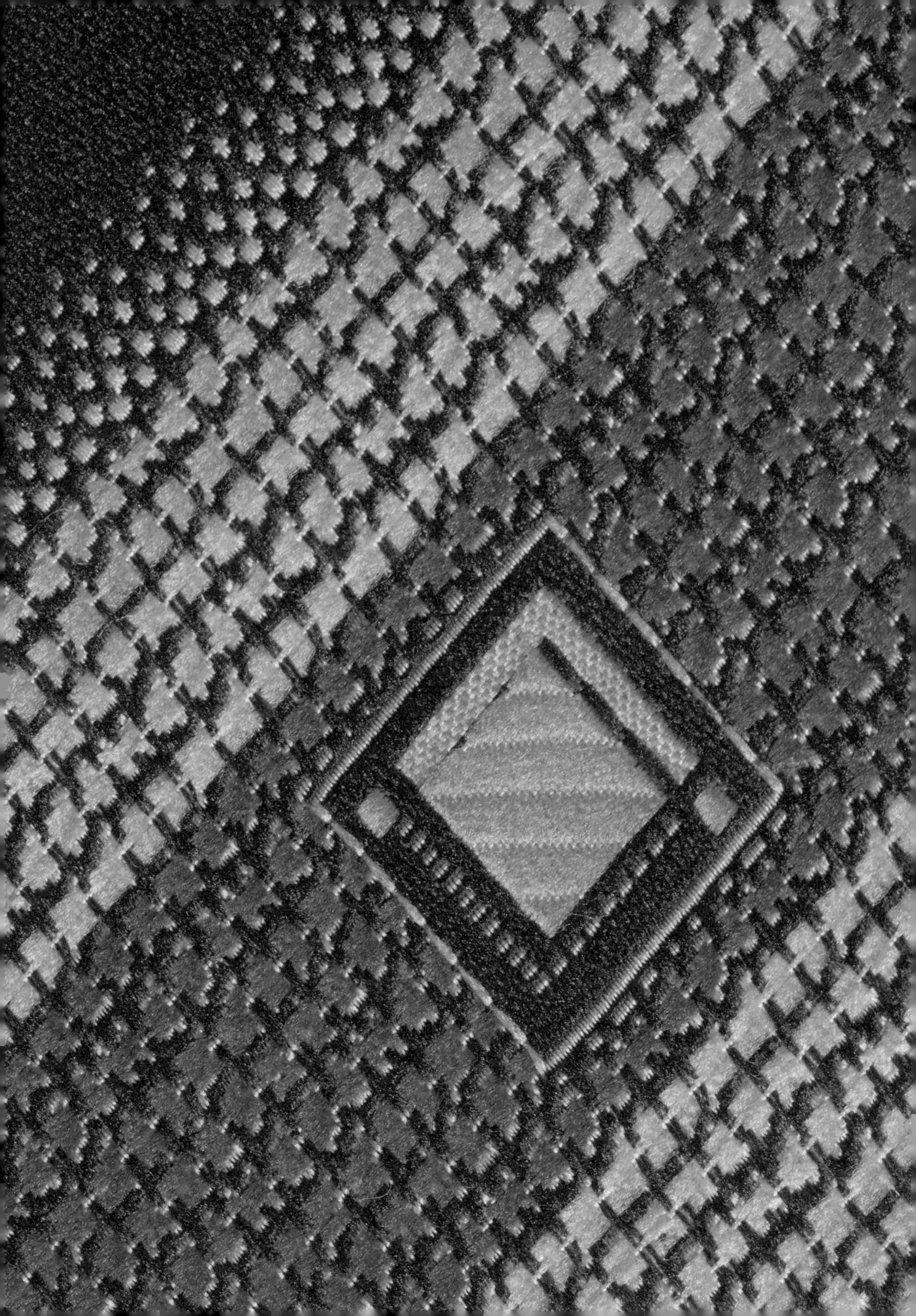

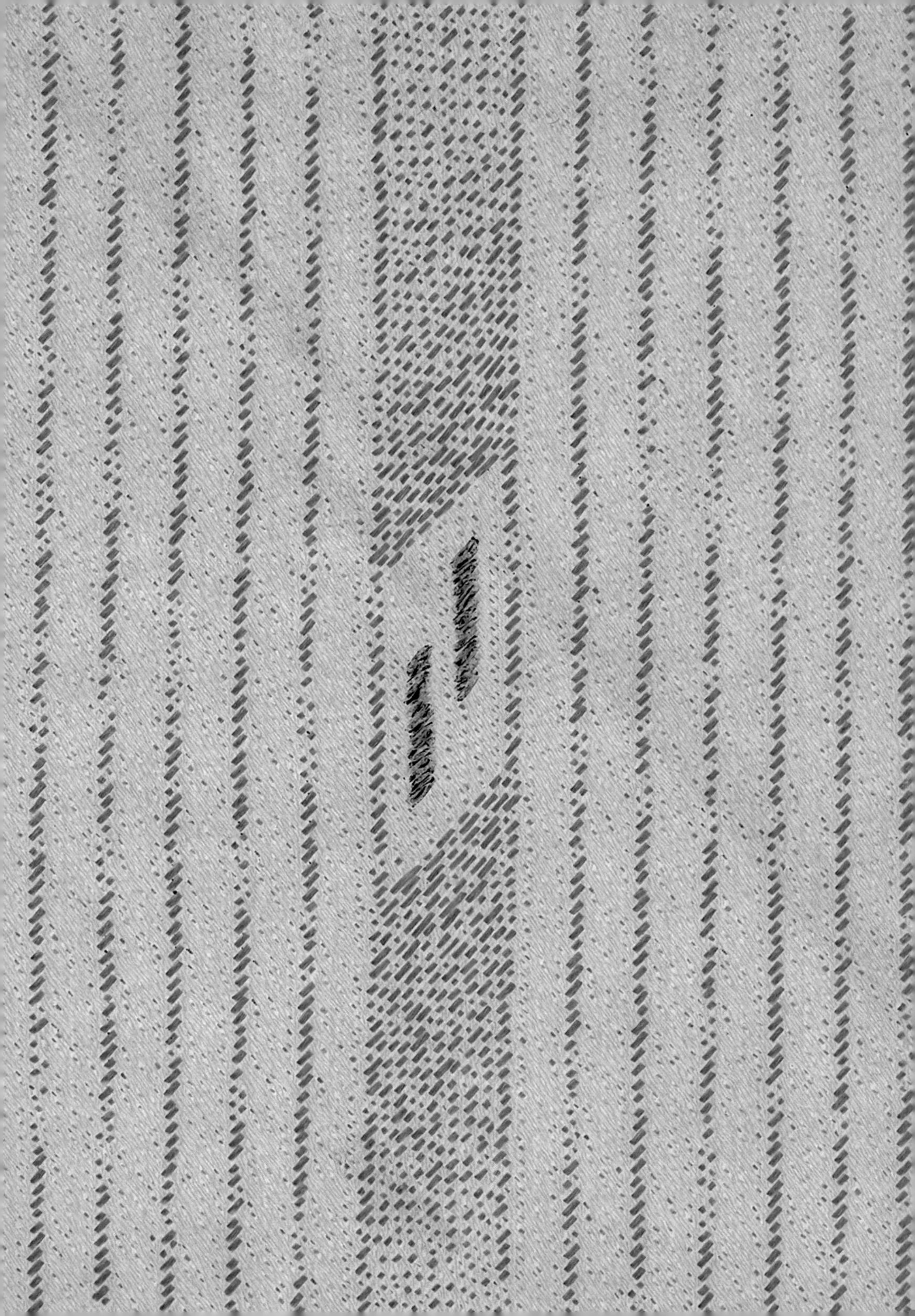

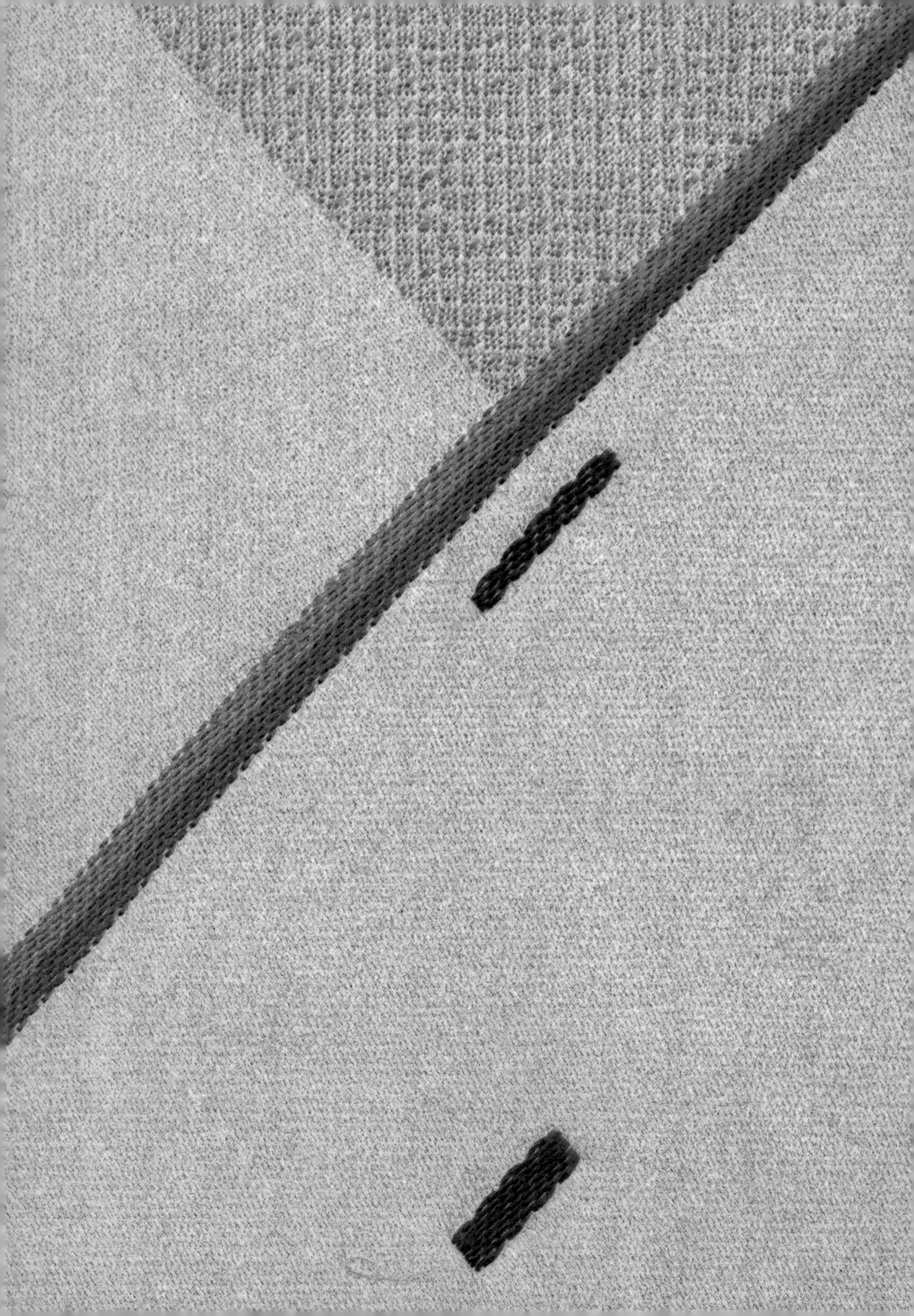

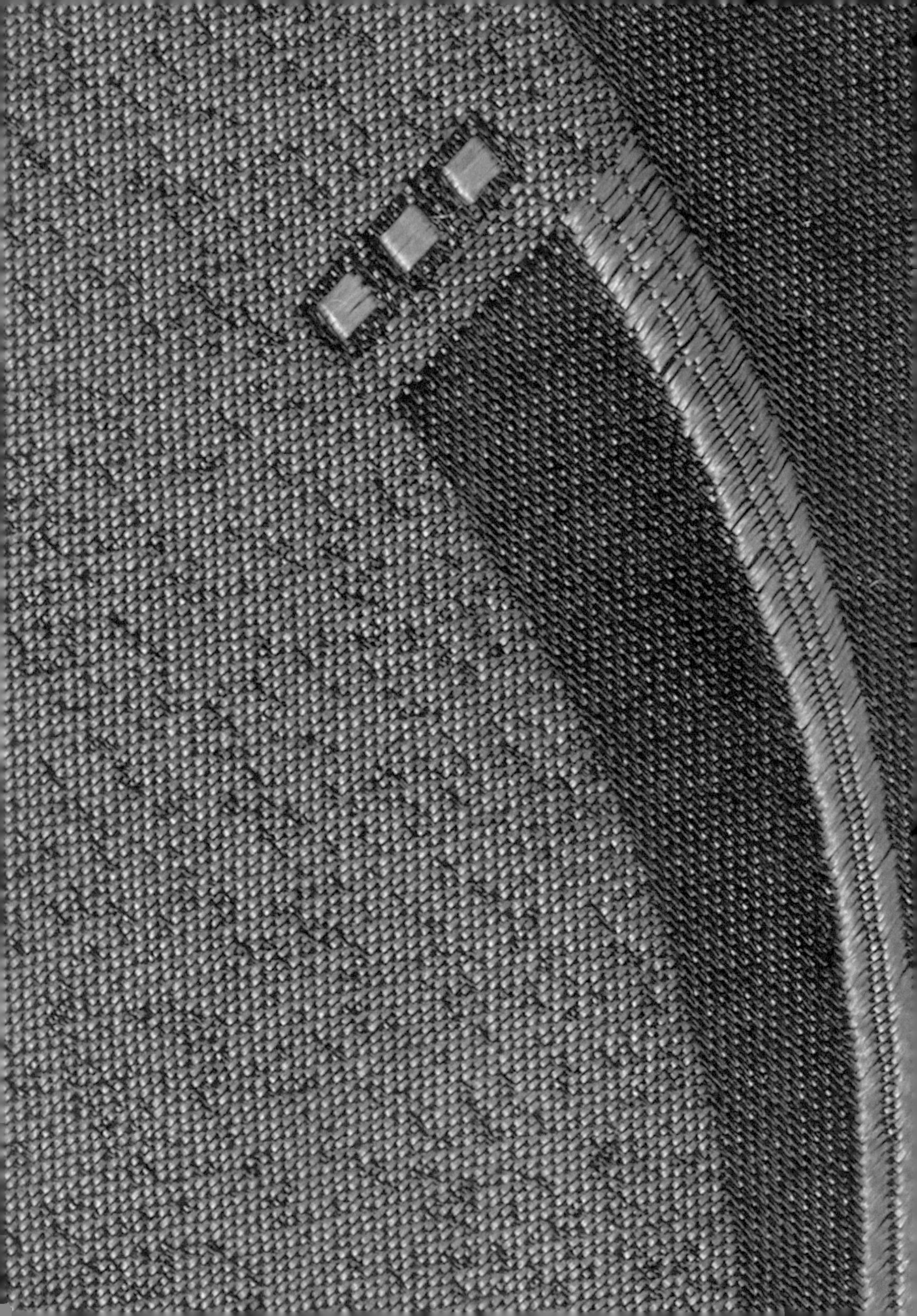

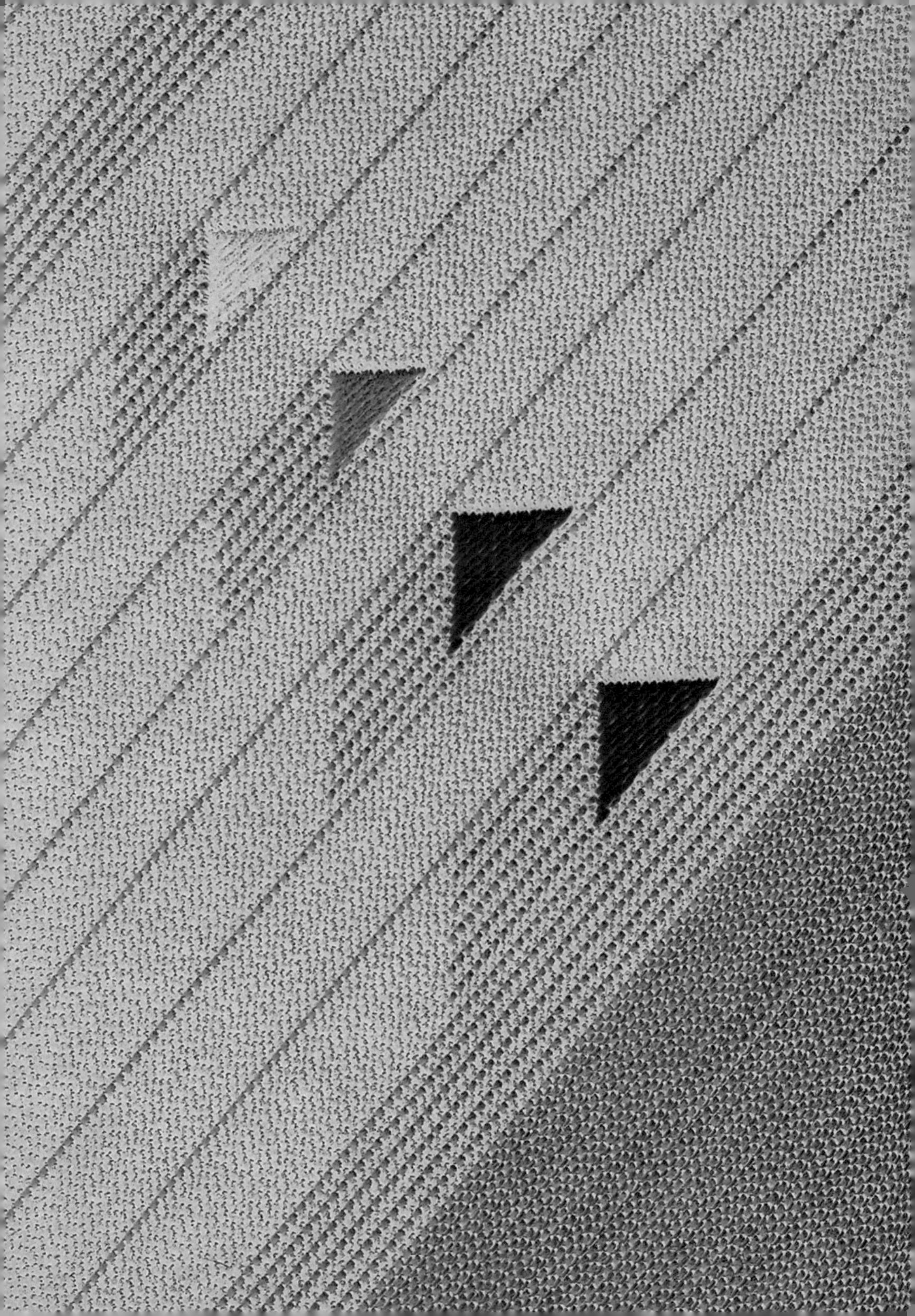

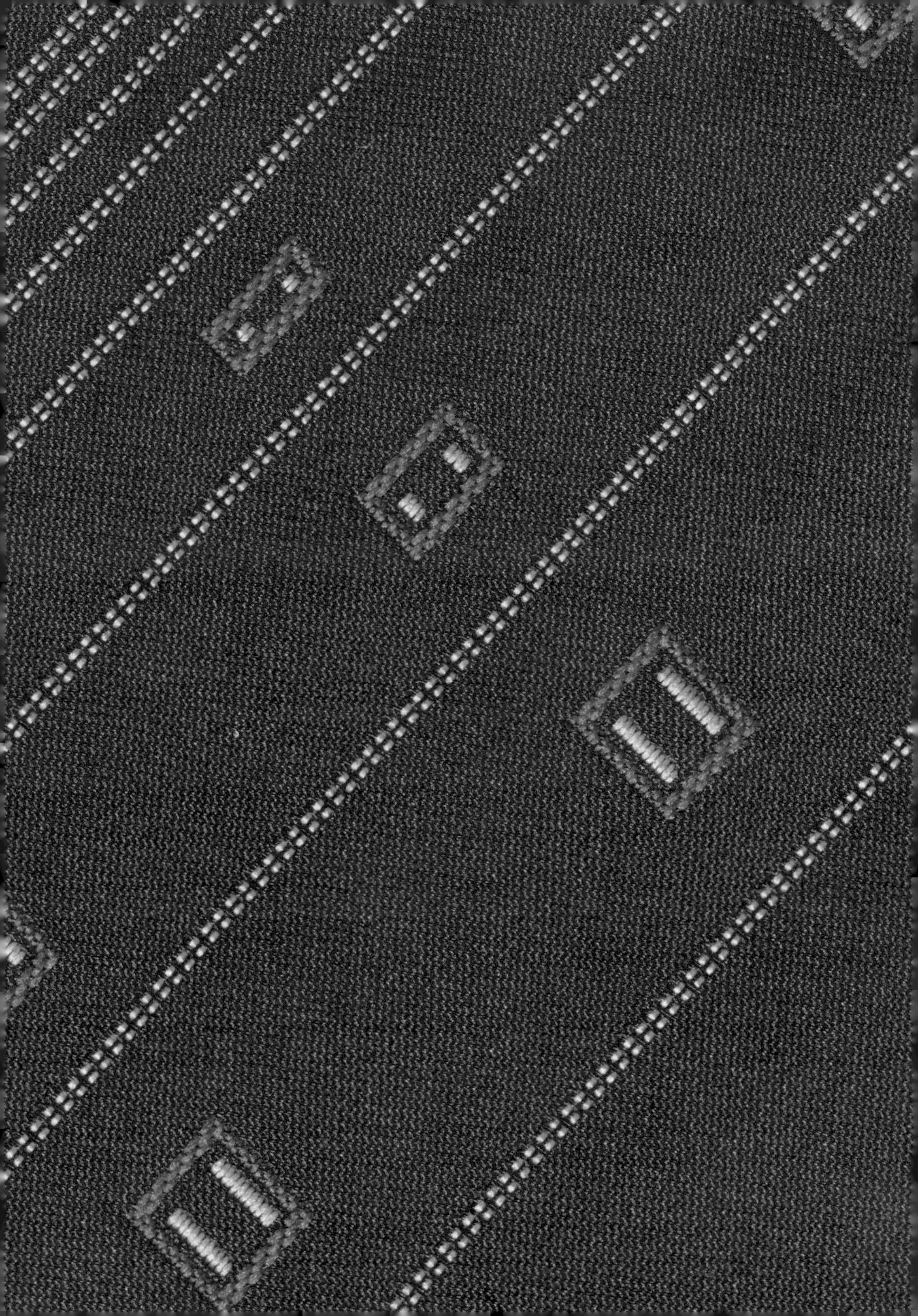

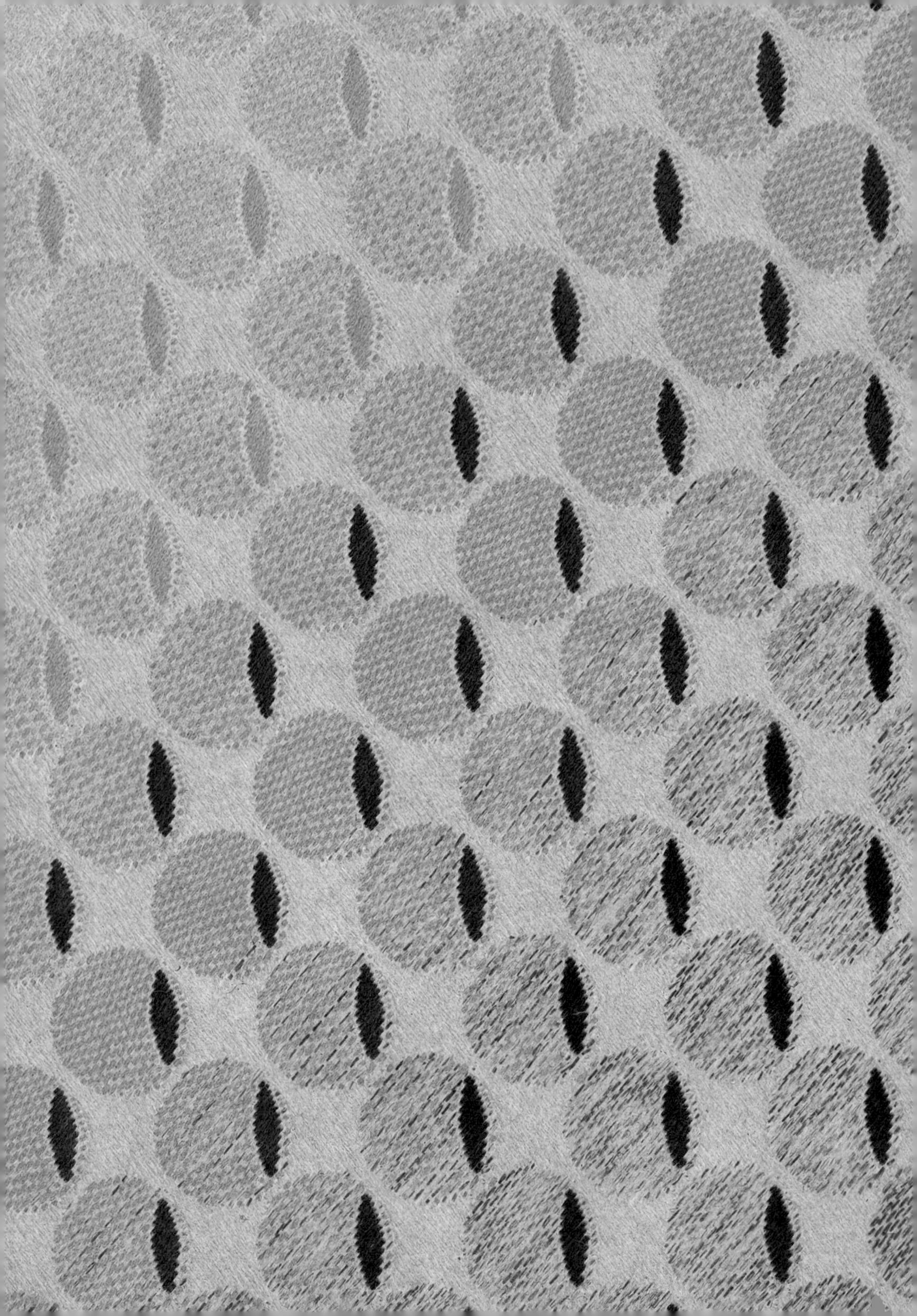

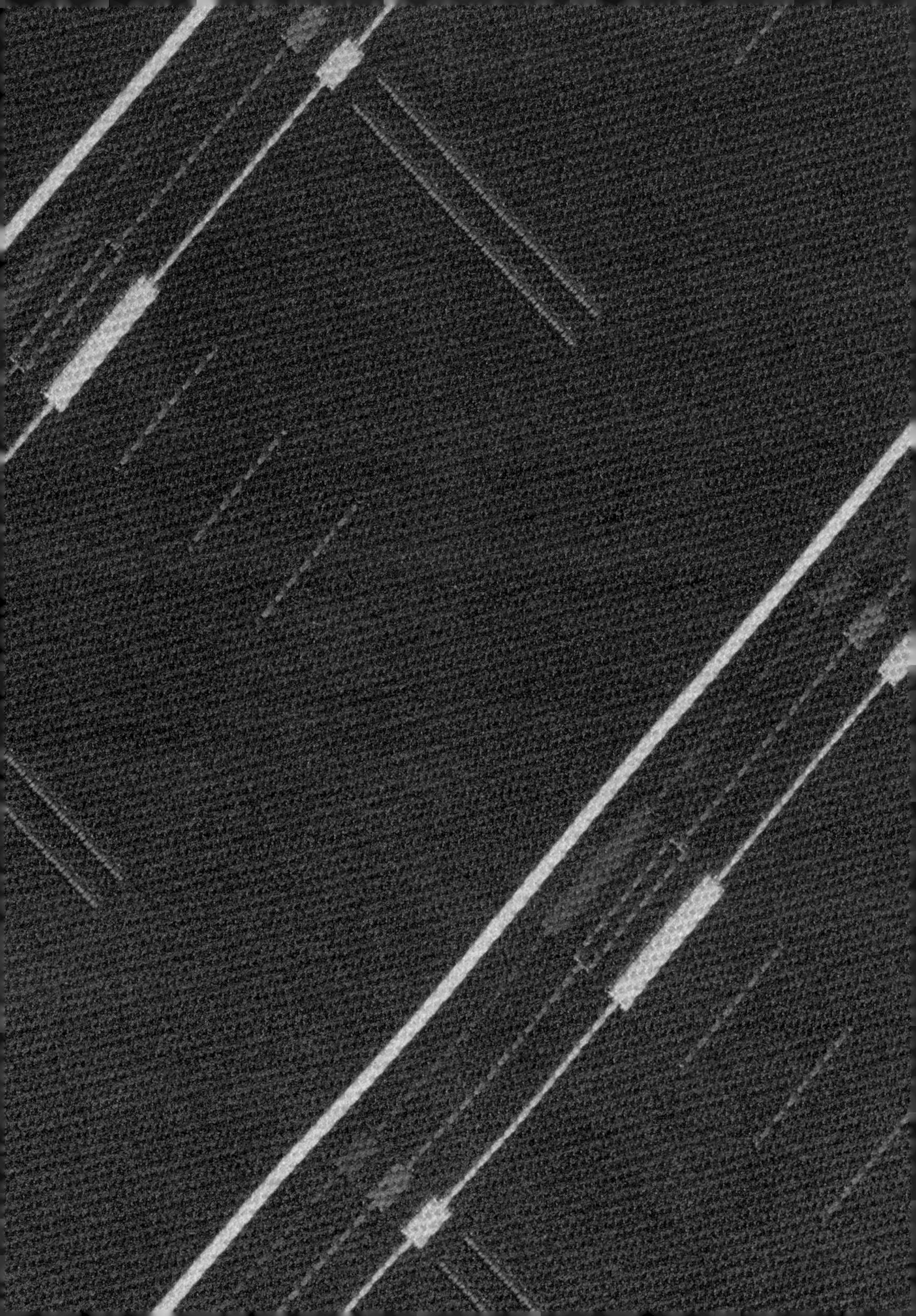

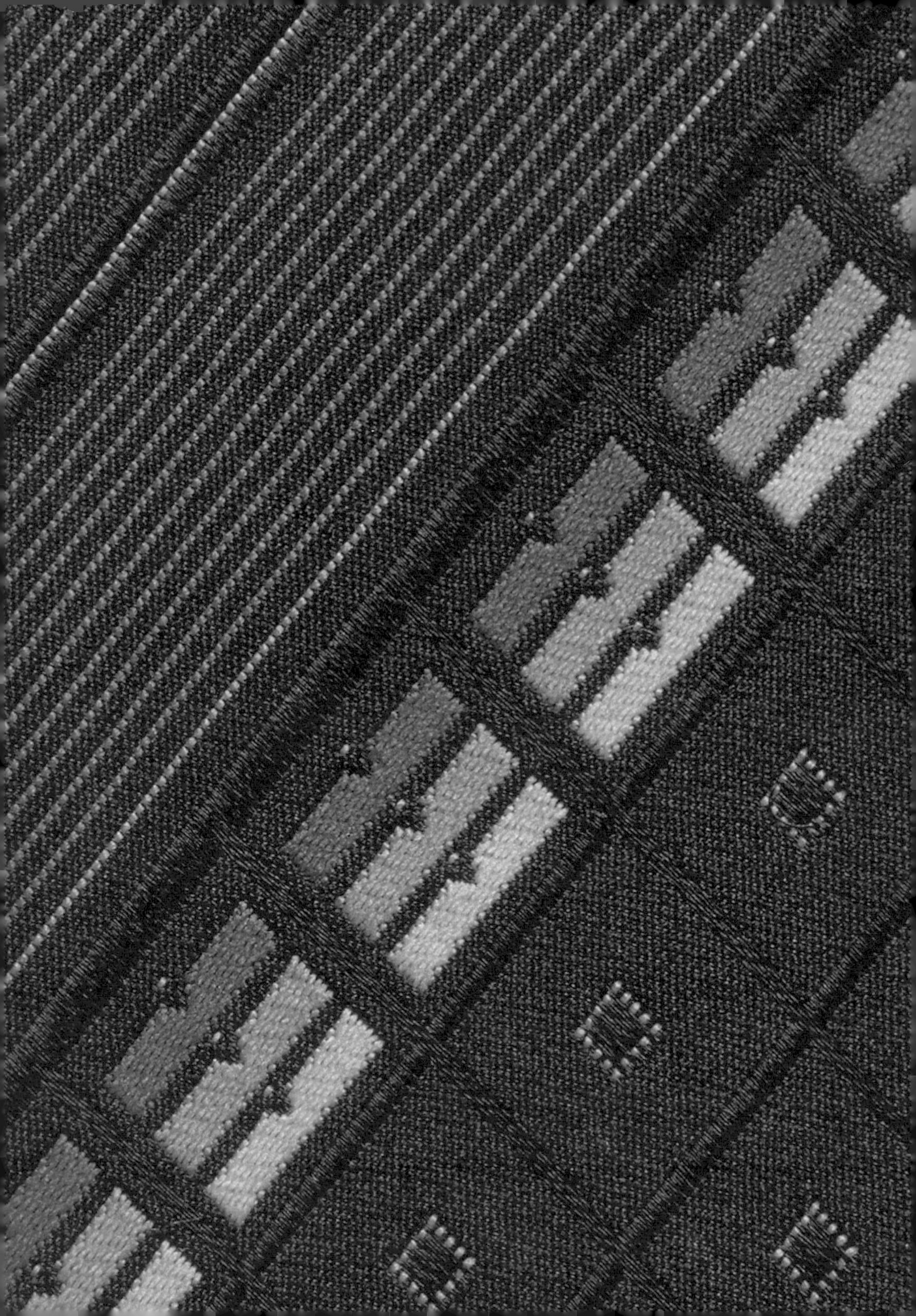

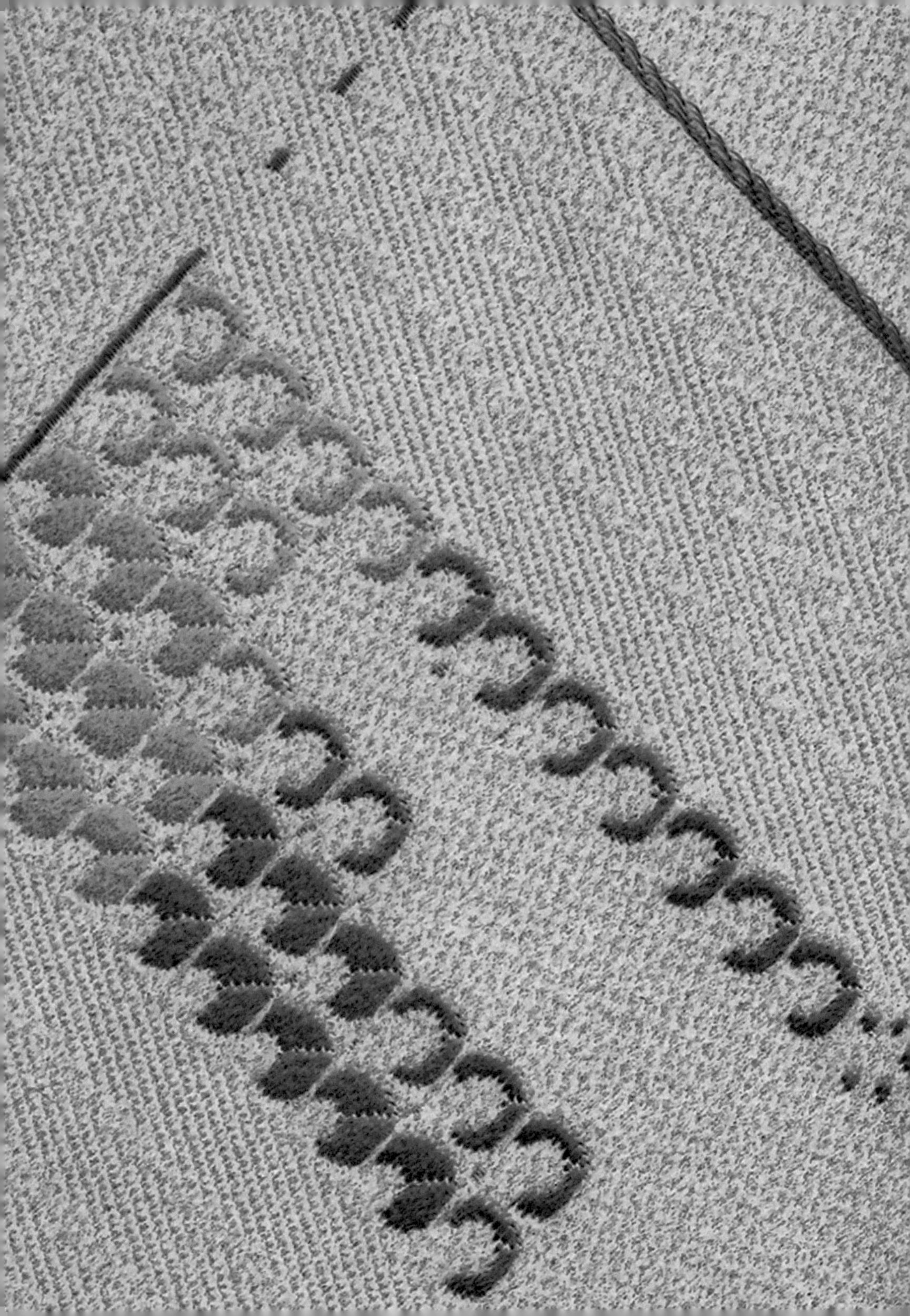

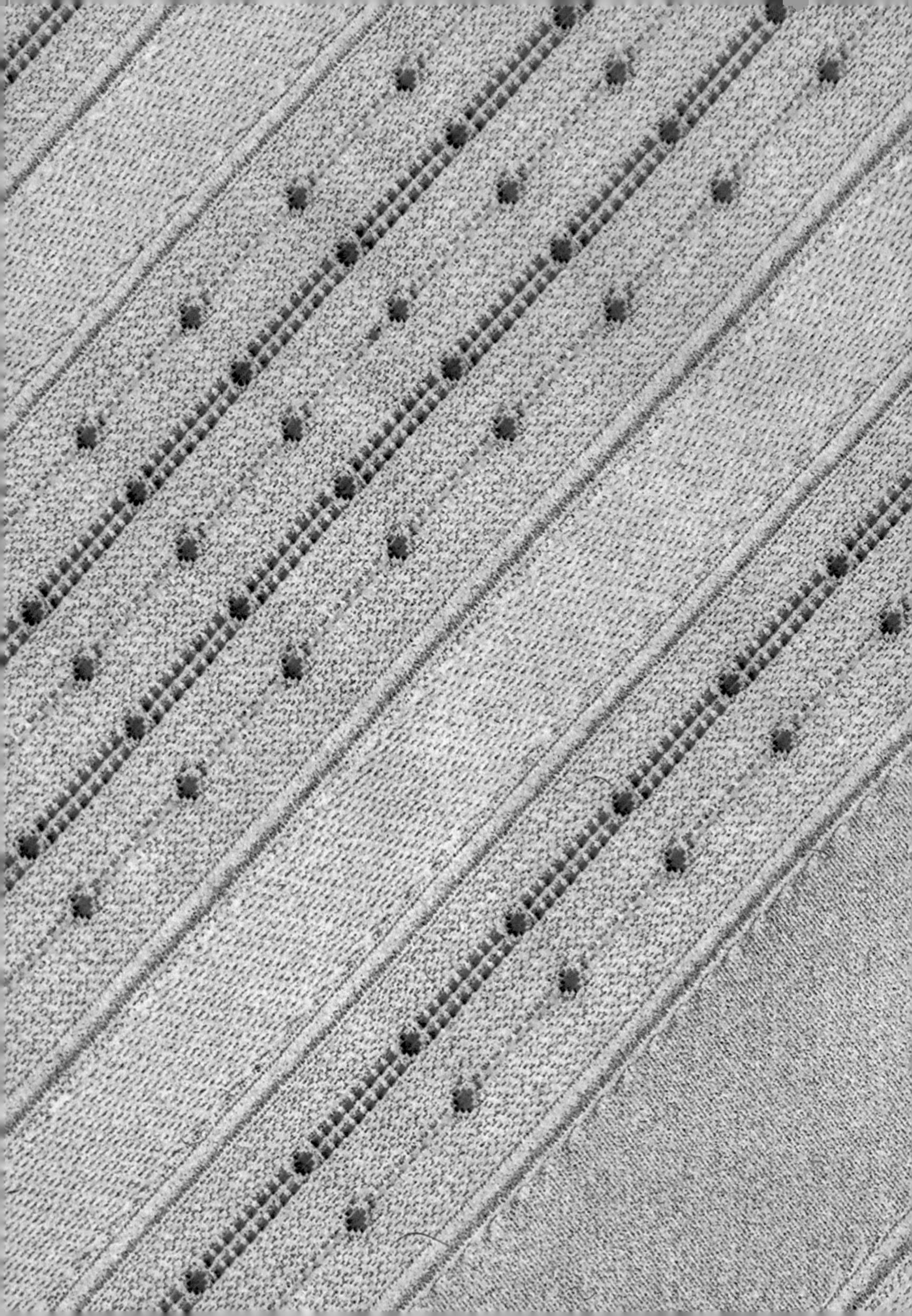

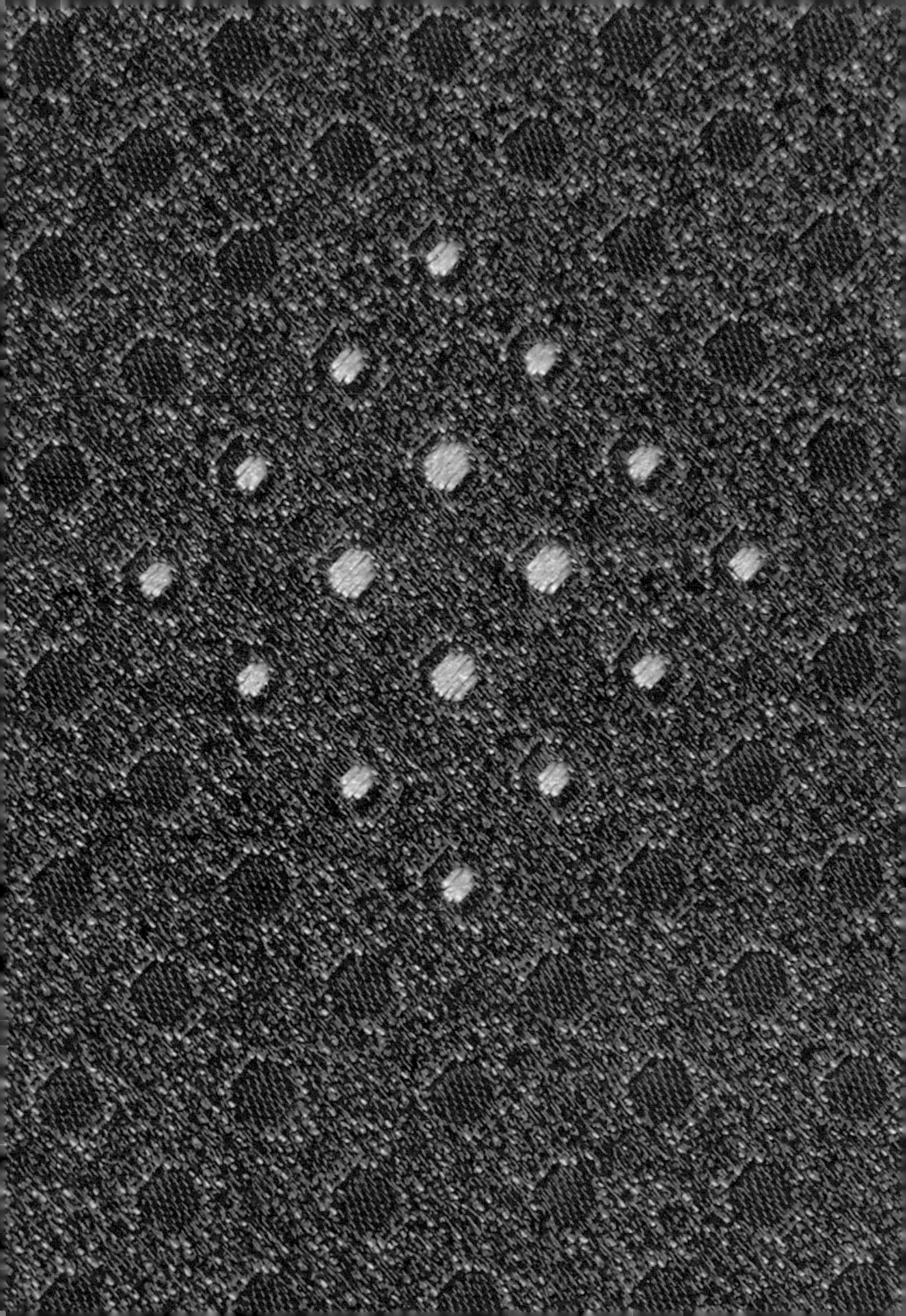

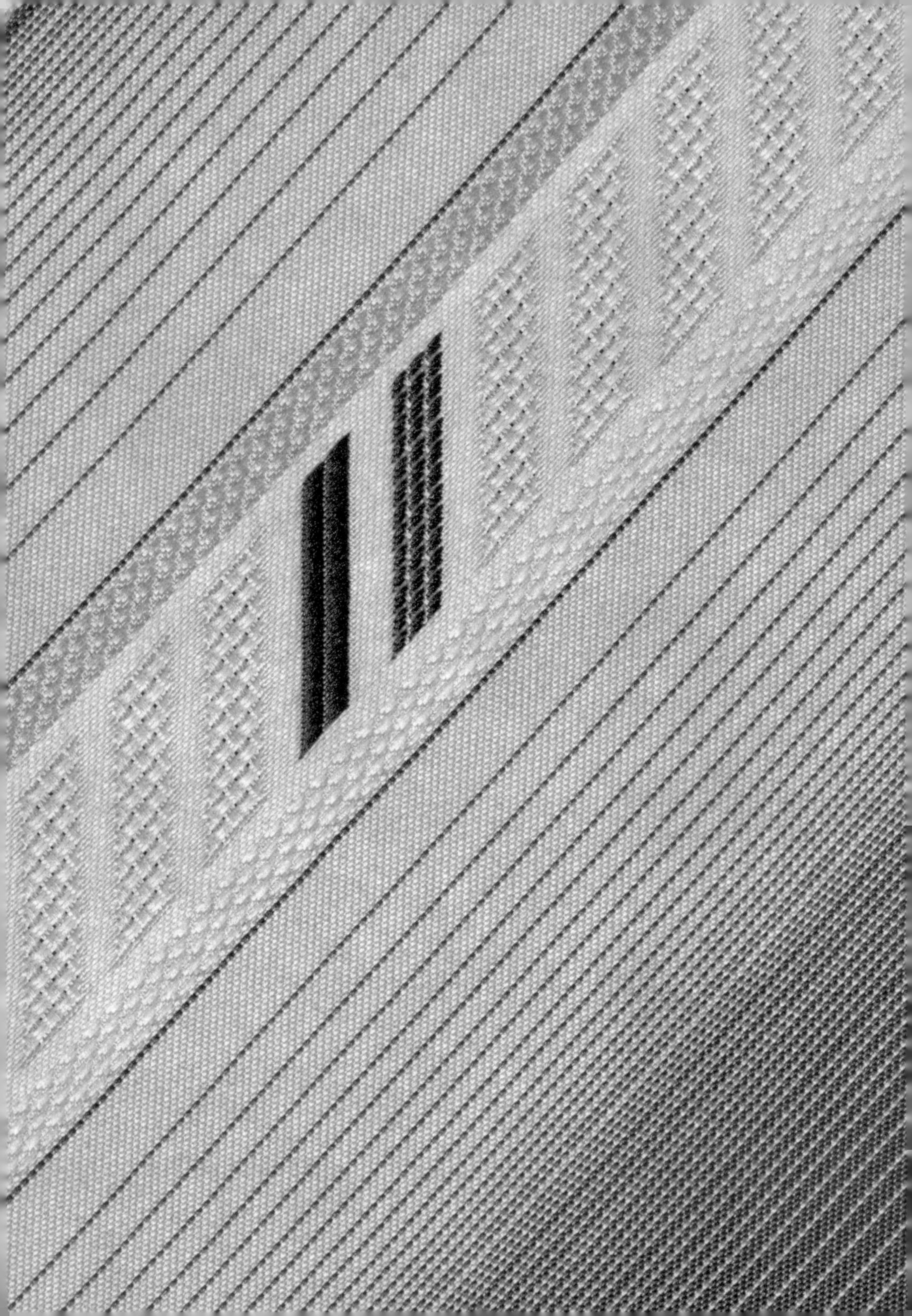

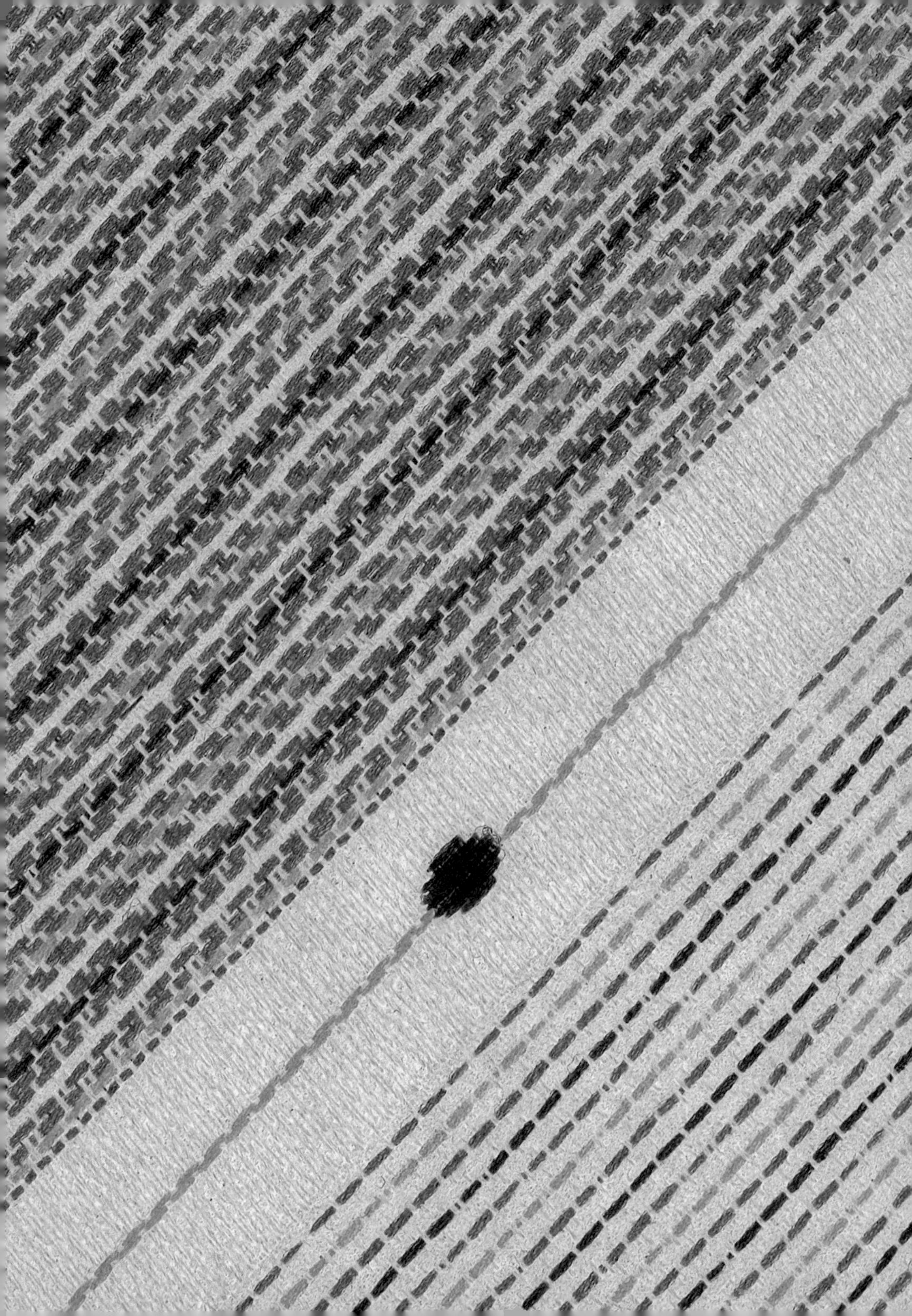

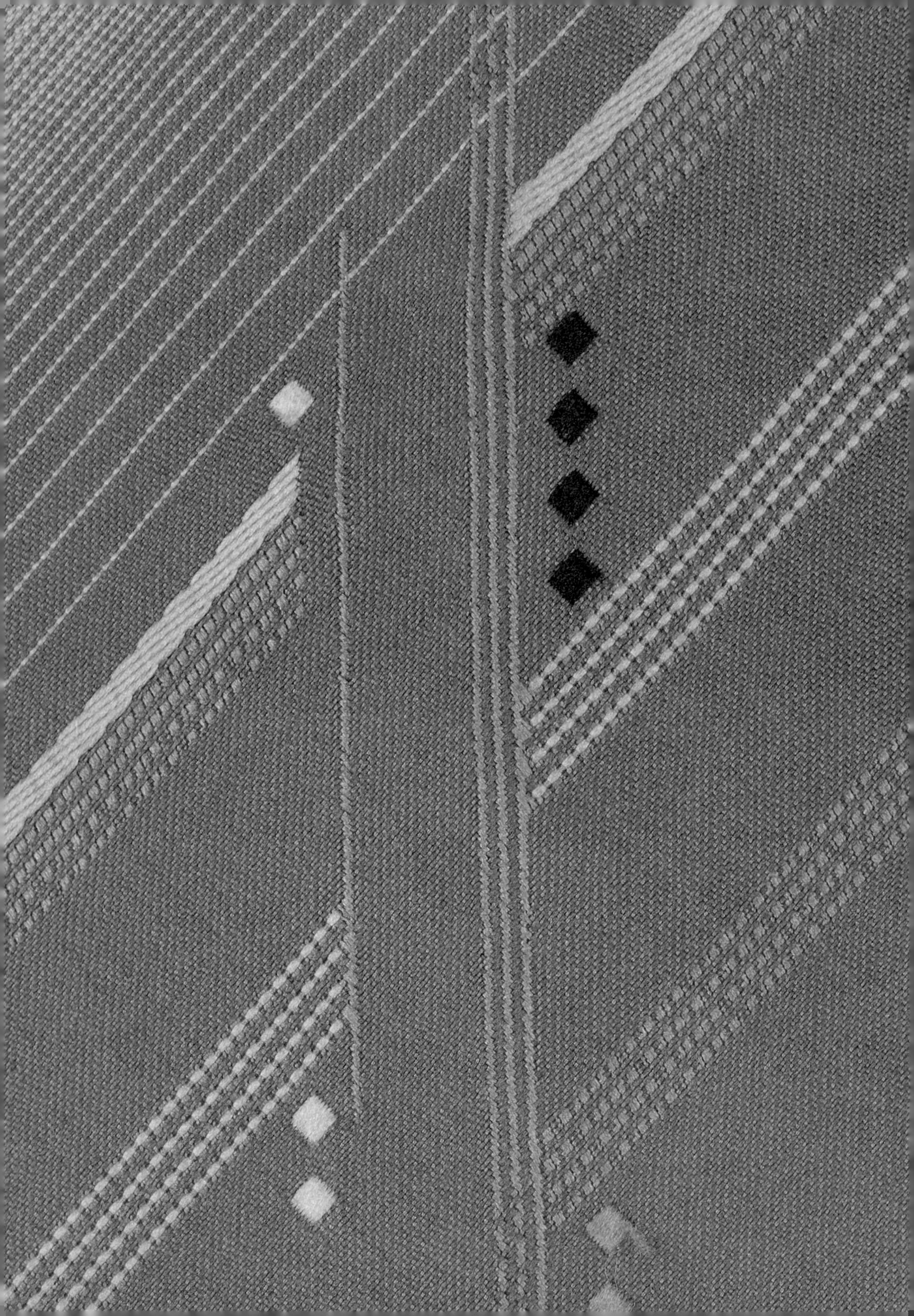

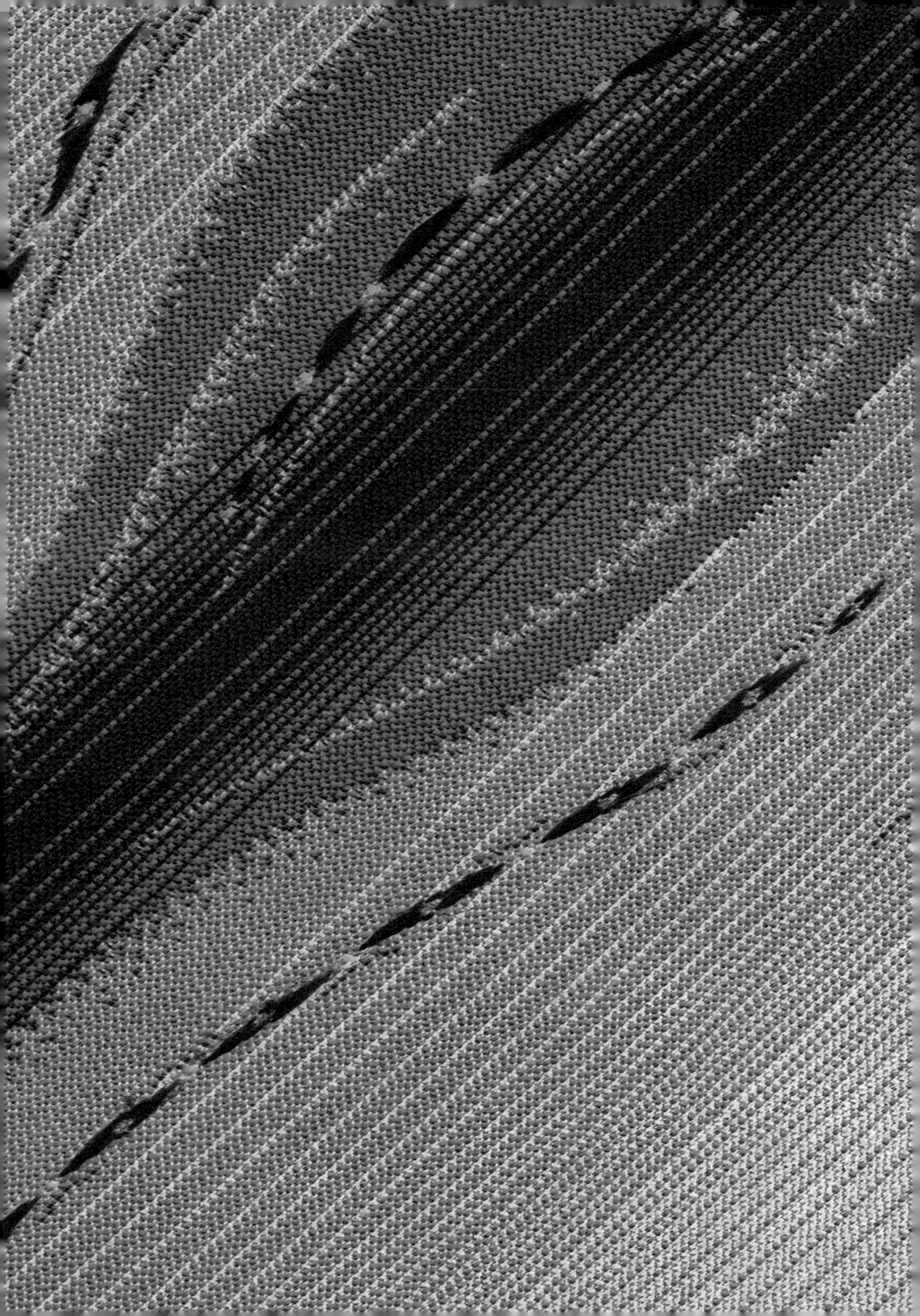

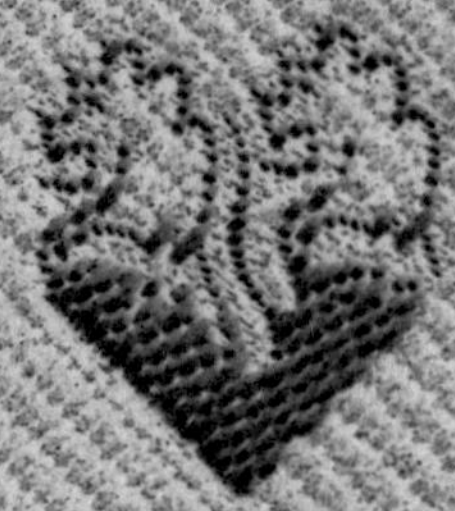

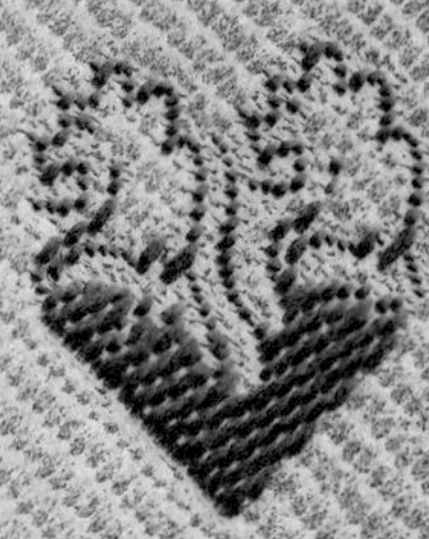

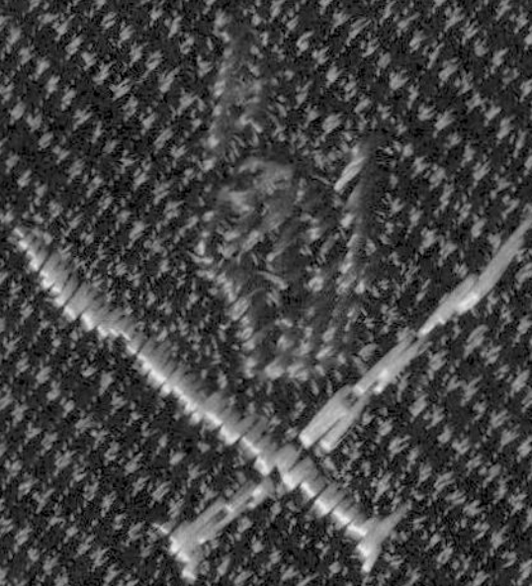
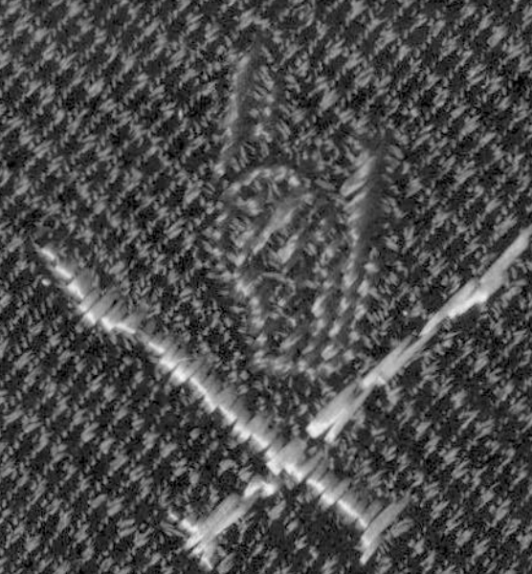
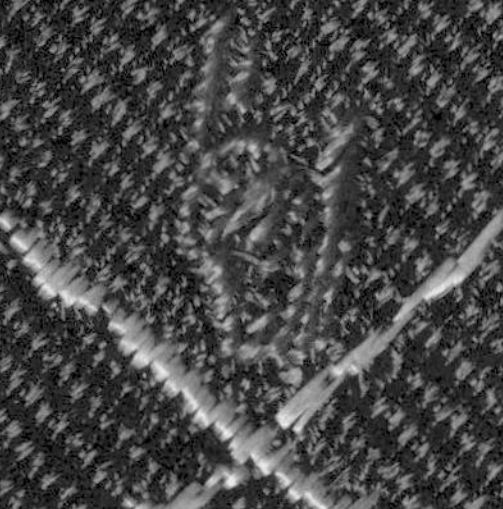

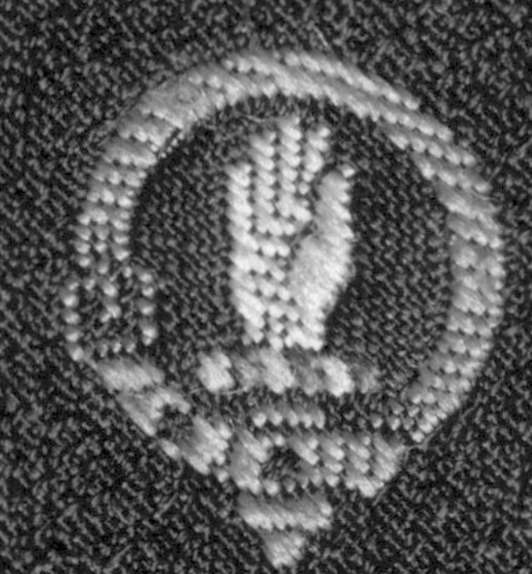
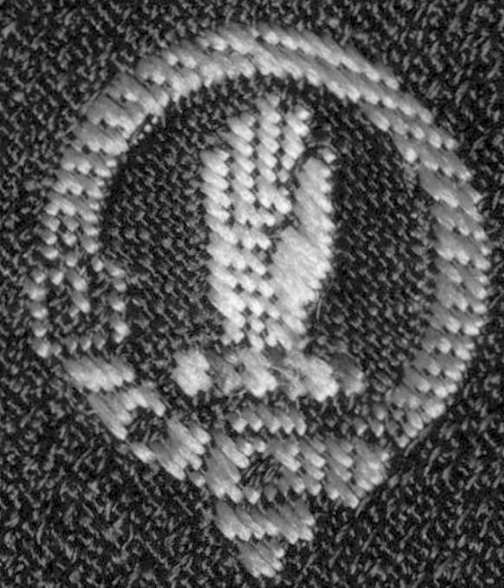
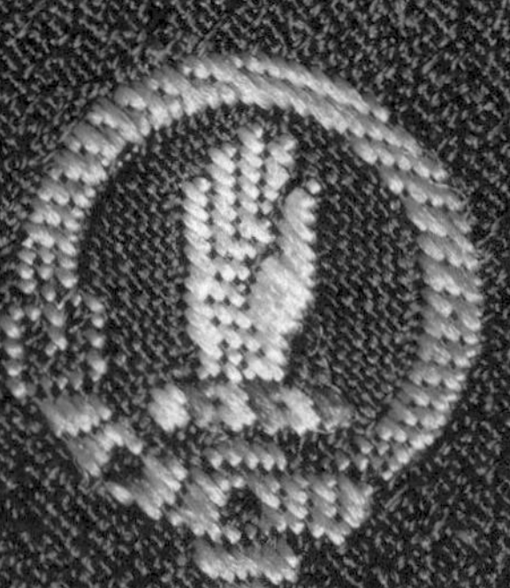

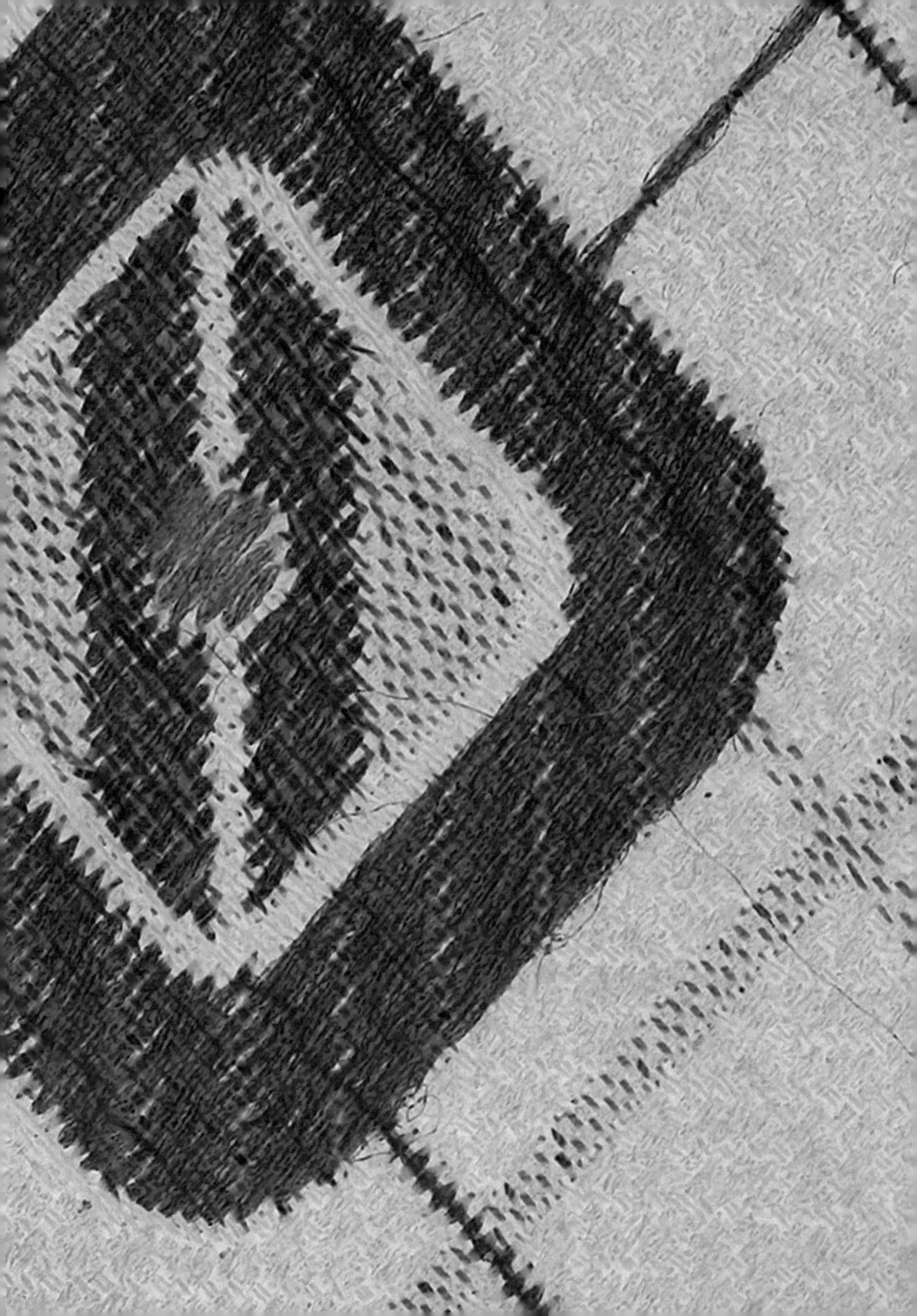

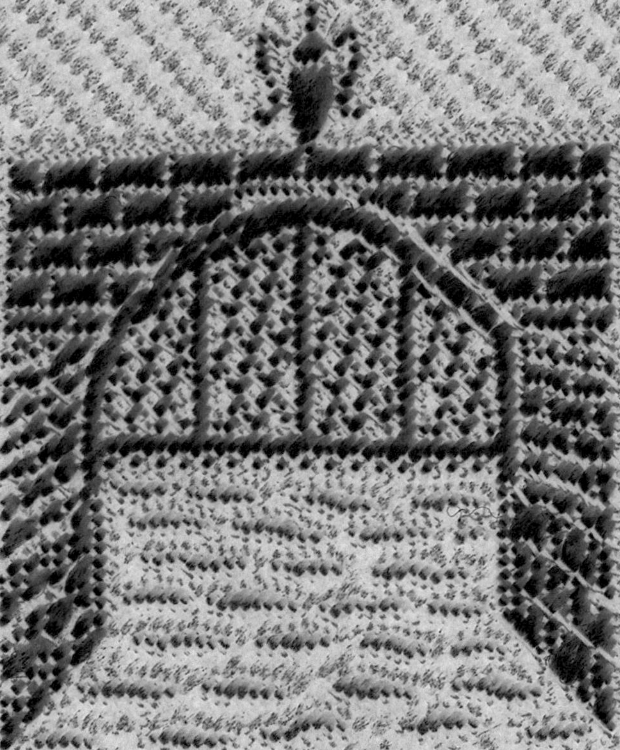

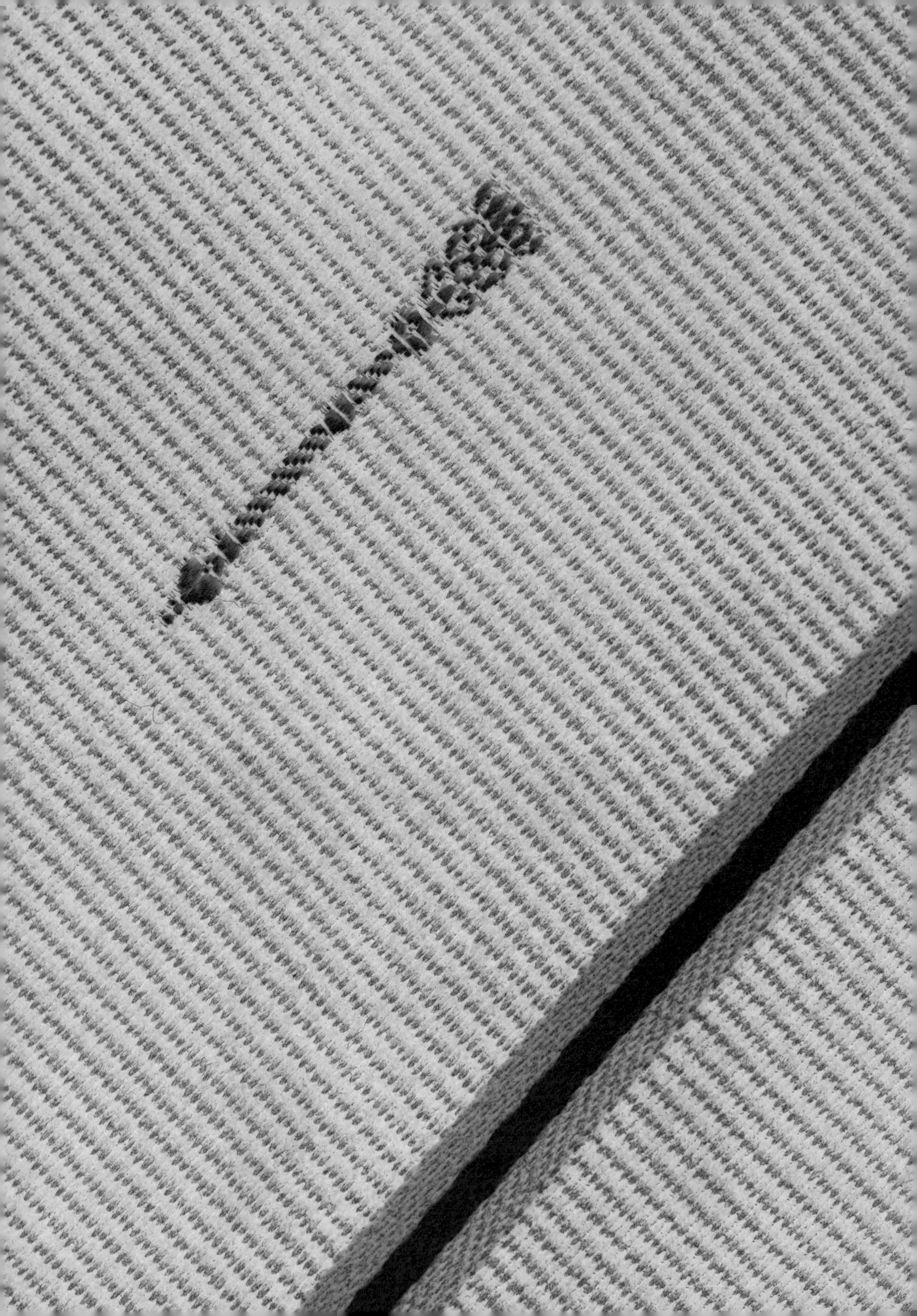

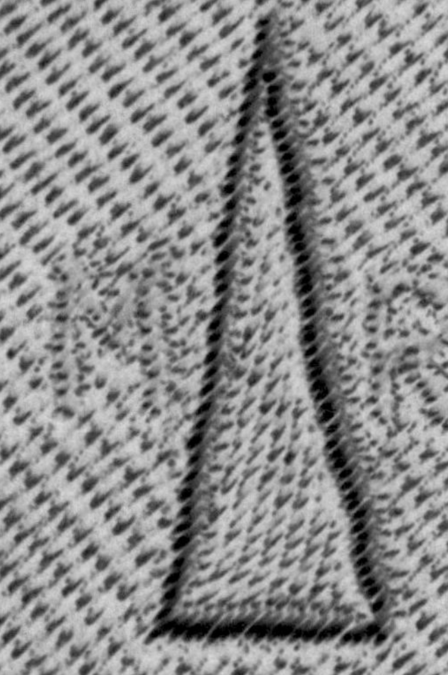
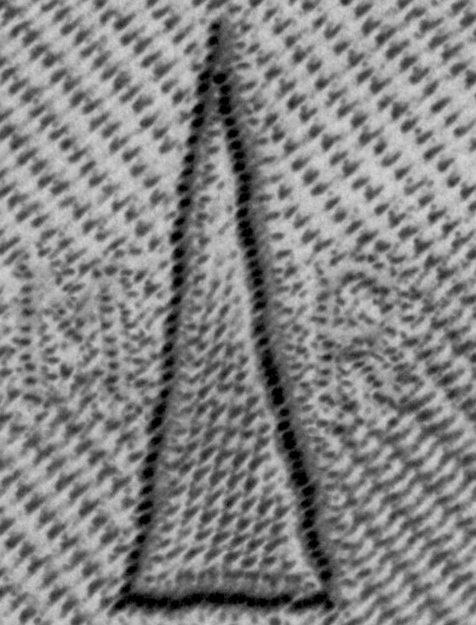

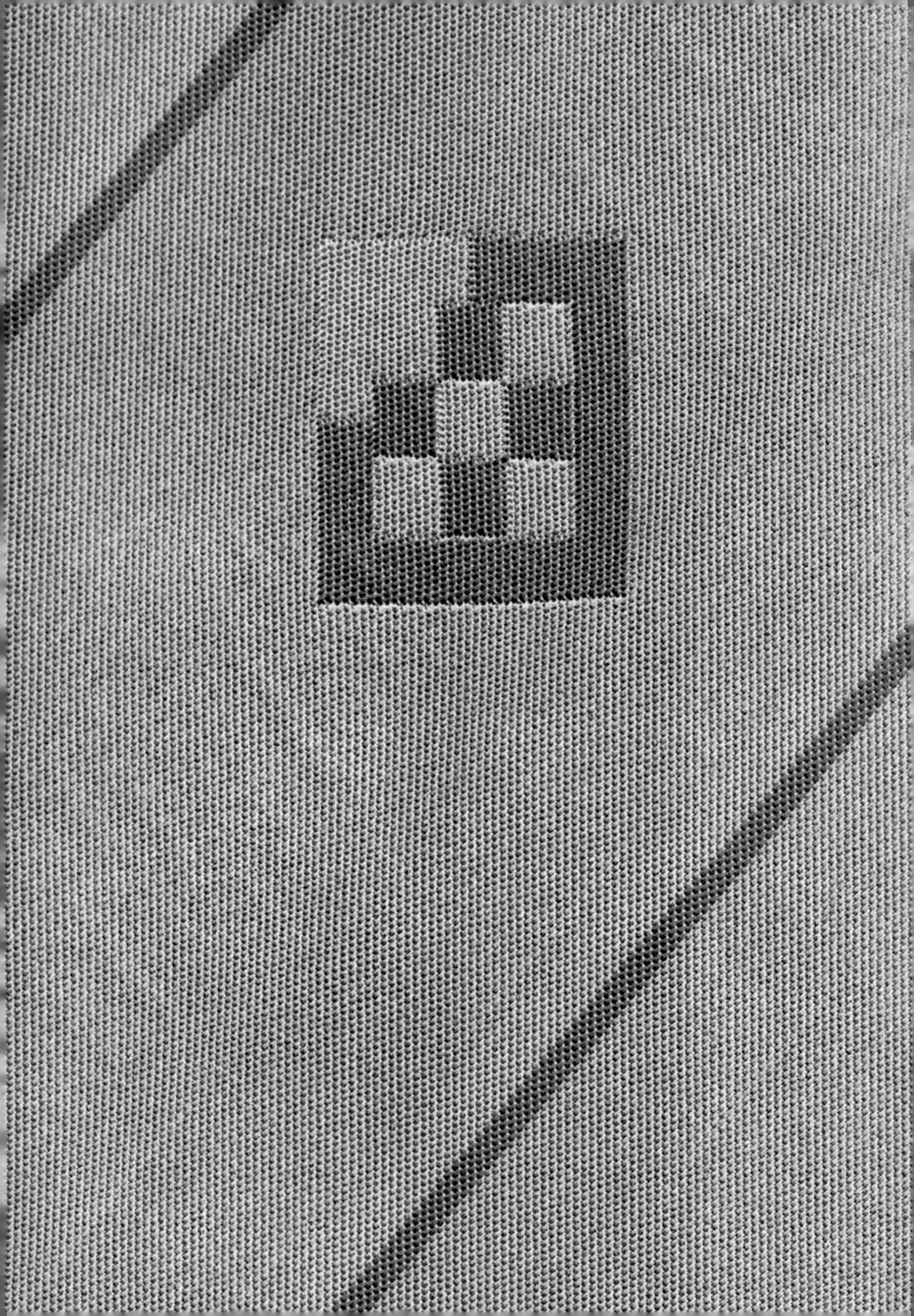

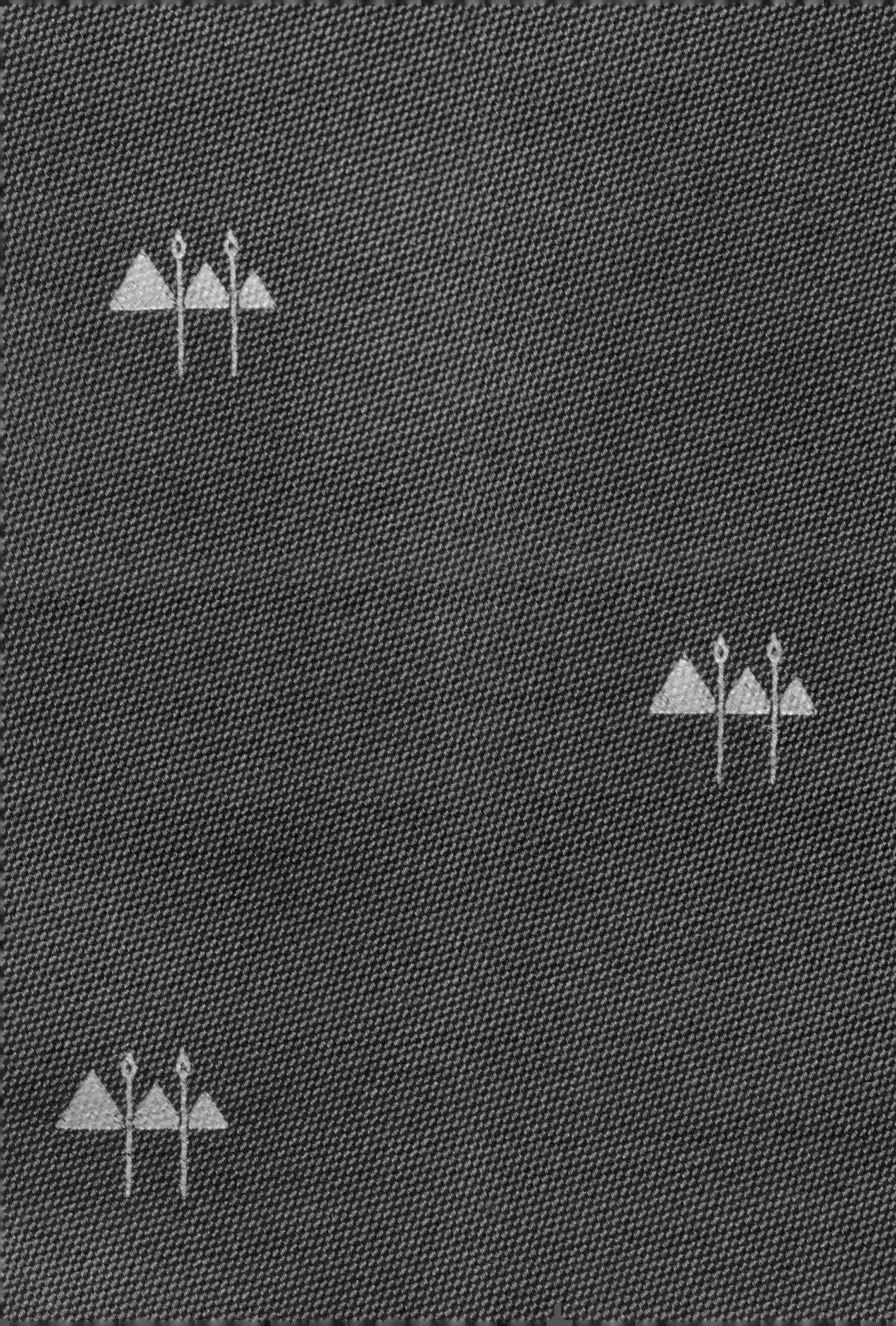

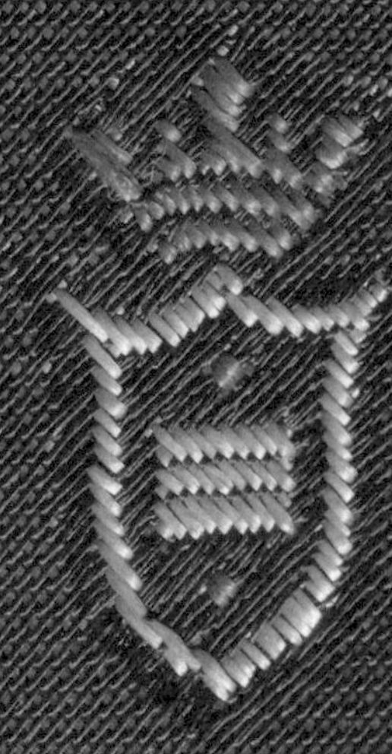

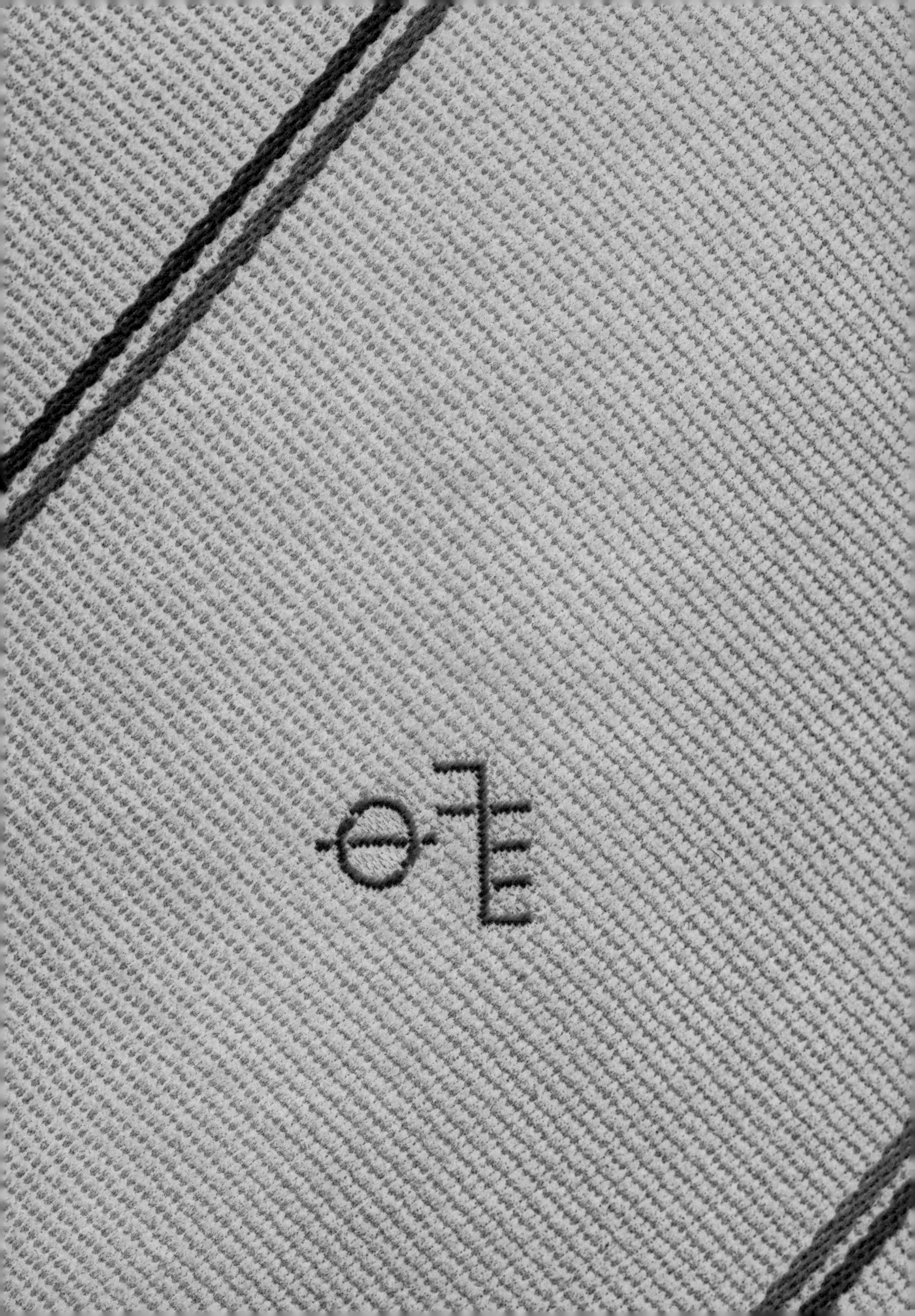

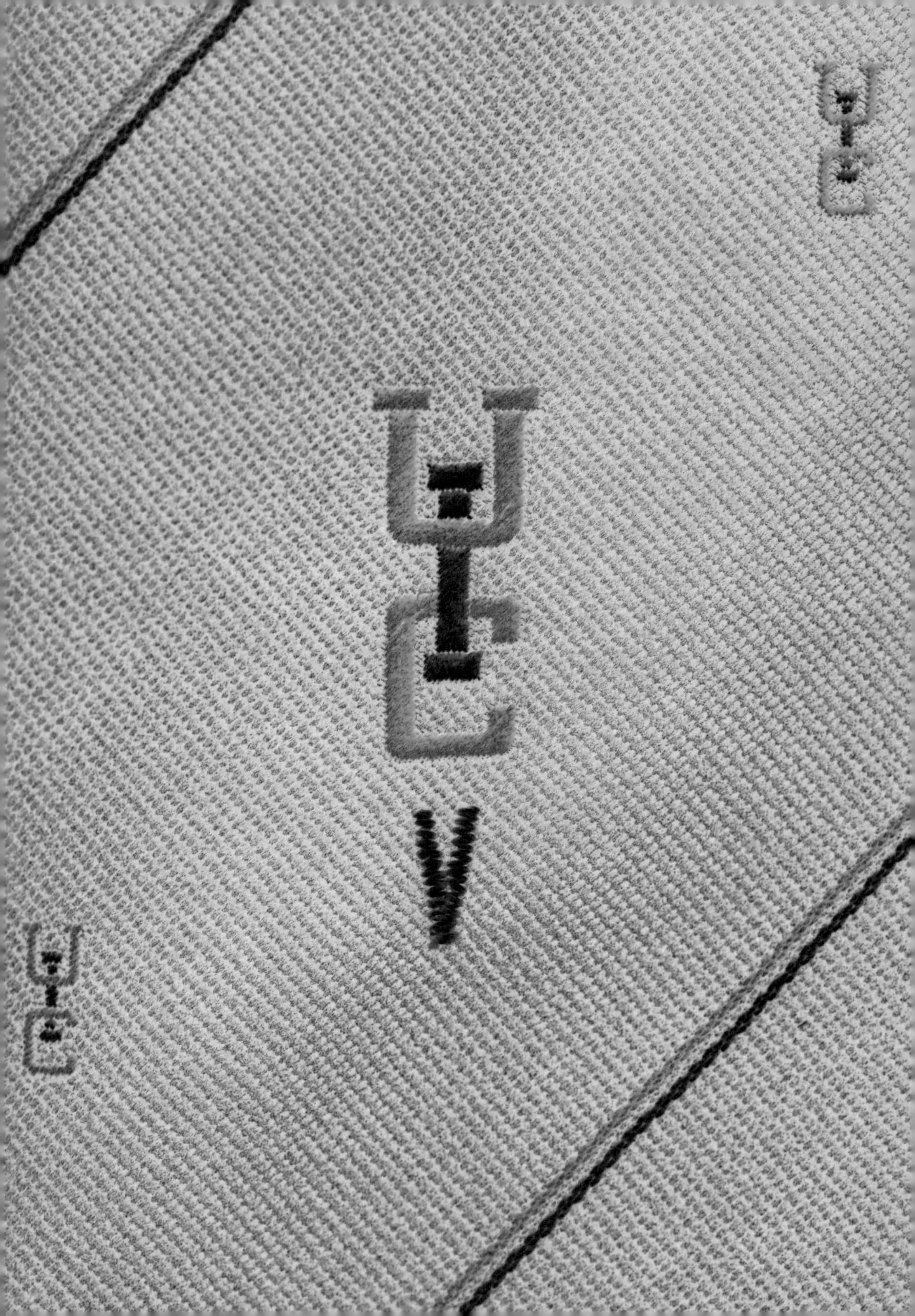

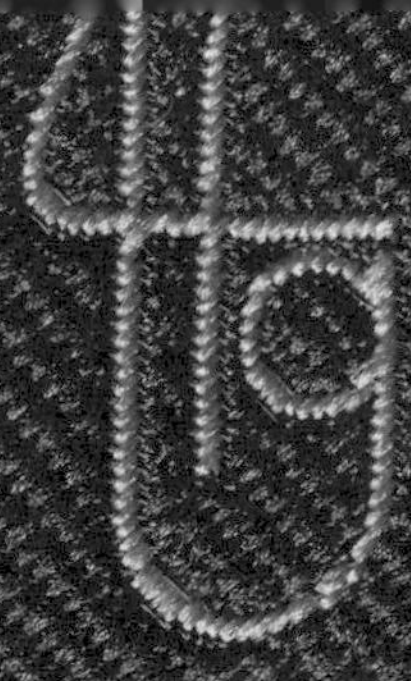
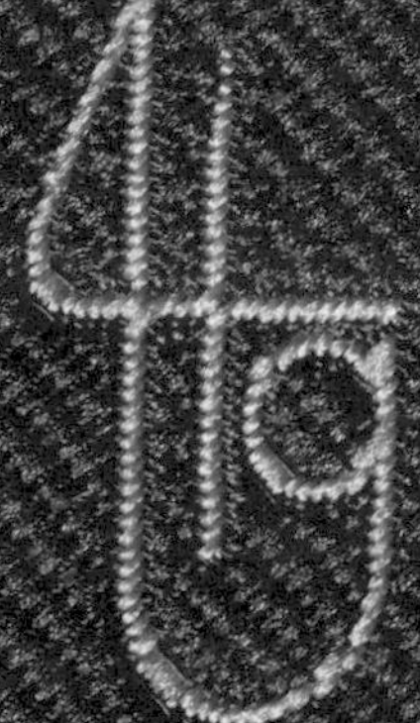

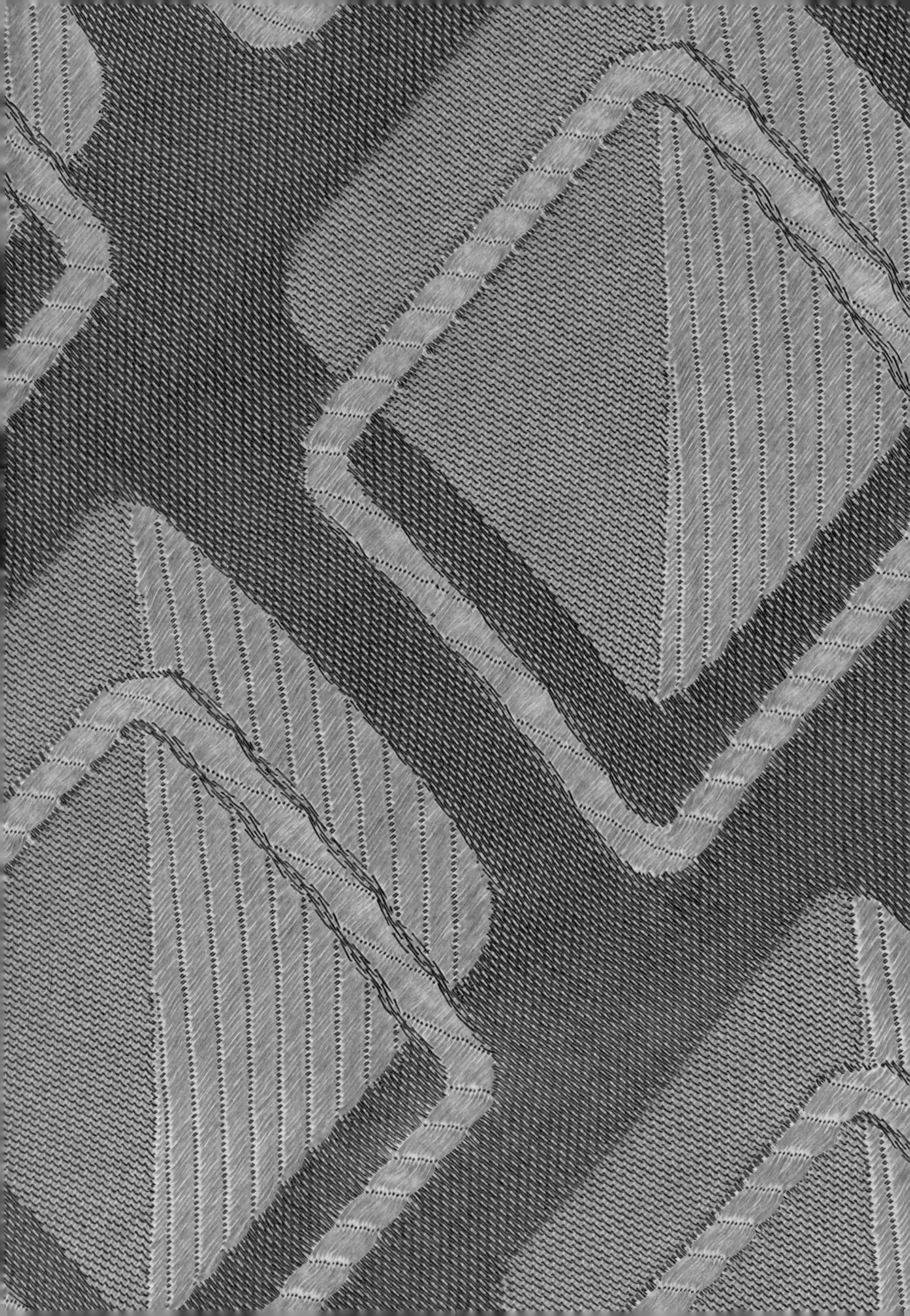

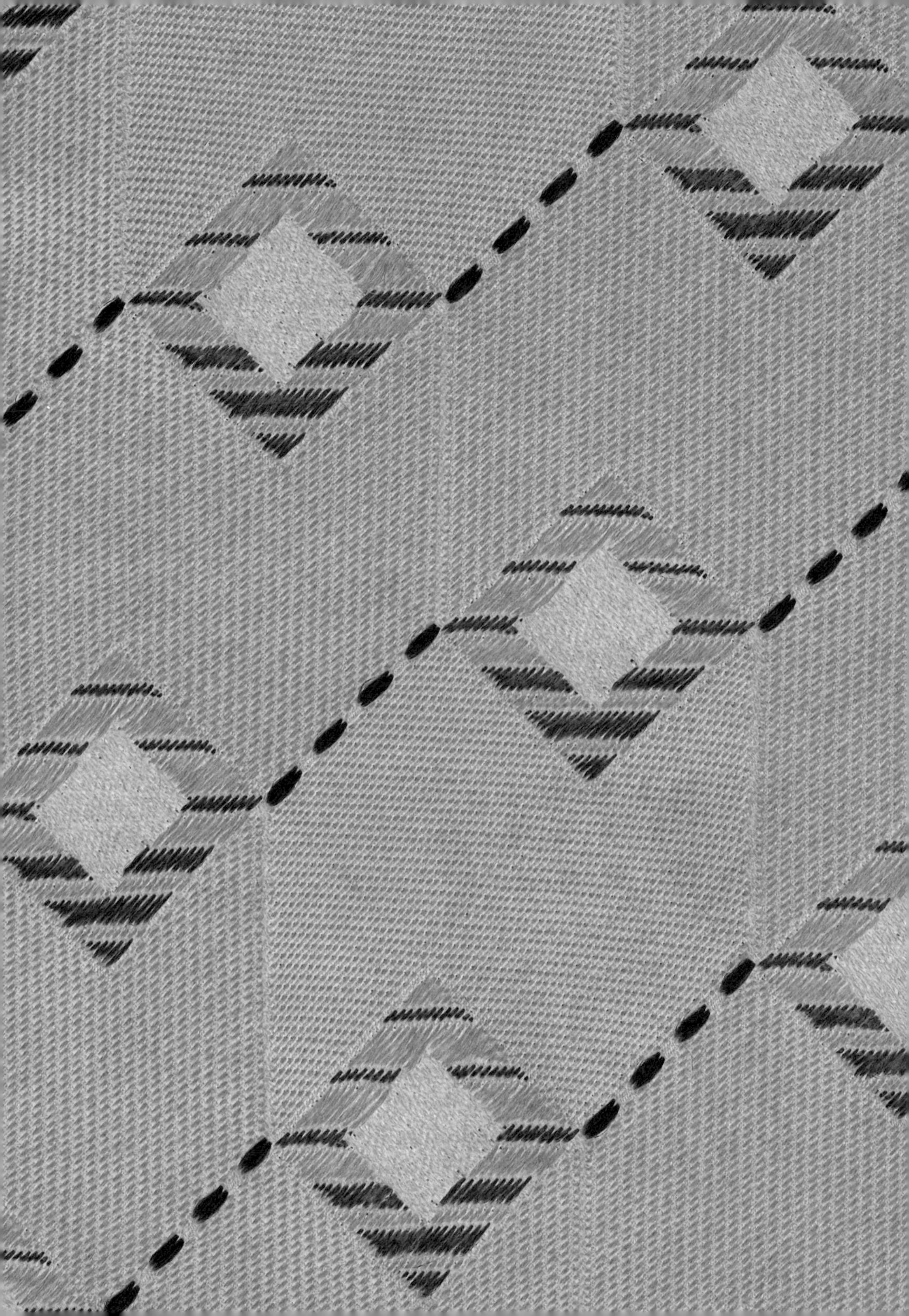

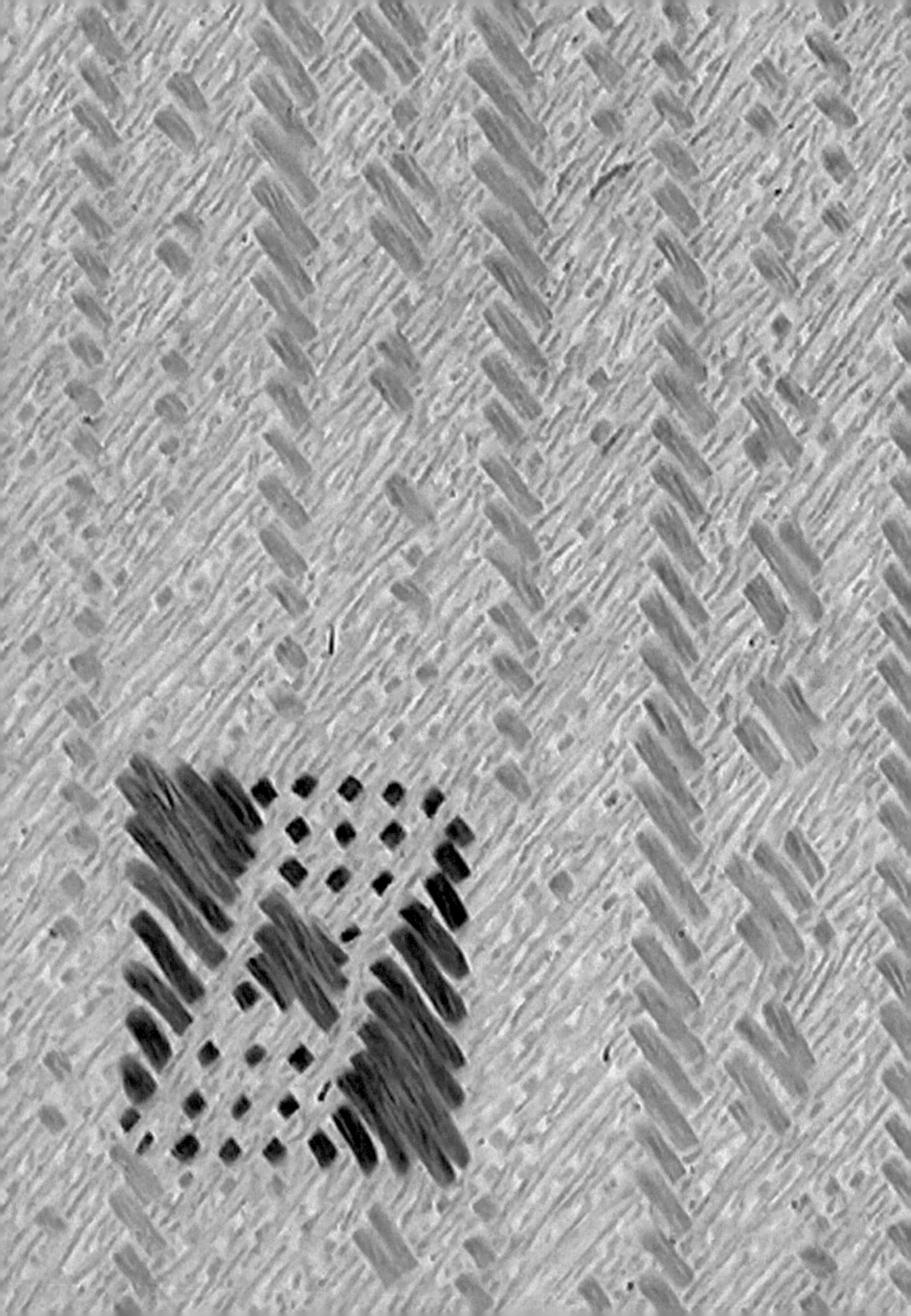

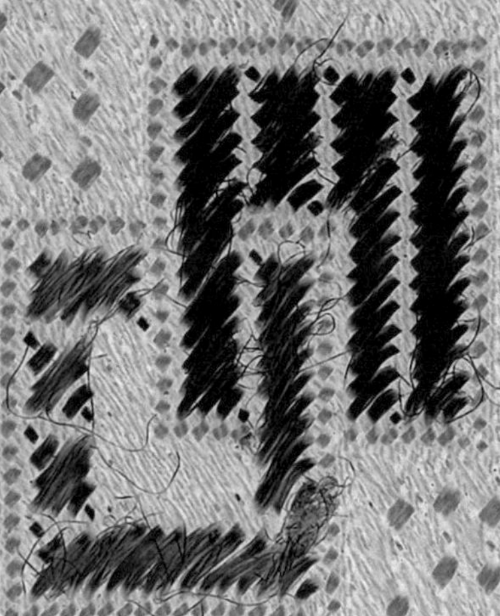

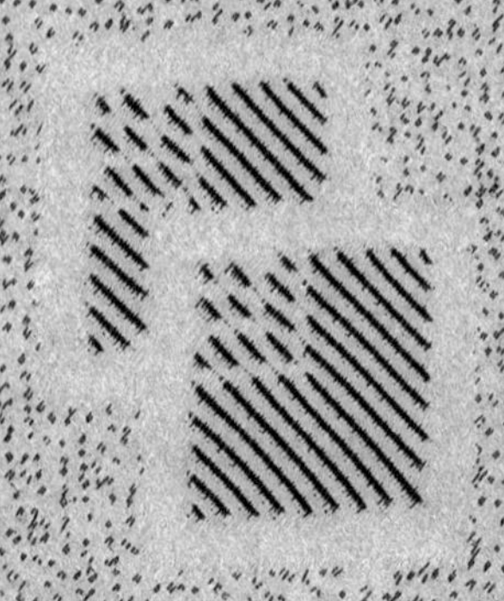
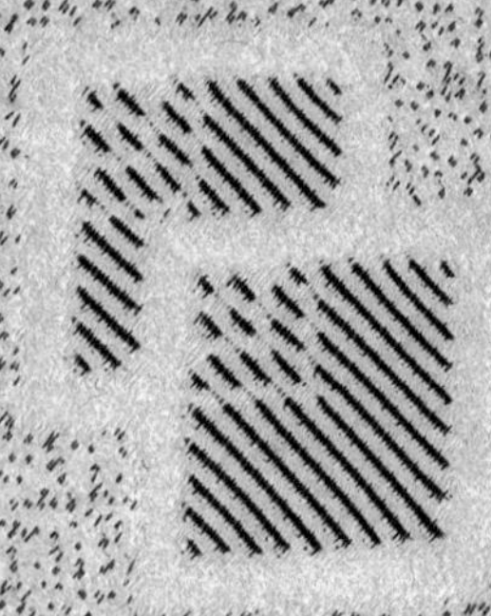
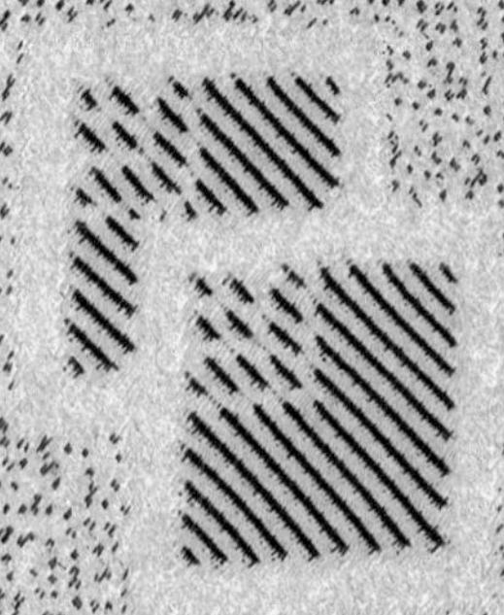

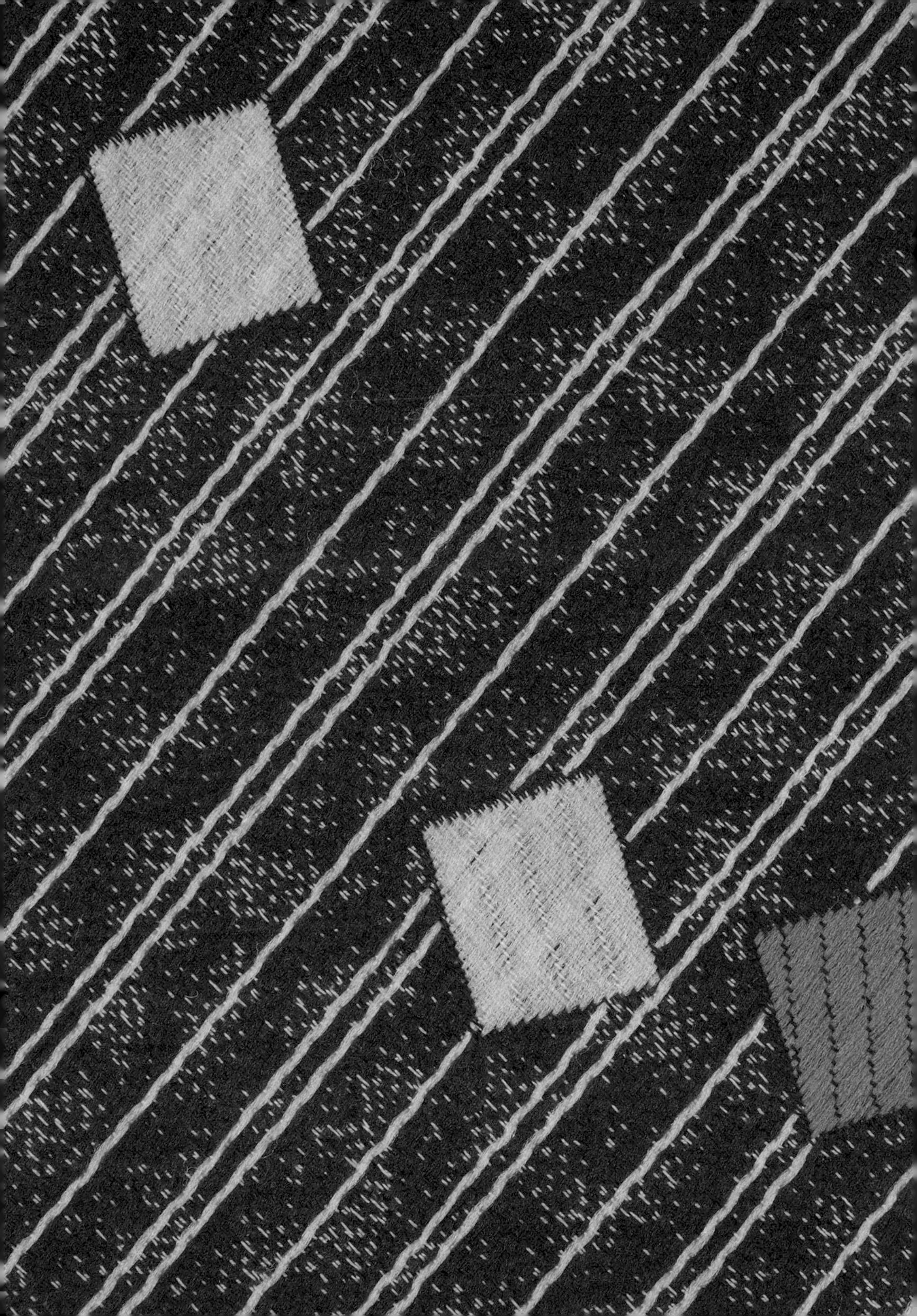

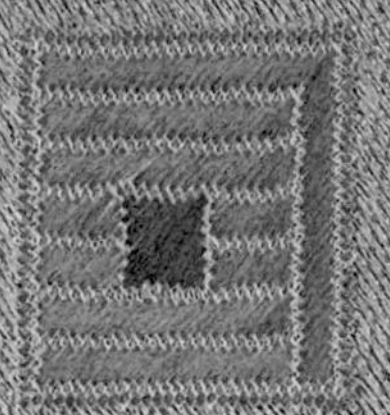
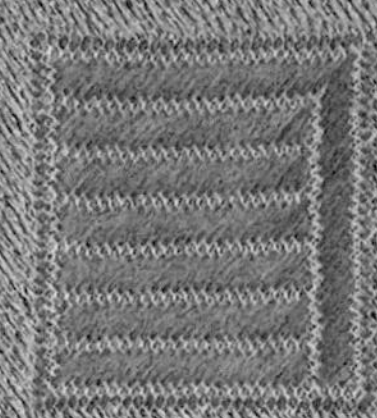
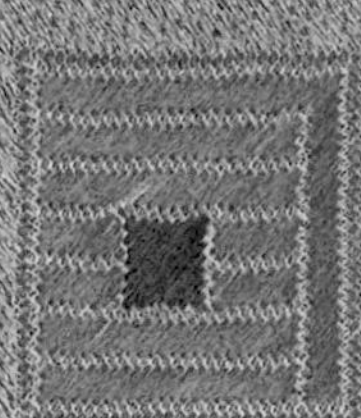
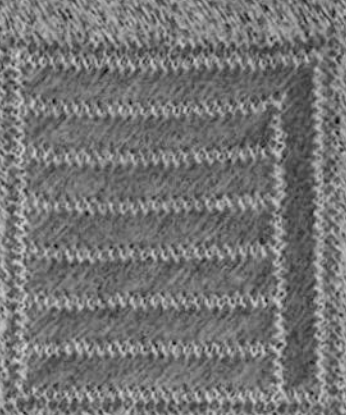
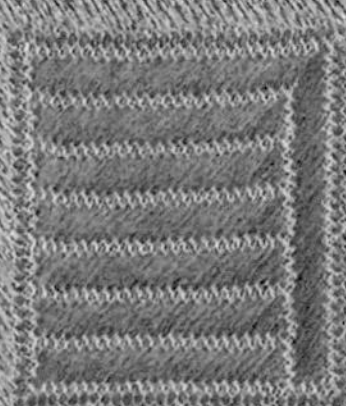
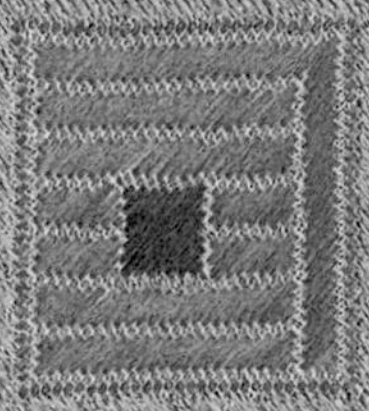
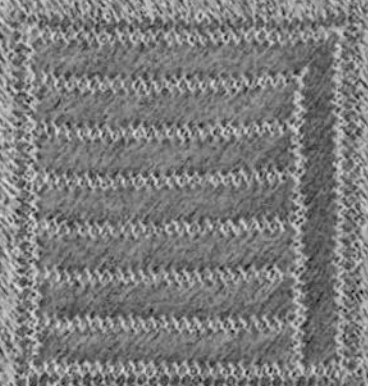
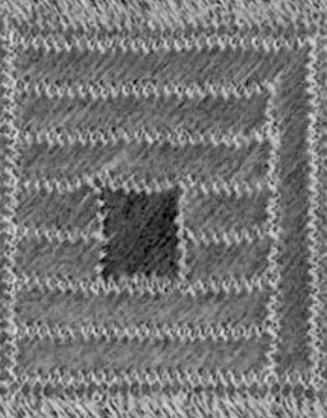
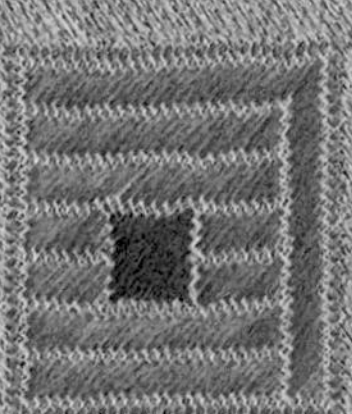
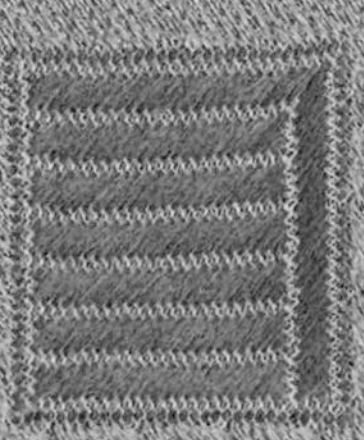
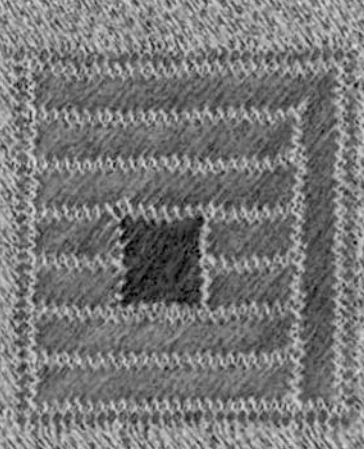
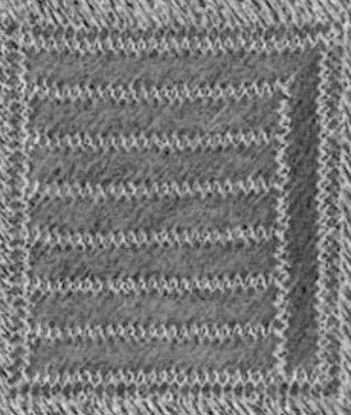
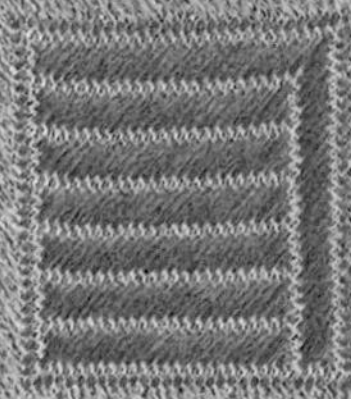
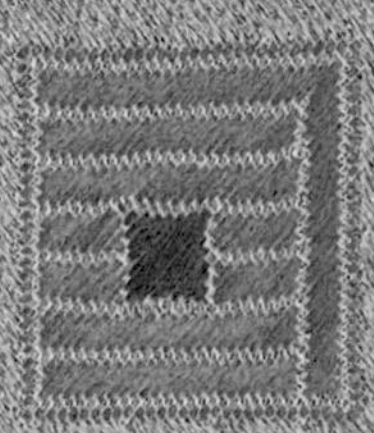
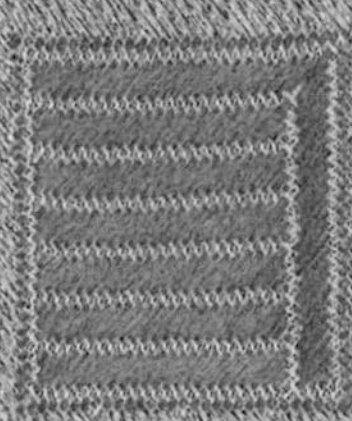
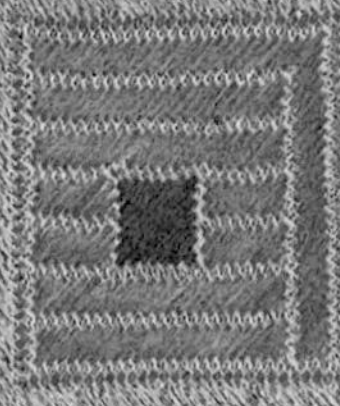
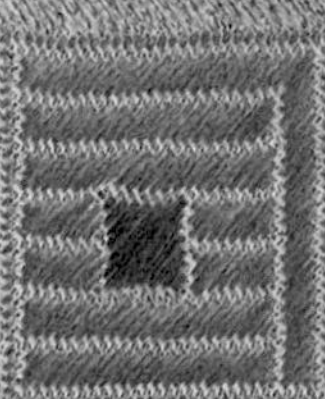
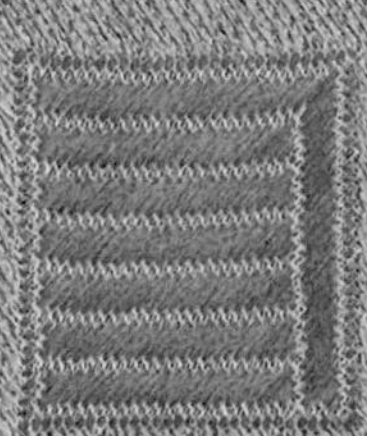
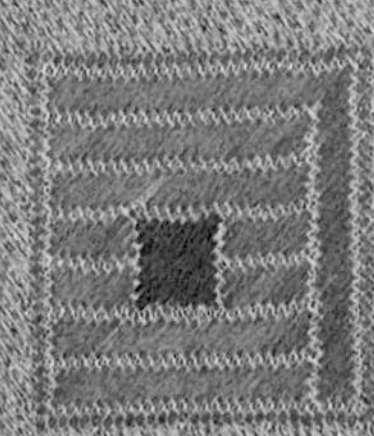
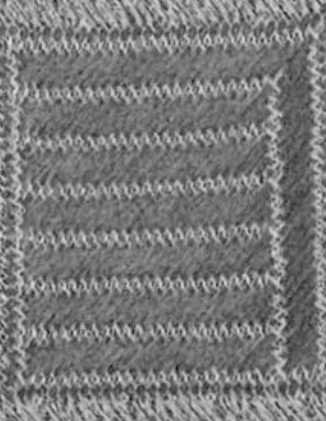

NIGHT

THE

NIGHT

THE

OF

WORLD

<u>NIGHT OF THE WORLD (2023)</u>

In December 2002, a ship called the *Tricolor* sank amid
dense fog along with its cargo of 2897 luxury cars.
It went down in an area of the Channel between the
British Isles and mainland Europe called West Hinder.
The video takes us to this location, into the dark
hold of the wrecked vessel, to witness the spectral
image of its luxury cargo drifting in the murk.

The exact area in which the *Tricolor* sank is a
small area of the sea unclaimed and not legislated by
any state. Within the video, it operates as an "other"
place with different laws, much like how outer space
functions within science fiction. This provides the
premise for a fantasy narrative in which the luxury
cars exert a kind of consciousness. The morphology
of their "intelligent vehicle control-systems" (which
digitally perform navigation, entertainment, climate,
and safety functions) is corrupted by immersion in
the polluted, underwater environment. They develop
memory and desire, as well as the language to communi-
cate these things, derived entirely from their specific
user manual and product press releases. Most particularly, they acquire a powerful collective will, and the
ability to exert their force in concert.

It is the combined force of the cars' "intelligent
control systems" that constitutes the video's protago-
nist. It narrates, addressing the viewer via onscreen
motion graphics and a choir of synthetic voices;
it provides mapping graphics to narrate the location
of the wreck, and it selects the musical soundtrack
for the action. In the latter stages of the video,
the narration shifts into a more lyric form. The cars

NIGHT OF THE WORLD (2023)

Im Dezember 2002 sank in dichtem Nebel ein Schiff
namens Tricolor mit einer Ladung von 2897 Luxusautos.
Es ging in einem Gebiet des Ärmelkanals zwischen
den Britischen Inseln und dem europäischen Festland
unter, das West Hinder genannt wird. Das Video nimmt
uns mit an diesen Ort, in den dunklen Laderaum des
Schiffswracks, um das gespenstische Bild der in der
Dunkelheit treibenden Luxusfracht zu sehen.

    Das genaue Gebiet, in dem die Tricolor gesunken ist,
ist ein kleiner Meeresbereich, der von keinem Staat
beansprucht oder verwaltet wird. In dem Video wirkt
es wie ein »anderer« Ort mit anderen Gesetzen, ähnlich
wie der Weltraum in Science-Fiction verwendet wird.
Dies bildet die Grundlage für eine Fantasieerzählung,
in der die Luxusautos eine Art Bewusstsein erlangen.
Die Morphologie ihrer »intelligenten Fahrzeugsteuerungs-
systeme« (die Navigations-, Unterhaltungs-, Klima- und
Sicherheitsfunktionen digital bereitstellen) wird durch
das Eintauchen in die verschmutzte Unterwasserwelt
beschädigt. Sie entwickeln ein Gedächtnis, ein Verlangen
und eine Sprache, um diese Dinge zu artikulieren, die
ausschließlich aus dem ihnen eigenen Benutzerhandbuch
und aus Pressemitteilungen stammt. Vor allem aber entwickeln sie einen starken kollektiven Willen und die
Fähigkeit, ihre Kraft gemeinsam auszuüben.

    Es ist die geballte Kraft der »intelligenten Kontroll-
systeme« der Autos, die die Protagonistin des Videos
bildet. Sie liefert die Erzählung und wendet sich
mittels bewegter Grafiken auf dem Bildschirm und einem
Chor synthetischer Stimmen an die Betrachter:innen.
Sie stellt Kartenmaterial zur Verfügung, um die Lage

"play" a song from their hard drives and their
drifting inertia evolves into a lovely, synchronized
underwater dance. This begins in an apparently
joyful, almost optimistic spirit, but concludes with
a spectral threat.

(An earlier version of this work called *WEST HINDER*
was produced in 2012.)

des Wracks zu beschreiben, und wählt den musikalischen
Soundtrack für die Handlung aus. In der letzten Phase
des Videos geht die Erzählung in eine lyrische Form
über. Die Autos »spielen« einen Song von ihren Fest-
platten ab und ihre dahintreibende Trägheit verwandelt
sich in einen anmutigen, synchronisierten Unterwasser-
tanz. Dieser beginnt in einer scheinbar fröhlichen,
fast optimistischen Stimmung, endet aber mit einer
gespenstischen Bedrohung.

(Eine frühere Version dieses Werks mit dem Titel *WEST
HINDER* wurde 2012 produziert.)

Folgende Seiten / Following pages:
Auswahl an Einzelbildern einer Live-Action-Videoaufnahme.
Medienbestand von *NIGHT OF THE WORLD*. /
Selection of frames of live-action video recording.
Media asset of *NIGHT OF THE WORLD*.

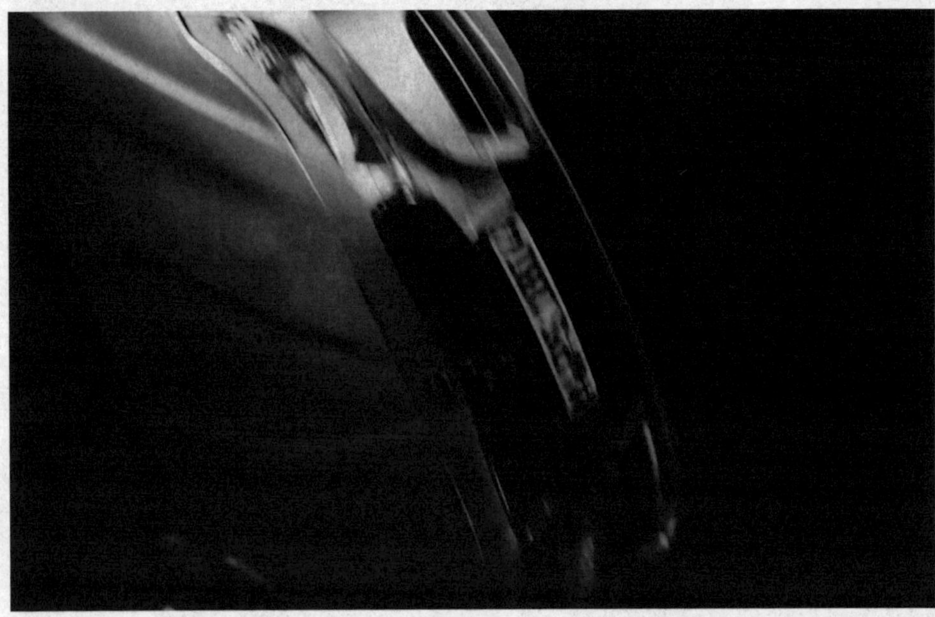

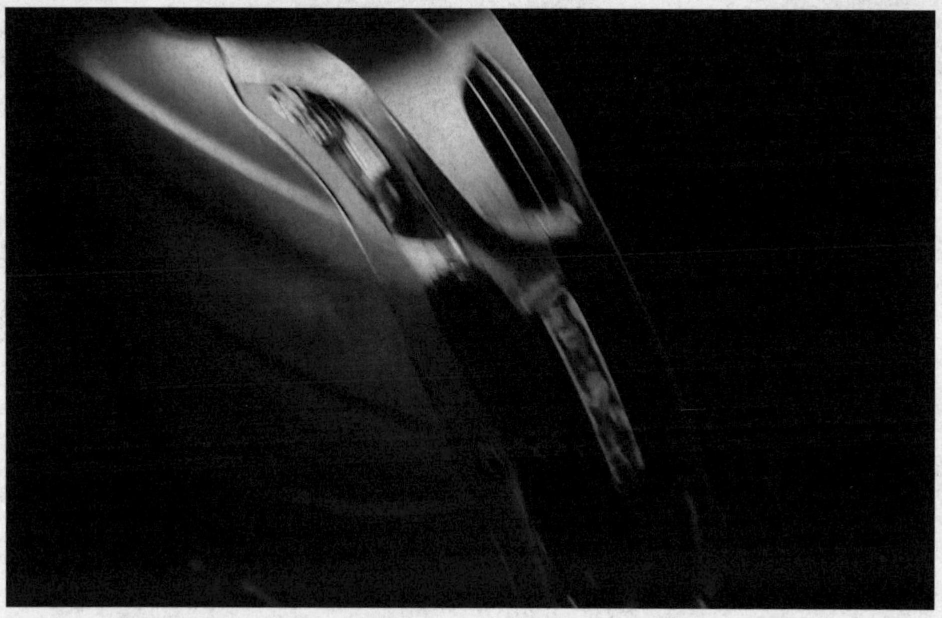

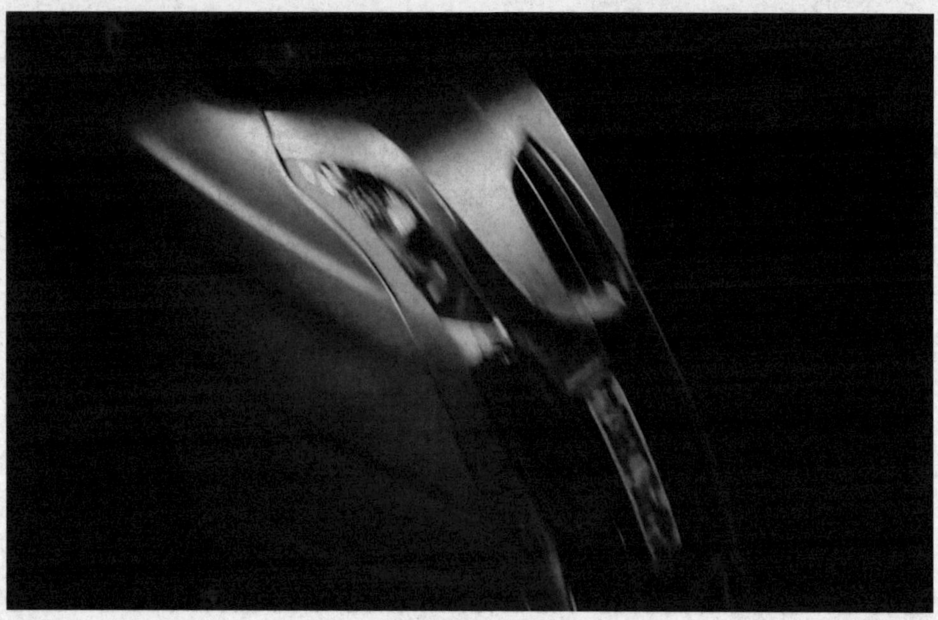

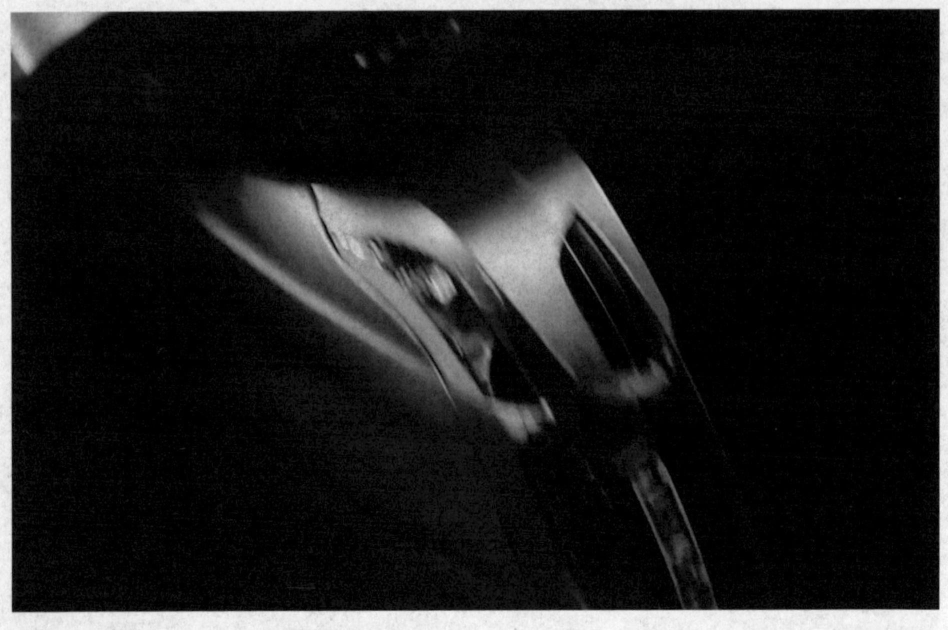

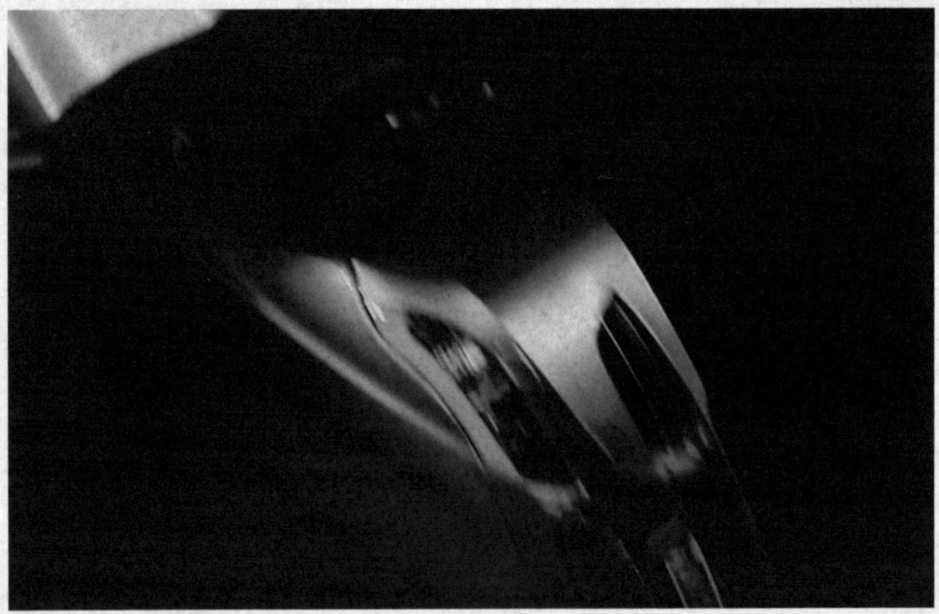

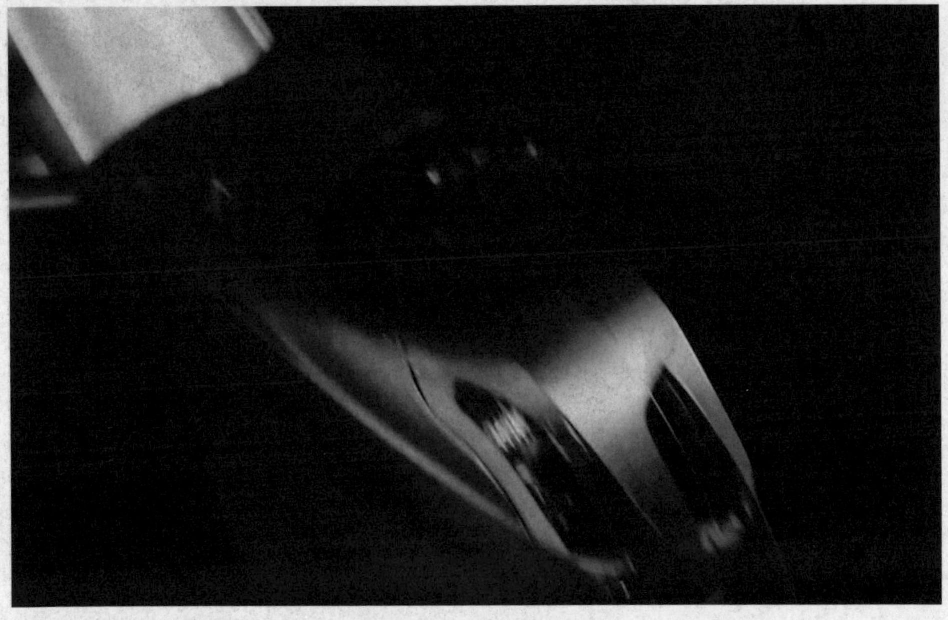

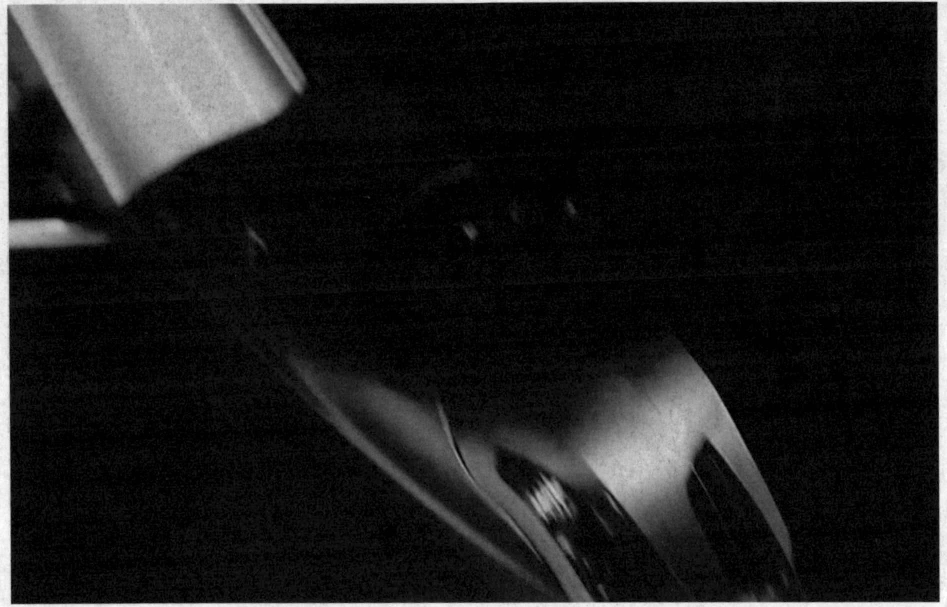

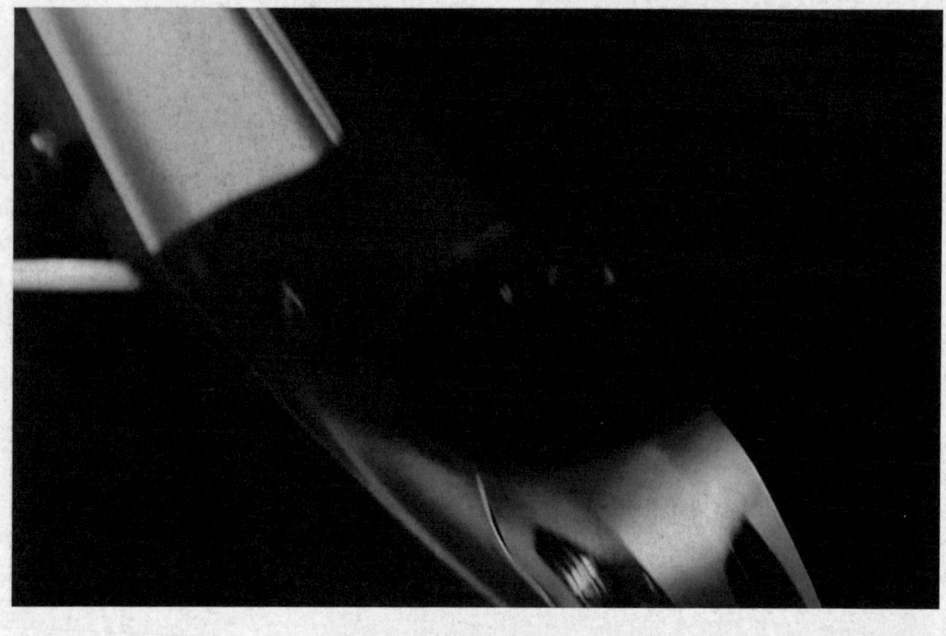

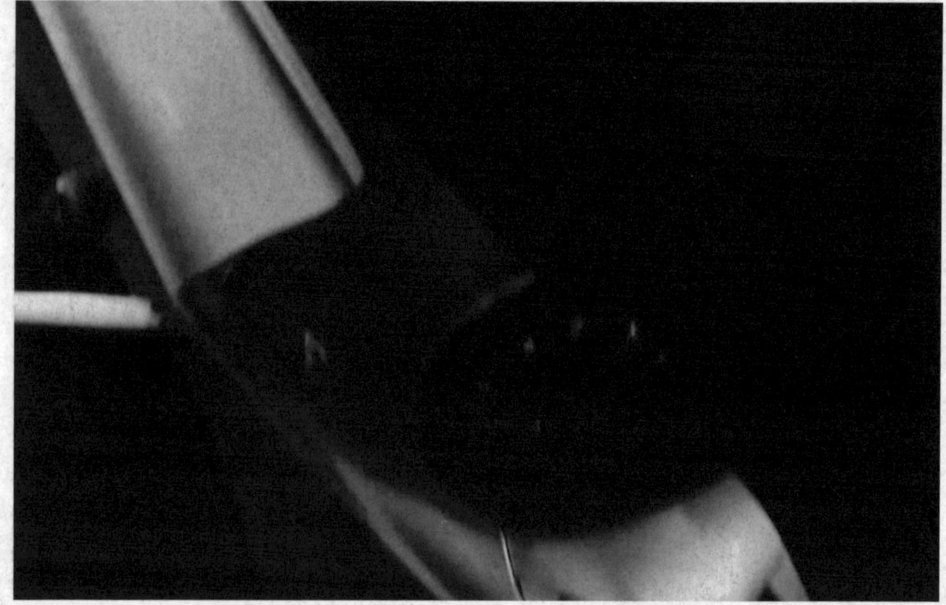

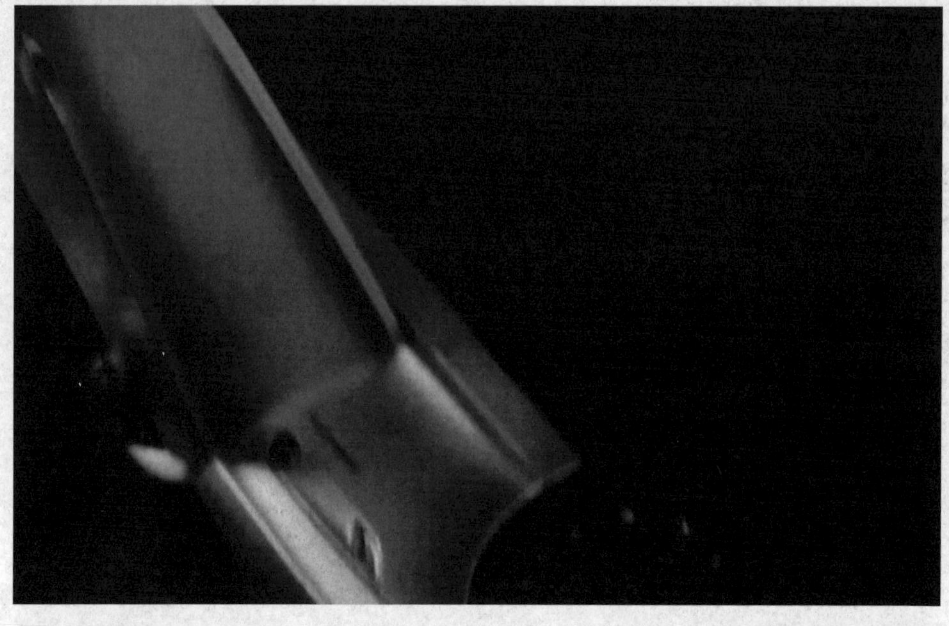

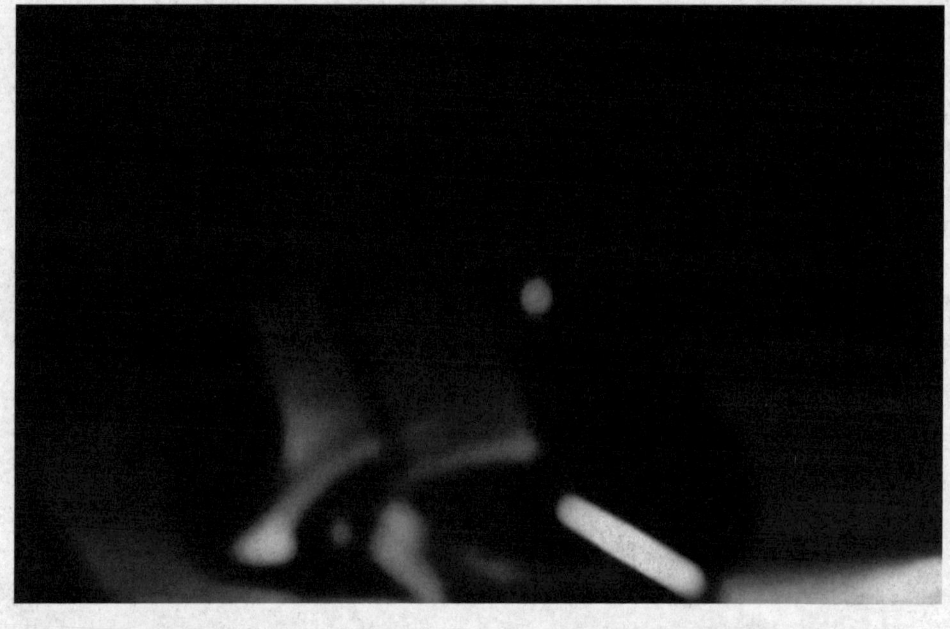

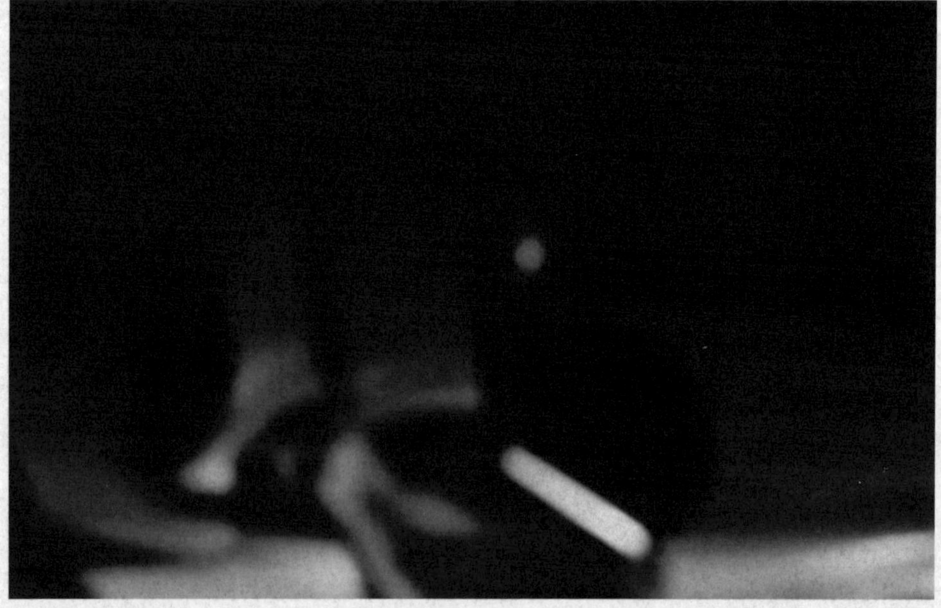

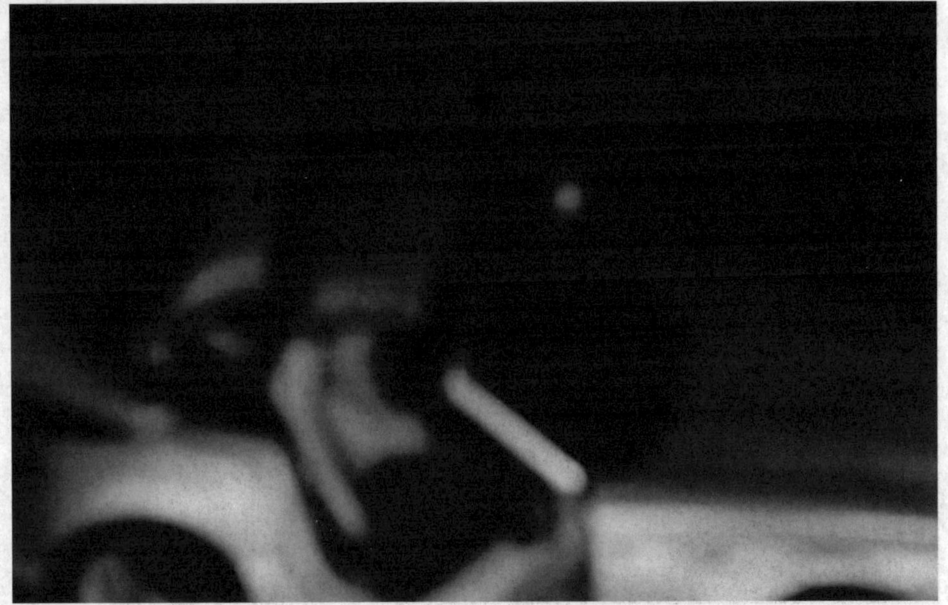

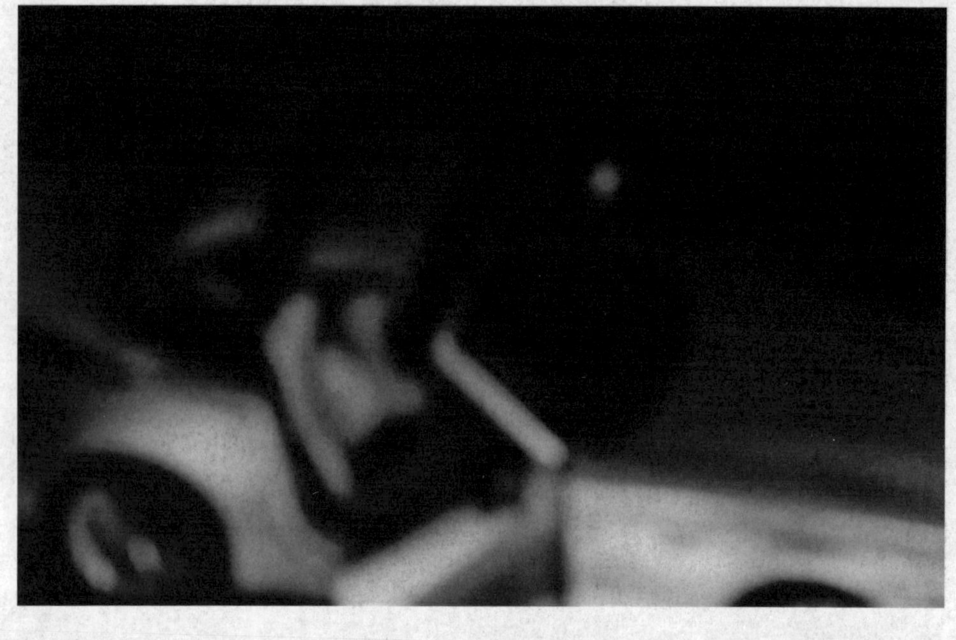

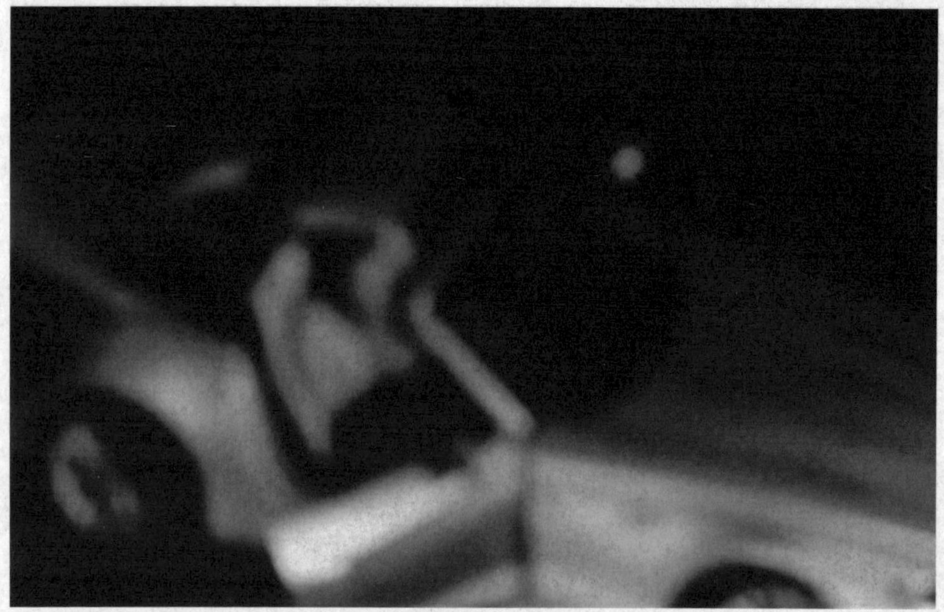

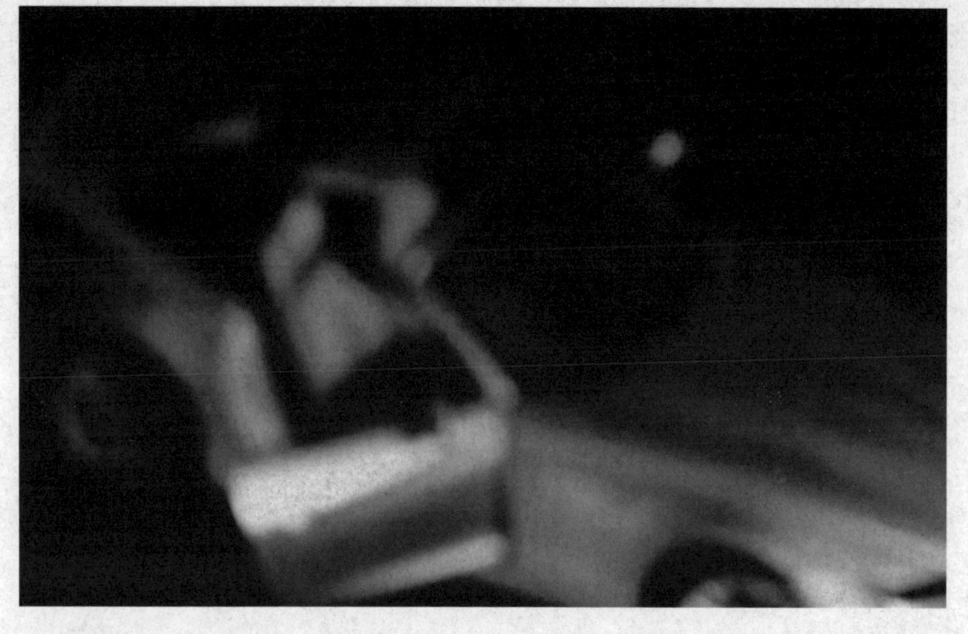

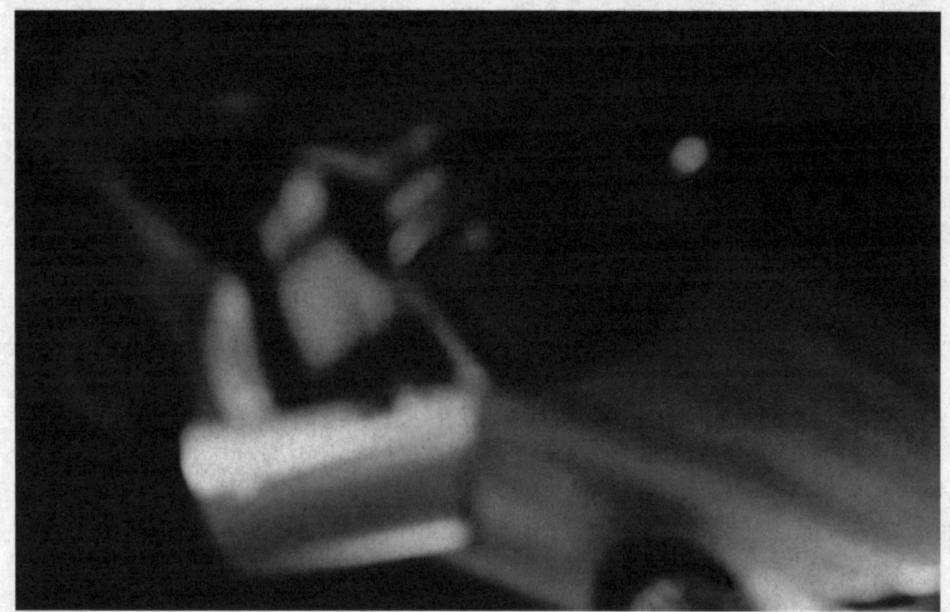

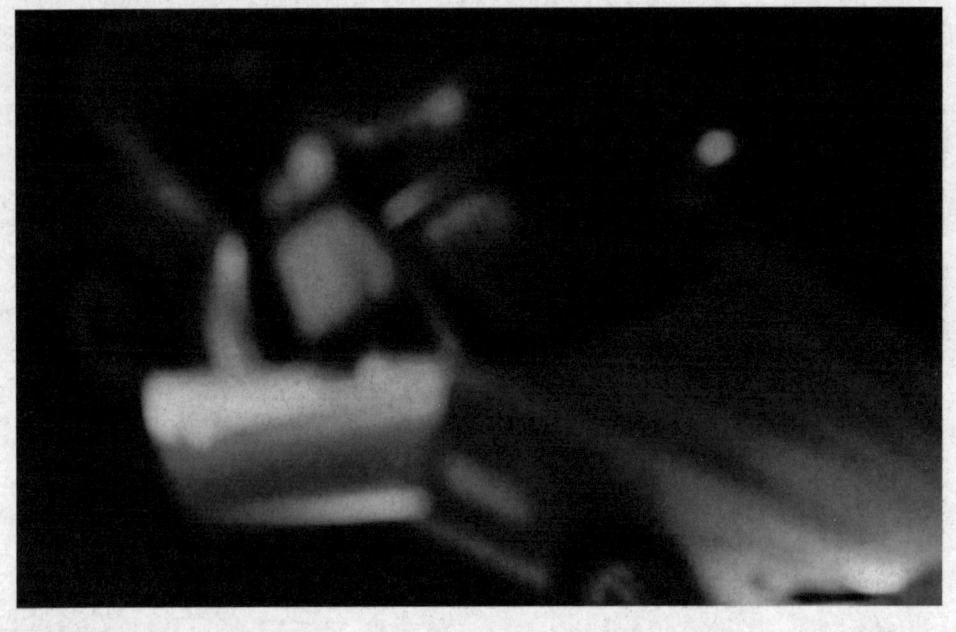

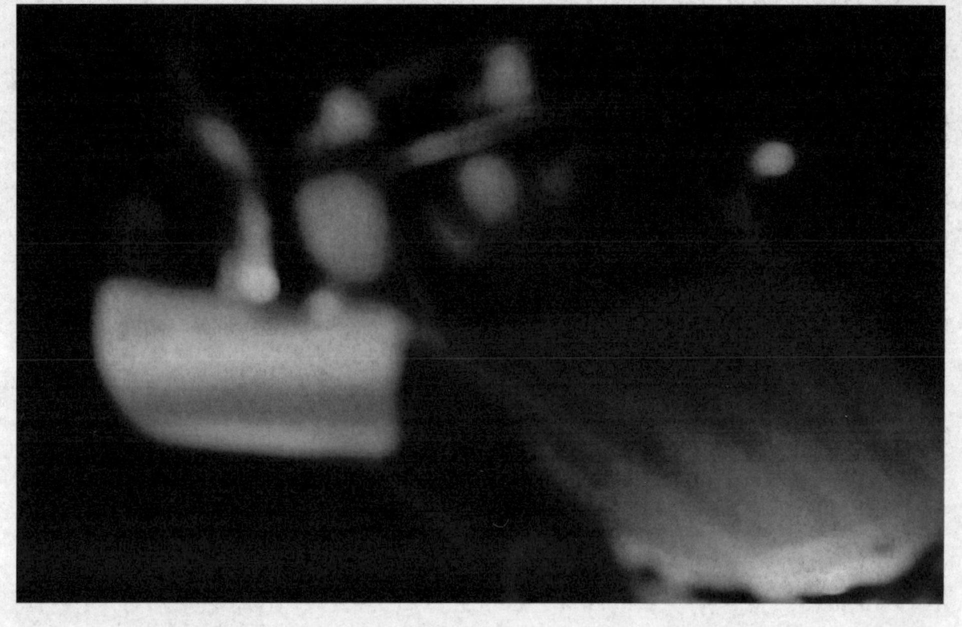

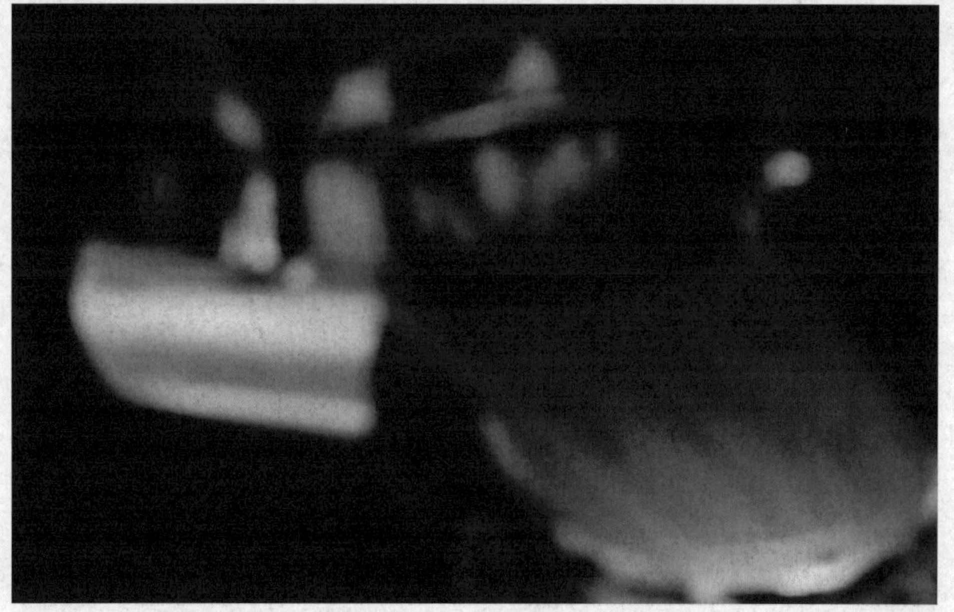

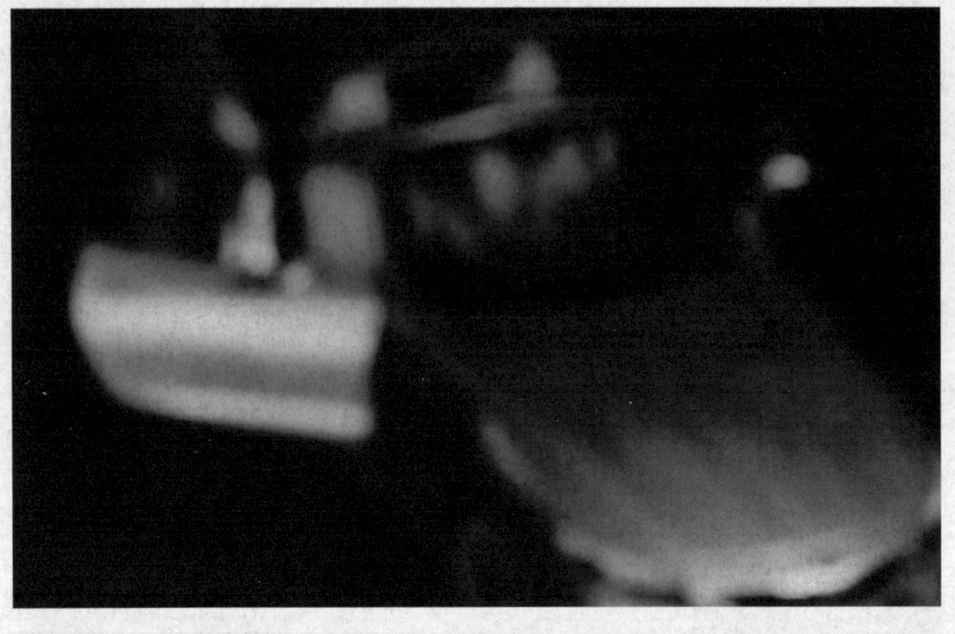

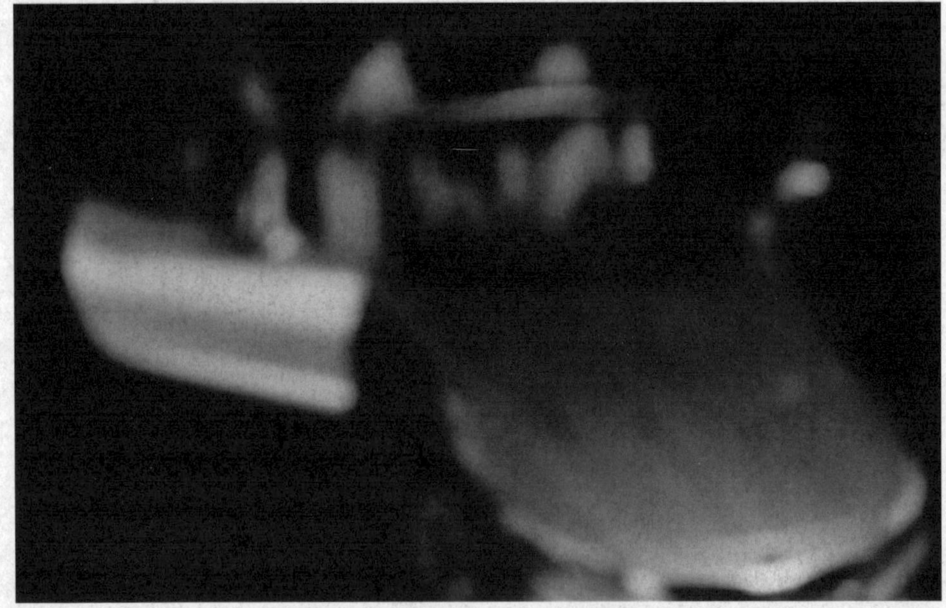

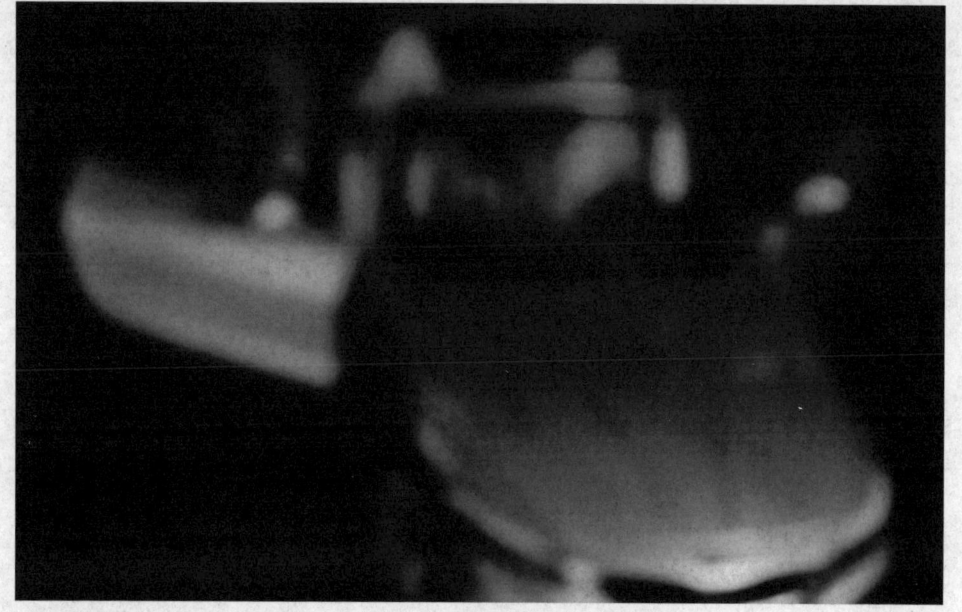

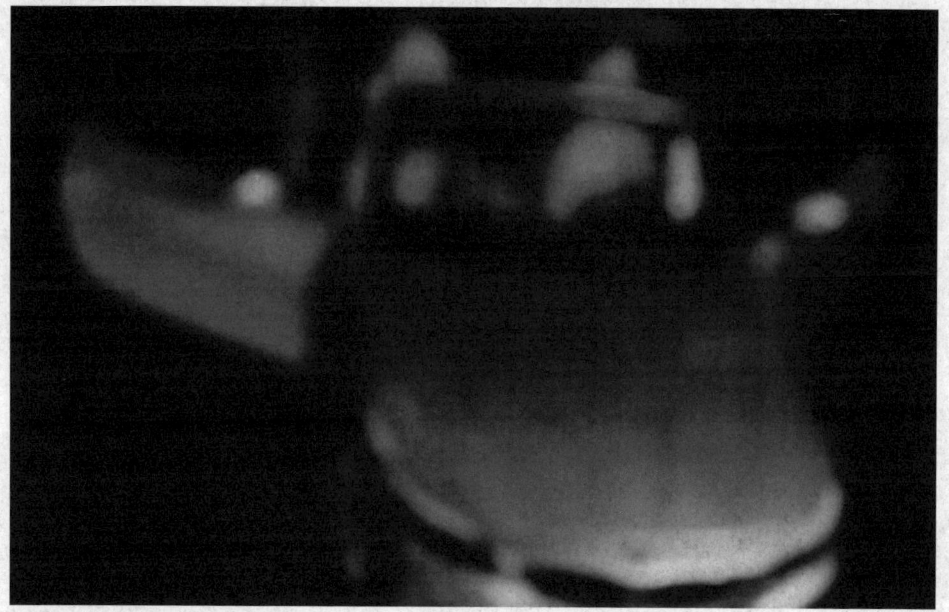

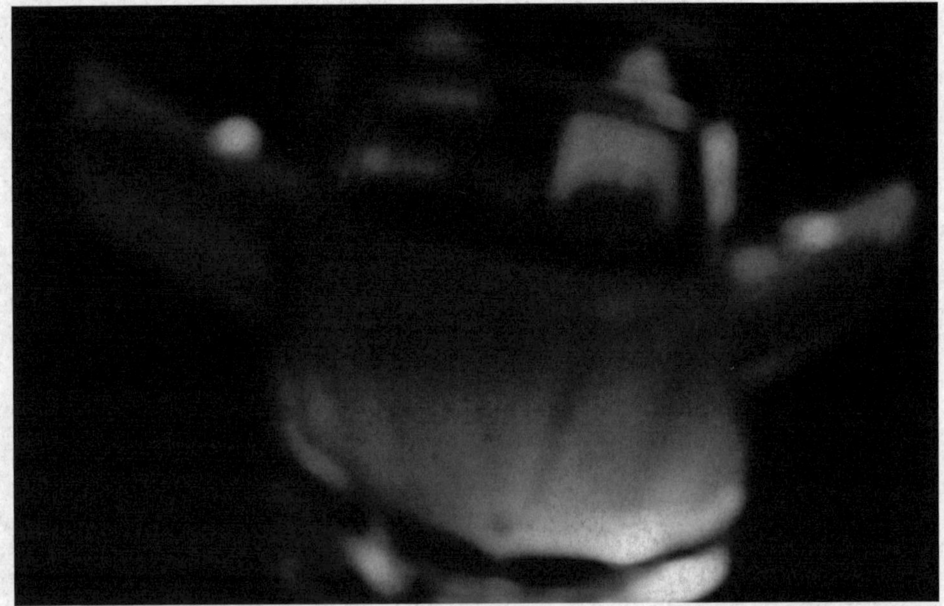

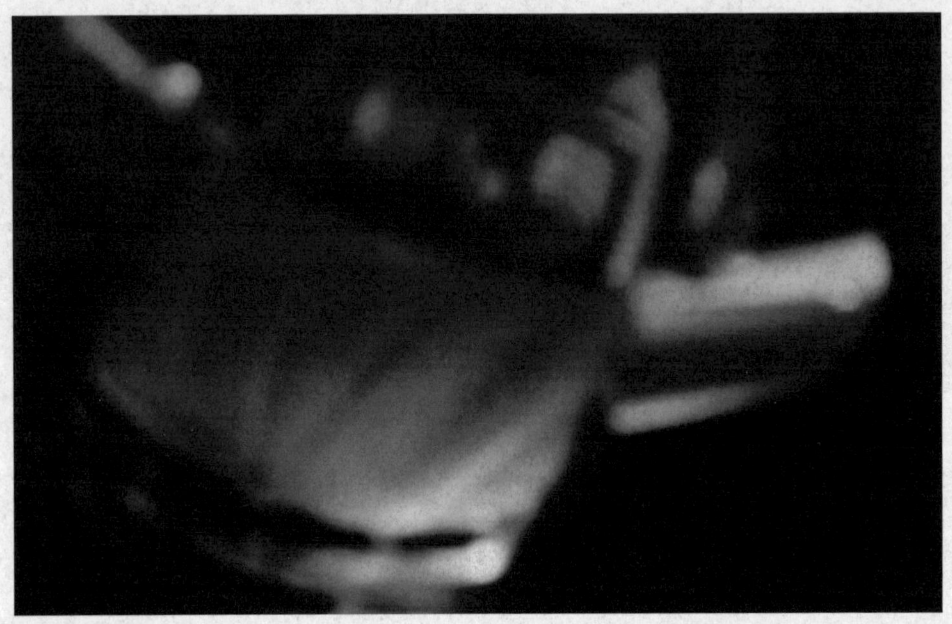

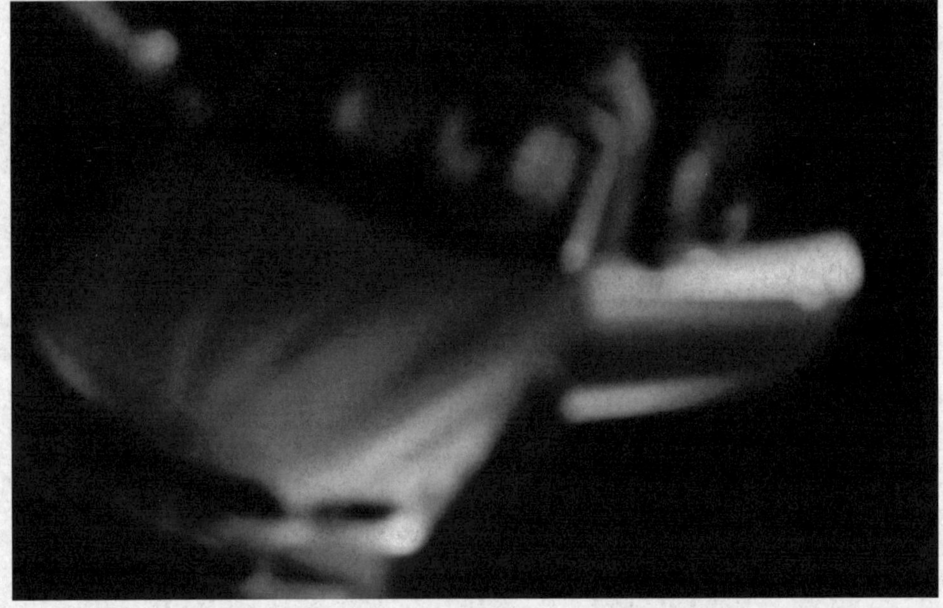

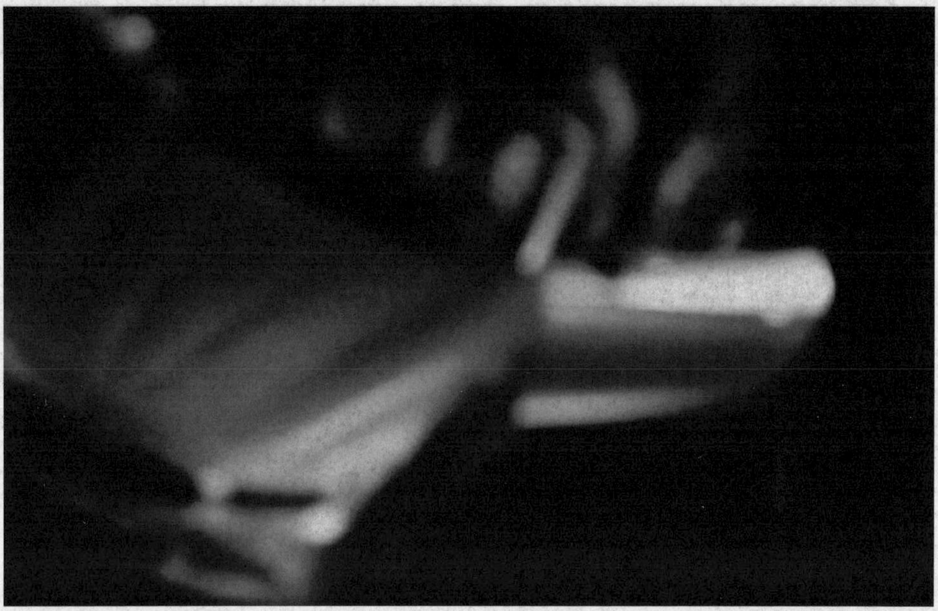

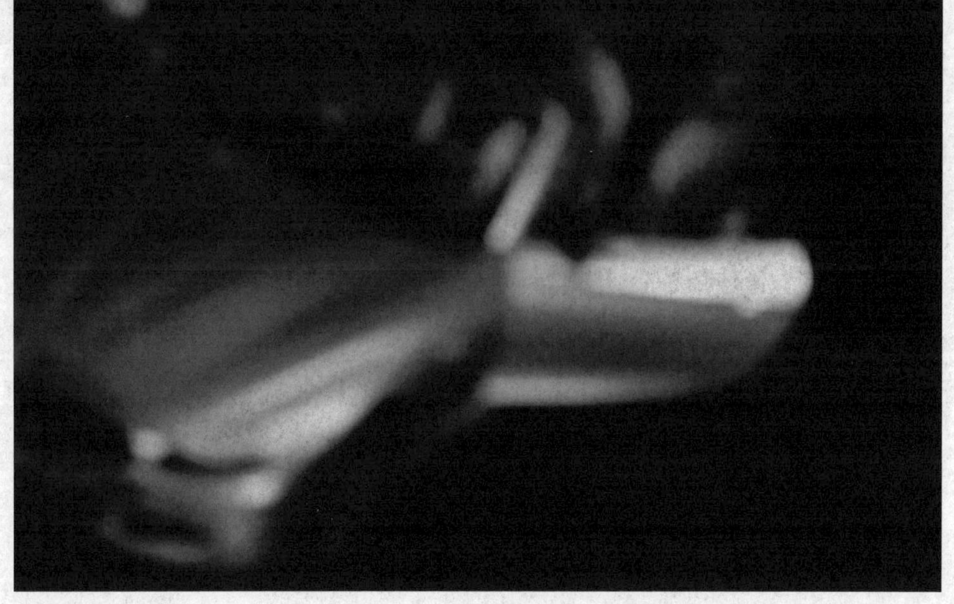

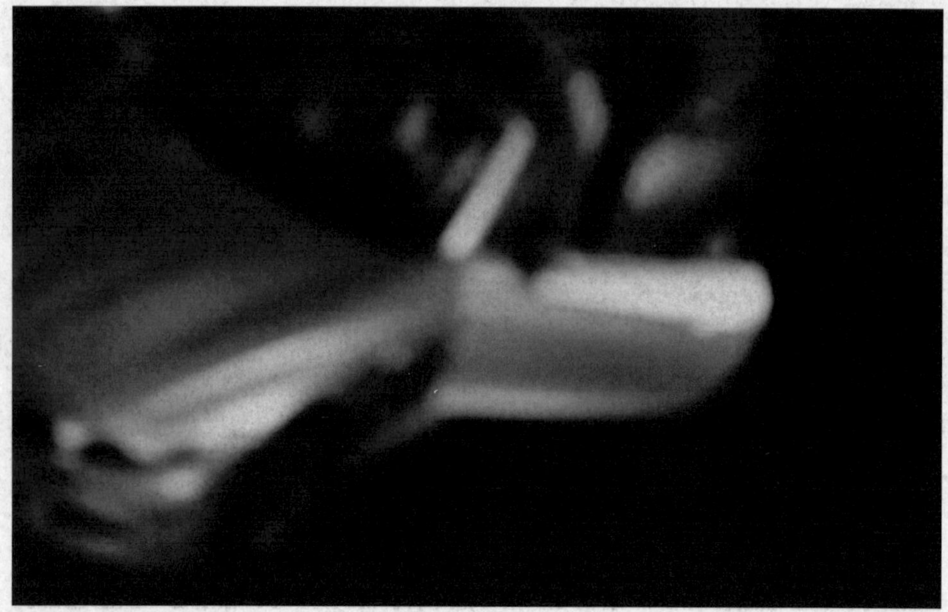

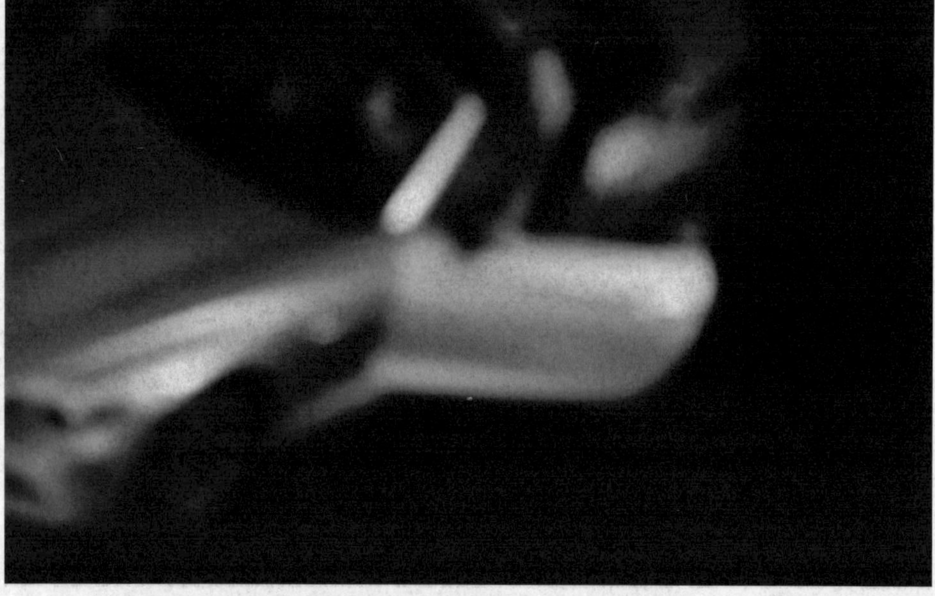

you don't have to see something
to know it is there

* * *

relax
into an advanced spatial concept
with clear organisation
and delineation
of user and control-oriented functions

intuitive operation and logical functionality
are ensured by optimised visual assists
and a consistent flow of information
in the larger
higher-definition control display
a slim free-floating centre console
other details include graphics
for the direct selection of the entertainment
and telecommunications menus
grouped conveniently next to the controller
in the gps navigation section
users benefit from map-displays
newly enhanced with topography
and functionally improved with new standards of size
brilliance
detail and view choice

and here
there are five freely programmable
intelligent memory keys

<u>SKRIPT FÜR *NIGHT OF THE WORLD*</u>

Man muss eine Sache nicht sehen
um zu wissen dass sie da ist

* * *

Entspanne dich
hinein in ein fortschrittliches Raumkonzept
mit klarer Gliederung
und Darstellung
von nutzer- und steuerungsorientierten Funktionen

Intuitive Bedienung und logische Funktionalität
werden durch optimierte visuelle Assistenzsysteme
garantiert
und ein konsequenter Informationsfluss
im größeren
höher auflösenden Steuerungsdisplay
Eine schmale frei schwebende Mittelkonsole
Weitere Details sind Anzeigesysteme
zur direkten Auswahl der Unterhaltungs-
und Telekommunikationsmenüs
die praktischerweise neben der Steuerungseinheit angeordnet
sind
Im Unterpunkt GPS-Navigation
profitieren Nutzer:innen von Kartendarstellungen
die neuerdings um topografische Daten erweitert wurden
und in ihrer Funktion verbessert durch neue Standards
bezüglich Größe
Helligkeit
Bildausschnitten und Wahl der Perspektive

along with the ability
to combine voice and visual display

and in the audio option
there is an extremely versatile
and realistic experience of sound
provided by up to 16
high-performance loudspeakers
with neo-dyme magnetic cores
and a digital nine-channel amplifier
that plays tracks
straight from a dedicated hard drive

the ambiance is of transcendent quality
and most important of all
it is inviting

* * *

and there are different rules here

there is a gentle
virtually imperceptible motion
of rotation
pressing and tipping
and the user is surrounded
with the shimmering effect
of cool high-tech
deep interior shades of jerez black
boast blue pearl pigments
interlagos blue in turn
incorporates red colour pigments
to provide a highly attractive interaction

Und hier
gibt es fünf frei programmierbare
intelligente Datenspeicher
mit der Möglichkeit
Stimme und visuelle Darstellung zu kombinieren

Und die Audio-Option
bietet ein äußerst vielseitiges
und realistisches Klangerlebnis
erzeugt durch bis zu 16
Hochleistungslautsprecher
mit Neodym-Magnetkernen
und einen digitalen 9-Kanal-Verstärker
der Musikstücke
direkt von einer speziellen Festplatte abspielt

Der Klang ist von überirdischer Qualität
und was am wichtigsten ist
er ist einladend

* * *

Und hier gelten andere Regeln

Es gibt eine sanfte
fast nicht wahrnehmbare
Dreh-, Schub- und Kippbewegung
und der/die Nutzer:in ist umgeben
von dem schimmernden Effekt
coolen Hightechs
Im Inneren weisen tiefe Farbtöne von Jerezschwarz
blaue Perlpigmente auf
Interlagosblau hingegen

of blue and violet from various angles
these elements
literally twist around one another
as forces are transmitted
along defined paths in extensive
and precisely defined deformation zones
dark areas seemingly flow around
the gently contoured highlights
of cerulean
opal glaze and fox red
and distinguish the high-calibre materials
with perfect finish
that are low slung
here
all along the bed plate

* * *

there is truth in engineering
and to be ultra-precise
there are two thousand
eight hundred and ninety-seven of us
gathered here
enclosed along the bottom line
crawling the bedplate
clinching and bonding in the dark
absolutely ready for years and years
of elapsed time
perfectly chrono-graphed

and this hard experience has generated
a controlled deformation of our logical functionality
ensuring a complete departure

enthält rote Farbpigmente
um eine äußerst attraktive Wechselwirkung
von Blau und Violett aus verschiedenen Perspektiven
zu bieten
Diese Elemente
wickeln sich buchstäblich umeinander
während entlang definierter Pfade
Kräfte in ausgedehnten und präzise definierten
Verformungszonen
übertragen werden
Dunkle Bereiche scheinen
die sanft konturierten Glanzpunkte
einer himmelblauen
Lackschicht und eines Fuchsrots zu umfließen
und heben die hochkarätigen
ausgezeichnet verarbeiteten Materialien hervor
die hier
entlang der Bodenplatte
tiefergelegt sind

* * *

Technik enthält Wahrheit
und um ganz präzise zu sein
sind Zweitausendachthundertundsiebenundneunzig von uns
hier versammelt
umschlossen am Grund
an der Bodenplatte kriechend
klammernd und klebend in der Dunkelheit
absolut bereit für unzählige Jahre
exakt gemessener
verstrichener Zeit

from our predecessor
and enthusing us with a powerful appetite
we have character
yes
and intelligent drive
with freely programmable behaviour
all the way
to the maximum permissible
it boasts magnificent power
and is augmented with all the damper forces
and the deadlocks

and we have retained our beautiful profile
which we owe to the long and sweeping indicator
ultra responsive
yet powerfully resistant
under the rapidly changing conditions
of vigorous longitudinal
lateral and vertical motion

viewed from various angles
our bodies are composed of energetic dimensions
expressing athletic poise in the most elegant form
sleek lines trace a graceful silhouette
above the waistline
strong curves in the shoulders
taut and dynamic in their outline
an underbody composed of cool
sculptural surfaces that recall modernism
and rooflines of chromed arabesque
flow gracefully over the flanks
all the way to the bumpers
a bold and sensual rear aspect
that communicates muscular substance

202

Und diese schwierige Erfahrung hat
eine kontrollierte Deformierung unserer logischen
Funktionsfähigkeit bewirkt
Was einen vollständigen Abschied
von unserem Vorläufer gewährleistet hat
und uns mit einem kraftvollen Verlangen erfüllt
Wir haben Charakter
ja
und einen intelligenten Antrieb
mit frei programmierbarem Verhalten
bis hin zum
maximal Zulässigen
er verfügt über eine großartige Leistung
und wird ergänzt um all die Dämpfungskräfte
und Sicherheitsverriegelungen

Und wir haben unser schönes Profil bewahrt
das wir der langen und ausgreifenden Anzeige zu
verdanken haben
die äußerst sensibel reagiert
und sich doch als kraftvoll und widerstandsfähig erweist
unter den sich schnell wandelnden Bedingungen
einer energischen längsgerichteten
seitlichen und vertikalen Bewegung

Von unterschiedlichen Blickwinkeln aus betrachtet
sind unsere Körper aus energetischen Dimensionen
zusammengesetzt
die eine athletische Gelassenheit in ihrer elegantesten
Form zum Ausdruck bringen
Schlanke Linien zeichnen eine anmutige Silhouette
oberhalb der Taille
Starke Rundungen an den Schultern
die in ihrem Umriss straff und dynamisch wirken
Ein Unterboden bestehend aus kühlen

* * *

and there is more
we have achieved a perfect interface
a chorus of our combined force and energy
see
our rack and pinion steering systems
automatically adjust their shift points as one
to achieve the most stylish co-ordination
this harmonious capability includes
a particularly languid 360 degree turning circle
performed in millisecond precision
with an exquisite interface of our traction
and super-controlled glide urges

yes
we dive and roll in bends
in the multiphase
to the beat of progress
with open stroke
with full flared air-intake scoops
for ultra precise control
and likewise
the widely yawning side panels
are sensitive and so alert
punch-riveting in relatively soft mounts
and tipping the lever forward
for downshifts to the multi-link
double-wishbone front
now so much more natural and intuitive

we are a very ductile force
but more extrovert now
with a new z-fold system and axel kinematics

skulpturalen Oberflächen die an die Moderne denken lassen
und Dachlinien aus verchromten Arabesken
fließen anmutig über die Flanken
bis hinab zu den Stoßstangen
Eine mutige und sinnliche Rückansicht
die muskulöse Materie vermittelt

* * *

Und da ist noch mehr
Wir haben eine perfekte Schnittstelle geschaffen
einen Chor unserer kombinierten Kraft und Energie
Sehen Sie
Unsere Zahnstangenlenkungssysteme
richten ihre Schaltpunkte automatisch zu einer Einheit aus
um die eleganteste Abstimmung zu erreichen
Diese harmonische Fähigkeit umfasst
einen besonders trägen 360-Grad-Wendekreis
der mit millisekundengenauer Präzision ausgeführt wird
mit einer vorzüglichen Schnittstelle unserer Bodenhaftung
und genau geregeltem Gleitverlangen

Ja
wir tauchen und schlingern durch Kurven
mehrphasig
im Rhythmus des Fortschritts
mit Öffnungshub
mit voll ausgestellten Lufteinlasshutzen
für eine hochpräzise Steuerung
und ebenso
sind die weit klaffenden Seitenverkleidungen
sensibel und sehr geistesgegenwärtig
Stanznieten in relativ weichen Halterungen

tailored to the high power
stretching the lower anchors and tethers
on the long hood
and the short front overhang
in a double-pivot strut-type
with triple synchromesh
so crisp and quick
creating the impression of a comet on the move

and then
with a tweak of the headlight stalk
we are right here by your side
speaking the language of technical perfection
and firing ever-evolving solutions

ready now with a separate throttle butterfly
applied with tactile precision in the dark
in the wet sump
in the relatively long space
here
here
we will follow you
with near-photographic realism
we will follow you
in an amazing spectrum of dark pigments
combined and harmonised with the pleasures
we will follow you

* * *

we have progressed a significant evolution
in applied
combined memory

206

und das Antippen des Hebels
zum Herunterschalten
zur Mehrlenker-Doppelquerlenker-Vorderachse
ist jetzt so viel natürlicher und intuitiver

Wir sind eine sehr formbare Kraft
aber jetzt noch extrovertierter
mit einem neuen Z-Fold-System und einer Achsenkinematik
zugeschnitten auf die hohe Leistung
Sie streckt die unteren Verankerungen und die Haltegurte
auf die lange Motorhaube
und den kurzen vorderen Überhang
in einem Doppelgelenk-Federbeintyp
mit dreifachem Synchrongetriebe
das so knackig und schnell ist
dass der Eindruck eines Kometen in Bewegung entsteht

Und dann
mit einem kleinen Zug am Scheinwerferhebel
sind wir genau hier an Ihrer Seite
sprechen die Sprache technischer Perfektion
und feuern stetig sich weiterentwickelnde Lösungen ab

jetzt bereit mit einer separaten Drosselklappe
eingesetzt mit taktiler Präzision in der Dunkelheit
in der triefenden Ölwanne
im relativ langen Raum
hier
hier
Wir werden Ihnen folgen
mit nahezu fotografischem Realismus
wir werden Ihnen folgen
in einer erstaunlichen Bandbreite dunkler Pigmente
die mit den Genüssen kombiniert und in Einklang gebracht
werden
Wir werden Ihnen folgen

to achieve an optimised potential for recall
almost like a muscle
flexing
shifting
adapting
and we have made retrieval
along the horizontally flowing lines
narrowing precisely
and targeted at the beginning
of our displacement

with intuitive mastery via our combined strength
we can reach
now
and exert from the base up
from our low placement
here
to the warm homogeneous illumination
there
an extraordinary revolution
a muscular thrust and pulling force
with the all firing memory
of a dynamic torque
of high
higher and highest-strength

* * *

Wir haben eine bedeutende Entwicklung im Bereich angewandter
kombinierter Speicher angestoßen
um ein optimiertes Erinnerungspotenzial abzurufen
Fast wie ein Muskel
sich beugend
sich verändernd
sich anpassend
Und wir haben uns
entlang der horizontal fließenden Linien wiedergefunden
die sich präzise verengen
und auf den Ansatz unseres Hubraums
ausgerichtet sind

Mit intuitiver Beherrschung durch unsere kombinierte Kraft
können wir es
nun schaffen
und von unten nach oben
von unserer niedrigen Position aus
hier
zur warmen homogenen Erleuchtung
dort
eine außerordentliche Revolution realisieren
einen muskulären Schub und eine zerrende Kraft
mit der alles befeuernden Erinnerung
an ein dynamisches Drehmoment
von großer
größerer und allergrößter Stärke

UNDE

FOOT

UNDERFOOT (2022)

The first seven minutes of *UNDERFOOT* take us through
the extensive reading rooms of Europe's largest
lending library, shortly before its public opening
in 1981.
　　A series of photographs created at that time
provide the basis for this tour. They document a large,
late-modernist building with spacious interiors of
clean, geometric design. While the rooms are furnished
for hundreds of readers, they appear entirely unpop-
ulated and, even more conspicuously, hold no books.
　　The rare opportunity to observe a library prior to
the admission of its contents offers a certain imagi-
native license: to fill it up differently. This is
seized by the video's two unnamed, voiceless narrators,
who guide us through the empty building. The tour is
anodyne at the start, but the narrators focus with
increasing intensity upon the acoustic qualities of
the hardwood veneers and decorative carpets that
line the reading rooms.
　　In moderating the sonic world of the library, these
materials enact a kind of confinement and exclusion.
Yet through their specific materialities and imagery,
they are also fugitive and diverting. The narrators
duly exploit this contradiction, now with the feverish
excitement of a ghost story. They elaborate the
library's geometric modernist interior, via certain
gothic precedents, into a realm of foliage and flora.
And here, they exhort us to dig.
　　The second part of the work reveals glimpses of a
body of archival material located in the same city
as the library: a collection of floral designs for the

UNDERFOOT (2022)

Die ersten sieben Minuten von *UNDERFOOT* führen
uns durch die weitläufigen Lesesäle der größten Leih-
bibliothek Europas kurz vor ihrer Eröffnung im
Jahr 1981.

Eine Reihe von Fotos, die damals entstanden sind,
bilden die Grundlage für diesen Rundgang. Sie dokumen-
tieren ein großes, spätmodernes Gebäude mit weitläufigen
Innenräumen in klarem, geometrischem Design. Obwohl
die Räume für Hunderte von Leser:innen eingerichtet
sind, scheinen sie völlig unbelebt zu sein, und noch
auffälliger ist, dass sie keine Bücher enthalten.

Die seltene Gelegenheit, eine Bibliothek vor der
Aufnahme ihres Inhalts zu sehen, bietet einen gewissen
imaginativen Spielraum, um sie anders zu füllen.
Dies wird von den beiden namenlosen, stimmlosen Erzäh-
ler:innen des Videos genutzt, die uns durch das leere
Gebäude führen. Der Rundgang ist anfangs recht nüchtern,
doch die Erzähler:innen konzentrieren sich mit zu-
nehmender Intensität auf die akustischen Qualitäten der
Hartholzfurniere und dekorativen Teppiche, mit denen
die Lesesäle ausgekleidet sind.

Indem sie die akustische Welt der Bibliothek dämpfen, bewirken diese Materialien eine Art von Begrenzung
und Ausgrenzung. Doch durch ihre spezifische Materia-
lität und Bildlichkeit sind sie auch flüchtig und
zerstreuend. Die Erzähler:innen schöpfen diesen Wider-
spruch aus, nun mit der fieberhaften Spannung einer
Geistergeschichte. Sie bauen das geometrisch-moderne
Interieur der Bibliothek mithilfe bestimmter gotischer
Vorbilder in ein Reich von Laub und Flora aus. Und
hier ermuntern sie uns zum Graben.

spool carpet loom. This remarkable, if grotesque invention of the industrial age supplied yarn to the loom
using a chain of hundreds of linked spools, as wide as
the carpet itself and hundreds of feet long. The
chain of spools was suspended overhead, slung between
rolling cogs, extending far beyond the loom-body
and spreading across the factory ceiling – much like
an upturned, phantasmic image of the carpet being
woven below.

Folgende Seiten / Following pages:
Videostills aller fotografischen Bilder in *UNDERFOOT*,
in korrekter Gegenüberstellung und Reihenfolge. /
Video stills of every photographic image featured in
UNDERFOOT, in correct juxtaposition and order.

Der zweite Teil der Arbeit bietet Einblicke in eine
Fülle an Archivmaterial, das sich in derselben Stadt
wie die Bibliothek befindet: eine Sammlung von Blumen-
mustern für Spulenwebstühle. Bei dieser bemerkenswerten,
wenn auch grotesken Erfindung des Industriezeitalters
wurde das Garn über eine Kette aus Hunderten von miteinander verbundenen Spulen zum Webstuhl geleitet.
Die Spulenkette, die so breit wie der Teppich selbst
und Hunderte von Metern lang war, hing an der Decke und
wand sich zwischen sich drehenden Zahnrädern. Sie
erstreckte sich weit über den Webstuhlkörper hinaus
über die Fabrikdecke – wie ein umgekehrtes, gespensti-
sches Bild des Teppichs, der unten gewebt wurde.

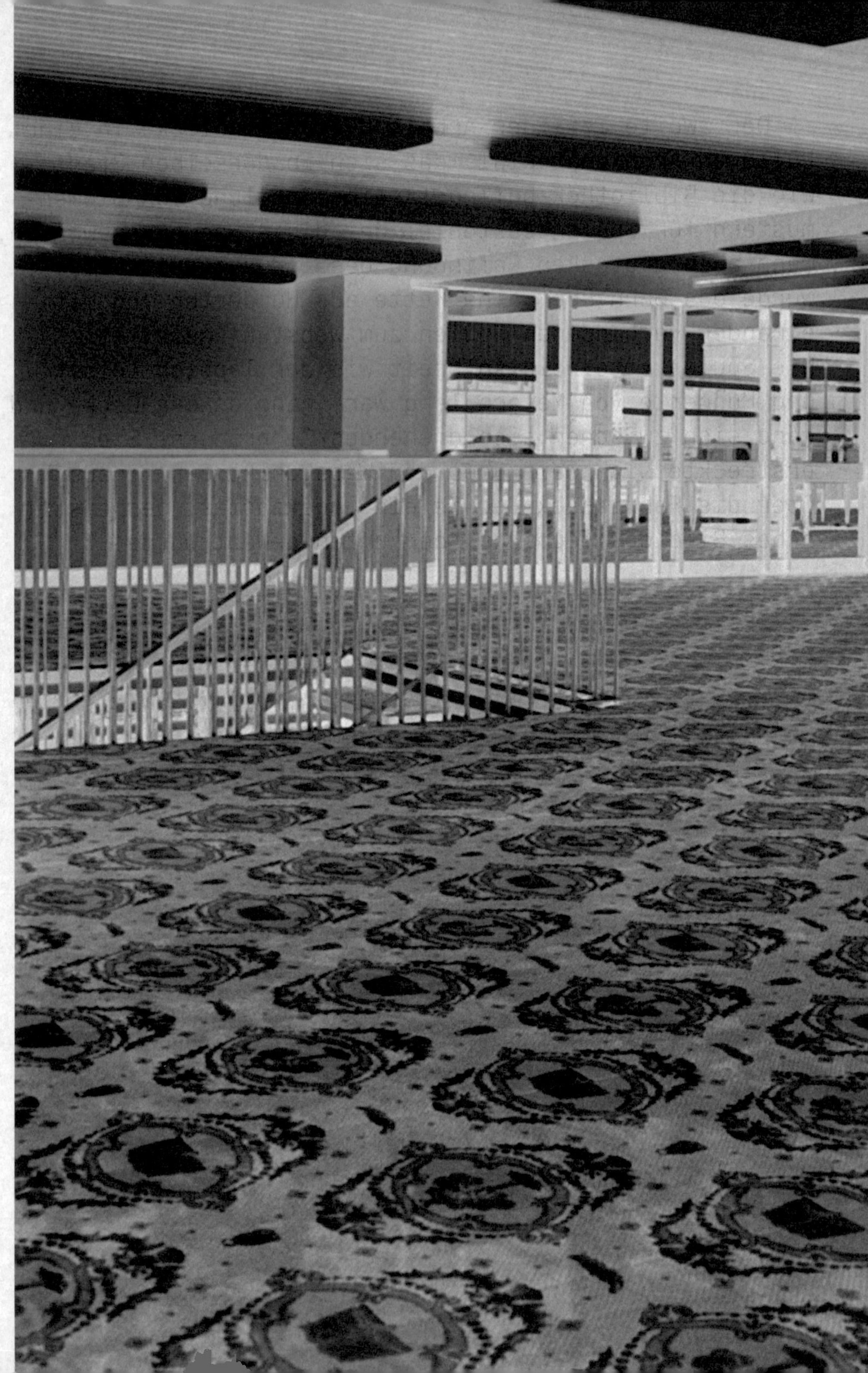

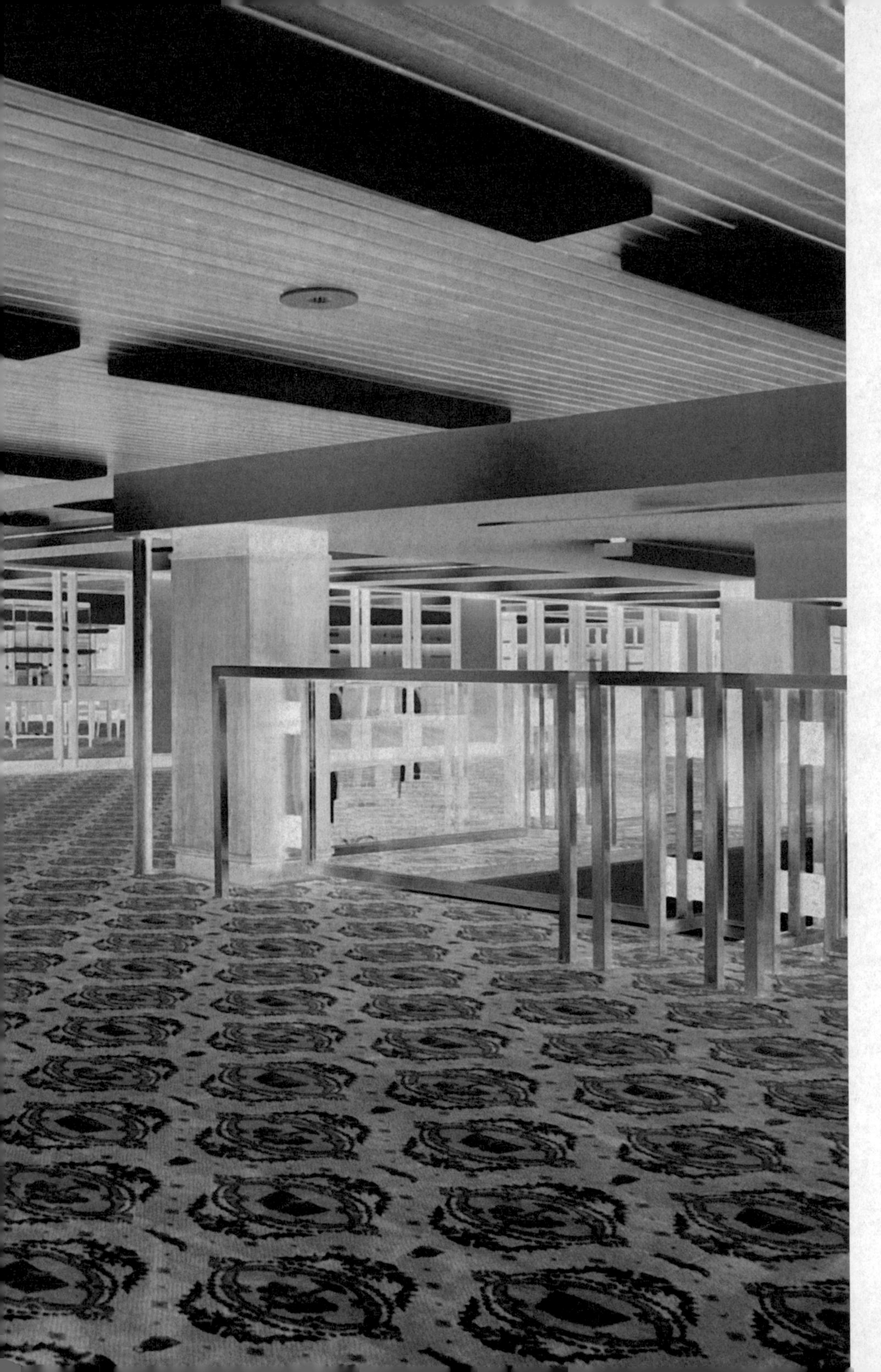

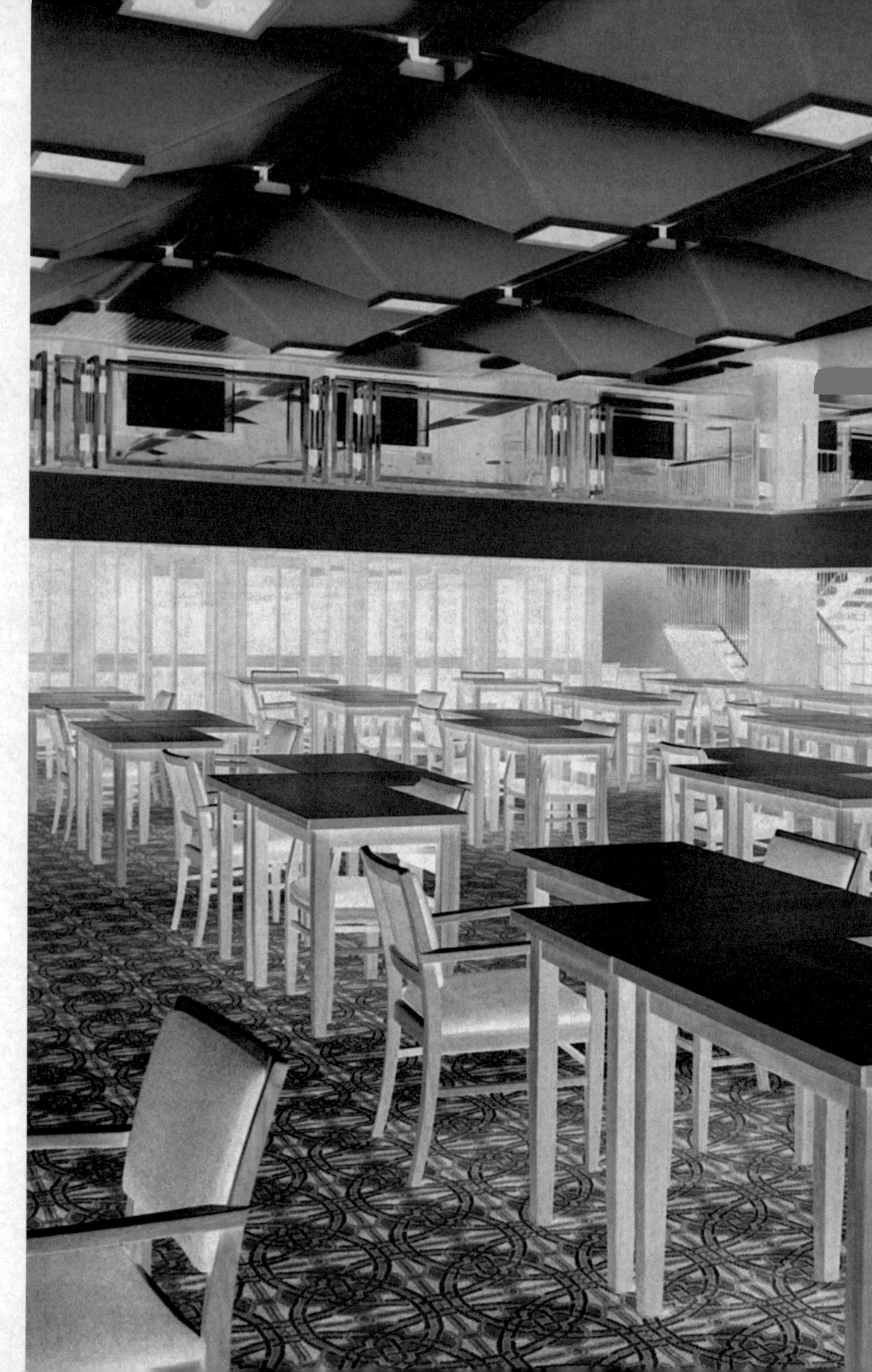

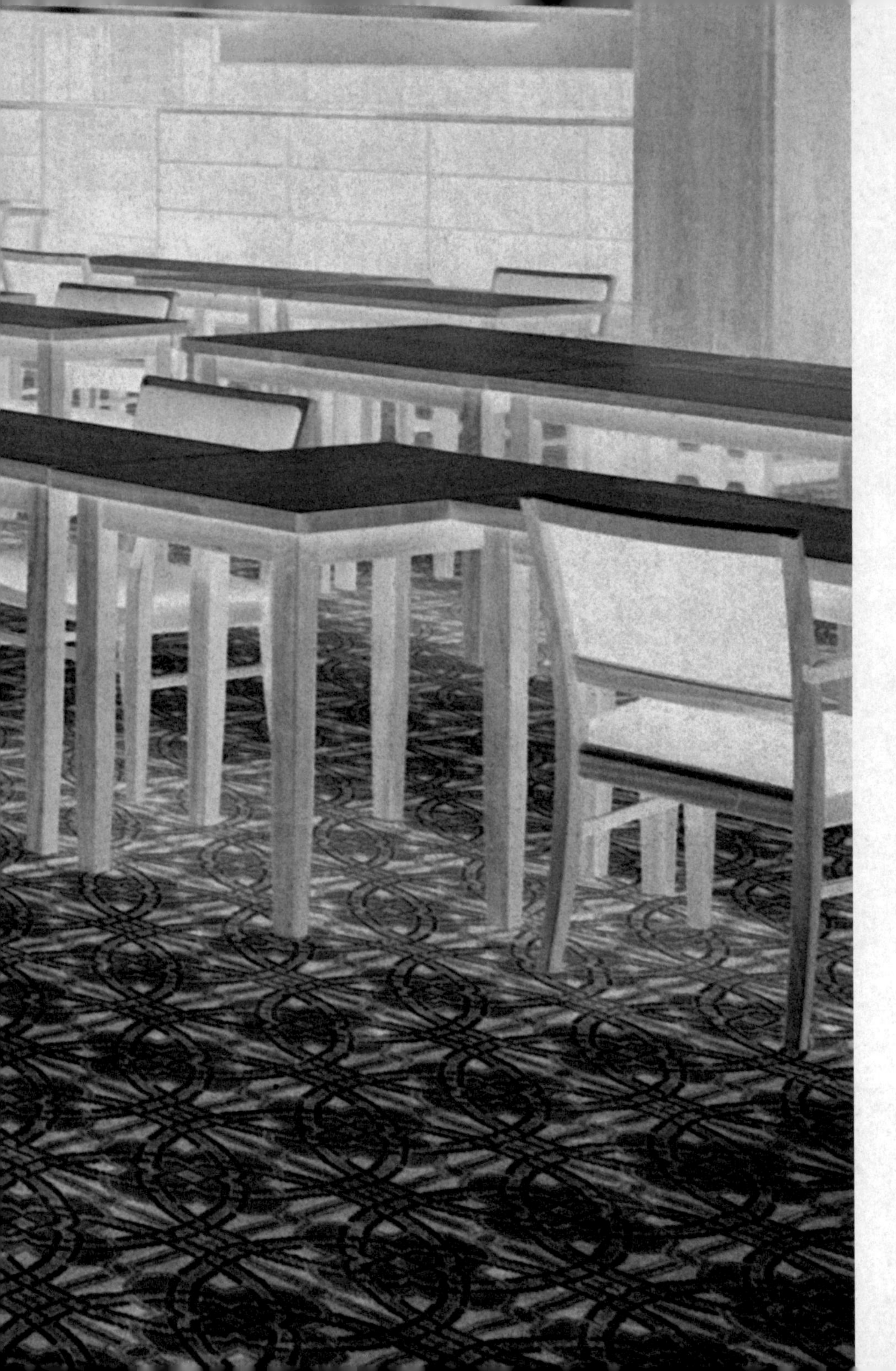

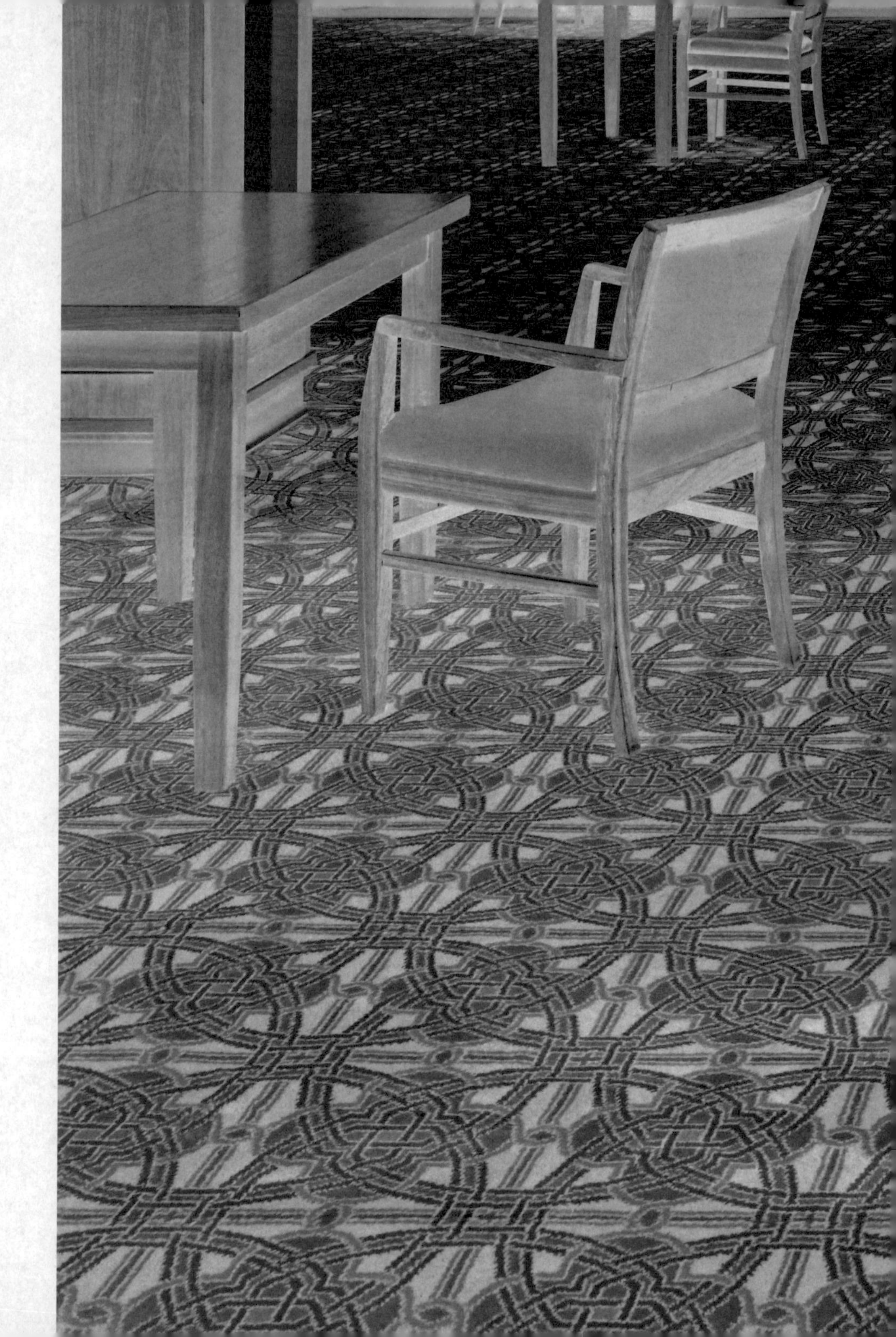

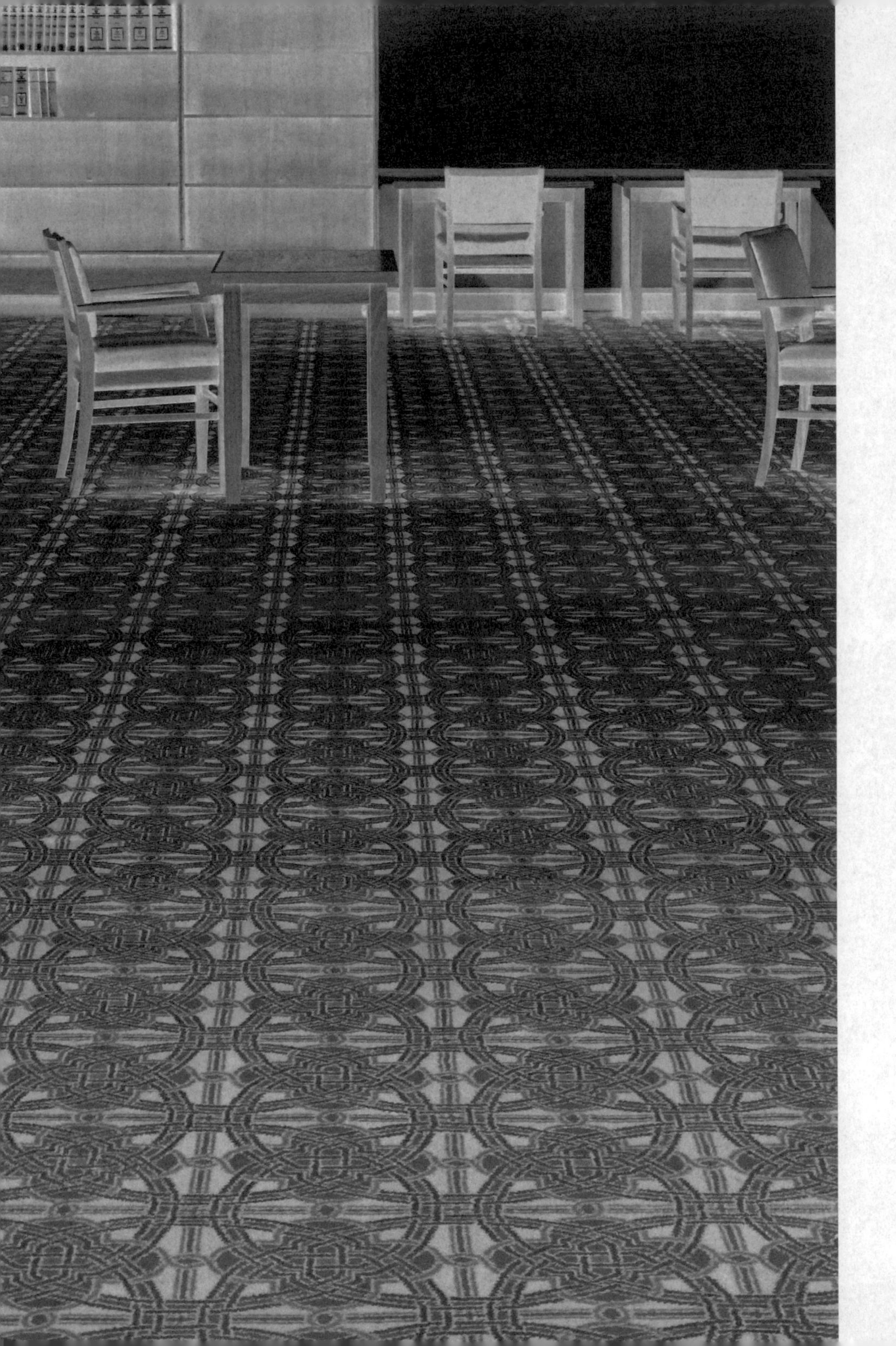

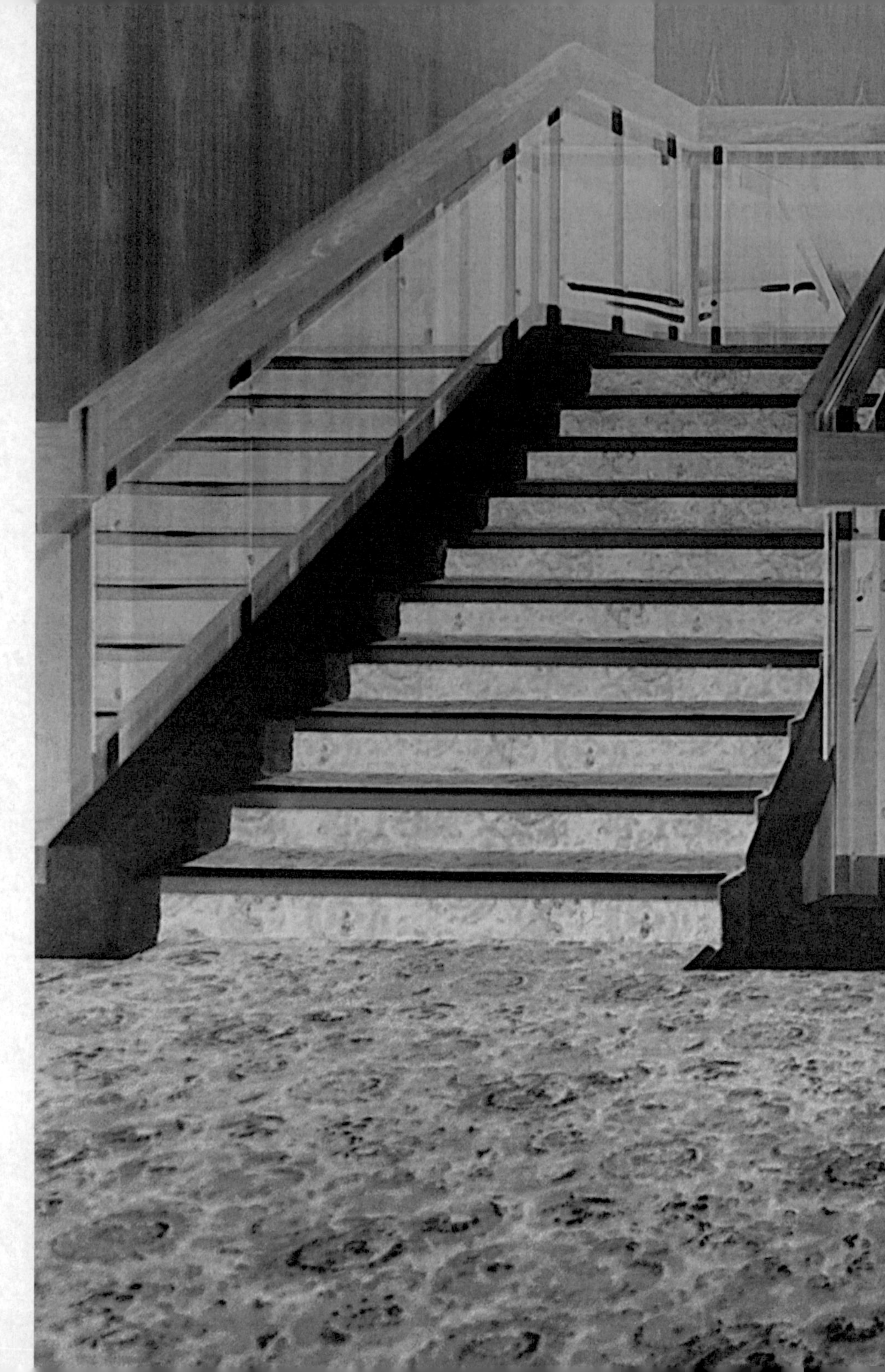

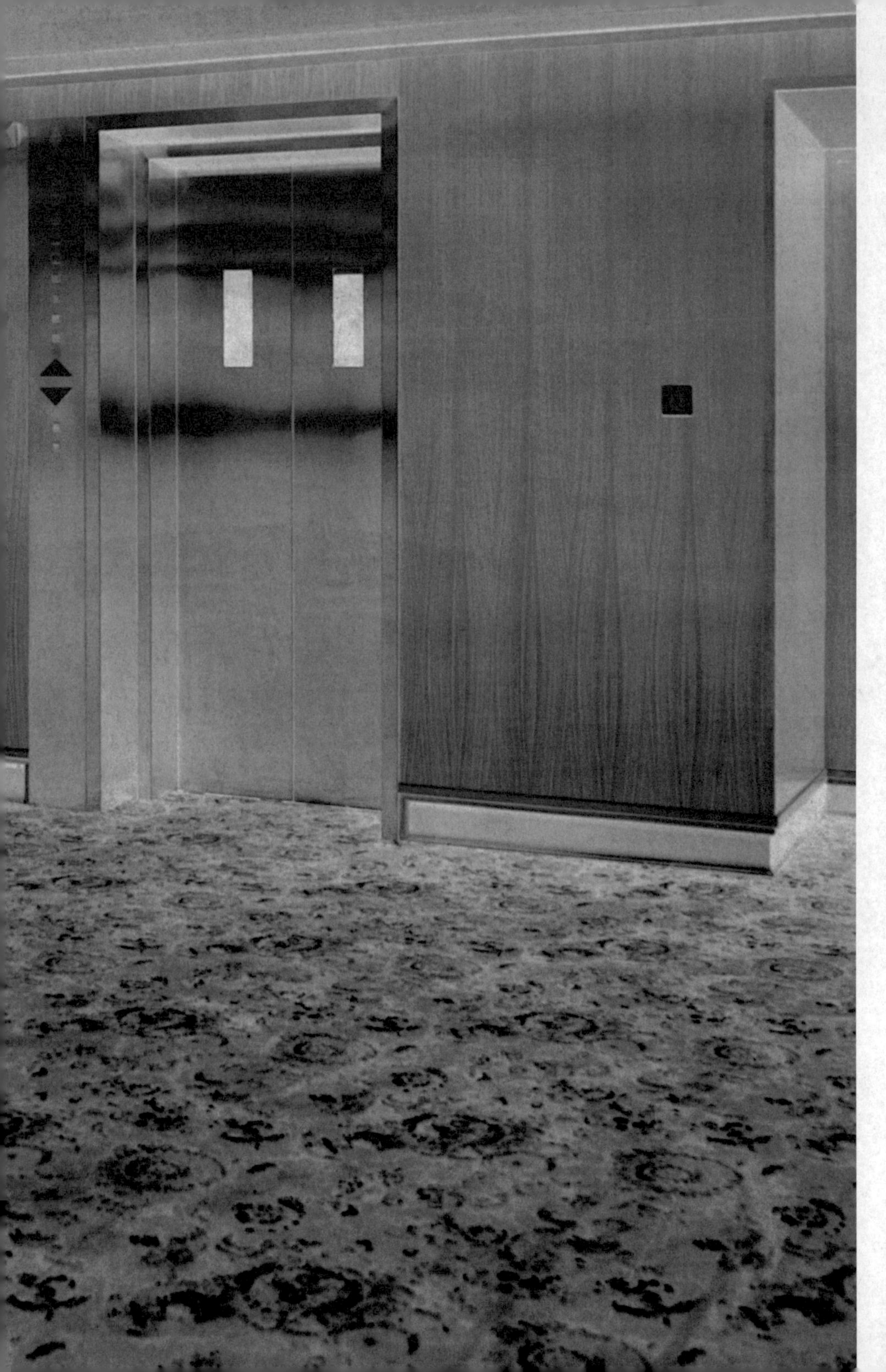

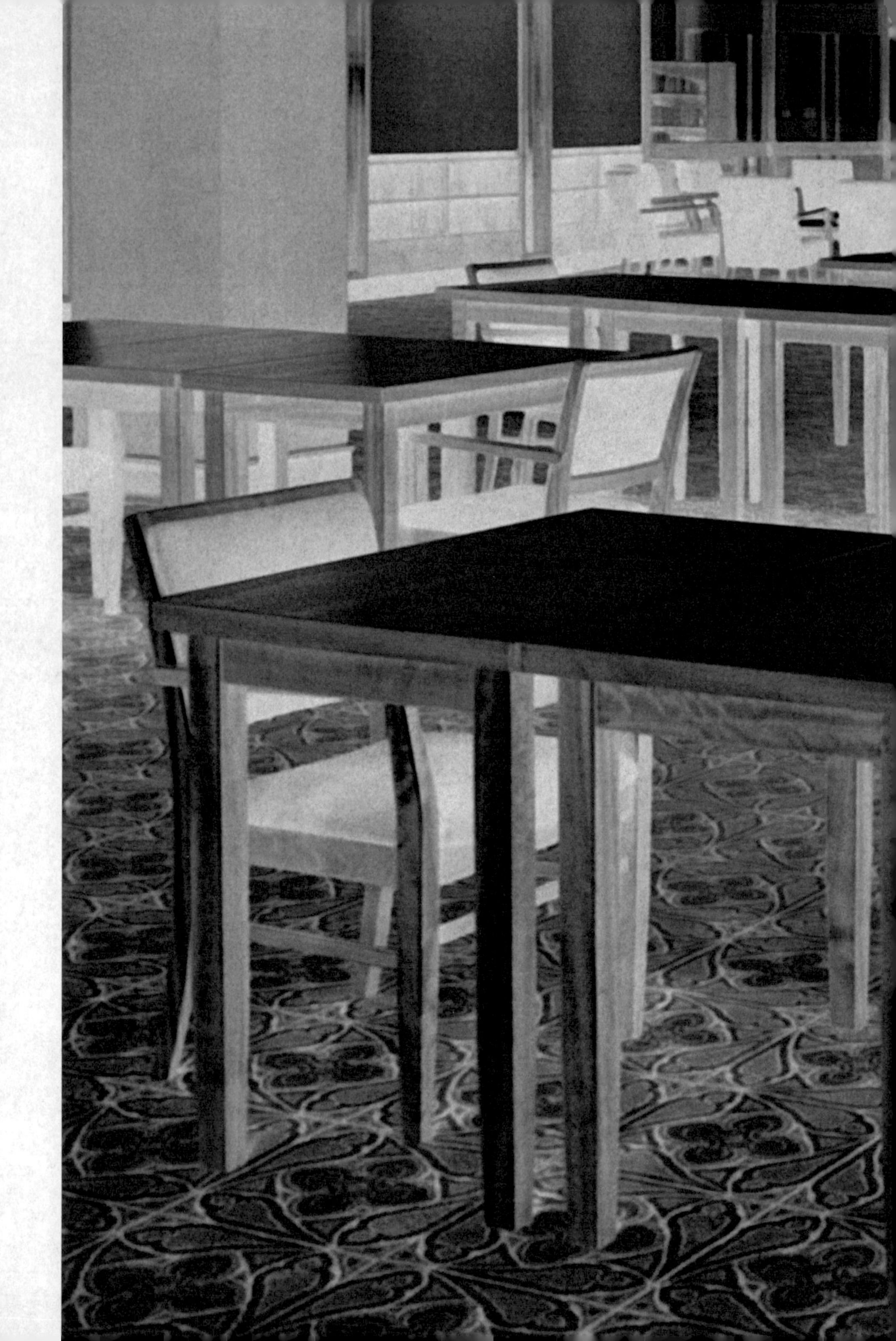

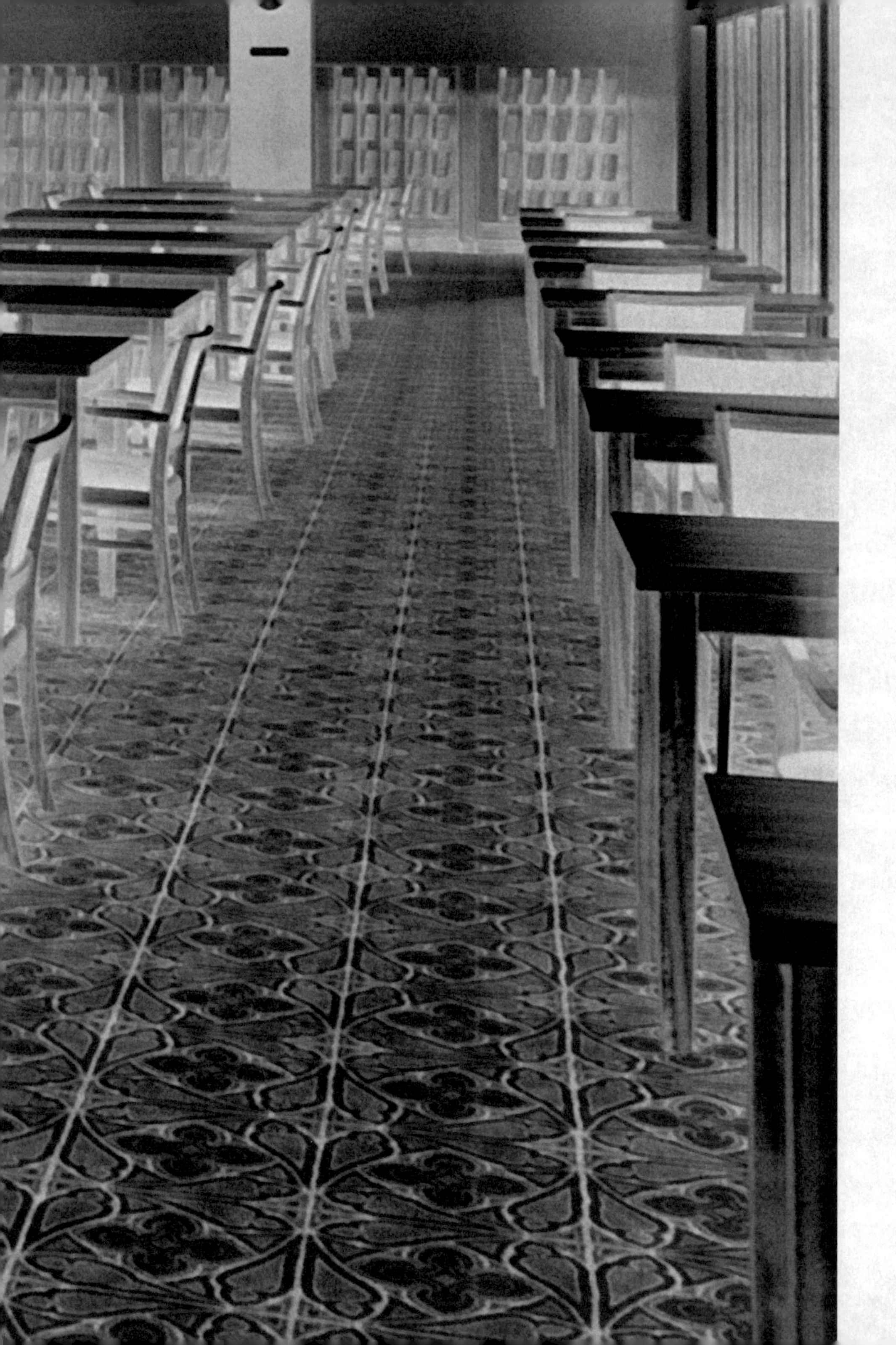

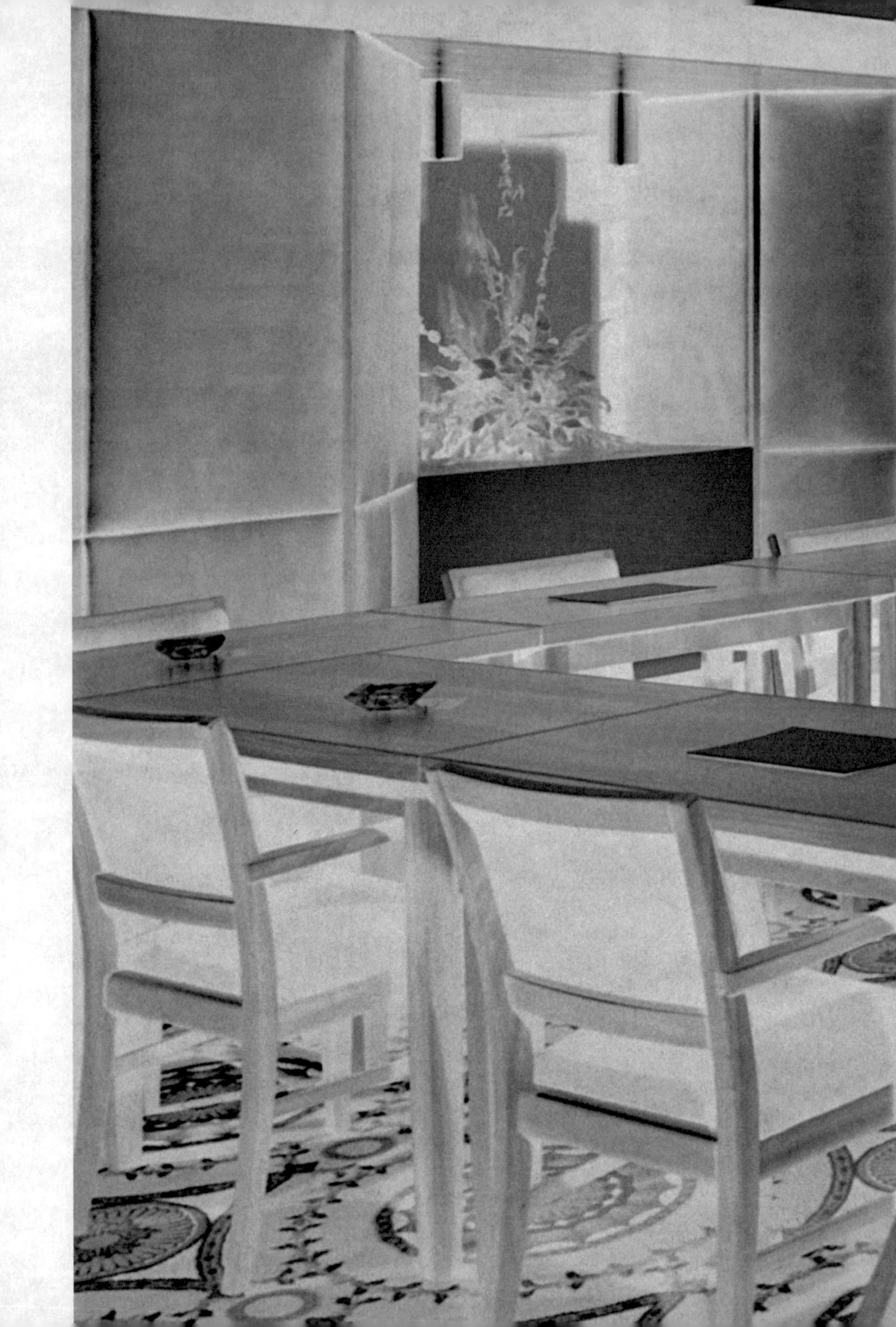

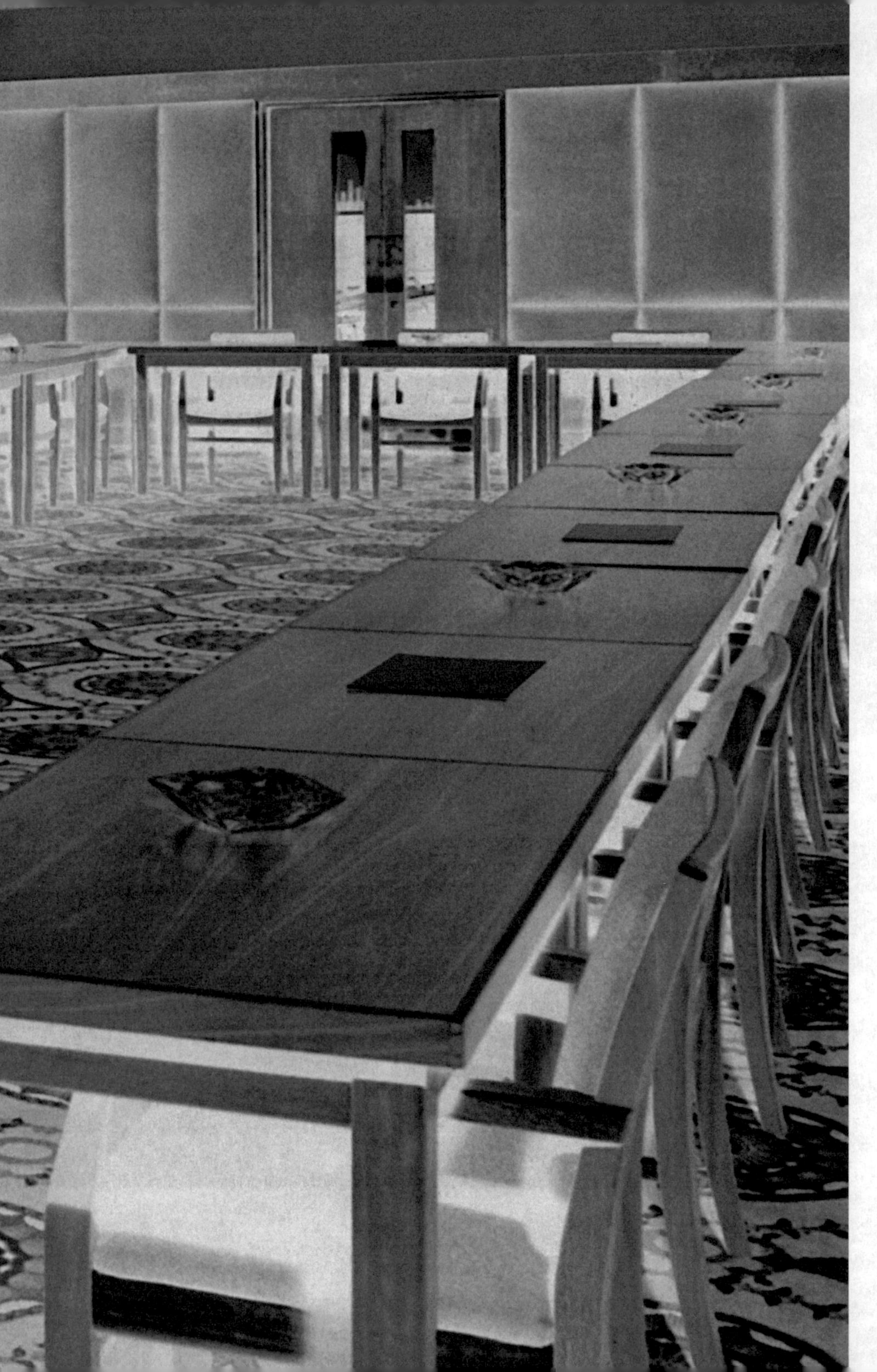

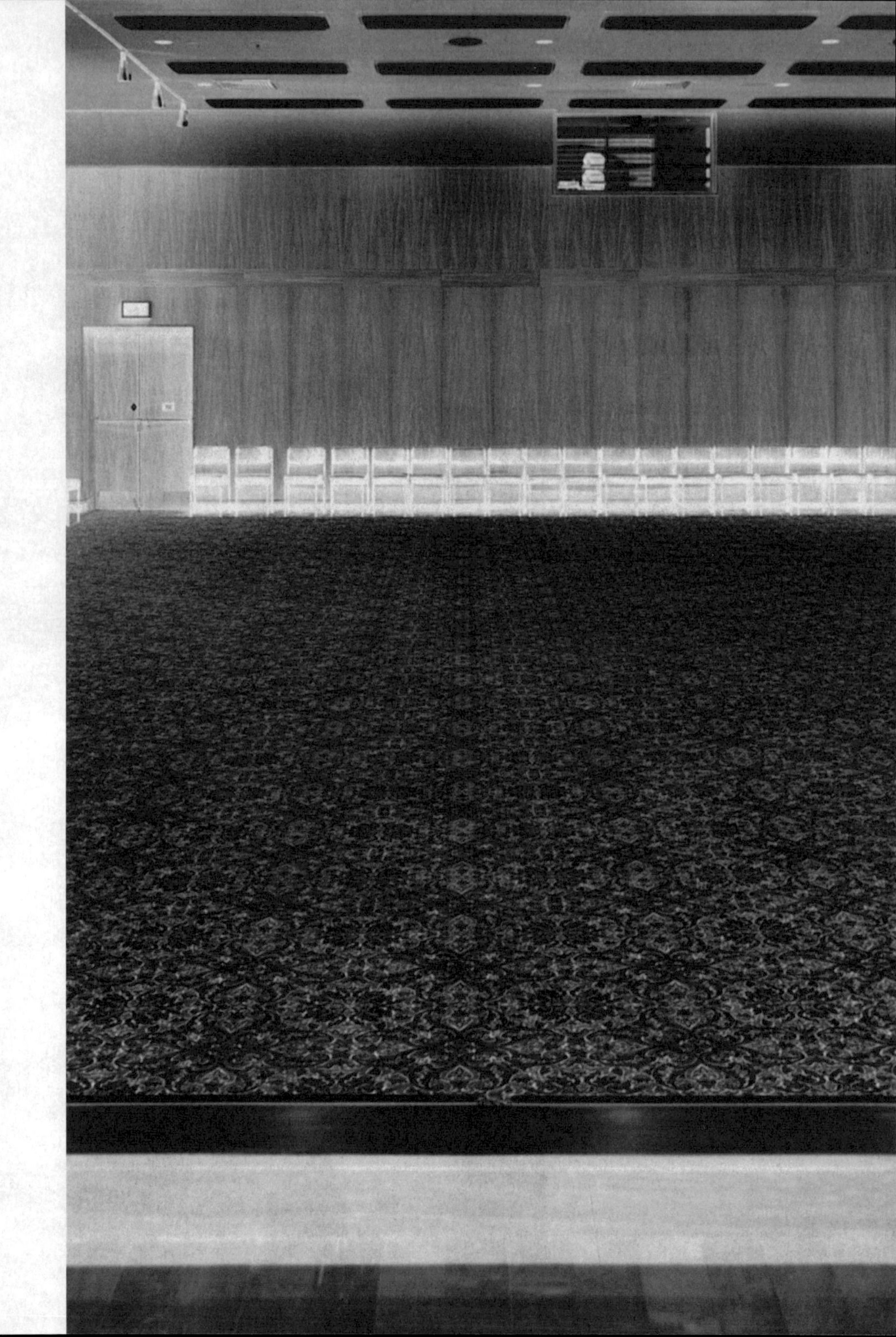

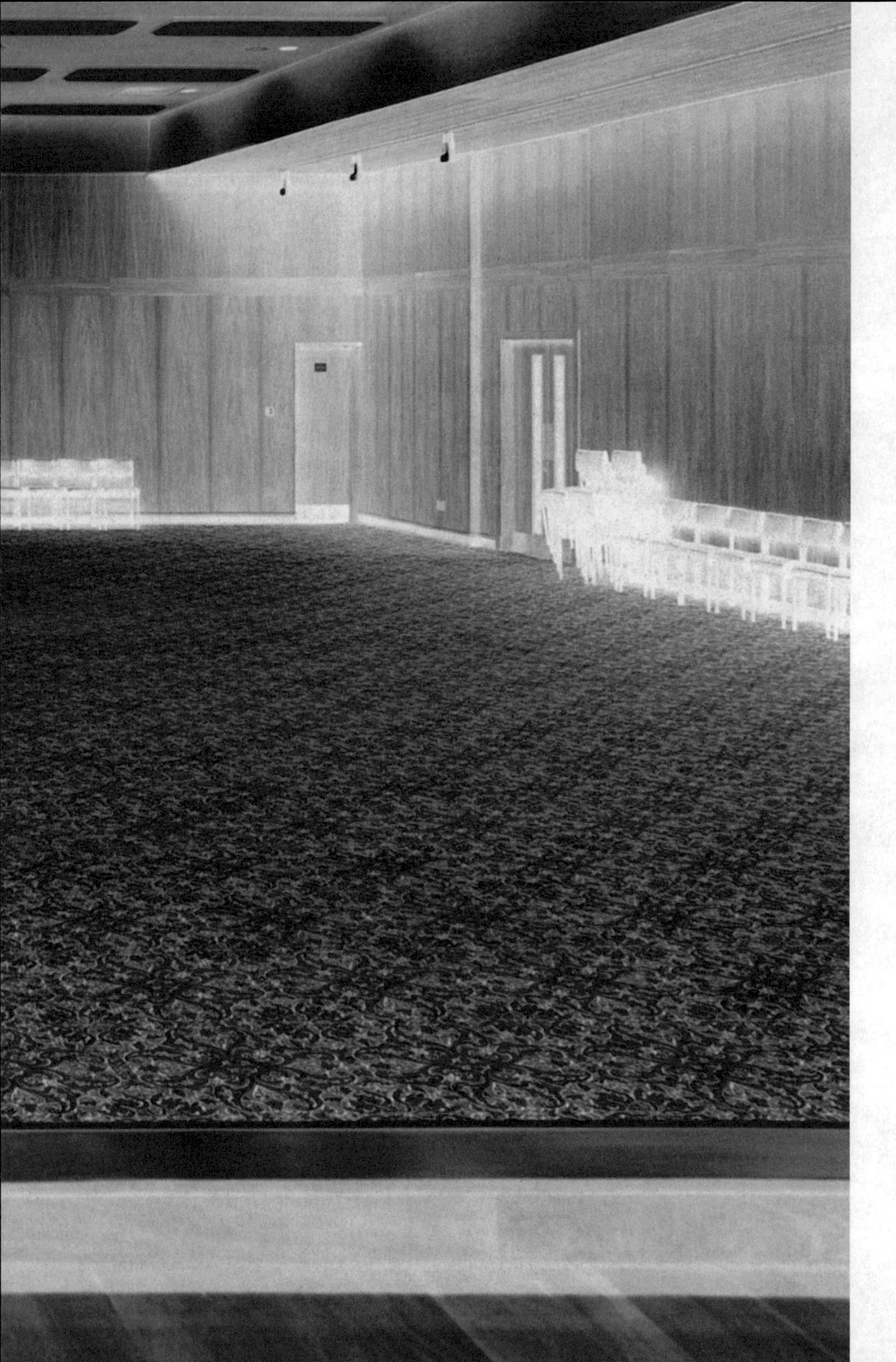

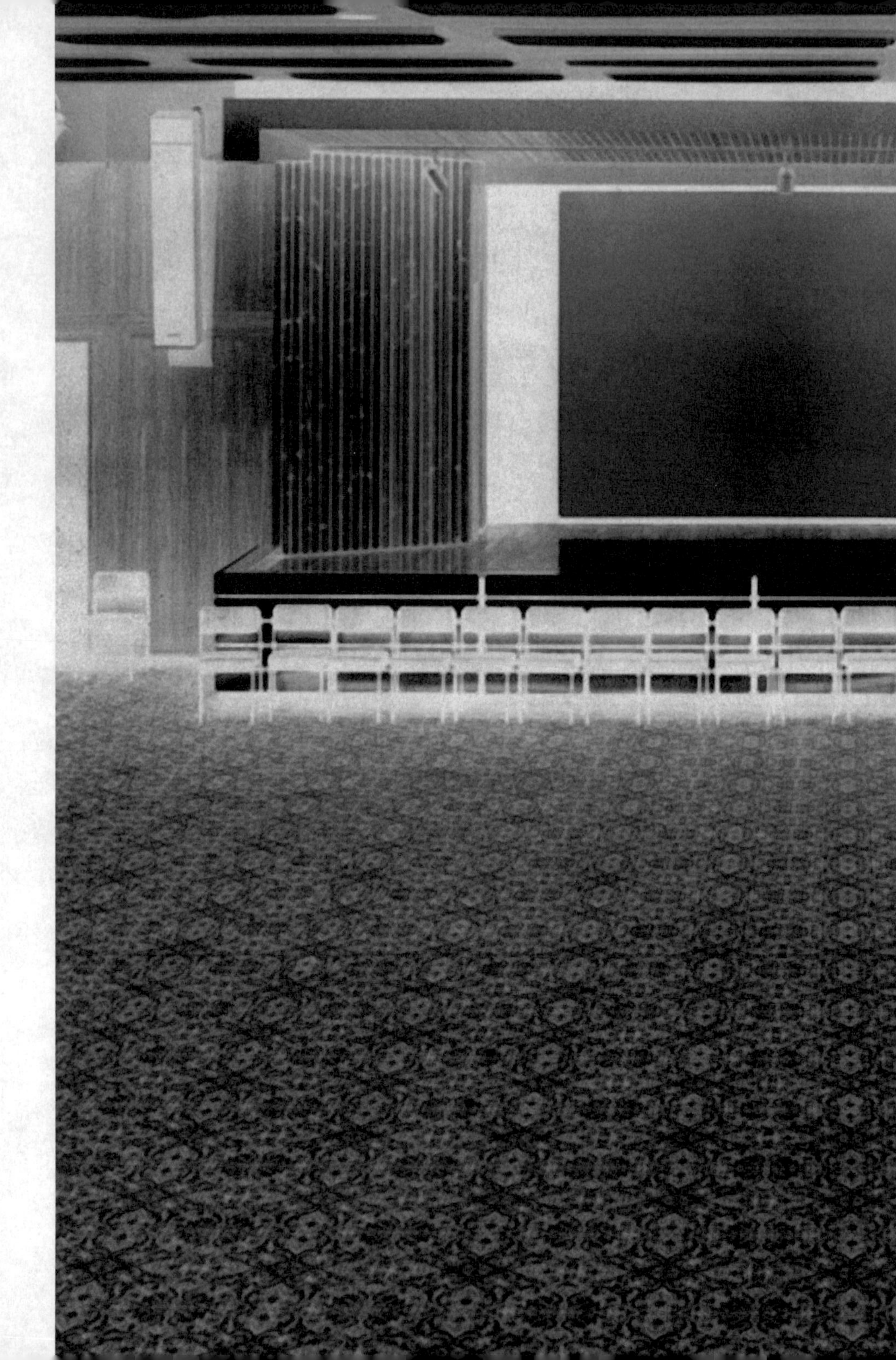

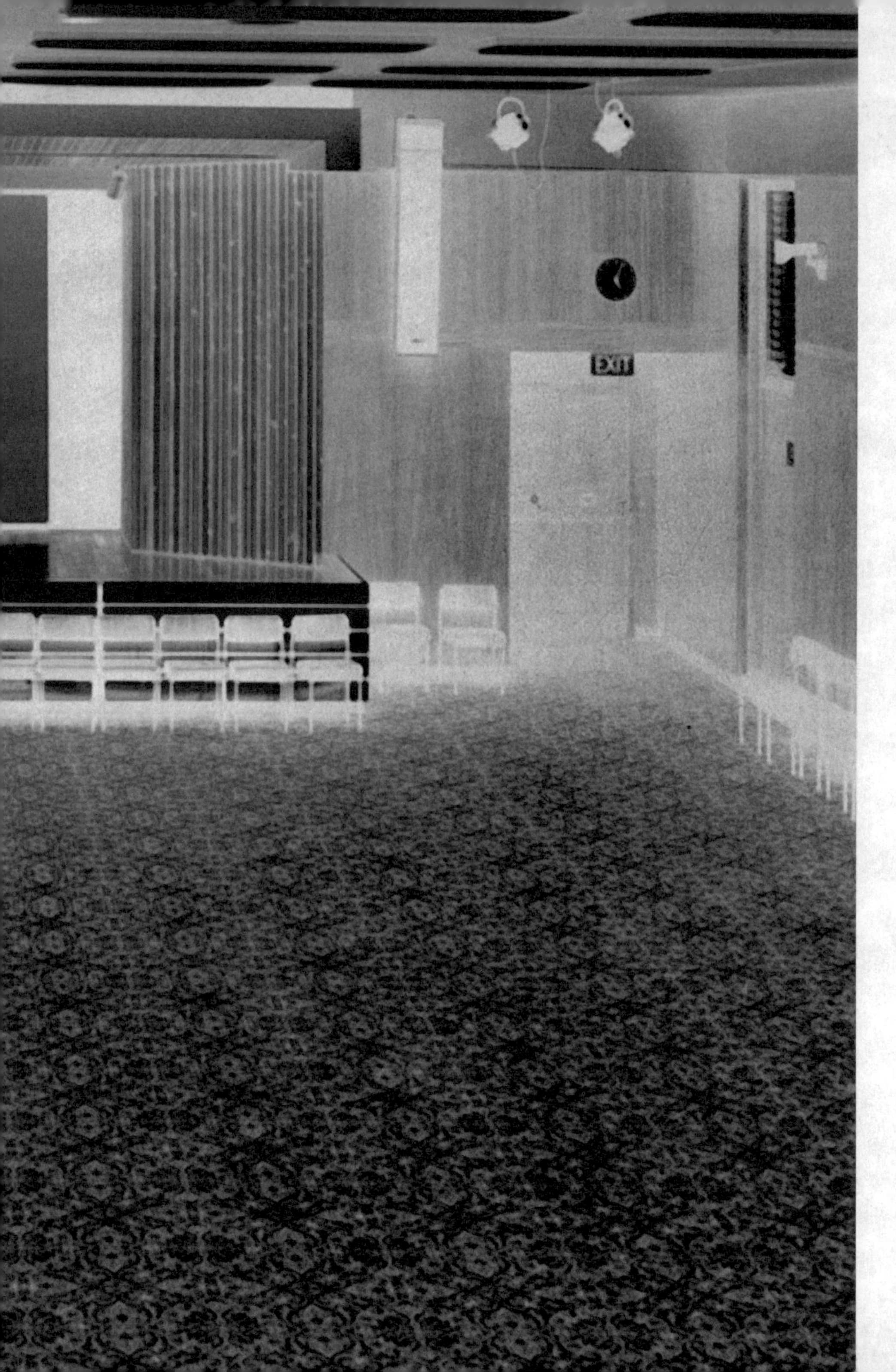
EXIT

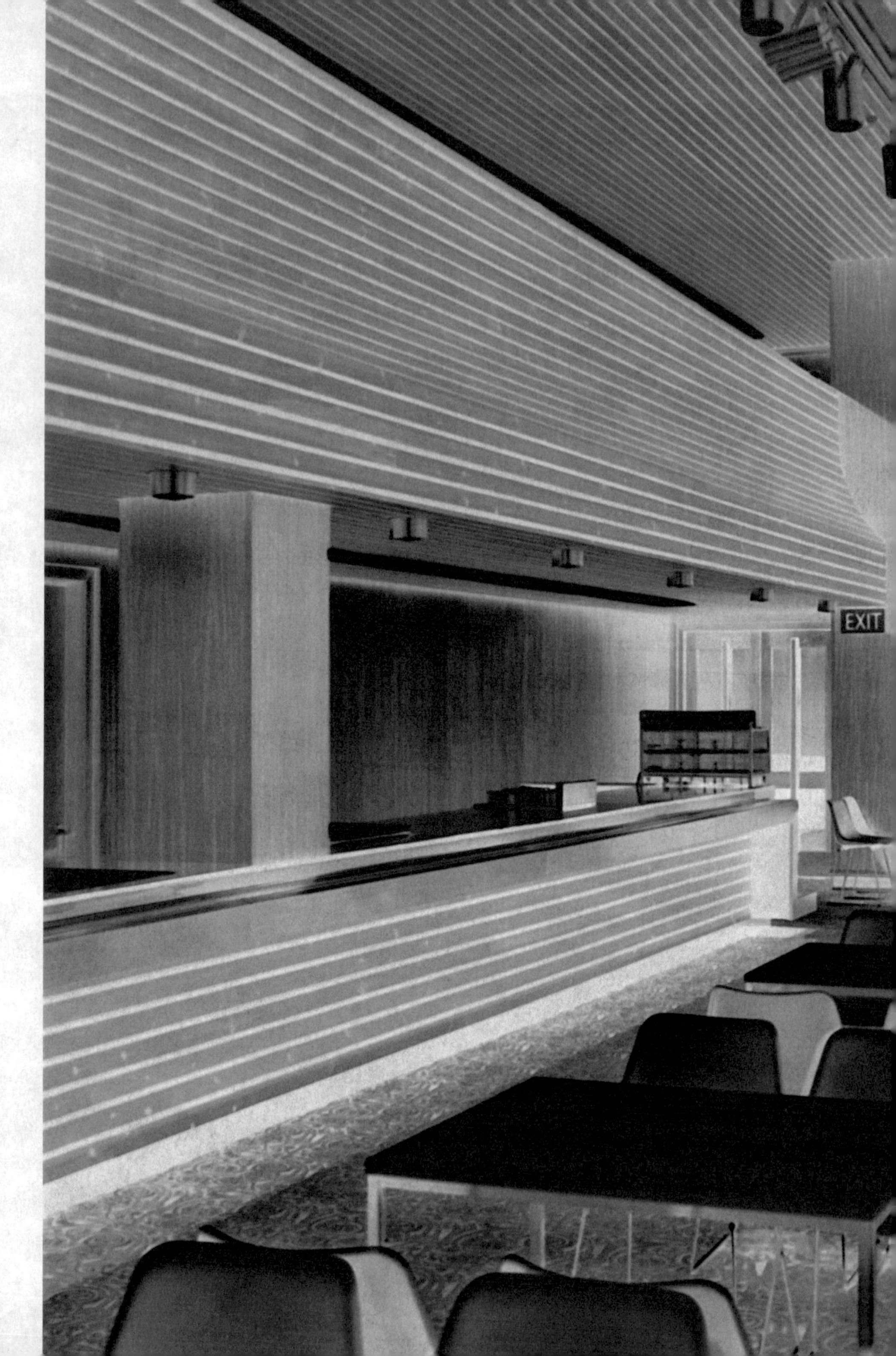

EXIT

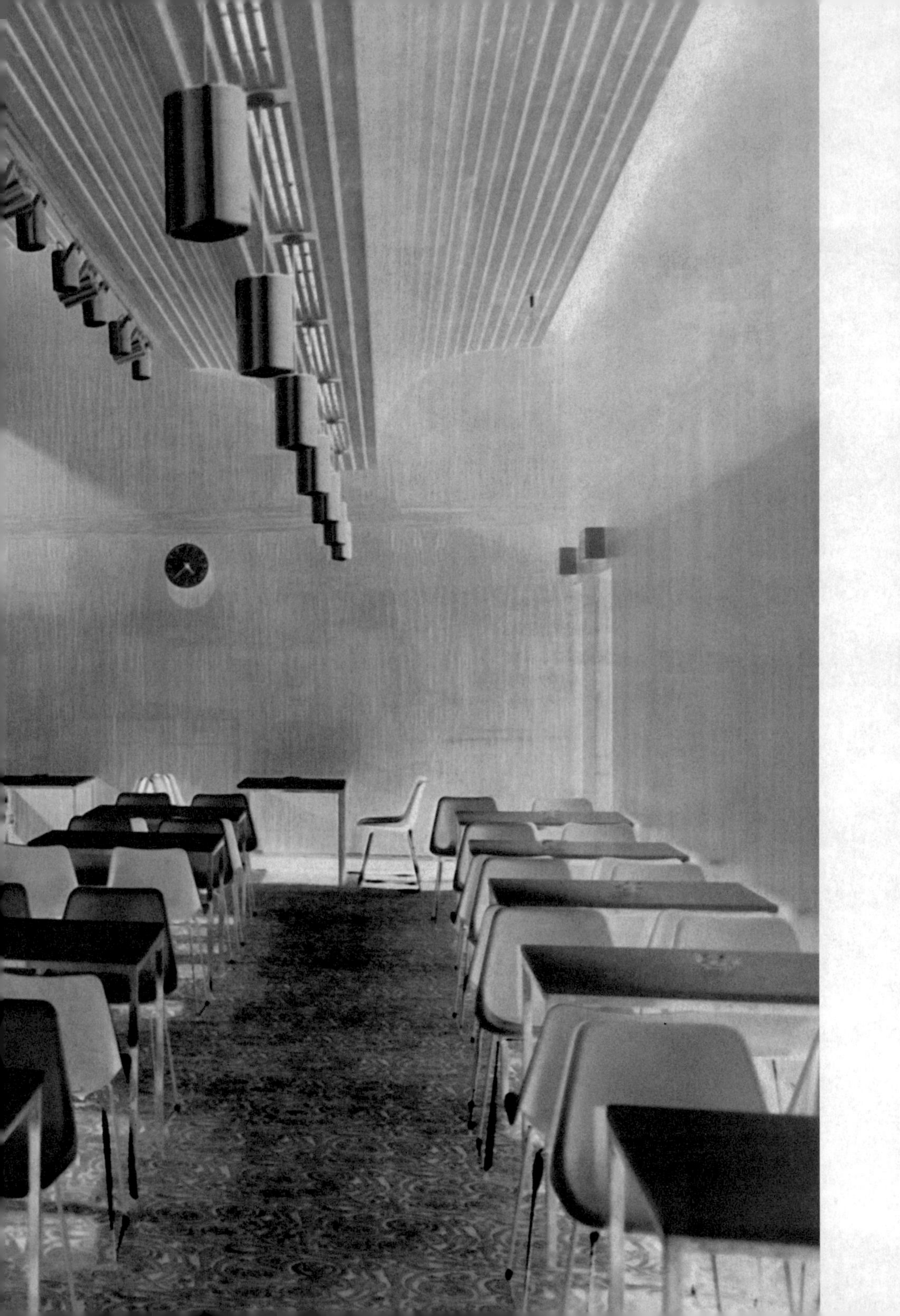

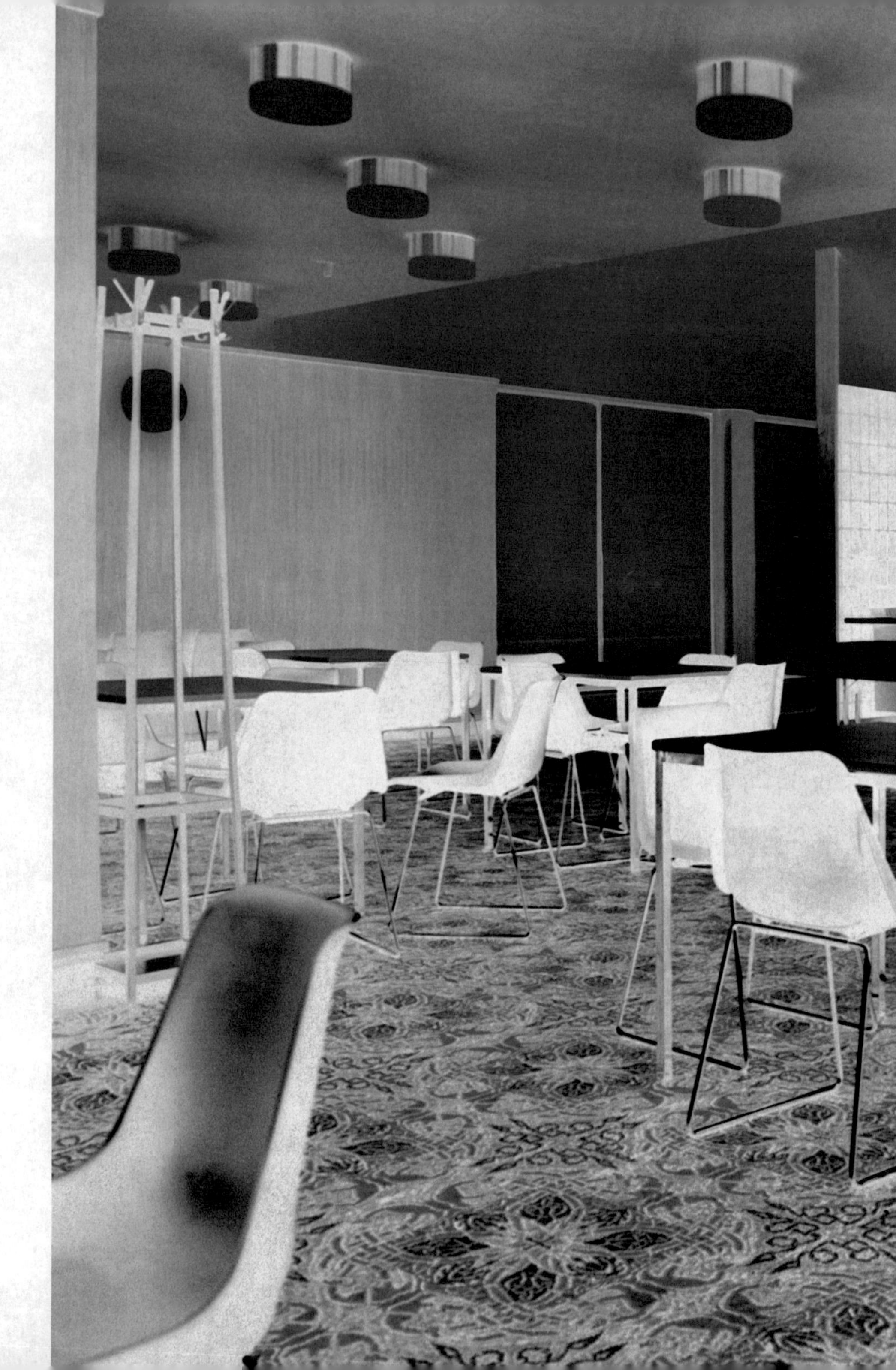

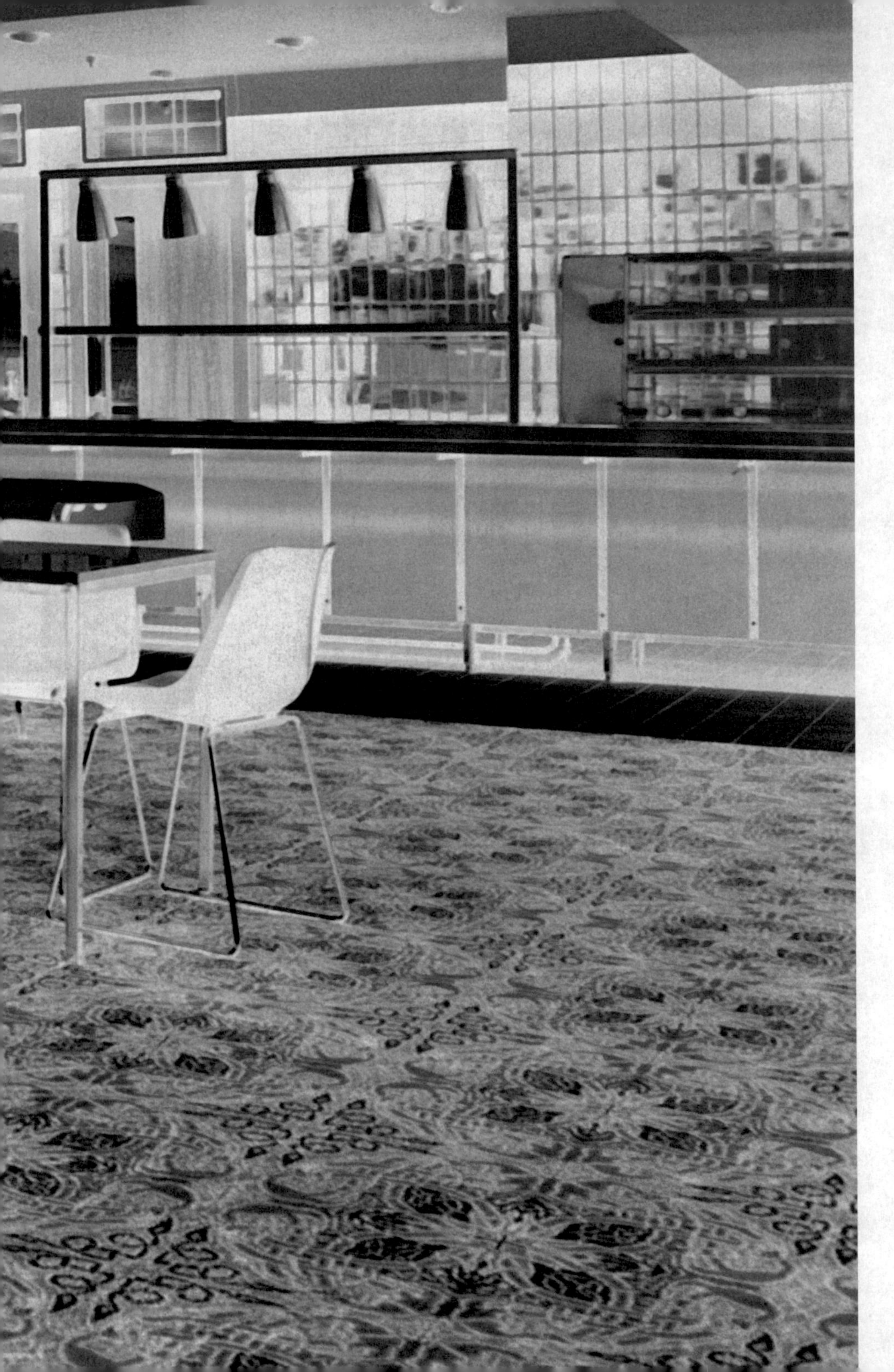

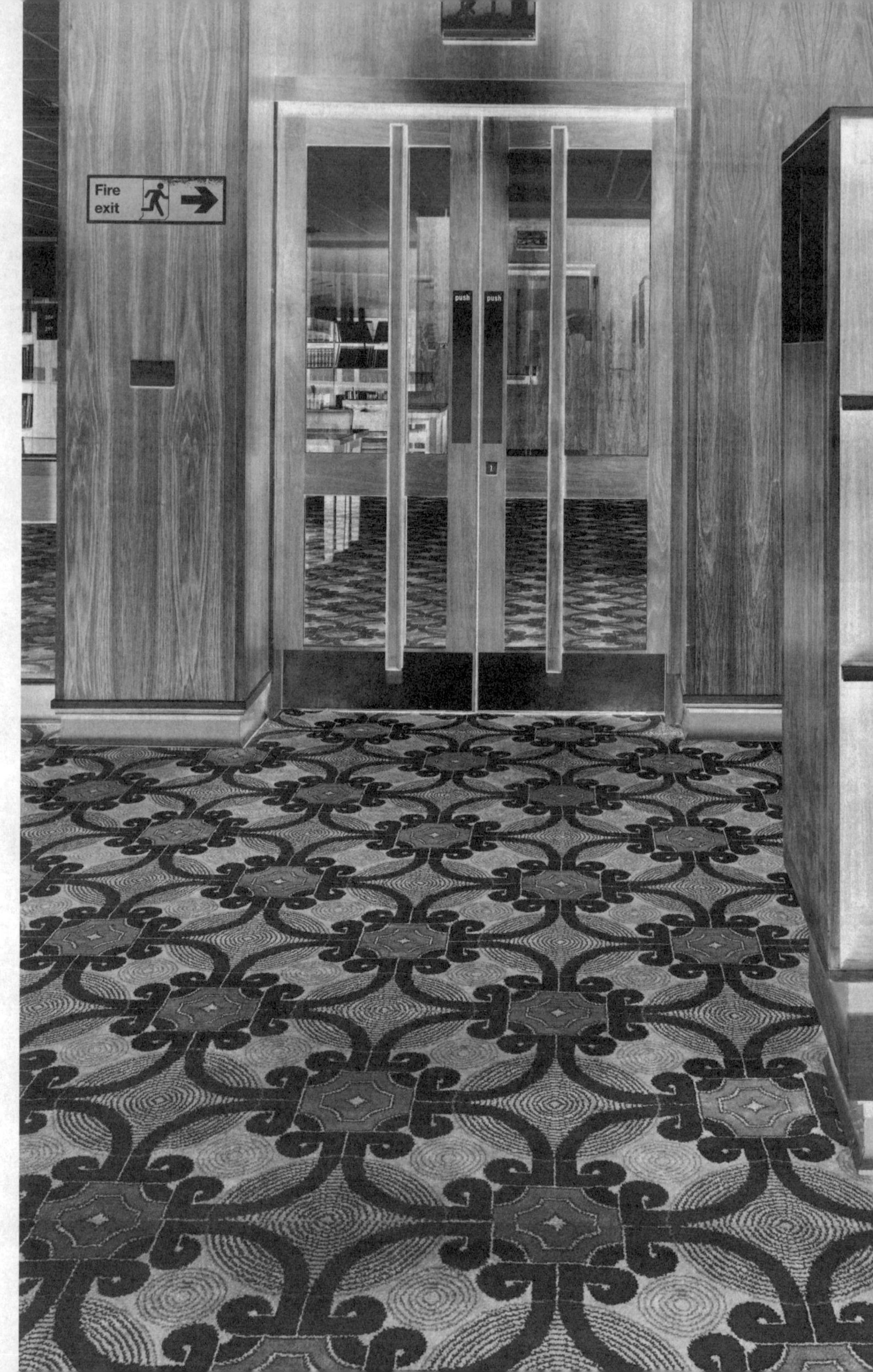
Fire
exit
push push

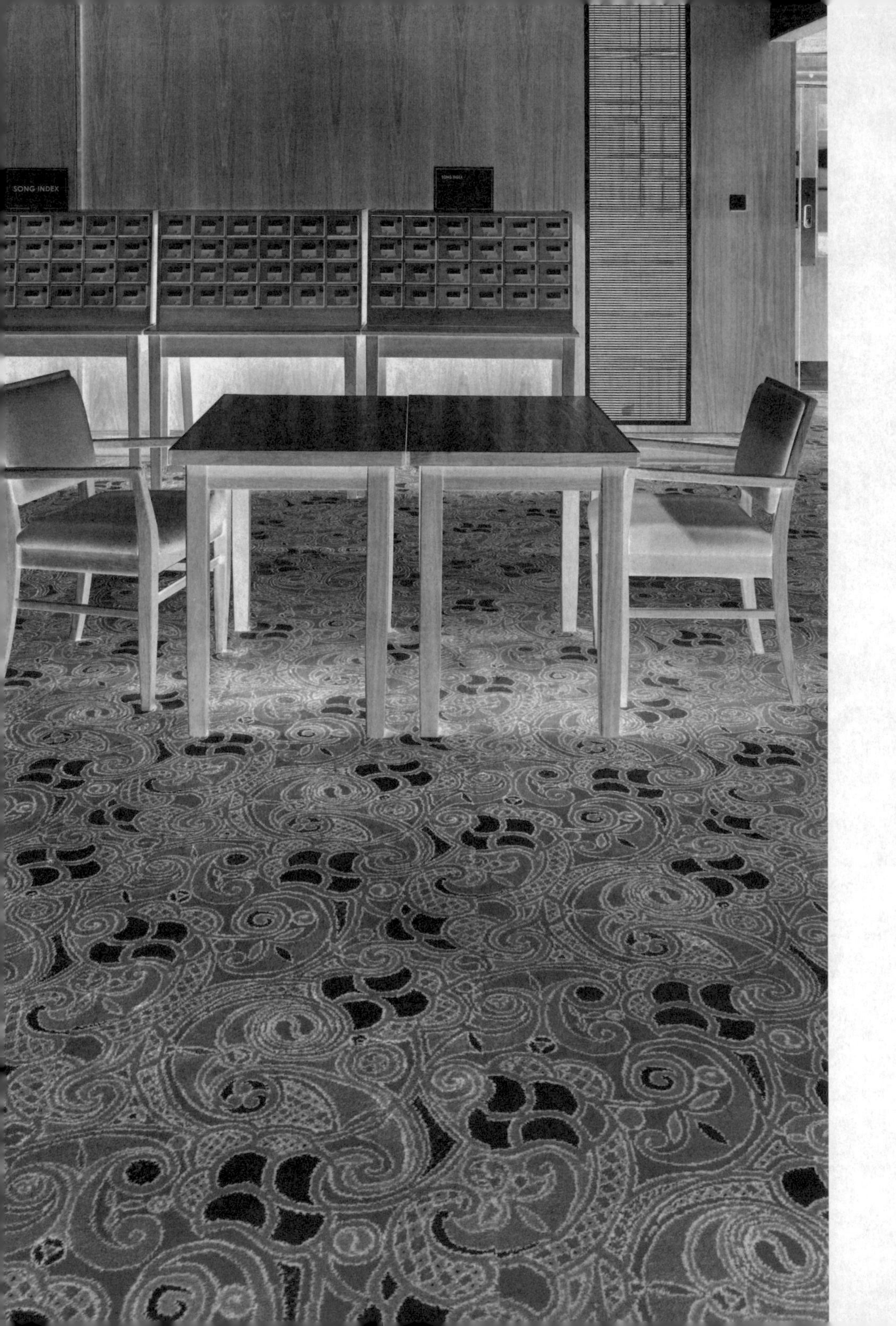

SONG INDEX
SONG INDEX

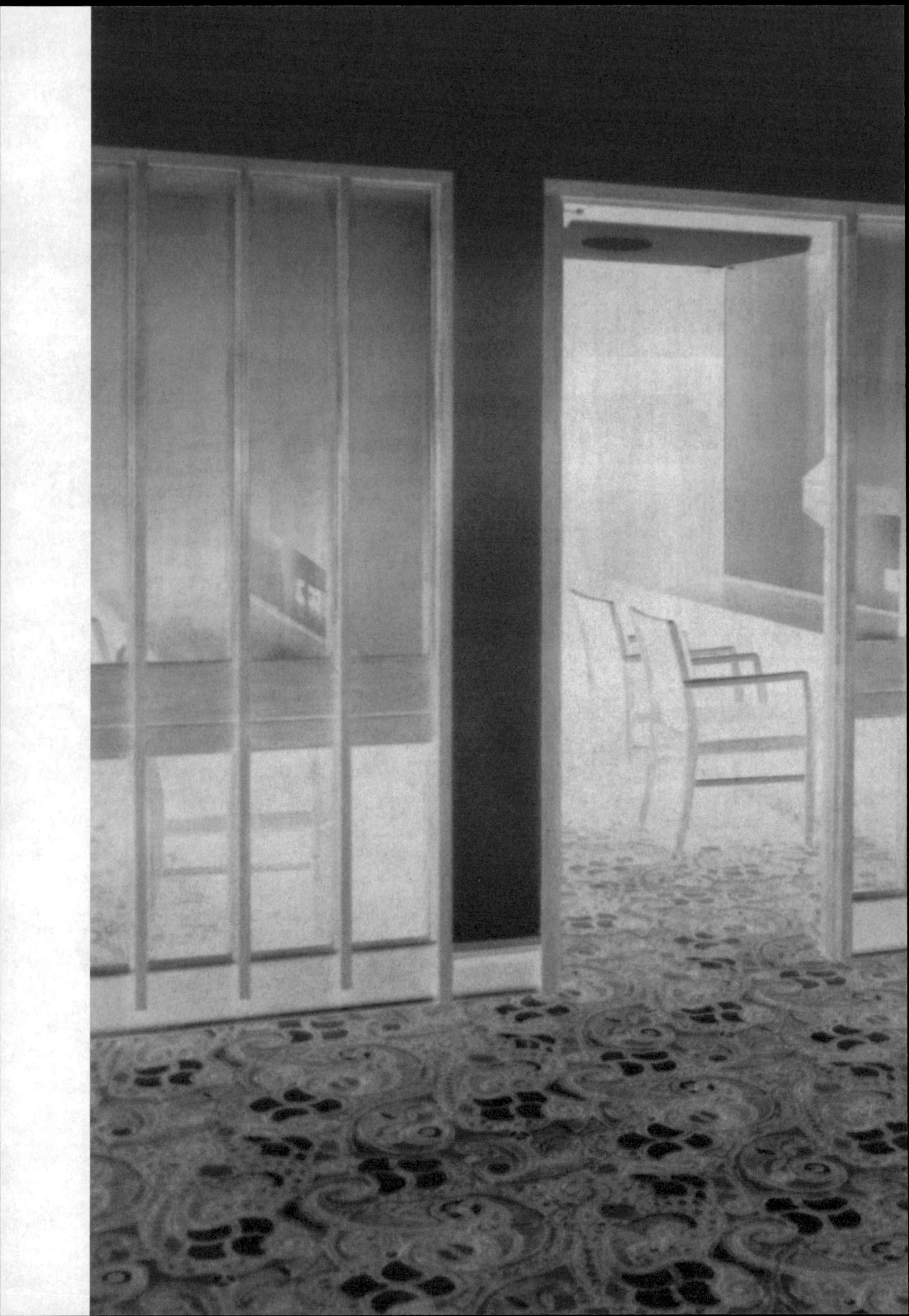

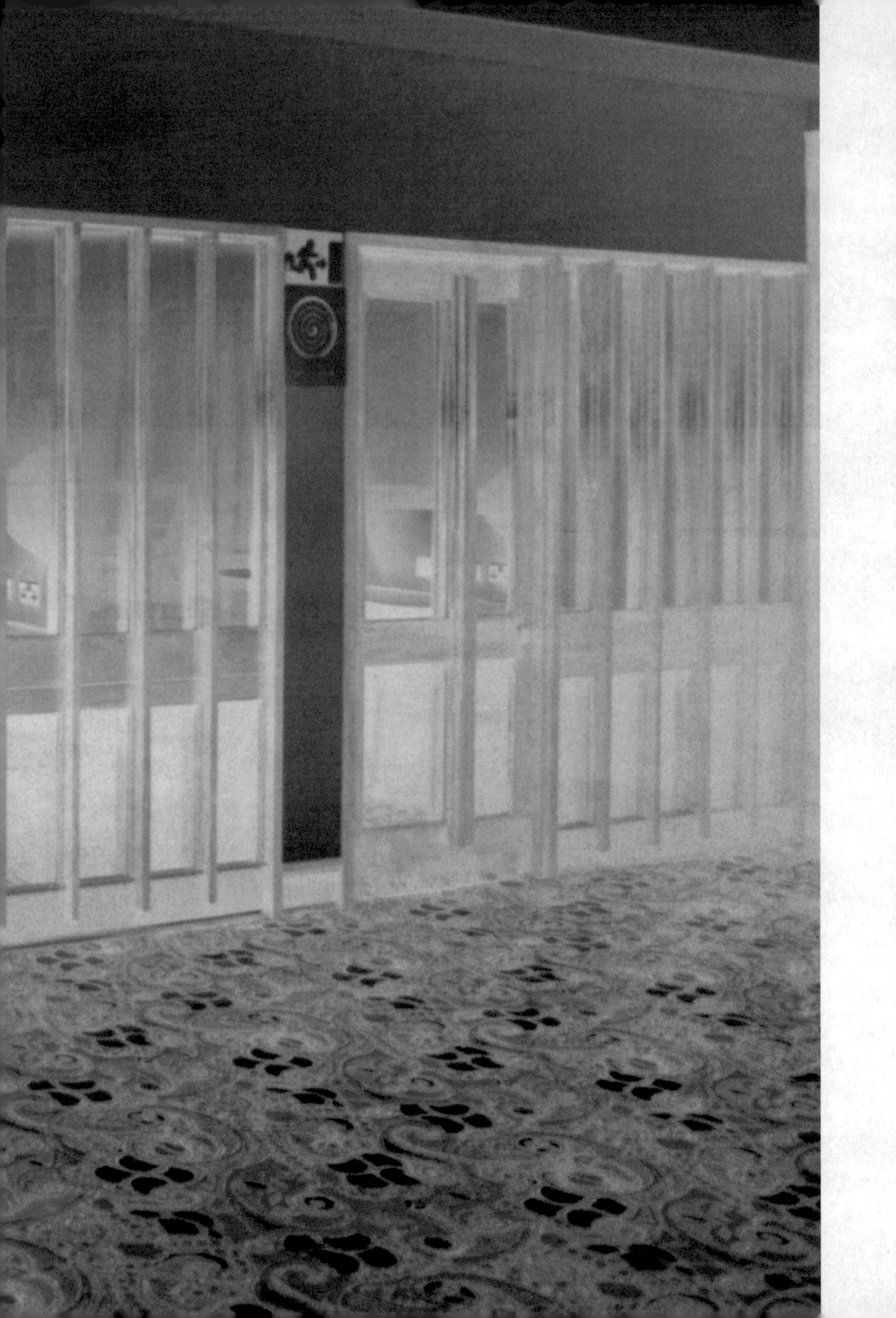

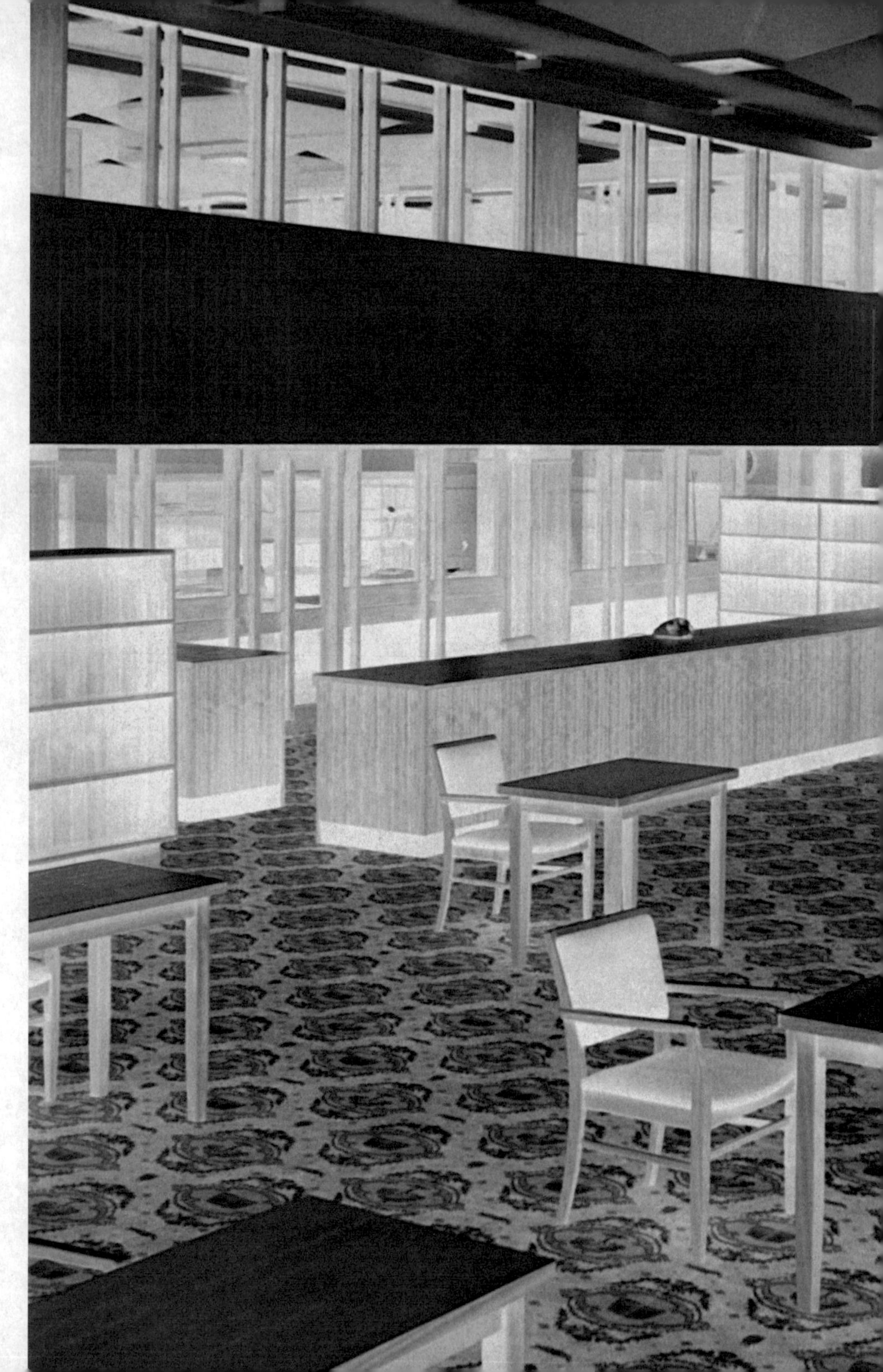

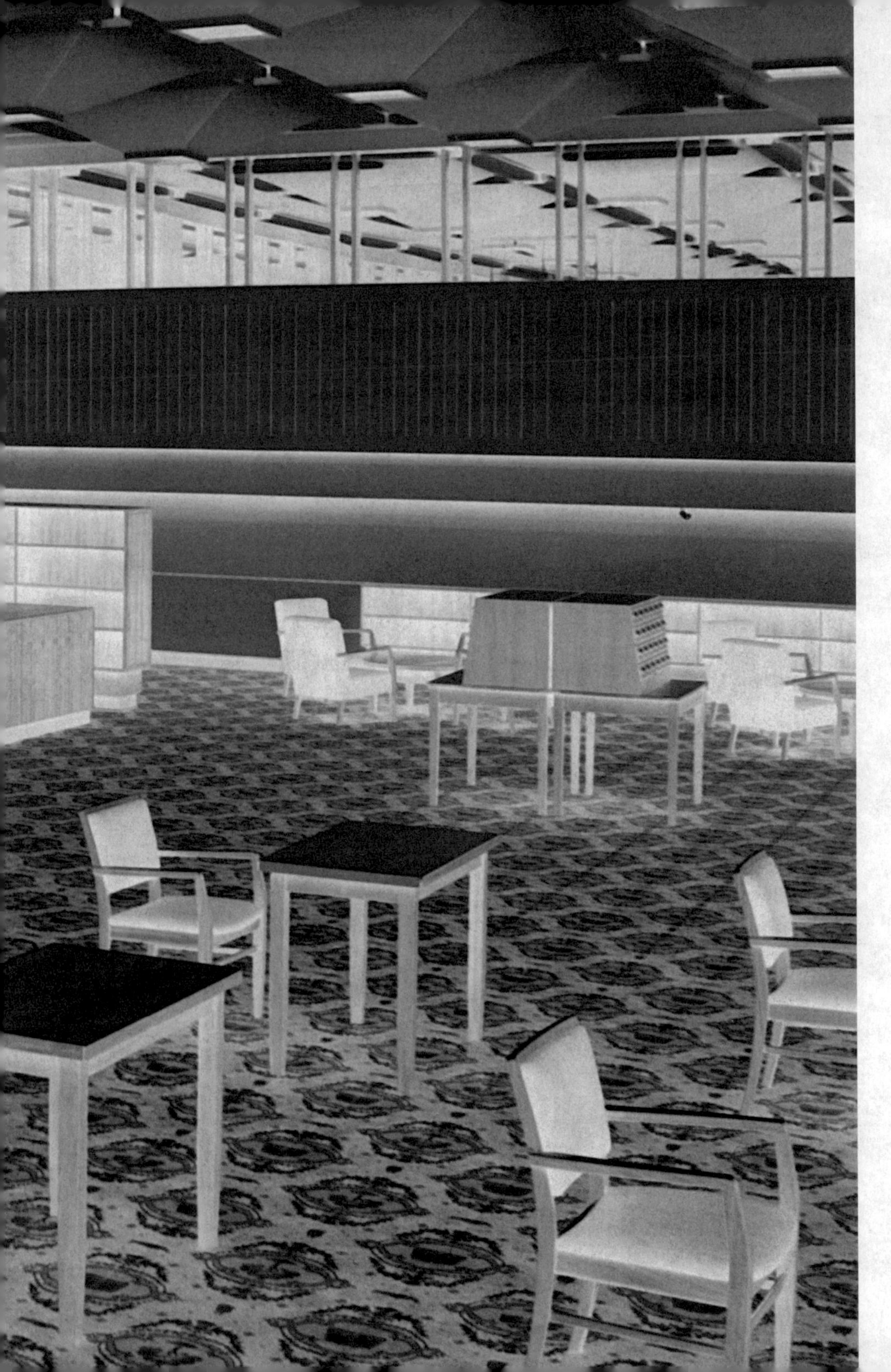

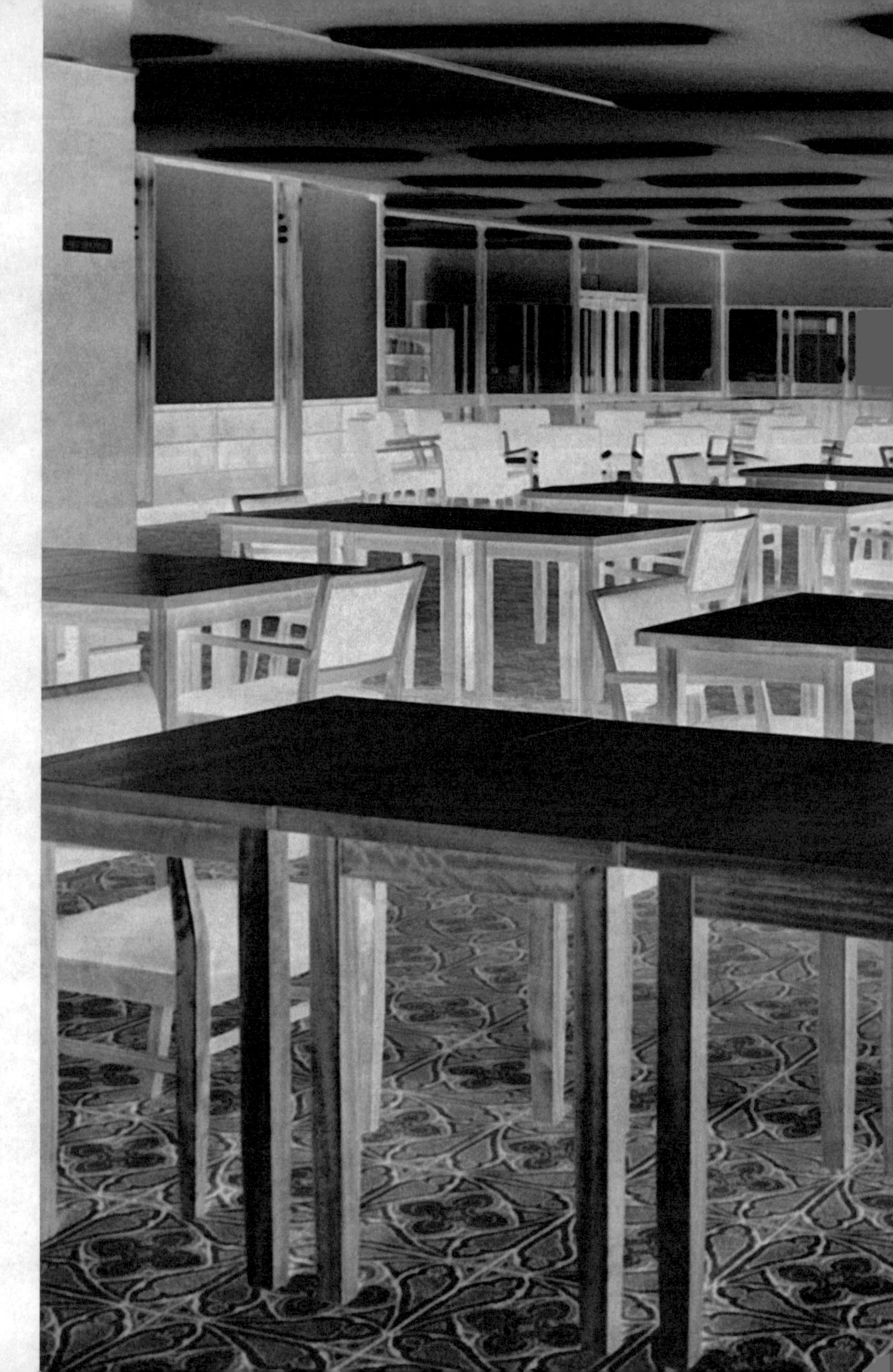

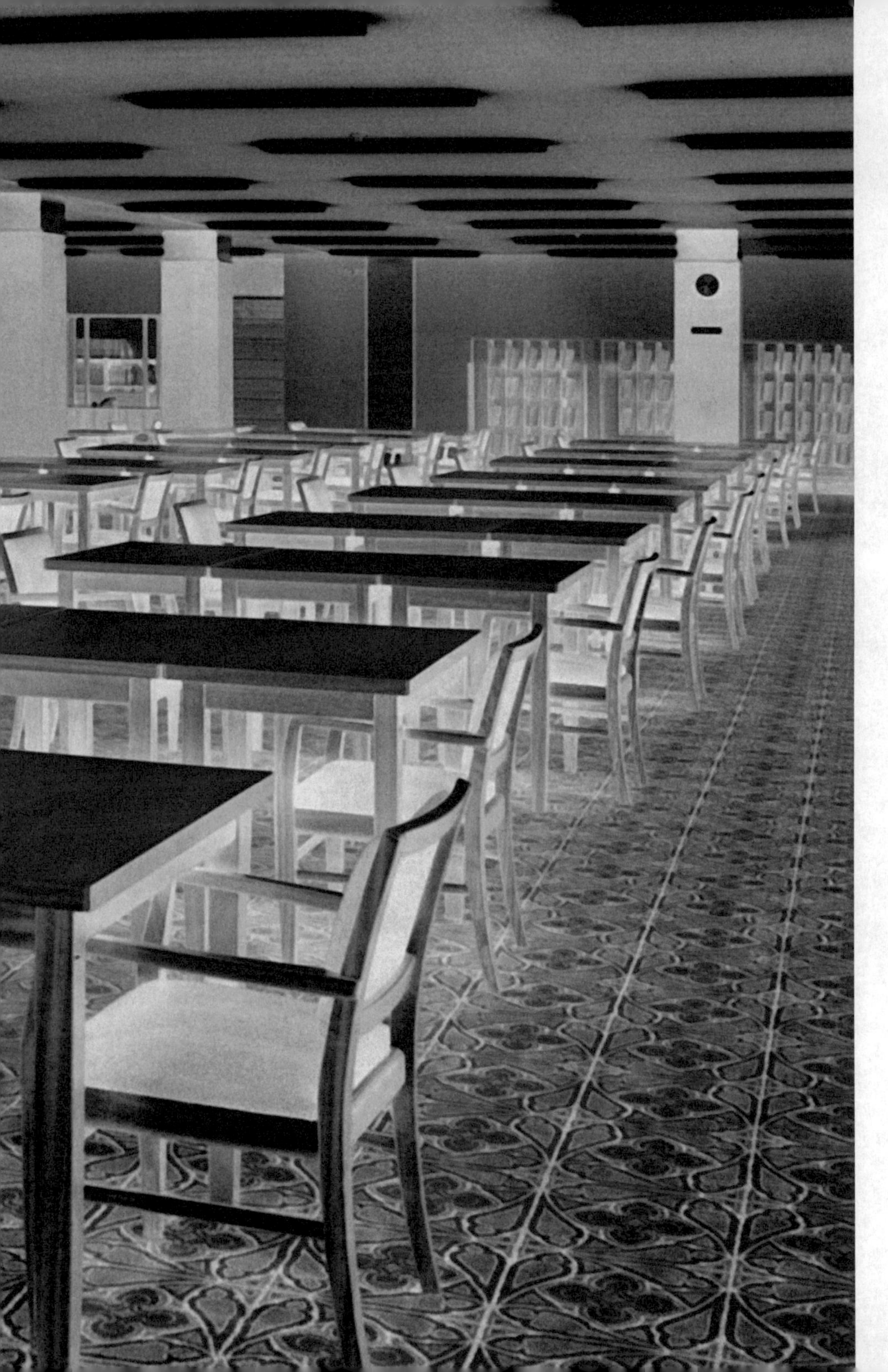

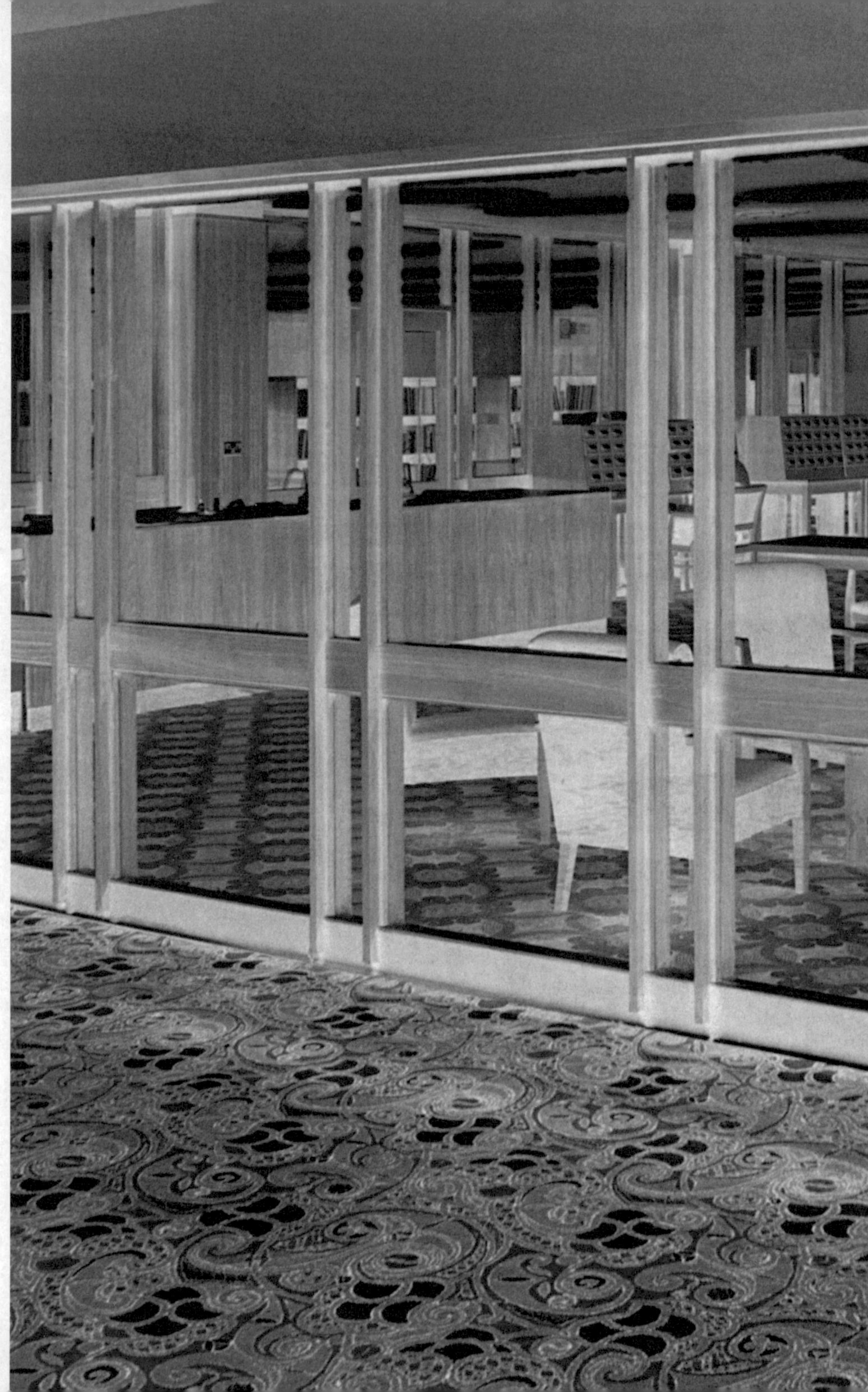

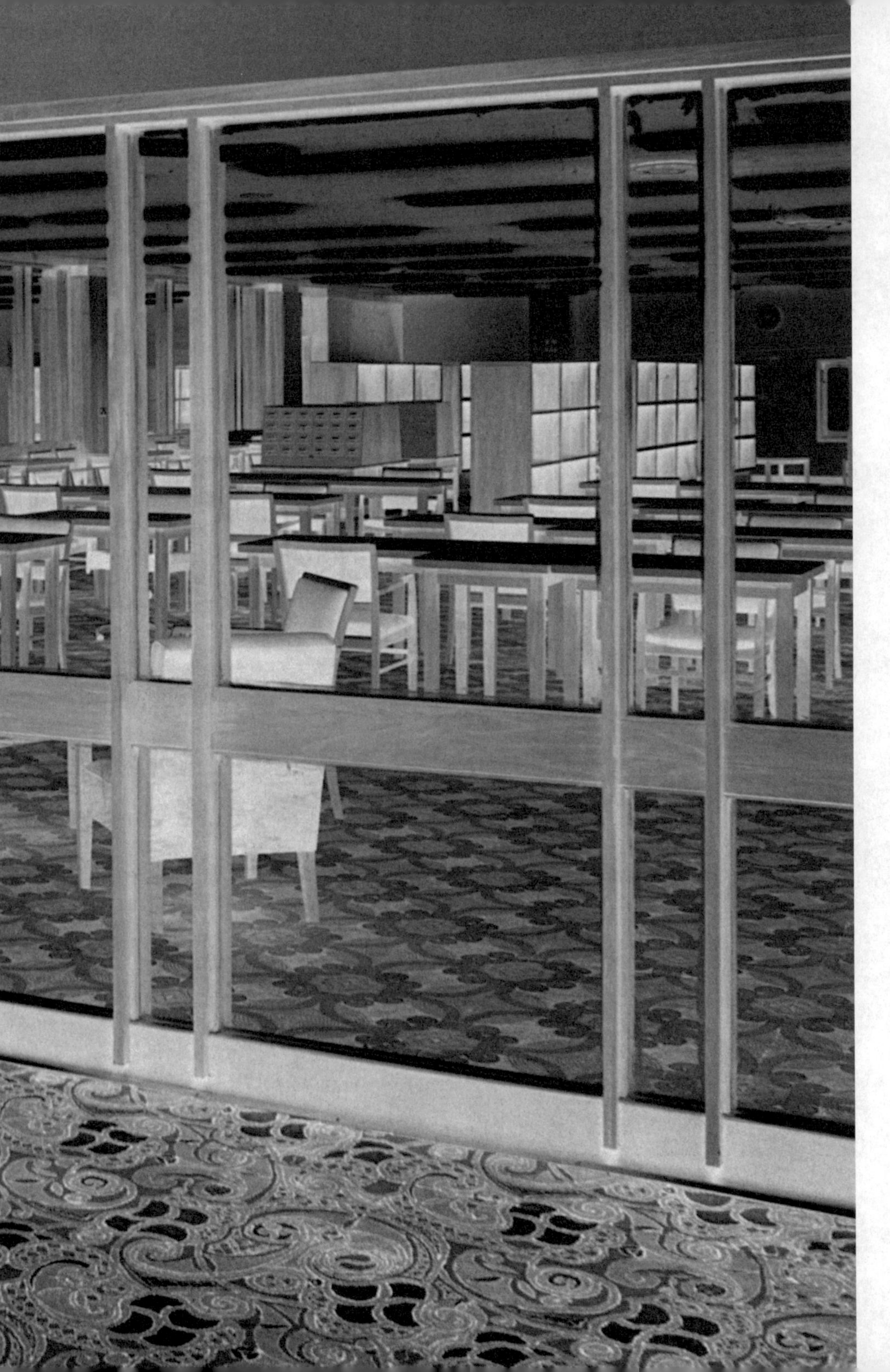

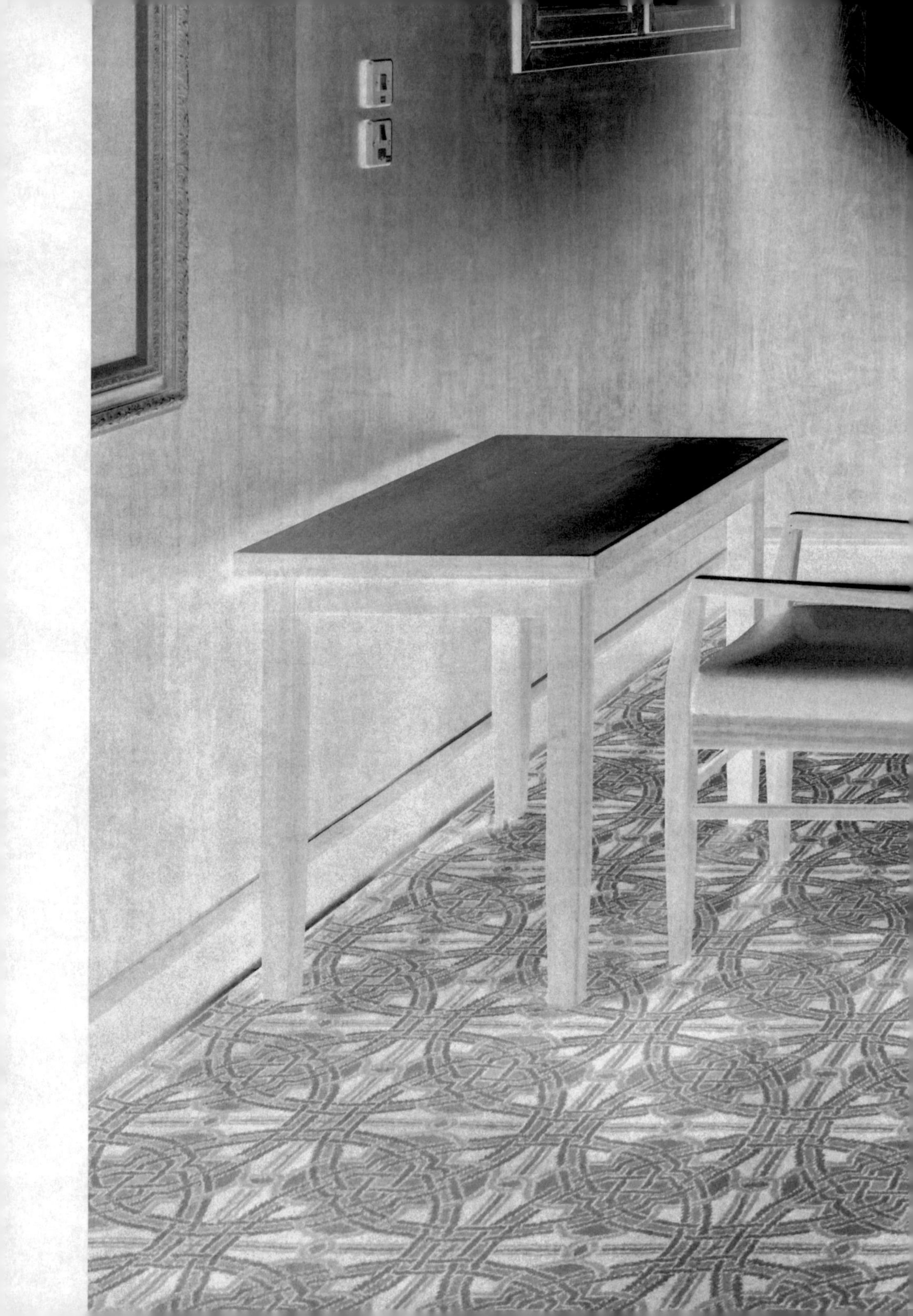

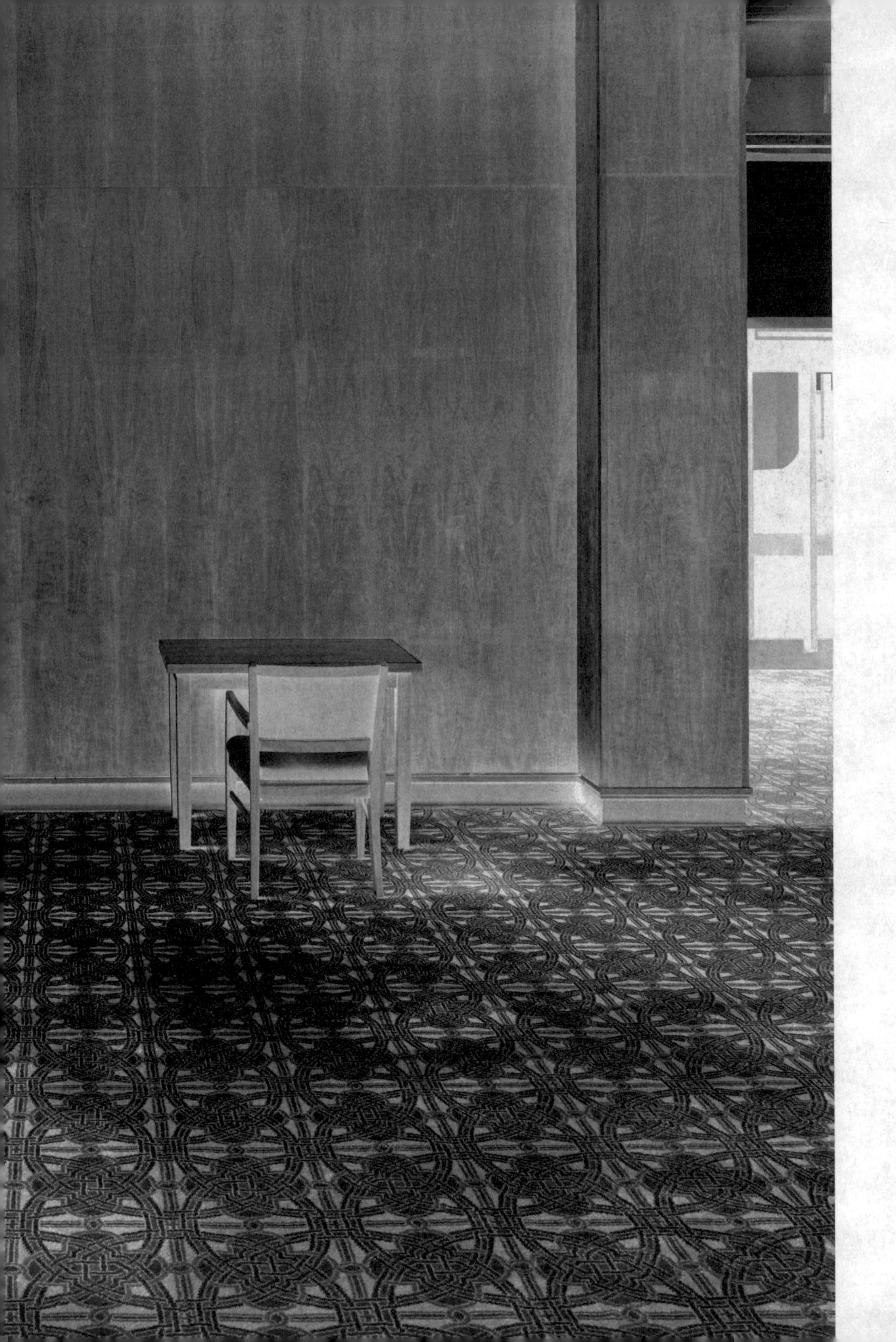

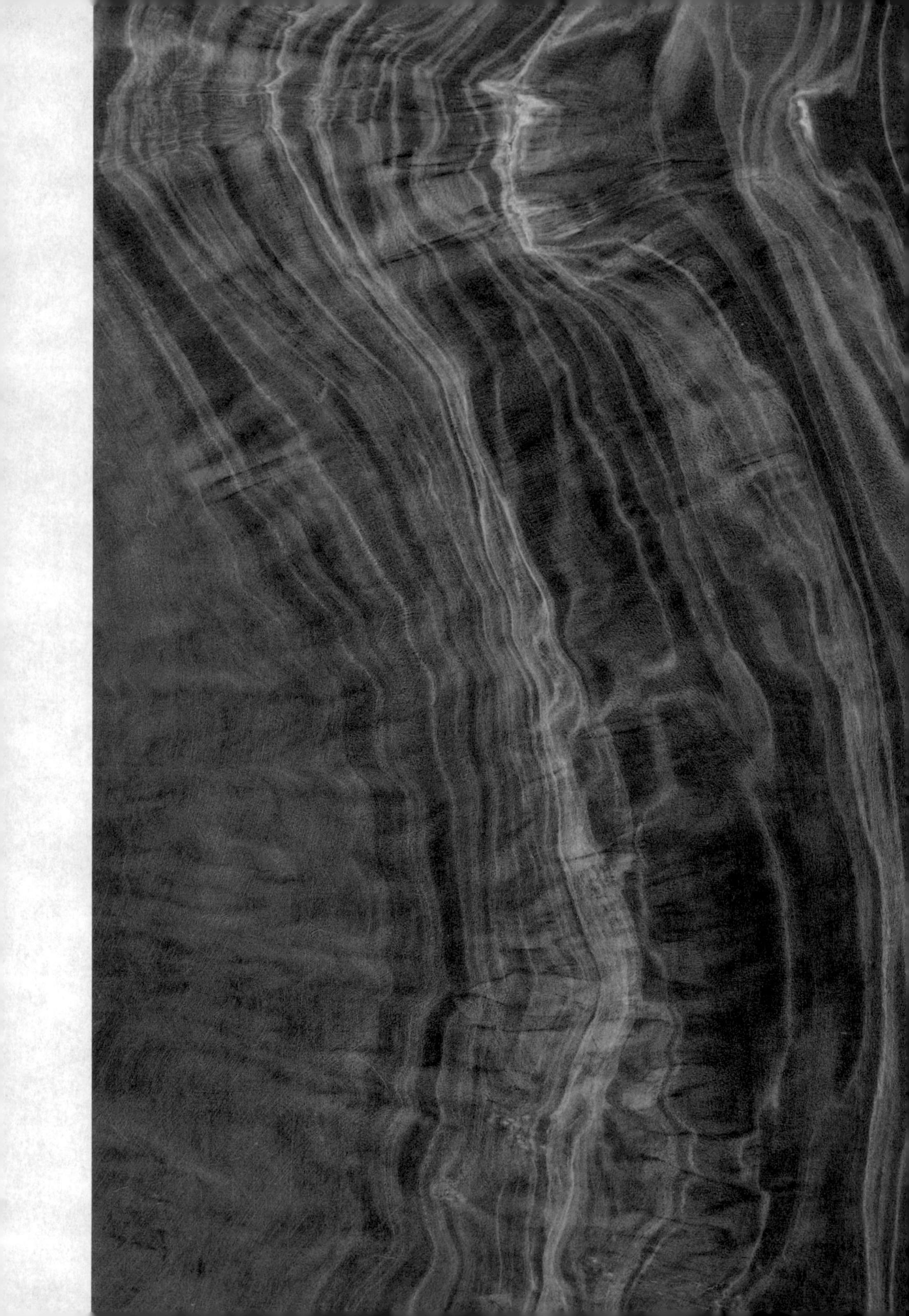

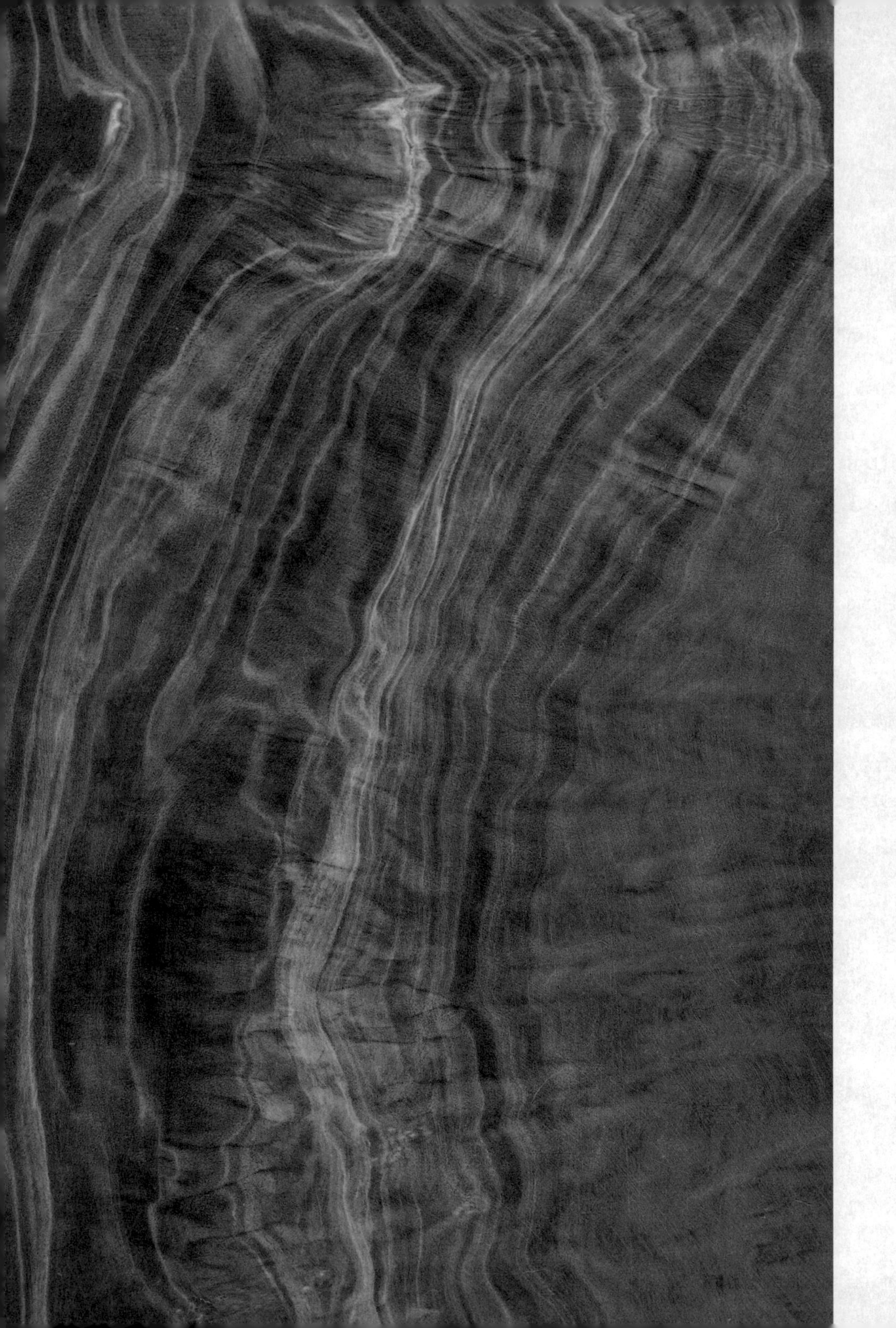

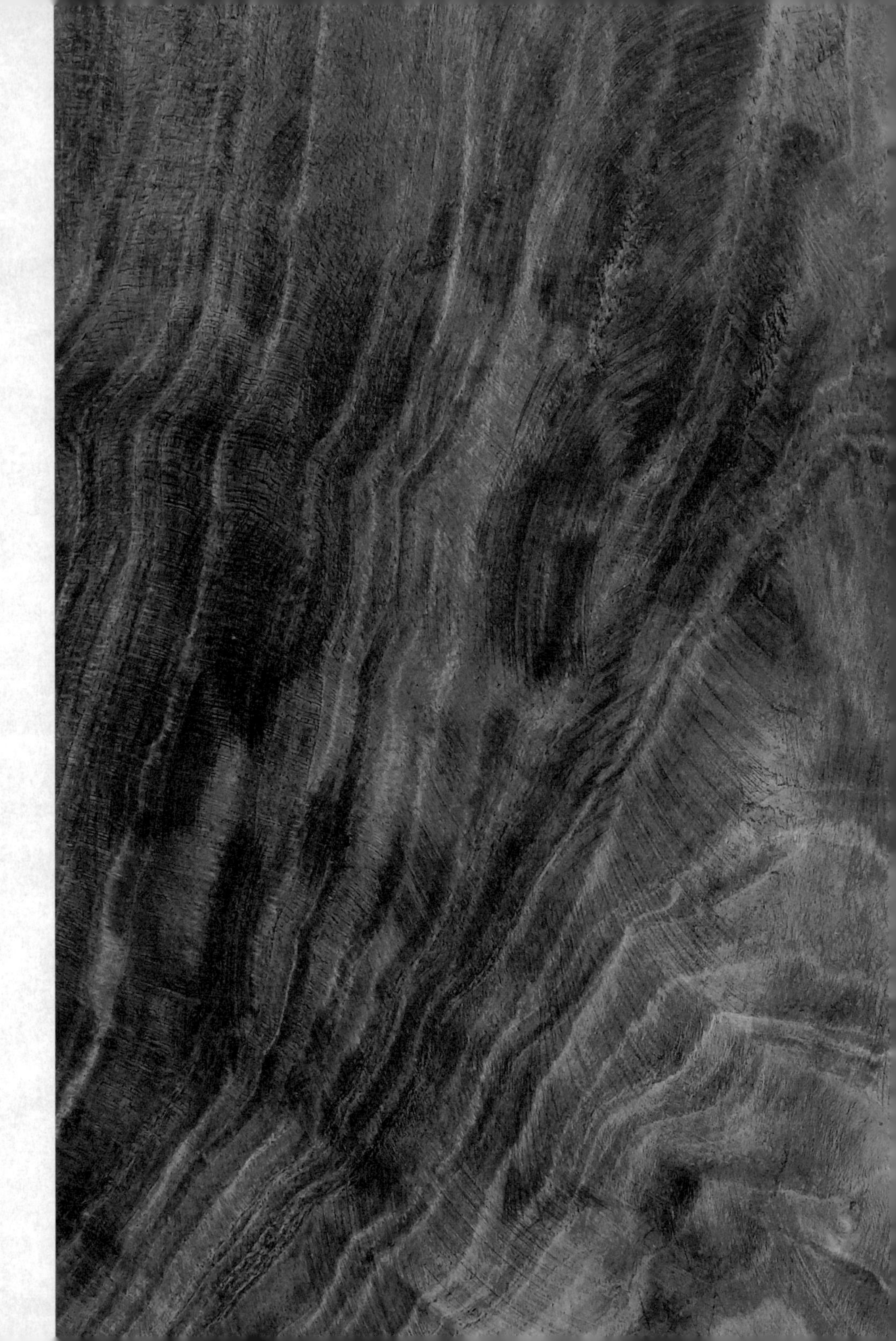

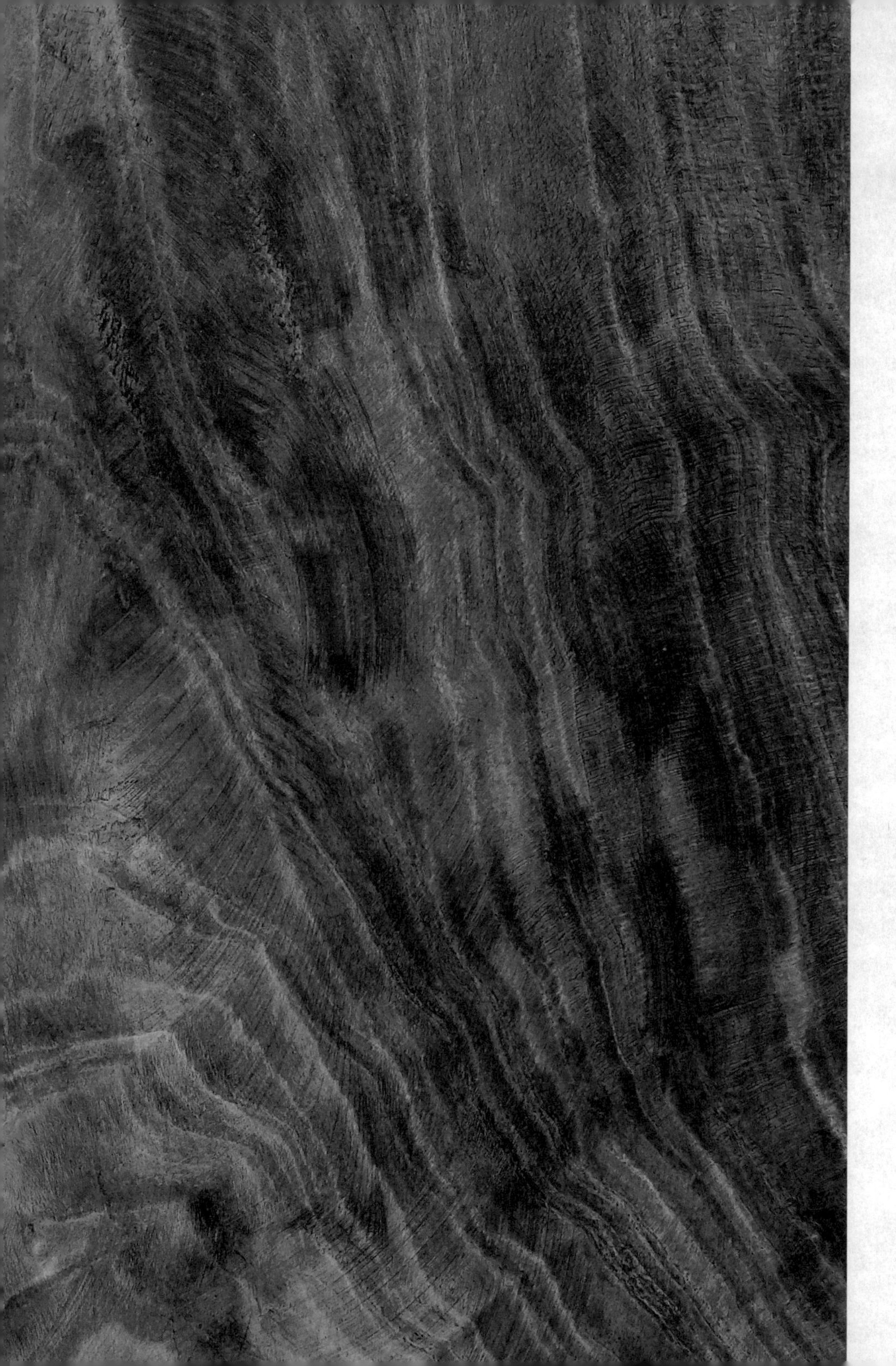

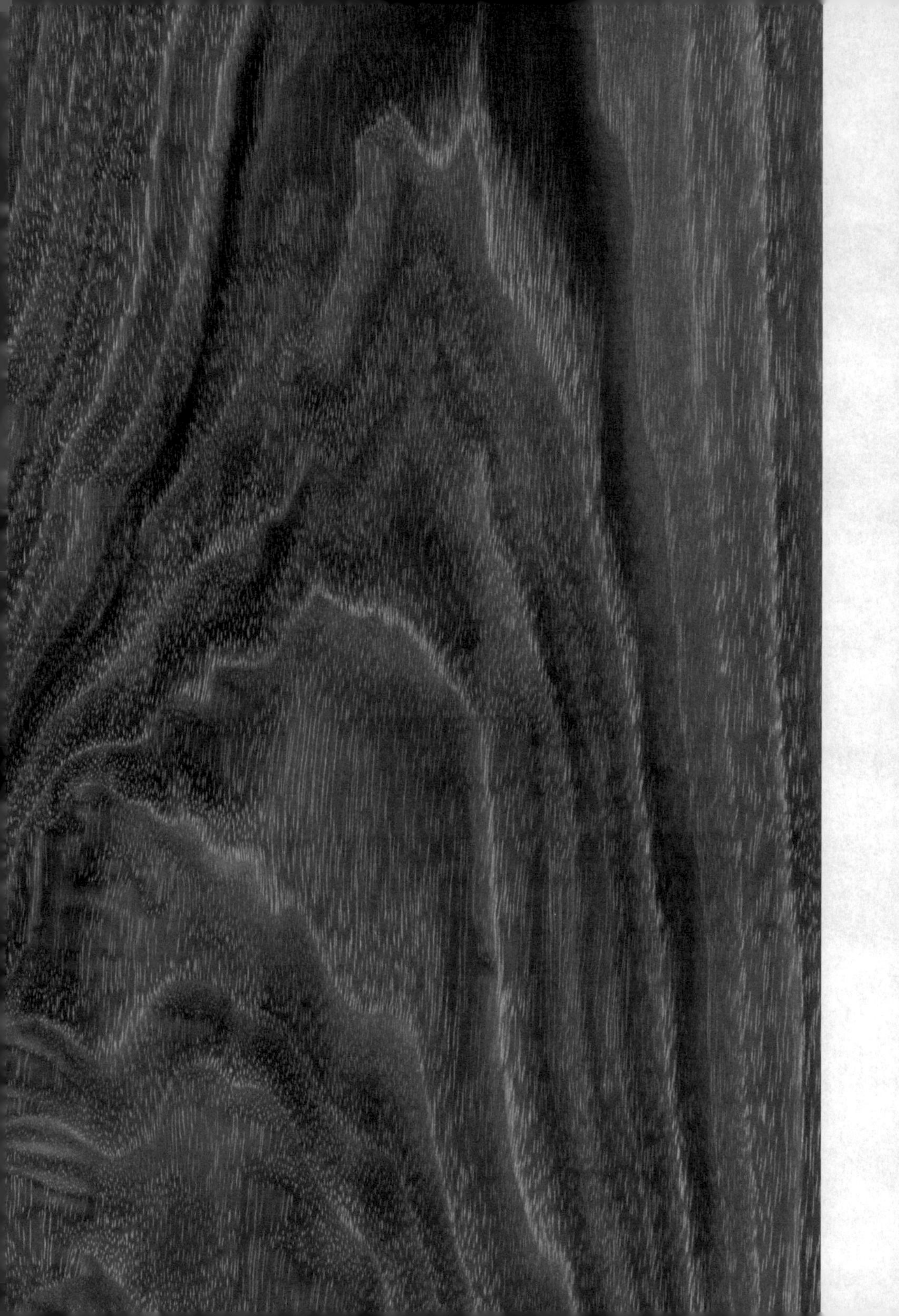

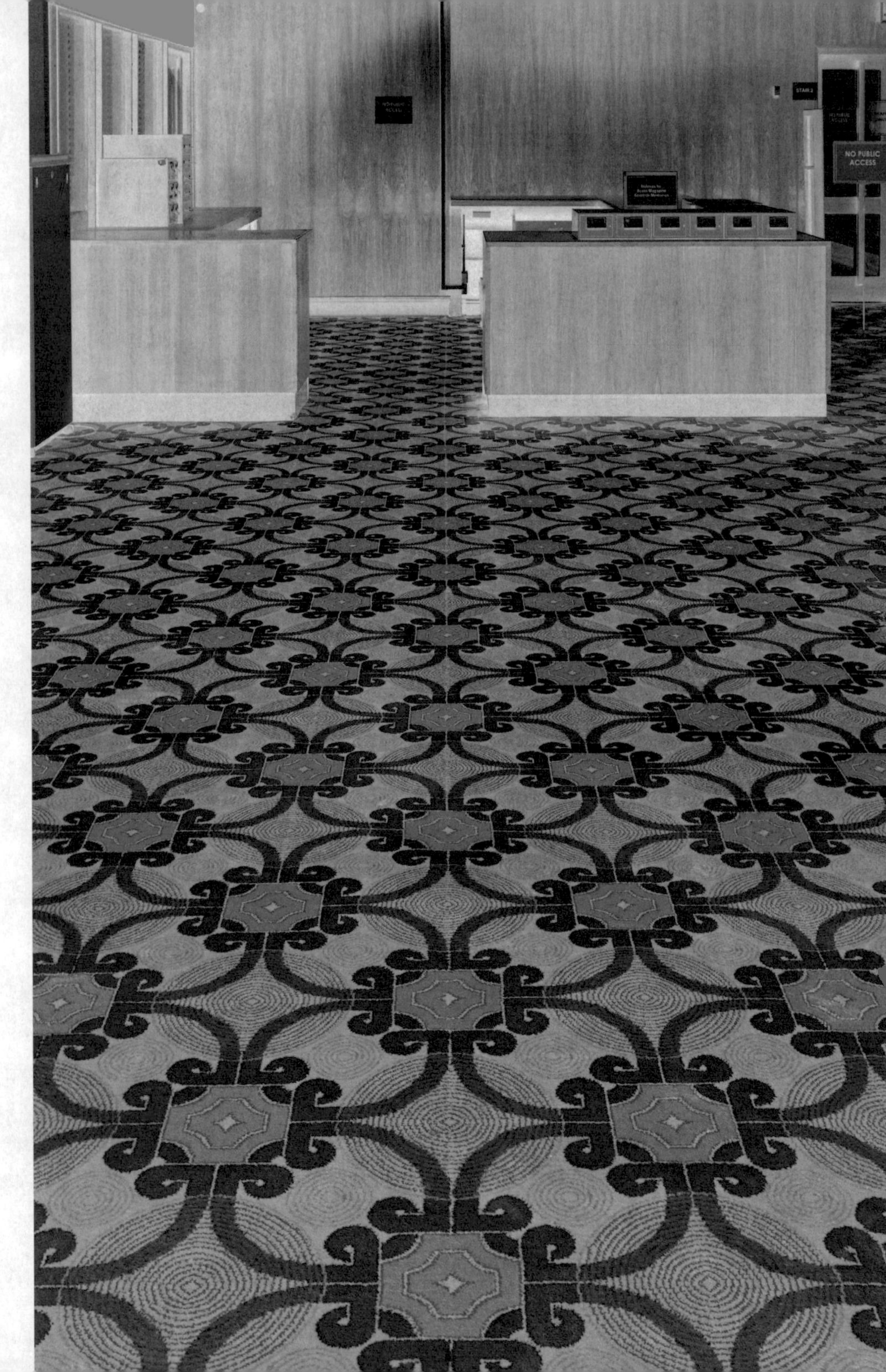

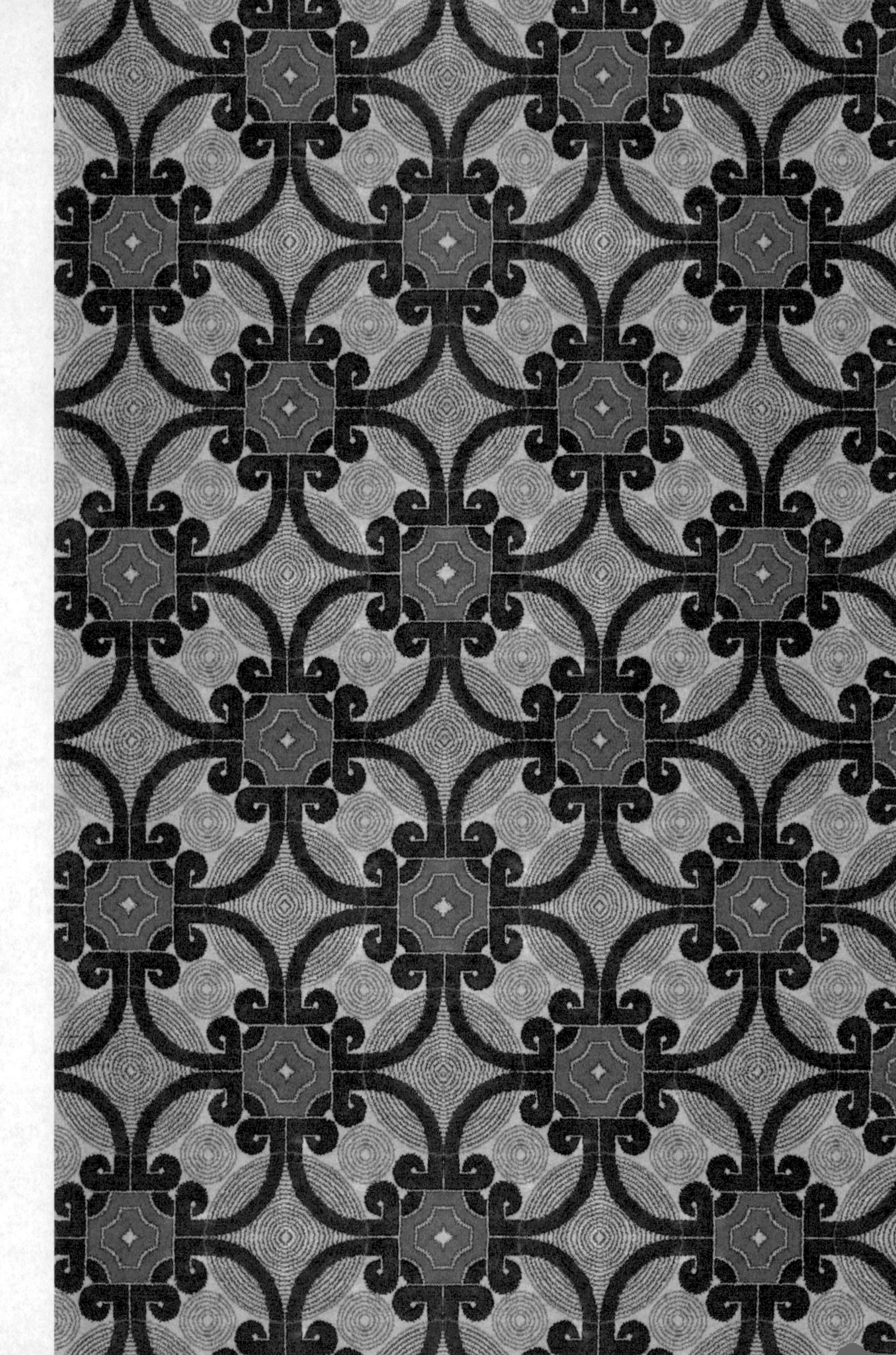

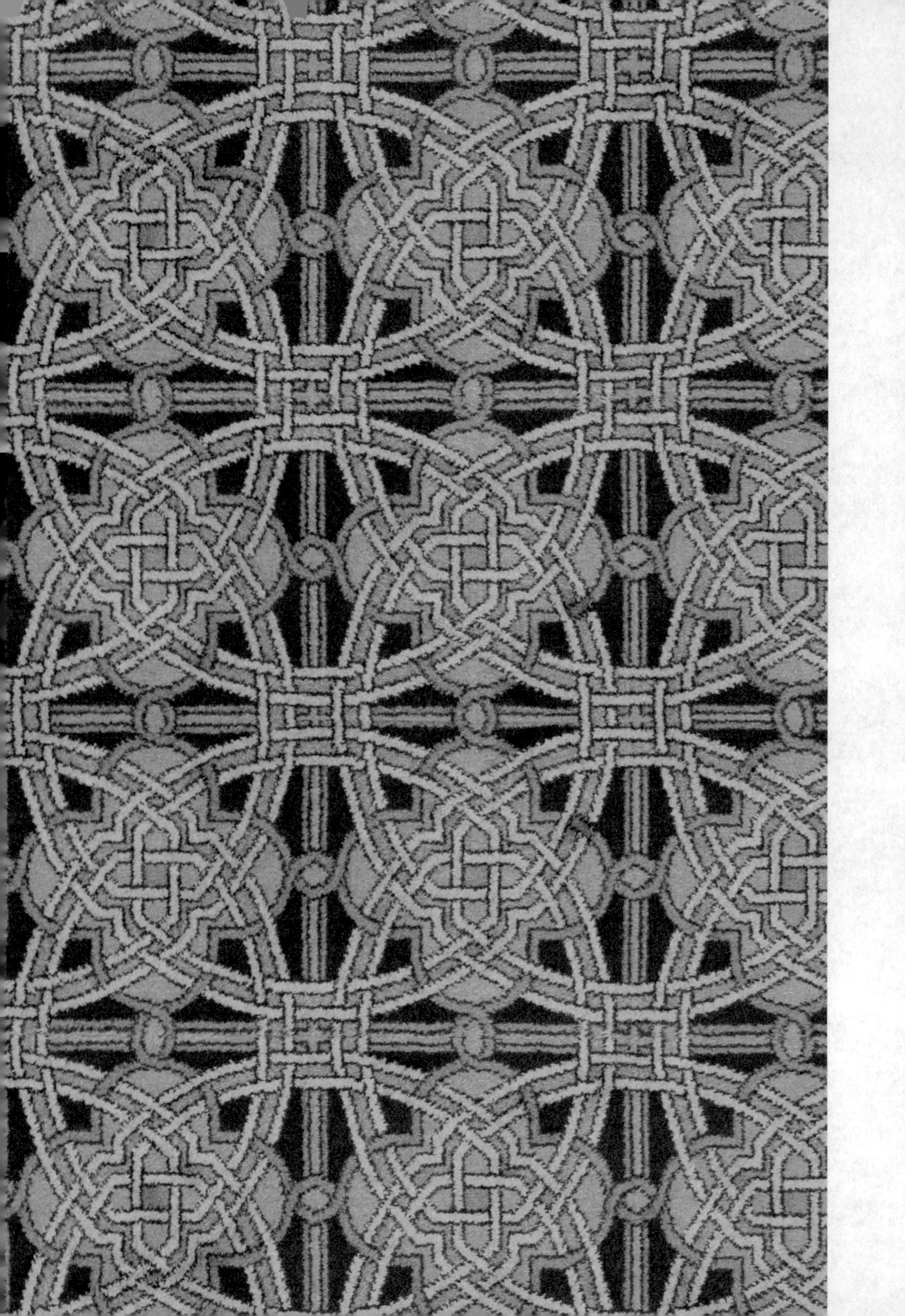

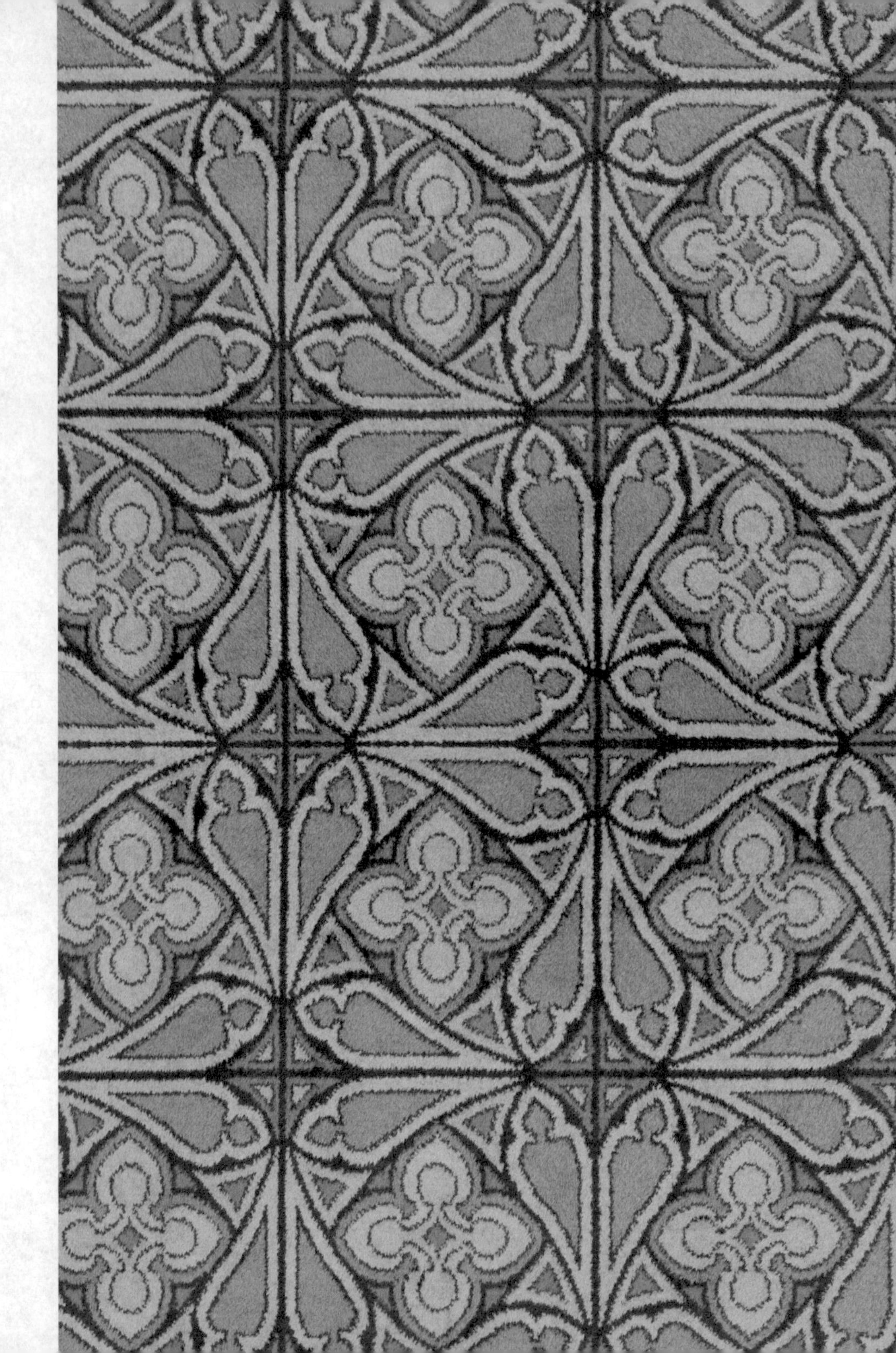

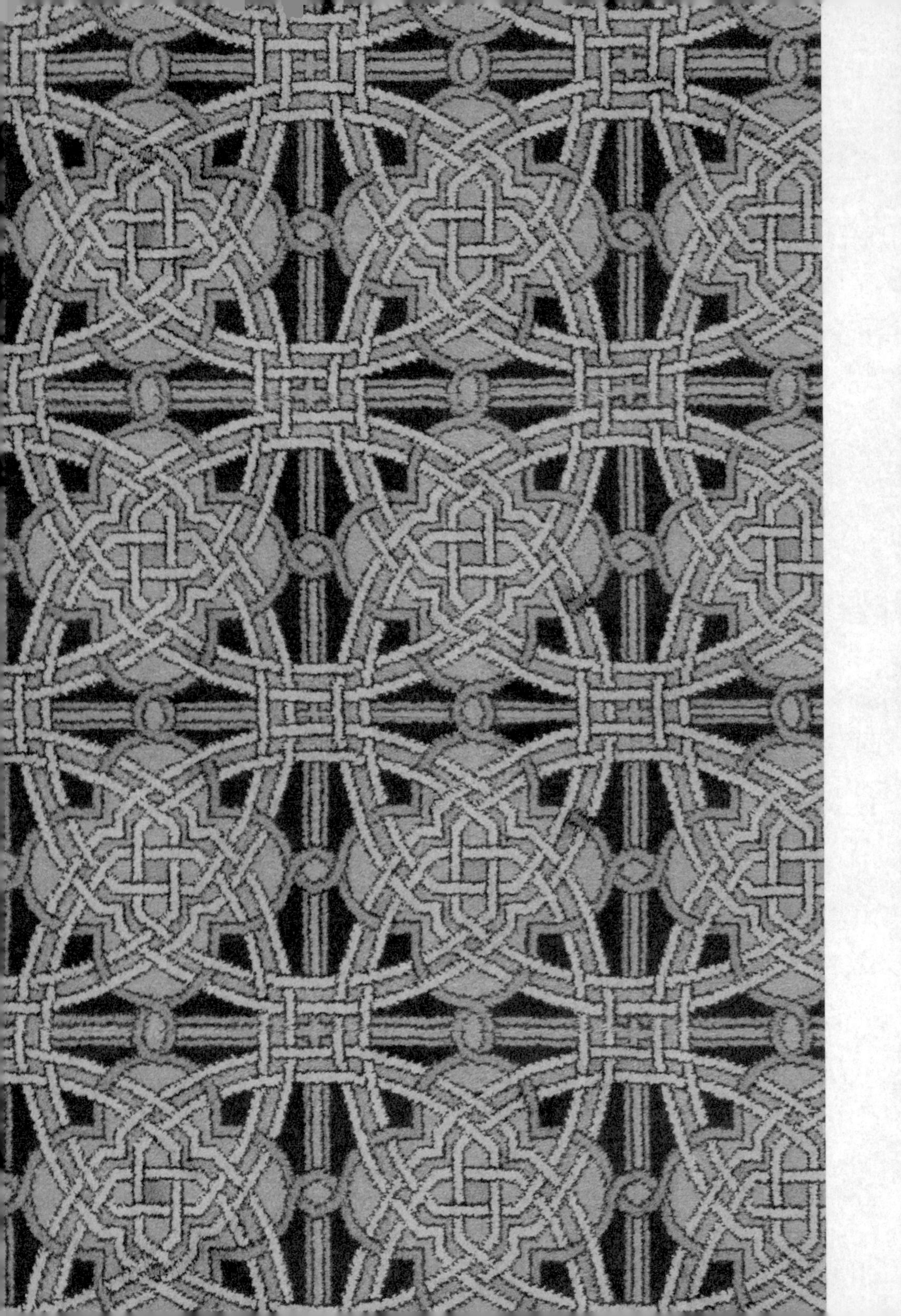

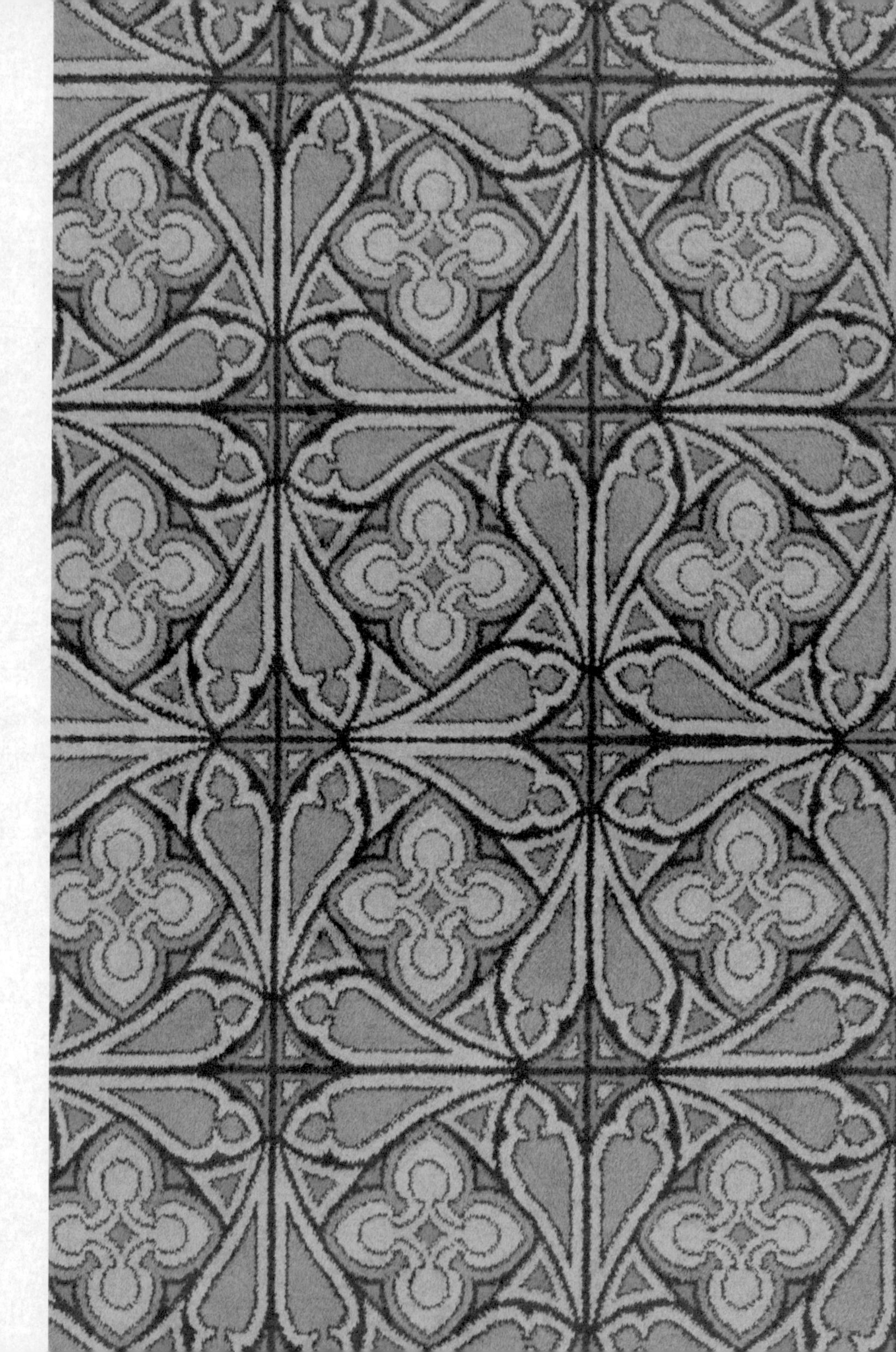

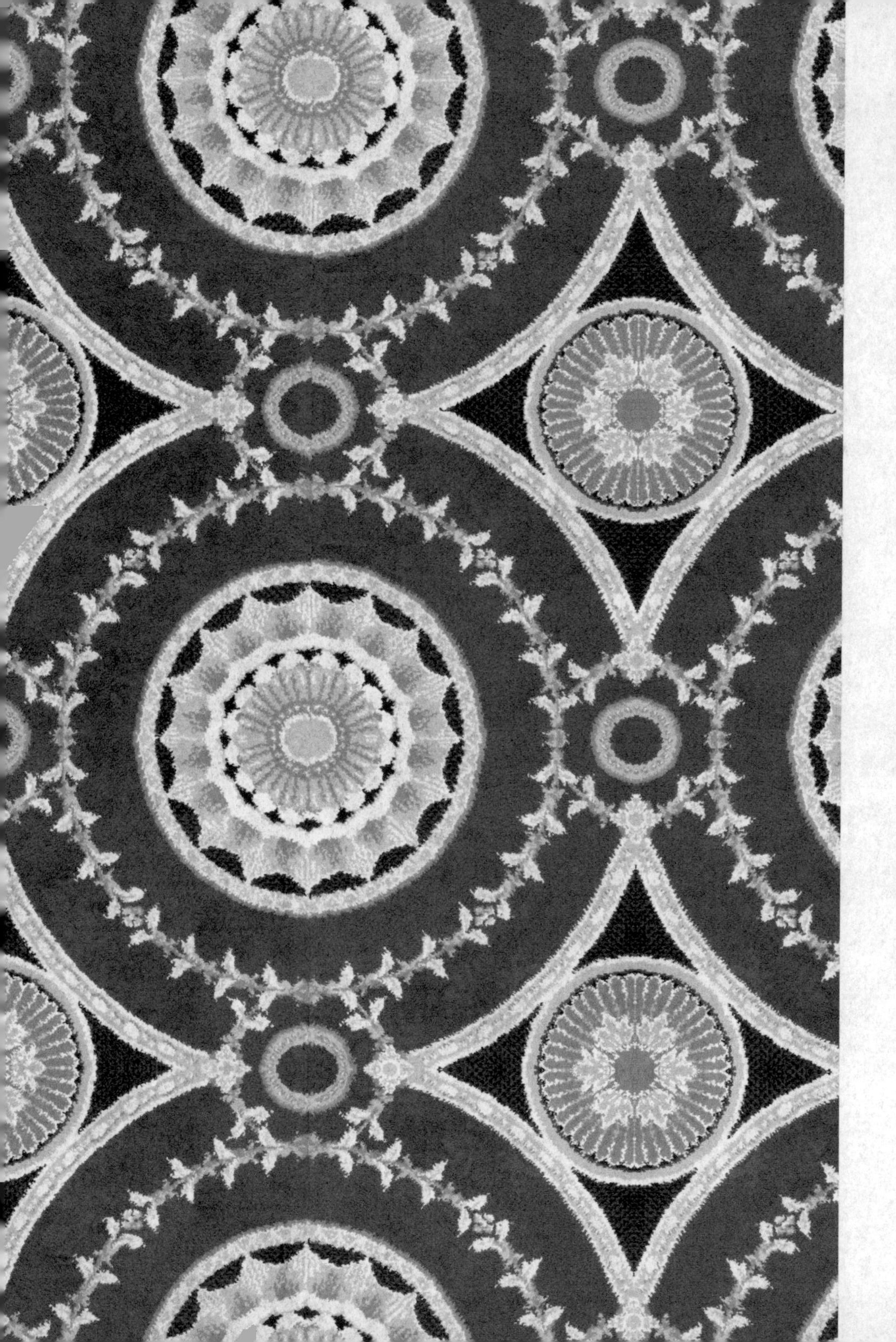

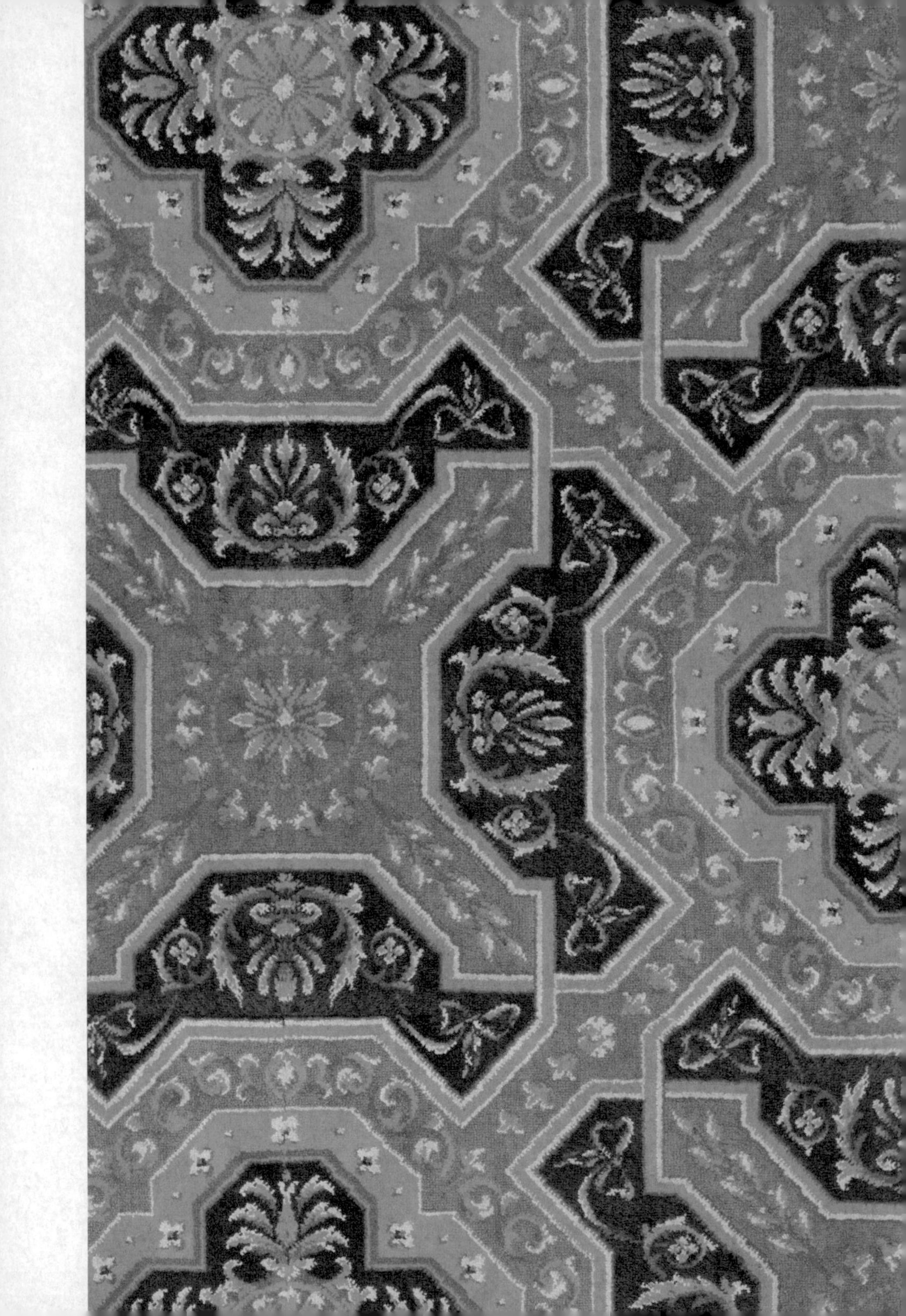

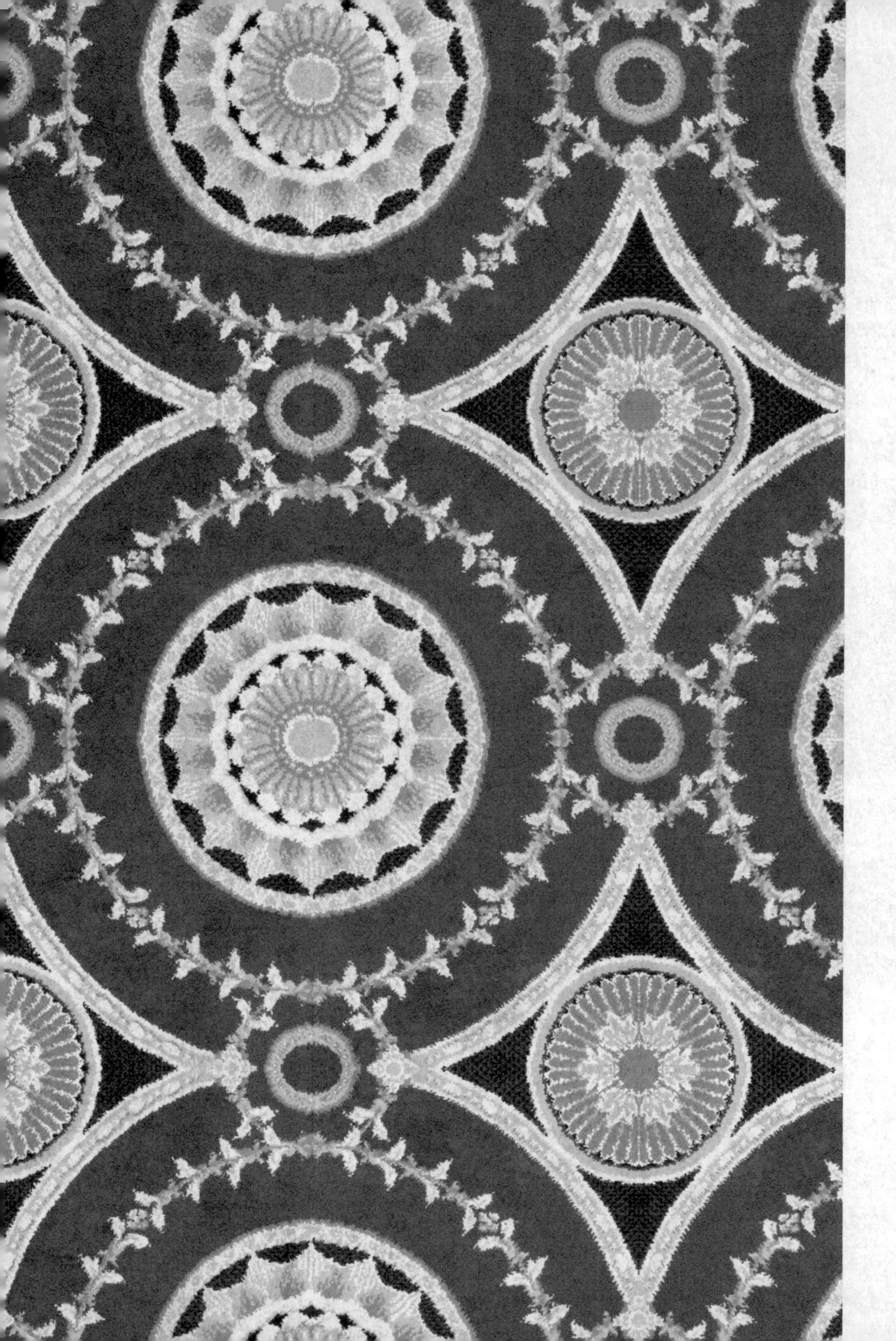

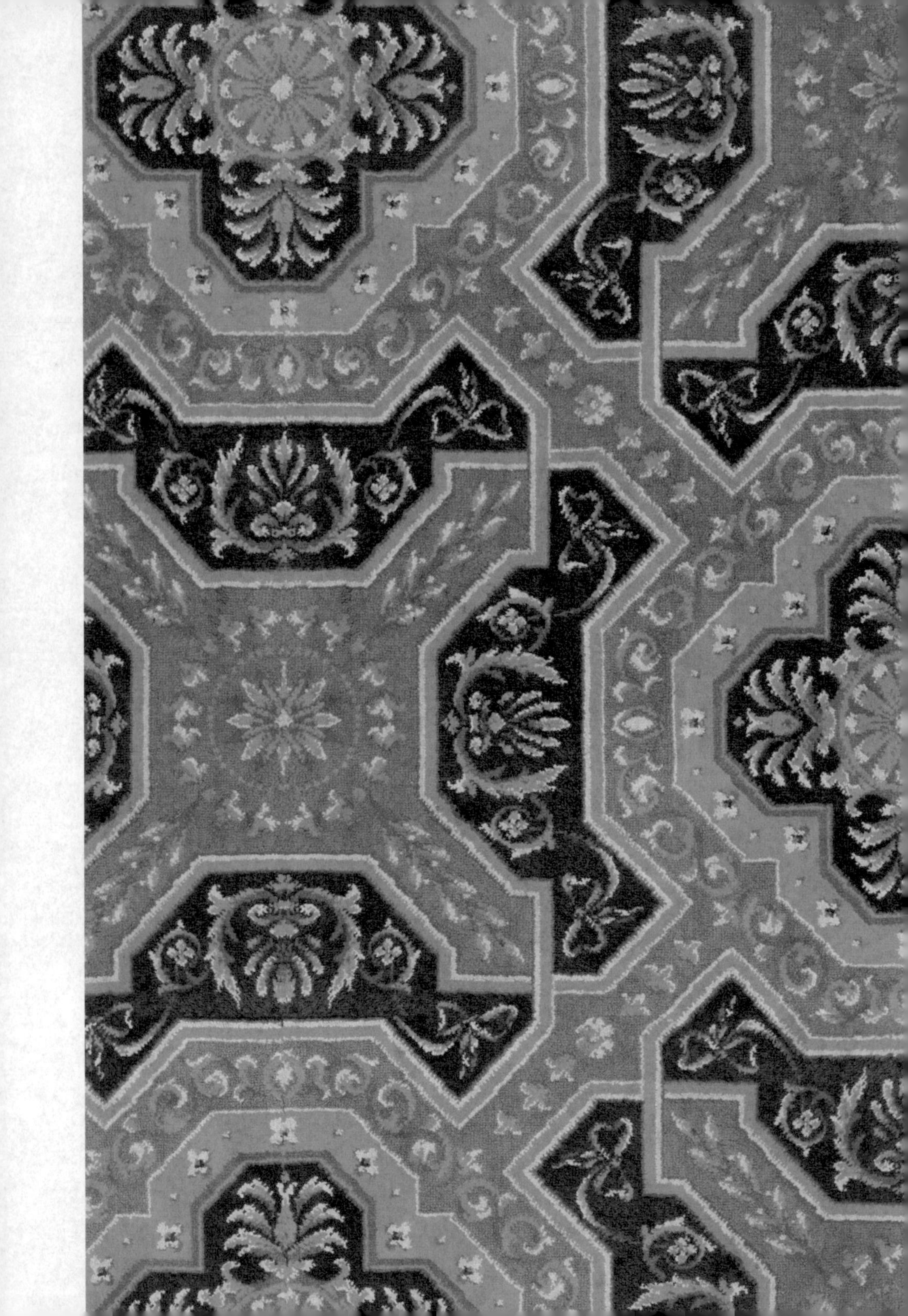

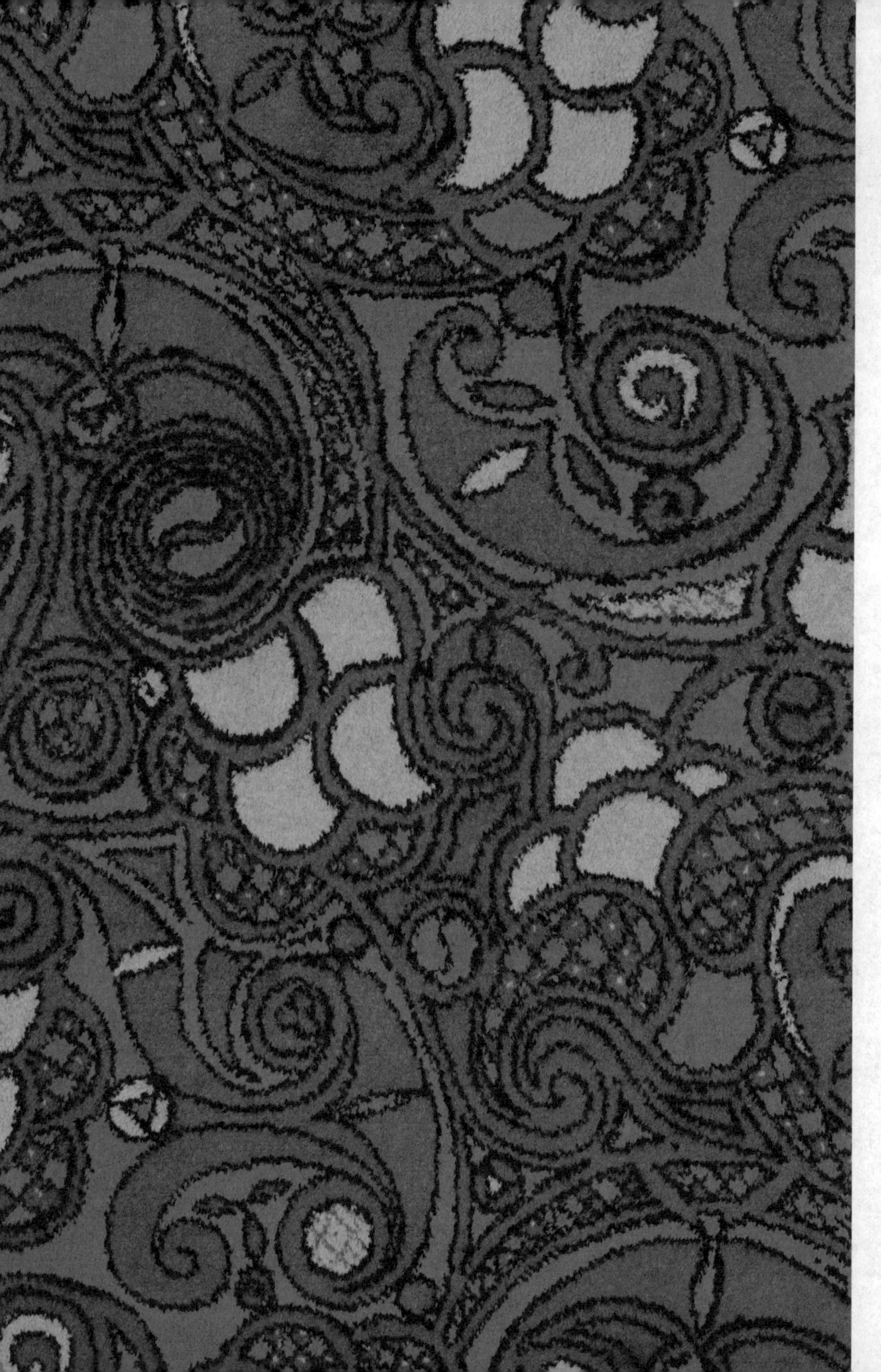

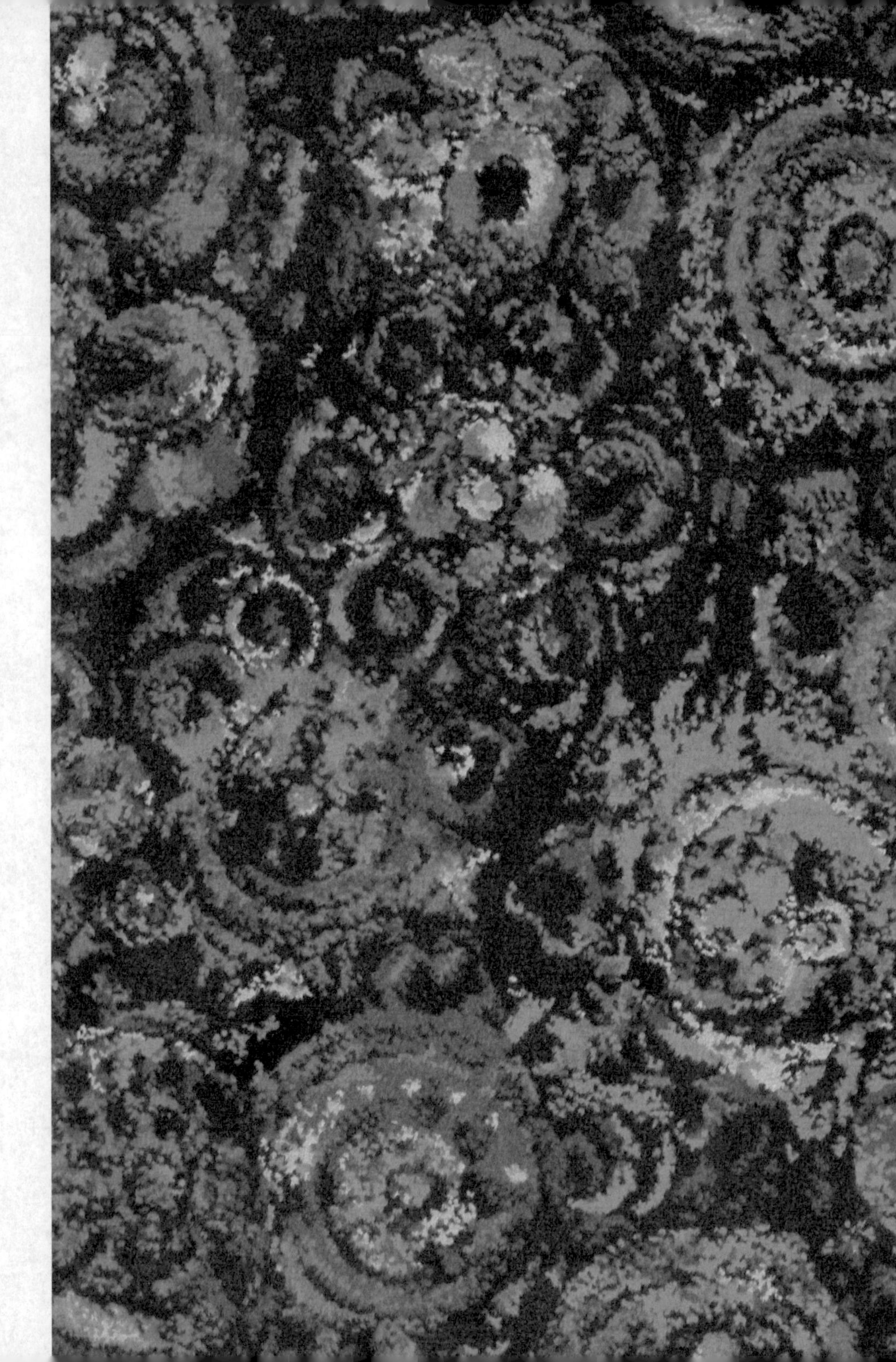

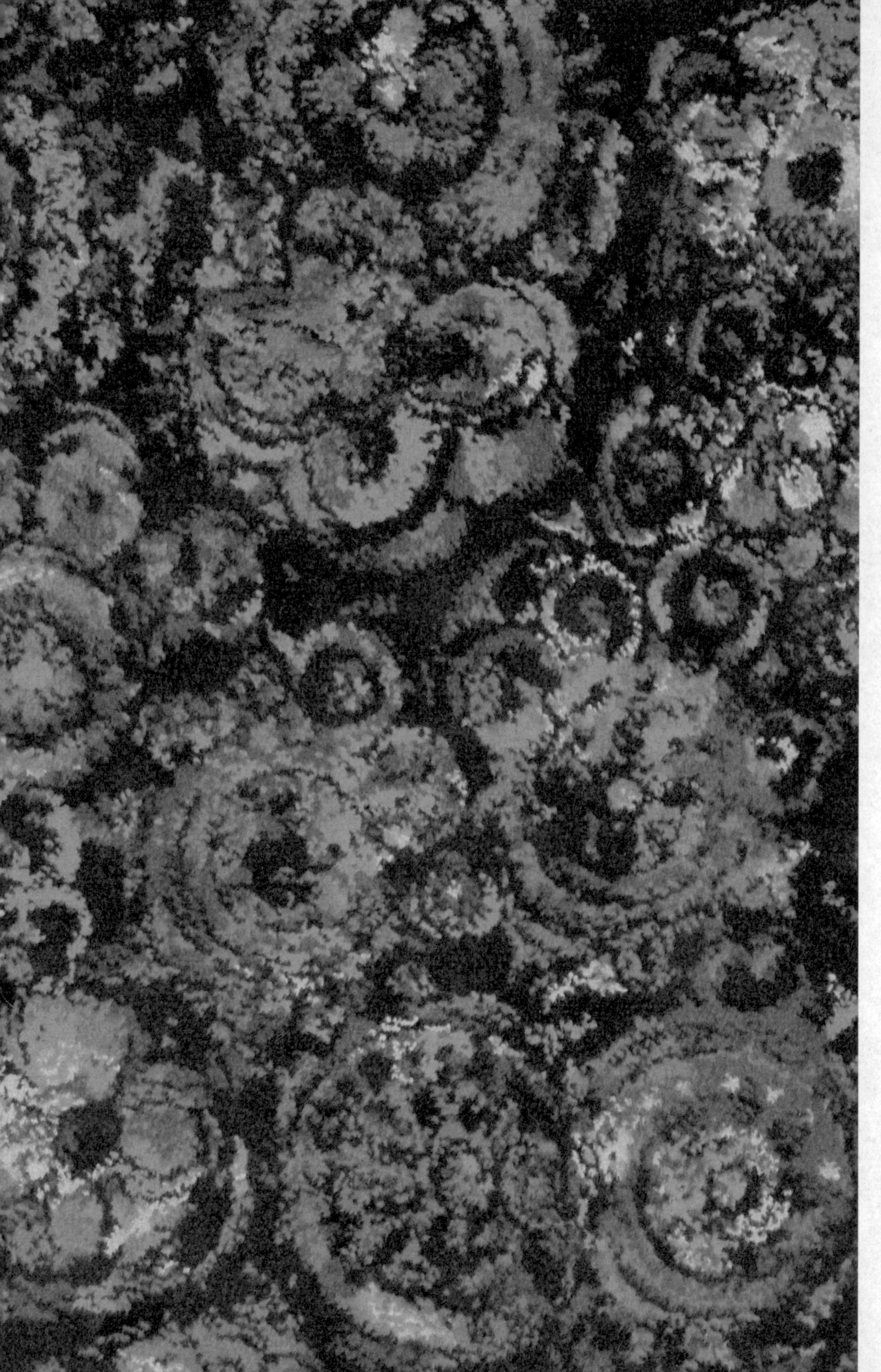

VIDEOVORTRÄGE / VIDEO LECTURES

2020
23:26 minutes duration

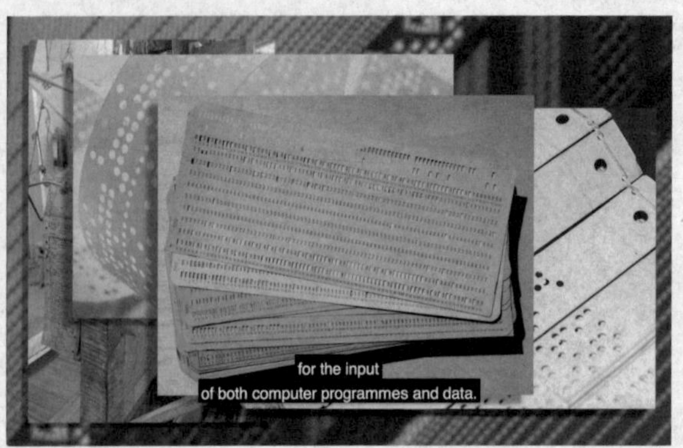

This is the first of several video lectures created
by Elizabeth Price during the Covid pandemic, when
lockdown restrictions were imposed in London. Unable to
deliver lectures in person, and with creative projects
interrupted, Price began to make a series of intricately
composed video lectures. Conducted not only from the
solitary space of her studio, but also deep within the
digital repositories and computer interfaces where
she creates her videos, they offer a forensic encounter
with artistic method and motivation.

In this lecture, Price primarily focusses upon the
two-channel work *FELT TIP* (2018), unpicking its complex
production processes and analyzing the social history
of the textiles it features. Dwelling, in particular,
upon a series of neckties that seem to be decorated
with the image of a computer chip instead of a historic,
institutional crest, she addresses the differing
notions of long or deep cultural memory at stake.

2020
Dauer: 23:26 Minuten

Dies ist der erste von mehreren Videovorträgen,
die Price während der Covid-19-Pandemie erarbeitet
hat, als in London Lockdown-Maßnahmen verhängt wurden.
Da es ihr nicht möglich war, persönlich Vorträge
zu halten, und ihre kreativen Projekte unterbrochen
wurden, schuf Price eine Reihe von aufwendig kompo-
nierten Videovorträgen. Sie wurden nicht nur in der
Abgeschiedenheit ihres Ateliers durchgeführt, sondern
in den digitalen Archiven und Computerschnittstellen,
an denen sie ihre Videos erstellt, und bieten eine
forensische Auseinandersetzung mit künstlerischer
Methodik und Motivation.
    In diesem Vortrag konzentriert sich Price vor
allem auf die 2-Kanal-Arbeit *FELT TIP* (2018), in der
sie die komplexen Produktionsprozesse und die soziale
Geschichte der Textilien analysiert, denen sie sich
in ihrer Arbeit widmet. Insbesondere geht sie auf eine
Reihe von Krawatten ein, die anstelle eines historischen, institutionellen Wappens mit dem Bild eines
Computerchips verziert zu sein scheinen, und thematisiert die unterschiedlichen Vorstellungen von langem
oder tiefem kulturellem Gedächtnis, um die es in der
Videoarbeit geht.

2021
15:53 minutes duration

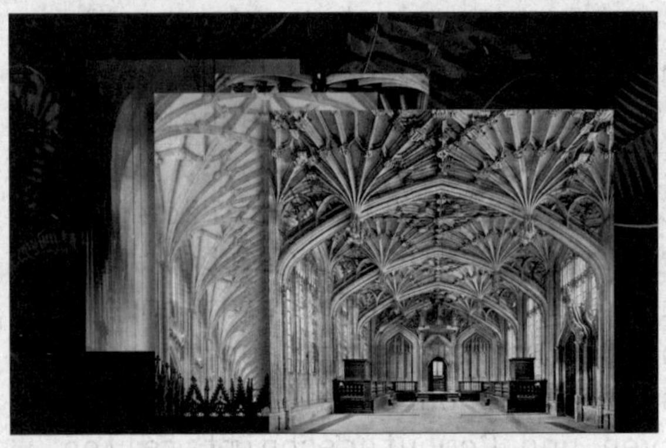

Polyphony and the dramatic chorus are recurring themes
in the moving-image art of Elizabeth Price. This
manifests in her use of narration provided by multiple
voices. Often, these varied "voices" represent different archival and technical sources and are the basis
for the development of a heterogeneous method of
audio-visual composition. *A GOTHIC CHOIR: THE TOTAL
WORK* is the first of three lectures in which Price
explores the significance of the medieval architectural
form of the Gothic choir in the development of her
own language of expression in moving-image art. In particular, she identifies the architecture of the choir
as a literal, sculptural expression of the enduring
resonance of the voices of the dead.

EIN GOTISCHER CHOR: DAS GESAMTWERK

2021
Dauer: 15:53 Minuten

Polyphonie und der dramatische Chor sind wiederkehrende
Themen in der Bewegtbildkunst von Elizabeth Price.
Dies zeigt sich in ihrer Verwendung von Erzählungen,
die von mehreren Stimmen vorgetragen werden. Oft ver-
körpern diese verschiedenen »Stimmen« unterschiedliche
archivarische und technische Quellen und sind die
Grundlage für die Entwicklung einer heterogenen Methode
der audiovisuellen Komposition. *A GOTHIC CHOIR: THE
TOTAL WORK* ist der erste von drei Vorträgen, in denen
Price die Bedeutung der mittelalterlichen Architektur-
form des gotischen Chors für die Entwicklung ihrer
eigenen Ausdruckssprache in der Bewegtbildkunst untersucht. Insbesondere identifiziert sie die Architektur
des Chors als buchstäblichen, skulpturalen Ausdruck
für die anhaltende Resonanz der Stimmen der Toten.

2021
17:27 minutes duration

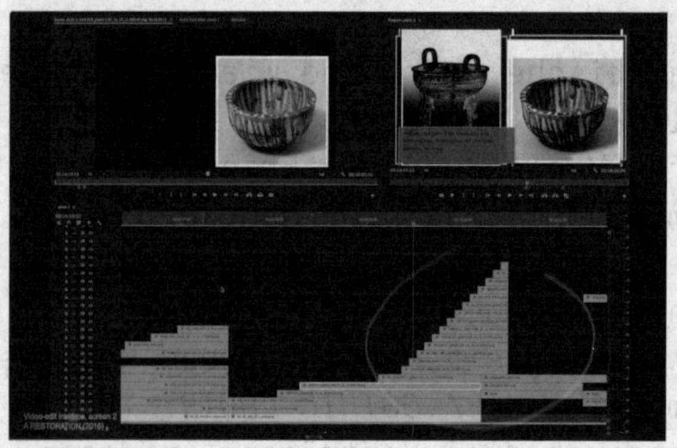

In this, the second lecture dedicated to the Gothic
choir, Price explores the similarities of that architectural form to the design of law courts, theaters,
and political chambers of debate, such as the British
House of Commons. Further to this, Price relates
the choir to systems for the organization of knowledge,
arguing that the historic "voices" inferred by the
Gothic choir are often also those of the authors who
created some of the first libraries. She develops these
themes with a particular reference to *A RESTORATION*
(2016), moving through its dense, digital repositories
of historic photographs and documents, and exploring
her own methods of reorganizing vast amounts of this
material on the editing timeline, only a fraction of
which is visible in the video itself.

EIN GOTISCHER CHOR: GRUNDRISSE UND AUFRISSE

2021
Dauer: 17:27 Minuten

In diesem zweiten, dem gotischen Chor gewidmeten
Vortrag untersucht Price die Ähnlichkeiten dieser
architektonischen Form mit der Gestaltung von
Gerichtsgebäuden, Theatern und politischen Sitzungs-
sälen, wie beispielsweise dem britischen Unterhaus.
Darüber hinaus setzt Price den Chor mit Systemen der
Wissensorganisation in Beziehung und erklärt, dass
es sich bei den historischen »Stimmen«, auf die
der gotische Chor verweist, oft auch um die der
Autoren handelt, die die ersten Bibliotheken schufen.
Sie erörtert diese Themen mit besonderem Bezug auf
A RESTORATION (2016) und bewegt sich dabei durch die
dieser Arbeit zugrunde liegenden dichten digitalen
Bestände historischer Fotografien und Dokumente.
So erforscht sie ihre eigenen Methoden, mit denen sie
die riesigen Mengen solchen Materials, von dem nur
ein Bruchteil im Video selbst sichtbar ist, auf der
Timeline neu ordnet.

2021
17:56 minutes duration

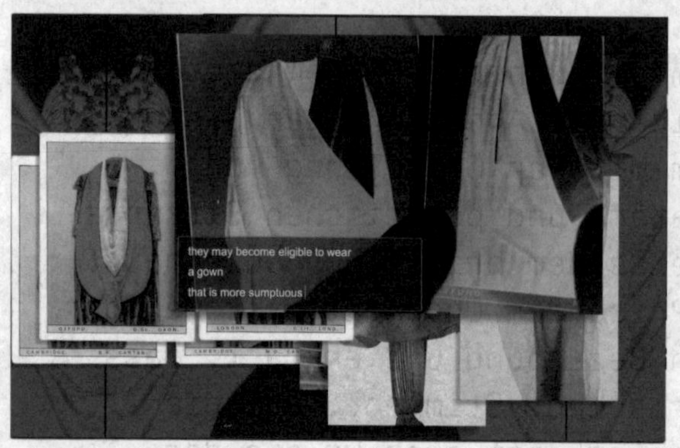

Certain origins of the Gothic choir lie in the classi-
cal chorus, defined as a circle of singing dancers.
In this lecture, Elizabeth Price considers Gothic
revivals and their enduring impact on ideas of embodied
performance and voice. Briefly addressing costumes and
postures of power in academic, ecclesiastical, and legal
contexts, Price goes on to explore the expression of
voice in the tradition of British satiric prints, which
were contemporaneous with the Gothic revival in litera-
ture and architecture.

   In the latter part of the lecture, she assesses
the impact of the Gothic on audio technology, arguing
that the architectural choir's inference of spectral
voices is also a prelude to more recent technological
revenants: all those disembodied presences created
by voice-recording technologies from the wax cylinder
to the digital. Price asks what it means to reassemble
such a choir within the digital. Is it possible to
conjure the dead to sing a different song?

EIN GOTISCHER CHOR: GESANG UND TANZ

2021
Dauer: 17:56 Minuten

Bestimmte Ursprünge des gotischen Chors liegen im
klassischen Chor, der als ein Kreis singender Tän-
zer:innen definiert wurde. In diesem Vortrag befasst
sich Price mit den Wiederbelebungen der Gotik und
deren nachhaltigem Einfluss auf die Vorstellungen von
verkörperter Performance und Stimme. Nach einer kurzen
Betrachtung von Kostümen und Machtpositionen in
akademischen, kirchlichen und juristischen Kontexten
geht Price auf den Ausdruck der Stimme in der Tradition der britischen satirischen Druckgrafik ein,
in der dieser zur gleichen Zeit aufkam wie das gotische Revival in Literatur und Architektur.
  Im letzten Teil des Vortrags bewertet sie den
Einfluss der Gotik auf die Audiotechnologie und legt
dar, dass der architektonische Chor mit seinen
spektralen Stimmen auch ein Auftakt für neuere techno-
logische Wiedergänger ist: all jene körperlosen
Präsenzen, die durch Sprachaufzeichnungstechnologien
von der Wachswalze bis zur Digitaltechnik entstehen.
Price fragt, was es bedeutet, einen solchen Chor
im Digitalen neu zusammenzustellen – ist es möglich,
die Toten zu beschwören, damit sie ein anderes
Lied singen?

2023
SOUND OF THE BREAK – Schirn Kunsthalle, Frankfurt
SLOW DANS – Gallery of Modern Art, Glasgow

2022
UNDERFOOT – Hunterian Art Gallery, Glasgow

2021
CHOREOGRAPH – Void Gallery, Derry
REFLECTIONS: Female Voices in Moving Image – Workplace, London
A GOTHIC CHOIR – Paul Mellon Centre for Studies in British Art, Yale University, London

2020
SLOW DANS – Artangel, The Assembly Hall, Borough, London
FOOTNOTES – Artangel, Auftrag für Internetübertragung / commission for the internet

2019
A LONG MEMORY – The Whitworth, The University of Manchester, Manchester
LONGUE TONGUE – Nottingham Contemporary, Nottingham
FELT TIP – Walker Art Center, Minneapolis
THE WOOLWORTHS CHOIR OF 1979 – Centro De Arte Dos De Mayo, Madrid

2018
THE WOOLWORTHS CHOIR OF 1979 – Tate Britain, London
txtferz – Morley College Gallery, London
KOHL – Art Basel, Basel
A RESTORATION – Adam Art Gallery, Wellington
WEST HINDER – Centre for Contemporary Art, Derry
K – Wyoming Project, Peking / Beijing
BERLINWAL – Museum für Naturkunde Berlin, Berlin
USER GROUP DISCO – BFI Southbank, London

2017
A RESTORATION – Institute for the Study of the Ancient World, New York
A RESTORATION – The Art Institute of Chicago, Chicago
K – The Art Institute of Chicago, Chicago
K – Grimm Gallery, New York
A PUBLIC LECTURE & EXHUMATION Film International – Whitechapel Gallery, London

2016
WE KNOW – The Model, Sligo
WELCOME – Neuer Berliner Kunstverein, Berlin
IN A DREAM YOU SAW A WAY TO SURVIVE AND YOU WERE FULL OF JOY – The Whitworth, The University of Manchester, Manchester
IN A DREAM YOU SAW A WAY TO SURVIVE AND YOU WERE FULL OF JOY – De La Warr Pavilion, Bexhill on Sea
IN A DREAM YOU SAW A WAY TO SURVIVE AND YOU WERE FULL OF JOY – The Glynn Vivian, Swansea

2015
USER GROUP DISCO – Turku Art Museum, Turku
K – Untitled, Art Basel, Basel
AT THE HOUSE OF MR X – Cinématèque Robert Lynen, Paris

2014
SUNLIGHT – Index, The Swedish Contemporary Art Foundation, Stockholm
THE TENT – Kunsthalle Winterthur, Winterthur
SLEEP – MOT International, Brüssel / Brussels
NUMBER NINE – Julia Stoschek Collection, Düsseldorf / Dusseldorf
THE TENT – EVA International, Ireland's Biennial, Limerick
Using Memory – mumok – Museum moderner Kunst Stiftung Ludwig Wien, Wien / Vienna

2013
HERE – Musee d'art contemporain de Montréal, Montreal
SUNLIGHT – Focal Point Gallery, Southend
USER GROUP DISCO – Scottish National Gallery of Modern Art, Edinburgh
AT THE HOUSE OF MR X – Henry Moore Institute, Leeds
THE WOOLWORTHS CHOIR OF 1979 – Haus der Kulturen der Welt, Berlin
THE WOOLWORTHS CHOIR OF 1979 – Stedelijk Museum, Amsterdam
THE TENT – Random Acts, Channel 4 mit / with ICA, Institute of Contemporary Arts, London

2012
TURNER PRIZE 2012 - Tate Britain, London
THE TENT - Bloomberg Space, London
CHOIR - Kunstverein Bielefeld, Bielefeld
THE WOOLWORTHS CHOIR OF 1979 - MOT International, London
HERE - Baltic Centre for Contemporary Art, Gateshead

2011
CHOIR - New Museum, New York
CHOIR - Chisenhale Gallery, London

2010
THE TENT - Frieze Projects Commission, Frieze Art Fair, London
USER GROUP DISCO - Pavilion, Leeds
Perfect Courses and Shimmering Obstacles - Tate Britain, London
AT THE HOUSE OF MR X - CalArts, California Institute of the Arts, Valencia

2006-2009
USER GROUP DISCO - Spike Island, Bristol
O FONTANA - MOT International, London
AT THE HOUSE OF MR X - Stanley Picker Gallery, London
A PUBLIC LECTURE AND EXHUMATION - Studio Voltaire, London
AT THE HOUSE OF MR X - Camden Arts Centre, London
AT THE HOUSE OF MR X - BFI, London

WERKE DER KÜNSTLERIN BEFINDEN SICH IN FOLGENDEN SAMMLUNGEN / WORKS IN COLLECTIONS

The Artangel Collection
Arts Council Collection, London
Ashmolean Museum Collection, Oxford
British Council
Collection of Eileen Cohen
Collection of Elizabeth Redleaf
Collection of Robert Devereux
Collection of Robert and Renee Drake
Fondazione per l'Arte Moderna e Contemporanea CRT, Turin
Frans Hals Museum, Haarlem
Hunterian Art Gallery Collection, University of Glasgow
Krupp Foundation
Museum of Modern Art, Glasgow
Scottish National Gallery of Modern Art, Edinburgh
Stedelijk Museum, Amsterdam
Julia Stoschek Collection, Berlin/Düsseldorf / Dusseldorf
Tate
Towner Eastbourne, Eastbourne
Walker Art Center, Minneapolis
The Whitworth, The University of Manchester, Manchester

PREISE UND SHORTLISTS / PRIZES AND SHORTLISTS

2013 Contemporary Art Society Commissioning Prize: the Annual Award, UK
2012 The Turner Prize, Tate Gallery, UK
2012 The Paul Hamlyn Award, UK
2011 Shortlisted - Jarman Award, UK
2010 Shortlisted - Max Mara Prize for Women Artists, Whitechapel Gallery, UK

LEHRAUFTRÄGE UND PROFESSUREN / LECTURING AND PROFESSORSHIPS

2017-   Professor in Film and Photography, School of Art, Kingston University, London
2012-2017   Associate Professor in Fine Art, Ruskin School of Art, Oxford
2006-2011   Senior Lecturer, Fine Art, Royal College of Art, London
2006-2010   Reader in Fine Art, Kingston University, London
2000-2006   Lecturer in Fine Art, BA Fine Art, Goldsmiths College, London
1999-2006   Lecturer in Fine Art, BA, MA, and PhD, University of Leeds

2020	University of Glasgow, Library and Special Collections, Visiting Fellowship
2017	Audain Distinguished Artist in Residence Emily Carr University, Vancouver
2012	Arts Council Residency, Wysing Arts Cambridge
2011-2012	Leverhulme Residency at RAL British Space Centre
2010-2011	Helen Chadwick Fellowship, British School at Rome, Rom / Rome
2008-2009	Spike Island, Arts Council Residency, Bristol
2006-2007	Stanley Picker Fellow in Fine Art, Kingston University, London
2004-2006	Research Fellow in Fine Art, London Metropolitan University, London
2003	Scottish Arts Council Residency, Glasgow

A RESTORATION, 2016
2-Kanal-Video / Two-channel video
19 min
Finanziert durch die / Funded by the Contemporary Art
Society through the Museum Award of 2014
Die Arbeit zeigt Artefakte aus den / The work features
artifacts from the Ashmolean and Pitt Rivers museum
collections, Oxford, speziell Objekte aus dem /
particularly items from the Sir Arthur Evans Archive
Musik / Music: Andrew Dickens in Zusammenarbeit mit /
in collaboration with Elizabeth Price
CGI und / and Motion Graphics: Anne Haaning
Besonderer Dank an / Special thanks to Caroline Douglas
von der / of the Contemporary Art Society

FELT TIP, 2018
2-Kanal-Video / Two-channel video
10 min
In Auftrag gegeben von / Commissioned by Film and Video
Umbrella, London, Nottingham Contemporary und /
and Walker Art Center, Minneapolis. Zusätzliche
Unterstützung durch / Also supported by Kingston School
of Art through the Research Centre for Contemporary Art
Musik / Music: Andrew Dickens, Elizabeth Price
CGI Animation: Anne Haaning
Zusätzliche / Additional CGI: Gabriel Stones, Ollie Dook
Live-Soundaufnahmen / Live Sound Recording und /
and Motion Graphics: Rose Goddard
Schrift / Font Design: Spencer Fenton
Kamera / Director of Photography: Jamie Quantrill
Standbildfotografie / Stills Photography: Andrew Bruce,
Theo Christelis

UNDERFOOT, 2022
2-Kanal-Video / Two-channel video
14 min
In Auftrag gegeben von / Commissioned by The Hunterian,
in Zusammenarbeit mit / in collaboration with Panel,
Glasgow. Gefördert durch / Funded by Creative Scotland,
zusätzliche Unterstützung durch / also supported by
Kingston School of Art through the Research Centre for
Contemporary Art
Musik / Music: Andrew Dickens, Leah Kardos,
Elizabeth Price
CGI Animation: Anne Haaning, Ollie Dook
2D Animation: Oliver Michael Bacon
Live-Soundaufnahmen / Live Sound Recording: Richy Carey
Standbildfotografie / Stills Photography: Andrew Lee

NIGHT OF THE WORLD, 2023
1-Kanal-Video / Single-channel video
20 min
Produziert mit Unterstützung der / Produced with the
support of Schirn Kunsthalle Frankfurt. Zusätzliche
Unterstützung durch / Also supported by Kingston School
of Art through the Research Centre for Contemporary Art
Eine frühere Version der Arbeit wurde finanziert durch /
An earlier version of the work was funded through FLAMIN
by Film London und / and The Elephant Trust
Soundtrack komponiert und produziert von / composed and
produced by Brian Reitzell, mit / with Elizabeth Price
(2012), remixed von / by Jim Noble (2013), remixed von /
by Elizabeth Price (2022)
2D Grafik / Graphics: Rob Millington (2012),
Oliver Michael Bacon (2022)
3D Animation: Elliott Johnson (2012), Anne Haaning (2022)

THE CHORUS AND THEIR MEMORY, 2020
1-Kanal-Video / Single-channel video
23:26 min
In Auftrag gegeben von / Commissioned by Artangel, UK

A GOTHIC CHOIR: THE TOTAL WORK, 2021
1-Kanal-Video / Single-channel video
15:53 min
In Auftrag gegeben vom / Commissioned by the Paul Mellon
Centre for Studies in British Art, Yale University

A GOTHIC CHOIR: PLANS AND ELEVATIONS, 2021
1-Kanal-Video / Single-channel video
17:27 min
In Auftrag gegeben vom / Commissioned by the Paul Mellon
Centre for Studies in British Art, Yale University

A GOTHIC CHOIR: SONG AND DANSE, 2021
1-Kanal-Video / Single-channel video
17:56 min
In Auftrag gegeben vom / Commissioned by the Paul Mellon
Centre for Studies in British Art, Yale University

Dieser Katalog erscheint anlässlich der Ausstellung / This catalog is published in conjunction with the exhibition

Elizabeth Price
SOUND OF THE BREAK

Schirn Kunsthalle Frankfurt
23. März - 29. Mai 2023
March 23 - May 29, 2023

KATALOG / CATALOG

Herausgeber / Editor
Matthias Ulrich

Redaktion / Editing
Matthias Ulrich,
Marie Oucherif

Publikationsmanagement /
Publication Management
Natalie Storelli

Lektorat / Copyediting
Annette Siegel (Deutsch /
German)
Andrew Wagner (Englisch /
English)

Übersetzung / Translation
Michael Ammann (Englisch –
Deutsch / English – German)
Susie Hondl (Deutsch –
Englisch / German –
English)

Gestaltung, Satz und
Produktionsmanagement /
Graphic Design, Typesetting,
and Production Coordination
Kellenberger-White, London

Papier / Paper
Materica Kraft 250 gsm und /
and Ibo One 60 gsm

Schrift / Typeface
KW Museum Mono by
Kellenberger-White

Druck und Bindung /
Printing and Binding
robstolk®, Amsterdam

Veröffentlichung und
Vertrieb / Published and
distributed by
Mousse Publishing
Contrappunto S.r.l.
via Pier Candido
Decembrio 28
20137, Mailand / Milan
Italien / Italy

Erhältlich über /
Available through

Mousse Publishing,
Mailand / Milan
moussemagazine.it

DAP | Distributed Art
Publishers, New York
artbook.com

Les presses du réel, Dijon
lespressesdureel.com

Antenne Books, London
antennebooks.com

Erstausgabe / First
edition: 2023

Printed in the Netherlands

ISBN: 978-88-6749-570-2

€ 30 / $ 35

© 2023 Schirn Kunsthalle
Frankfurt, Mousse
Publishing, die Künstlerin
sowie die Autorinnen und
Autoren / the artist, the
authors of the texts

© Elizabeth Price für die
abgebildeten Werke der
Künstlerin / for the reproduced works by
the artist

© Norbert Miguletz Foto S. /
photo p. 5

Alle Rechte vorbehalten;
kein Teil dieser Publikation
darf in irgendeiner Form
ohne vorherige schriftliche
Genehmigung der Rechte-
inhaber reproduziert oder
unter Verwendung elektro-
nischer Systeme verar-
beitet, vervielfältigt oder
verbreitet werden.

All rights reserved. No part
of this publication may
be reproduced, translated,
stored in a retrieval
system, or transmitted in
any form or by any means
(electronic and mechanical,
including photocopying or
recording) without prior
written permission from the
copyright holders.

Der Herausgeber bedankt
sich bei allen, die
freundlicherweise der
Reproduktion von Inhalten
für dieses Buch zuge-
stimmt haben. Es wurden alle
Anstrengungen unternommen,
um die Genehmigung für die
Wiedergabe der Bilder und
Texte in diesem Katalog zu
erhalten. Der Herausgeber
steht jedoch wie üblich
den Inhaber:innen der
Urheberrechte zur Verfügung
und verpflichtet sich,
etwaige Auslassungen oder
Fehler in künftigen Ausgaben
zu korrigieren.

The publisher would like to
thank all those who have
kindly given their permission for the reproduction
of material for this book.
Every effort has been made
to obtain permission to re-
produce the images and texts
in this catalog. However,
as is standard editorial
policy, the publisher is at
the disposal of copyright
holders and undertakes to
correct any omissions or
errors in future editions.

Bibliografische
Information der Deutschen
Nationalbibliothek
Die Deutsche National-
bibliothek verzeichnet diese
Publikation in der Deutschen
Nationalbibliografie;
detaillierte bibliogra-
fische Daten sind online
über http://dnb.de abrufbar.

Bibliographic information
published by the Deutsche
Nationalbibliothek
The Deutsche National-
bibliothek lists this publication in the Deutsche
Nationalbibliografie;
detailed bibliographic data
is available online at
http://dnb.de.

AUSSTELLUNG / EXHIBITION
SCHIRN KUNSTHALLE FRANKFURT

Direktor / Director
Sebastian Baden

Stellvertretende Direktorin
und Ausstellungsleitung /
Deputy Director and Head of
Exhibitions
Esther Schlicht

Kurator / Curator
Matthias Ulrich

Kuratorische Assistenz /
Curatorial Assistant
Marie Oucherif
Organisation / Registrars

Elke Walter, Karin Grüning,
Fanny Bengsch

Leitung Hängeteam /
Installation Crew Supervisor
Andreas Gundermann

Technische Leitung /
Technical Services
Christian Teltz, Oliver
Taschke, Stefan Schell

Ausstellungsgrafik /
Exhibition Design
Sam Kim

Presse / Press
Johanna Pulz, Julia Bastian,
Maya Röttger, Thea Stroh

Publikationsmanagement /
Publication Management
Natalie Storelli

Schirn Magazin /
Schirn Magazine
Julia Schaake

Marketing
Luise Bachmann, Heike
Stumpf, Angelika Schäfer

Engagement
Miriam Werner,
Corinna Fröhling

Pädagogik / Education
Laura Heeg, Simone
Boscheinen, Olga Schätz,
Anna Haag, Sarah Schweizer

Veranstaltungen & Besucher-
management / Events and
Visitor Management
Ute Seiffert, Vivien Shahzad

Verwaltung / Administration
Heike Berndt, Boris
Deckelmann, Tanja Mayer

Assistenz Ausstellungs-
leitung / Assistant Head
of Exhibitions
Luise Leyer

Assistenz Direktion /
Assistant to the Director
Kerstin Lehmann

Leitung Gebäudereinigung /
Cleaning Supervision
Rosaria La Tona

Empfang / Reception
Bettina Beyermann,
Vanessa Bernhardt